THE HUSTLERS

Douglas Thompson is the bestselling author of
more than twenty books. A biographer, broadcaster and
international journalist, he is a regular contributor to major
newspapers and magazines worldwide. He divides
his time between Los Angeles and London.

Douglas Thompson

THE HUSTLERS

Gambling, Greed and the Perfect Con

PAN BOOKS

First published 2007 by Sidgwick & Jackson

First published in paperback 2008 by Pan Books
an imprint of Pan Macmillan Ltd
Pan Macmillan, 20 New Wharf Road, London N1 9RR
Basingstoke and Oxford
Associated companies throughout the world
www.panmacmillan.com

ISBN 978-0-330-44951-9

1 3 5 7 9 8 6 4 2

A CIP catalogue record for this book is available from
the British Library.

Typeset by SetSystems Ltd, Saffron Walden, Essex
Printed and bound in Great Britain by
Mackays of Chatham plc, Chatham, Kent

Visit **www.panmacmillan.com** to read more about all our books
and to buy them. You will also find features, author interviews and
news of any author events, and you can sign up for e-newsletters
so that you're always first to hear about our new releases.

For Lesley and Dandy

– a winning double

Contents

Acknowledgements

Doc Holliday said, or was said to have said, that a 'friendly' game of cards was a misnomer: 'Play to win, or don't bother. Check friendship at the door. If what you want is camaraderie, there is the bar. If it is companionship you seek, there are any number of likely whores.'

I learned to play cards, three-card brag, usually 'blind' bets, in the bagpipe room of an Edinburgh higher education establishment. I was often lucky.

The luck stayed with me when I met John Burke and Bobby McKew. Doc was wrong: you can have a friendly game. I thank them both for their grand help, their inspiration, and, most of all, for their stories. I'd also like to thank Mark Sykes, Mark Birley, David Pritchett, Michael Caborn-Waterfield, Bobby Buchanan-Michaelson, Caroline Gray, Theresa Follet, Cathy Maxwell-Scott, Raymond Nash, Claus Von Bülow, Nancy Gillespie, Charlie Richardson, Frankie Fraser and Diane Guinan-Browne for their help and time.

As always, Ingrid Connell at Pan Macmillan was patient, polite and a superb help at all times, as was my agent Sheila Crowley. Thanks are also due to Bruno Vincent at Pan Macmillan for his inspired help with the manuscript and photographs.

Life is six-to-five against? It depends who you're playing with.

A big, winning hand for them all.

Picture Acknowledgements

Credits are by page number in order from left to right and top to bottom.

1: © PA Photos (both). 2: Courtesy Bobby McKew; Mirrorpix. 3: Courtesy Bobby McKew (both). 4: Getty Images (both). 5: © PA Photos; Getty Images. 6: Getty Images; Topfoto. 7: Getty Images; Topfoto. 8: Getty Images. 9: Getty Images; courtesy John Burke. 10–11: Courtesy John Burke. 12: Topfoto; Mirrorpix. 13: Mirrorpix; Emma Giacon. 14: Desmond O'Neill Features; @ popperfoto.com; Mirrorpix. 15: Courtesy Bobby McKew (both). 16: Getty Images.

Preface

The race is not always to the swift,
nor the battle to the strong,
but that's the way to bet.

DAMON RUNYON'S PARAPHRASE OF ECCLESIASTES

More than a dozen years or so ago I wrote a series of newspaper articles about the ongoing mystery of Lord Lucan. At the time my inquiries involved the Clermont Club, and I heard the name John Burke mentioned. A one-time director of the club, he knew all the famous and infamous members and their stories but had 'retired; the word was he wanted to protect his secrets. There were 'reasons'.

Later, when I worked with Christine Keeler on her bestselling autobiography, *The Truth At Last*, she told me of the characters who inhabited the Star Tavern in Belgravia, including John Burke, whom she liked. He was, she said, a gentleman, who knew everybody but also knew how to keep secrets. At the same time a series of rather racy drawings by Stephen Ward, considered by some the most important and central character in the Profumo affair, were put up for sale.

I traced the seller, Michael 'Dandy Kim' Caborn-Waterfield. One of the more colourful characters in the country, he told me endless stories of London in the 1950s, 1960s, and 1970s. One involved a man called Bobby McKew with whom Kim had spent time in jail in the South of France – a little something to do with a robbery at Hollywood film tycoon Jack Warner's Riviera mansion.

McKew, it transpired, was as legendary as Kim, but in a far less flamboyant way. He knew people that people didn't want to know. He played his cards quietly, kept his own counsel. Against all his instincts Bobby joined me and Kim for lunch on the King's Road in Chelsea. With him was his long-time friend and fellow Irishman John Burke.

It was then that the two men, who had met in Dublin, began to tell me the story of the 'Big Edge', one of the most outrageous but brilliant crooked schemes of the twentieth century. It was also hugely successful, generating tens of millions of pounds in profits in today's money. As John Burke put it: 'It was brilliantly designed. It was psychologically and mathematically brilliant. Einstein would have been proud of it.'

The story involved a colourful cast of characters: rogues, villains, chancers, con men, aristocrats, people who delighted in devilment. Almost all were gamblers of one sort of another, a gallery of eccentrics worthy of Dickens at his most ingenious and Damon Runyon at his most fanciful.

In truth, it was a tale not just stranger but far more fascinating than fiction, more intriguing than the legend so far recorded about the people and events involved.

This, then, is the story of the 'Big Edge'.

Douglas Thompson, 2007
www.dougiethompson.com

Under the influence of uncontrollable ecstasy,
the players gamble their wives, their children
and ultimately themselves into captivity.

TACITUS, *GERMANIA*

Chemin de Fer

The Rules for Those Who Wish to Follow Them

Chemin de fer, known as chemmy, is utterly extravagant in its madness. It is a game of daring and nerve, of impetuosity – a true game of chance. It's as simple as betting on which number of bus will come around the corner first.

All face cards and tens count as zero. The aces count as one, and the rest as they are numbered: two, three, four, five, six, seven, eight, and nine.

If in counting the cards the total amounted to double figures, the ten would be dropped, a seven and six would count as three, a six and four as zero.

Nine is the best number, and called, along with a count of eight, as a 'natural'. The gamble is an even-money bet on which of two players is closest to nine.

Even if a player draws a third card, that decision involves no talent. The rules of the game, the tableau, which in casinos must be followed exactly, dictates mathematically correct play: whether to draw or rest.

Six packs of cards are normally used for a shoe. The croupier never handles the cards directly before a 'coup', a hand; he may move them down the table with his palette. Before the start of every shoe he shuffles the cards, a player cuts them by placing one card at random in the deck (something a clever croupier can 'break'), and places them in the shoe.

The cards in each coup, initially two each, are dealt by whichever player holds the 'bank'; he strokes them singly from the wooden shoe, which has a weight at the back and a metal mesh in front. He is gambling against whoever at the table calls '*banco*', and any player can do that. If the player who calls '*banco*' loses he can immediately call '*suivi*' and play again. This can go on until the bank loses.

Chemin de fer (French for 'railway' – the image of the shoe as a train travelling around the table) is the companion game of baccarat, once the grand gambling game in French casinos. The house provides a croupier to advise players of the rules. It also supplies all the necessary gaming equipment: table, chairs, the shoe (called the *sabot*) and the cards. For that, the house takes a percentage commission (the *cagnotte*, or rake) of 5 per cent on all winning bank hands. The house also guarantees to pay the winners.

Each player can be a banker in turn. The player who is acting as the bank is responsible with his/her own money for all losing bets, as well as collecting all winning bank bets.

The instructions and terms used in the game are in French. In a casino or gambling club chemmy is played on a kidney-shaped table covered with a green beige cloth. The croupier sits in the middle; there are nine seats for the players, the space on the table in front of them being marked with the numbers one to nine. There can be fewer players seated at the table, but never more than nine.

There is a slot in the table beside the croupier's place leading to a cabinet locked into the table into which the croupier drops the *cagnotte* (later a table charge). There is also a nine-inch-diameter hole in the centre of the table into which a removable, cylindrical metal container, flat on top and about two feet deep under the table, is placed. It has a slit into which the cards are dropped by the croupier after each coup.

The first bank goes to the player sitting at the right of the croupier, at number one. He puts in the middle of the table chips (cash is never seen in smart games) to the value for which he wishes to open his bank (his bet).

The player sitting at number two seat has first choice of taking the bet and after that precedence to do so moves anticlockwise – but anyone at the table can call the bet by saying '*banco*'.

The bank deals two cards alternately to his opponent and himself. They are dealt face down. The caller looks at his cards and if the joint count is either eight or nine he turns them over, as does the bank. There is then no further action; the better hand wins.

If there are no 'naturals', the caller can stay put – *reste* – or ask for a third card. The bank has exactly the same judgement to make.

The tableau, a copy of which is usually attached to the chemmy shoe, tells both players what is mathematically the correct strategy to adopt in almost every situation. There are a few situations where mathematically the alternatives of resting or drawing (*avalante*) make no difference to the chance of winning, and the gambler makes a choice. In casinos it was obligatory to adhere strictly to the tableau; in London, the games did not always hold as closely to the rules.

After a winning coup or coups the bank remains with the same person; after the first losing coup it passes automatically one place to the right – the train moves around the table.

Prologue: The Edge of Wonderland

Cheats don't prosper, but they have a big edge.

SYDNEY SUMMERS, 1955

They led the American Ray Ryan up the exquisite staircase, one of architect William Kent's most applauded achievements, to the *Salle Privée* which sat off a landing between the first and second floor at 44 Berkeley Square, London.

It was after dinner at the Clermont Club, and by 10.20 p.m. some of the other card players, in dinner jackets and dark lounge suits, had already arrived. Chatter, thick unfiltered cigarette smoke and the clink of iced drinks drifted around the classically elegant room.

Ryan was the tough, laconic 'founder' of Palm Springs in California. Once an oil wildcatter, he was now a wealthy man, the friend of movie stars, co-owner (with Oscar-winner William Holden) of the Mount Kenya Safari Club and boyfriend of Princess Alexander Hohenlohe (one-time actress and society playgirl Patricia 'Honeychile' Wilder). This particular evening he was extremely relaxed. He was a regular player when in London and was regarded by everybody at the Clermont as an all-round good guy.

Yet the plan that Christmastime in 1963 was not just to lead him up Kent's architectural wonder of a staircase, but up the garden path; to cheat him of £50,000, the equivalent in 2007 of £1 million.

It was a question, John Aspinall, the owner of the Clermont, told his fellow director and long-time gambling partner John Burke, of 'needs must'. At that time gambling clubs were allowed to give long-term credit, so, despite the extravagantly affluent appearance of the Clermont, the company's cash profit was poor.

John Aspinall had borrowed $200,000 from Ryan in May 1963, to cement the Clermont's reputation as the city's most exclusive gambling club and support his own position in London society. He had assumed that when Ryan returned to London he would ask for the loan to be repaid. The snag was that Aspinall could not afford to pay Ryan back. Instead he would 'win' back his debt, with some interest.

Which was why when Ryan took his seat to the right of the croupier, at number one, at the *chemin de fer* table in the *Salle Privée*, an Italian card sharp called Biondi sat at the croupier's left, at number nine. The salon had been turned into a private gaming area that evening for the first time.

Around the table, Ryan could see John Aspinall and other players like John Ambler, publisher John 'Mike' Ryan, the stockbroker Stephen Raphael and his protégé Richard John Bingham, the future 7th Earl of Lucan, whom Raphael had taught to play poker at the Hamilton Club in Park Lane. But tonight, 20 December 1963, it was chemmy, the game of choice in the London of the day, the ultimate game of chance when players went one to one. Players can swiftly win – or lose – enormous amounts of money.

The table set-up had been arranged so that Ryan couldn't make much eye contact with Biondi, who Aspinall had recruited through an international businessman, a questionable golf gambler and shady precious metals dealer who was said to be the inspiration for Ian Fleming's Bond villain Goldfinger. With his agile imagination Aspinall had introduced Biondi, who looked like a sleek, middle-aged, mild-mannered European businessman, as a friend of the Italian car tycoon Gianni Agnelli.

Biondi had collected the specially patterned, cellophaned Caro playing cards (every casino had its own upmarket 'brand' delivered regularly from the company's headquarters at 252 Boulevard Voltaire, Paris) from his contact at the Clermont on 19 December. He then 'treated' the cards so he could 'read' them and they were returned, seemingly innocent and untampered with, on the day of the private game.

For Ray Ryan it was meant to be a night of fun. He was an easy-going, colourful character; a seasoned gambler, he'd been around. Aspinall kept up the conversation at the table with typical embellishments. Biondi was a professional, and when he took the bank he stroked the cards out of the shoe with a practised, pink and manicured hand.

The cards turned for around ninety minutes in the private salon while downstairs in the stunning, splendid Grand Salon, other players, overseen by John Burke on this busy evening, chanced their luck at two chemmy tables.

In the Ray Ryan game, luck had nothing to do with it. Every play made by Biondi was dictated by his ability to 'read' the cards. He creamed off the winning coups and left the losing ones to his victim. With everyone playing on credit in the small, exclusive casino, Ryan began to call for more credit slip 'markers' and only a short time into the game had signed four, each for £5,000. (He had originally staked himself with a £5,000 'marker' for playing chips.)

But Ryan was no easy 'mark'. He'd been involved in the early days of gambling in Las Vegas when most of the desert town was controlled by the Mob. He'd grown up in the toughest gambling schools and had played with sharks before. Biondi just wasn't a good enough mechanic to fool and steal £50,000 from this man who had won, and lost, massive sums of money at gaming tables around the world. Less than two hours had gone by when Ryan sensed something was wrong. Or maybe he spotted a wrong movement. Perhaps it was simply his gambler's antennae warning him that all was not as it should be. He put down his cards and with his hands flat on the table raised himself from his chair. His grey eyes narrowed and he looked over at John Aspinall, who still wore his shameless, engaging smile. Quietly, he said: 'Can I have a word, John?'

The two men left the private salon. Ryan took Aspinall downstairs and into a little room at the back of the *caisse*, the cashier's office. In a quiet voice he told Aspinall that he knew what was going on. Aspinall said nothing, made no attempt to deny it.

Then Ryan asked for his 'markers'. There was a lot going on around the *caisse*. Aspinall called to John Burke and asked him to retrieve them from the *caissier*, the cashier Jim Gore, who had just returned from a tea break. Nearby was a watchful, helpful man who lent the cashier a hand on busy nights like this, allowing Gore to take short breaks.

The part-time cashier was not a man to whom John Aspinall or John Burke paid much attention, although he was very useful. To them, to Aspinall especially, he had the status of a well-connected concierge. Certainly this night Aspinall, as he was confronted by Ray Ryan, did not notice him in the background, his eyes constantly frisking the casino. Neither did John Burke, who was busily explaining to the concerned Jim Gore – who didn't just dish out signed papers to anybody and was nervous because he had to keep exact books – that Aspinall would take responsibility.

Aspinall, still silent, handed the markers to Ryan, who tore them up and put them in his pocket. A careful man, he didn't like the idea of having his signature even on torn pieces of paper in the Clermont. Aspinall remained quiet. What could he say?

Ryan looked at him and said, 'John, steal whatever you want, but don't rob the man who saved your life.'

With that Ryan walked out into the cold night air. He made no fuss. If he had done so it could have been the end of the Clermont, then arguably Europe's most glamorous gambling club, and of Aspinall's social and financial ambitions: Ryan, had he wanted, could have brought down the whole house of cards.

'He was an amazing man,' said John Burke. 'He could have caused a major scandal but he just shrugged it off; he had been around and expected people to try and cheat him in casinos, but John Aspinall he considered a friend. That annoyed him but he never once raised his voice. His attitude was one of disappointment, of being let down. He had a remarkable philosophy.'

As did Aspinall. He was a tough guy. Although badly shaken by what had happened, his first concern was that the show must go on. There was still a game to play upstairs, where there were two empty seats. Biondi, fearful that he was going to be caught up in a scandal, had vanished. The Clermont's star 'house' player, Peter West, was recruited to take his place at the table, and Aspinall rejoined the game and played on as if nothing at all had happened.

Biondi took with him £7,550 worth of Clermont chips that he had 'won'. He returned to the Clermont on 23 December and attempted to cash in. A furious Aspinall – Biondi had failed in his mission – instructed the cashiers to refuse to pay.

A week later the Secretary of the Clermont Club received a solicitor's letter, from Summer and Co., 25 Dover Street, Piccadilly, demanding payment of the £7,550. It was ignored.

Another letter was delivered by hand on 10 January 1964. It, too, was ignored, but behind the scenes a £1,000 payoff was made to Biondi in return for his 'chips'.

The settlement was engineered by a gambler called Leslie Price but known to Aspinall and Burke and everyone else in the gambling world as the Vicar. Price had his own reason for enjoying Aspinall's discomfort and it was he who had introduced Biondi to the West End legal firm. When that got no result he made a phone call to the Clermont:

'Aspers, I hear you're in a spot of bother.'

'What would that be, Vicar?'

'Difficult chaps, these Italians.'

'What can you do about it, Vicar?'

'I can fix that for a couple of grand. That'll get your chips back and you'll never be bothered about it again.'

'Five hundred pounds.'

'Let's call it a grand and be friends.'

'A thousand pounds it is.'

Biondi accepted this. He also, somewhat reluctantly, accepted some advice to leave the country and never return to England again. It was, in the circumstances, astute of him. The man who had told him to get out of town was the quietly intimidating Billy Hill, the controller of London's underworld and one of the most powerful gangsters in Europe.

One of his senior henchmen drove former boxer and 'minder' Bobby Warren to call on Biondi at the flat he was staying at in Chelsea Reach with some travel hints. Biondi didn't require any more encouragement to find his passport.

'Perhaps Biondi wasn't much of a card cheat,' said John Burke, 'but he wasn't a total fool. Better to get out than end up in the Thames.'

Hill, who looked as sleek as Humphrey Bogart in his gangster movie heyday, was quietly spoken but could be so chilling it was said he peed iced water. Like the screen idol, he almost always had a cigarette, a Capstan Full Strength, in his hand or in the corner of his mouth. He was 14 when he committed his first stabbing, and since then he had bullied and battered and cut his way to the top of London's gangland; had carved his place in crime history, often using his shiv to place a V for Victory on his victim's face. He specialized in protection rackets earning from West End nightclubs, drinking dens, bookmakers and illegal gambling joints known as spielers. He had powerful connections with the French and American Mafia.

Now, at the age of fifty-three, he was supposedly 'retired'. The reality was that from his home in Moscow Road, Bayswater, he was simply more careful and corporate in his dealings; he was London crime's chief executive officer, who would advise and finance robberies and other enterprises but found even richer pickings available from Britain's growing casino culture.

Which is why Biondi had to be thrown out of the country. What if there had been a scandal at the Clermont? It would just have drawn unwanted attention to Hill's own endeavours at other gambling clubs in London and Glasgow. The Italian had to go, before he messed up on the doorstep again.

The Ray Ryan debacle had seriously annoyed Billy Hill, something sensible people did not do, because he himself had always wanted to operate within the Clermont. Previously, he had asked his number two, Bobby McKew, to contact his friend and fellow Irishman John Burke. Hill also knew Aspinall's confidante from drinking with him at the Star Tavern in Belgravia where spivs, questionable toffs and Scotland Yard officers mingled most evenings with the pub's rich and respectable clientele.

'I told Bill that John Burke would never go for it, that he

was six-and-eight, straight,' said Bobby McKew. 'Bill accepted that and we pursued our business elsewhere. He didn't put it out of his mind though.'

Hill knew all about the Ray Ryan affair because he had a man inside the Clermont Club who monitored everything, as he had everywhere there was profit to be made. This was the part-time cashier, a clever shadow of a player, whose motivation was never compromized. It was always financial. He changed name according to country, and had so many different ones that they just called him Mr Money. That was his business: making money, moving money. Mr Money connected those who inherited wealth, those who got lucky with it and even some who earned it, with those who would casually take it away from them.

A refugee from Hitler's regime, with almost perfect English, he was a currency operator and jewellery fence. Aspinall was one of his better customers for stolen items, bought for the 'fence' price but insured for the full price against a rainy day.

Mr Money had first established his financial credentials in London, making his first big stake though a simple con. His girlfriend worked as maid to the wife of a shipping tycoon who liked to gamble in Monte Carlo. There was strict currency control at the time, and it was a serious criminal offence to break the rules. Yet, for a fee, Mr Money could do just that. His girlfriend introduced the tycoon to her 'Swiss banker', who was given £25,000 – a vast sum in the 1950s – to transfer to the South of France. When Mr Money and the cash vanished the victim could not go to the police. He was an accessory to a crime, and was not the kind of person to employ gangsters to retrieve his cash from the con man, so he had to accept what had happened.

Although a stocky figure, Mr Money was clever at remaining in the background, an unpretentious chameleon; working both sides of the street, as it were, he was on Billy Hill's weekly payroll as well as the Clermont's. Neither Aspinall nor John Burke was aware of his underworld connection.

Mr Money lived only a short walk from Moscow Road. He would visit Billy Hill regularly – Hill often didn't leave his flat for weeks at a time – to offer information and to be rewarded with two or three hundred pounds: the amount always depended on Hill's mood rather than on the information itself. Still, on the morning of 21 December as he rushed over to Moscow Road, Mr Money anticipated much profit in the news he had to share about the previous evening's entertainment at the Clermont. He knew that, although the Clermont was smaller than other London casinos, the enormous amounts of money gambled there every evening made it the ultimate prize.

Hill was enjoying a pot of tea when his breathless informant arrived. The gangster called for another cup as Mr Money hurriedly made him aware of Aspinall's attempt to rob Ryan and his desperation for cash.

Over that midmorning pot of tea, the wily Billy Hill sensed an opportunity.

1. THE PLAYERS

Picturing a teenaged Bobby McKew digging up turf board to fuel the fires of his home city of Dublin, it's difficult to imagine he'd later be known as 'the Chelsea Scallywag': dapper, with perfect manners, clever, quick-witted, a man whose sociability and tact would allow him to be Billy Hill's lieutenant, the son-in-law of South African millionaire industrialist 'Lucky' Jack Gerber and the close friend of movie stars and aristocrats. Yet he's always been a man of single-minded enterprise. Whatever has been thrown at him he has dealt with in a no-nonsense, practical way. He has accepted the knocks – and there have been a few, mostly self-inflicted – and ridden them out.

His father was in the movies. Robert McKew Senior worked for Rank and was in charge of the distribution of films to Irish cinemas. The powerful film executive thought his son might follow him into show business, which, in some ways, he eventually did. He lived with his father and his mother, Iris, and his two older sisters, Joy and Paddy, in the highly respectable Dublin suburb of Blackrock. The adored only boy in this comfortable, successful family went to Mountjoy College, a prominent Protestant school, but says his father got fed up with paying for him to do little but play sport and told him: 'I'm not sending you to Trinity College to play bloody rugby.'

The solid-thinking businessman hoped his son would join him at Rank, but instead Robert Junior got a job as a labourer, taking what work came around, but especially digging turf board, which kept him fit and put money in his pocket. When not working, he'd meet up with friends in the pubs around town, usually Davy Byrne's just off Grafton Street. Bobby often encountered John Burke, as they moved in a similar set. They were both restless young men, keen for company and intrigued with the world. Bobby McKew wasn't sure what he wanted, other than more excitement than he was getting in Dublin. John Burke simply wanted to play cards, to socialize, but also yearned for a bigger playing board. Among the friends they'd meet most evenings was John Ryan, the brother of the actress Kathleen Ryan.

Kathleen was renowned as a great beauty of her time. Her prominent Tipperary family had opened a shop on Dublin's Parnell Street in the 1920s, the first of a chain known as the 'Monument Creamery'. She was a prize in every way. In her decade-long career she appeared in several films, including her 1947 debut opposite James Mason in Carol Reed's eloquent classic, *Odd Man Out*.

One of her admirers was the gifted safe-cracker and Second World War double agent Eddie Chapman, who was more colourful than a rainbow and a dab hand with gelignite and the ladies. He treated them both delicately and to good effect. The safe-cracker came to Ireland to pursue Kathleen Ryan and one evening in Davy Byrne's her brother introduced Chapman to his 19-year-old friend Bobby McKew.

'Eddie always wanted the best,' said McKew. 'She was an utterly gorgeous, long-red-haired girl and Eddie was friendly with her. She lived with her mother Agnes Veronica and Eddie had to be careful with his courtship. But he didn't mind. He was a handsome man and had great charm and birds used to throw themselves at him.'

The young Dubliner was fascinated by Chapman and his incredible, seductive stories of events which were still fresh in everybody's minds. This was contemporary excitement, lavish true-life adventure. Eddie Chapman, the only Englishman to have been awarded the Iron Cross, directly from Hitler, had much to teach. He'd worked for Winston Churchill stealing Nazi secrets, and MI5 regularly had to decline his offers to assassinate Hitler. In 1997, his MI5 wartime files were released by the UK Public Records Office. Christopher Plummer had played Chapman in the rather wooden 1966 film, *Triple Cross*. The British Intelligence file on the agent codenamed 'ZigZag' is much more entertaining:

'The story of many a spy is commonplace and drab; the story of Chapman is different. In fiction it would be rejected as improbable. The subject is a crook, but as a crook he is by no means a failure and in his own estimation is something of a prince of the underworld. He plays for high stakes and would have the world know it. Of fear he knows nothing. Adventure to Chapman is the breath of life. Given adventure, he has the courage to achieve the unbelievable.'

Chapman, who was born in a village near Newcastle, had deserted from the Coldstream Guards in the 1930s and metamorphosed from a professional soldier into a highly successful professional crook, leader of London's infamous 'Gelignite Gang', whose trademark was to use the newly popular American chewing gum to attach the explosives. His MI5 personal file disclosed new details of his life before he became a spy. He had served a series of prison sentences, mostly for robberies, although one came after 'he behaved in Hyde Park in a manner likely to offend the virtuous public and was caught in flagrante delicto'.

He was arrested in Scotland after blowing the half-ton Chubb safe of the headquarters of the Edinburgh Cooperative Society. After endless scrapes and scraps he fled to Jersey, where he was eventually jailed for cracking the safe of a large dance hall. In prison he used his burglary knack to make keys that allowed him to move freely at night between the men's and the women's prisons and pursue the only thing he enjoyed more than blowing up safes.

After the Germans occupied the Channel Islands in 1940, he saw an opportunity for some form of freedom and offered his services to the Germans as a spy. He was convincing enough for the German authorities to move him from Jersey to France, where he was trained in the dark arts of espionage. As a subterfuge, the Nazis pretended to have executed him. In reality, he was sent back into Britain with orders to blow up the De Havilland aircraft factory in Hatfield, Hertfordshire. He handed himself over to MI5, who decided to play him back against the Germans, using him to provide false information as part of the Double Cross system. They staged a fake explosion at the aircraft factory and Chapman returned to Germany a hero. He was then sent back to England as an agent for the second time and fed his German handlers false information about the effects of the V-1 and V-2 rockets blitzing Britain. He is credited with saving the lives of many, many Londoners.

'The Germans came to love Chapman but although he went cynically through all the forms he did not reciprocate. Chapman loved himself, loved adventure and loved his country, probably in that order.' His MI5 file continues, 'The outstanding feature of the case is the courage of Chapman.'

Bobby McKew, who in 2007 regularly visited Chapman's widow Betty, has no doubts about that: 'They never admitted how good he was. My goodness, he went back to Germany! How crazy was that! And then he returned supposedly to guide in the V-bombs. He misled the Nazis and saved thousands of lives. To me he was a big hero. Yet the authorities didn't even give him a pension until 1994 – three years before he died.'

The charges against Chapman (for emptying more than forty safes) were dropped after the war, saving him a possible twenty-year prison term. In time, Chapman became the young Bobby McKew's mentor. Bobby told me the story over afternoon tea at a hotel near his home in Chelsea: 'Eddie became like an older brother to me. I stayed friendly with him all his life. He taught me how to blow up safes, dope greyhounds and a lot more.'

Much, much more.

Chapman was also tough, as Bobby McKew learned early on in their friendship. In those early days in Dublin it was common for young men to get into a fight after a pint too many, but it was carried out in a gentlemanly way. The two combatants would take their coats off, go outside, knock the hell out of each other, and then go back into the pub with missing teeth or a bust-up nose, but the best of friends. It was, Bobby acknowledges now, pointless and stupid. Yet there would be more serious arguments in his life with which he learned to deal more effectively. The lesson came from Chapman.

'One night, I was 21 then, I was in the bar with Eddie and I got into a ruck with this fella about I don't remember what, and we did the usual and went outside. He was a big lad but big people have never frightened me – you can't miss 'em. We were standing off before going at it when Eddie appeared. He had a tyre iron in his hand and he just bounced it off the side of the other guy's head. He dropped like a sack of potatoes. People were watching, had never seen anything like it. Eddie said, "Now, that'll save you a lot of trouble." He was right, and I've never forgotten that. What's the point of getting broken about and your teeth knocked out? Better to get in first and get it over and done with.'

In the weeks that followed Bobby felt stifled by Dublin, and to ease his boredom – and to please his parents – he agreed to take a job with the publicity department of the Rank Organization in London. He found it less than fascinating, but lasted nine months.

Bobby knew few people in London but he would meet Eddie Chapman for a drink. Chapman made some introductions, one of them to Billy Hill.

John Burke was 6 years old when he first picked up a pack of playing cards at the family home in the south of County Tipperary, and the mathematics and thrill of games of chance became a lifelong obsession.

He was born into a prominent Irish family, many of whose members devoted a large part of their lives to horses, racing and hunting. The family money came from business and property investments. His father, Richard Burke, was Master of the Tipperary Fox Hounds, one the premier packs in the country, for more than thirty years.

It was still the nineteenth century when Richard Burke graduated in law from Trinity College and took the long trip to San Francisco to practise. His only connection there was his former nanny, Helen O'Brien, who was now working for a wealthy Californian family. He decided to visit her. It proved to be a romantic decision. Her charge then was the 18-year-old beauty Margaret Donahue, daughter of one of the founders of the Bay city. It was, say the family, love at first sight and they were soon married.

The Donahues owned a bank and many of the streets of San Francisco. A superb horseman, Richard Burke introduced fox-hunting to California, in the Donahue-owned Menlow Park which is now part of Silicon Valley. However, says his son, Richard Burke MFH was not a man of business, and despite all the opportunities offered by the Donahue family yearned to hunt back home in County Tipperary. With his new wife he returned to Ireland and they set up home and enjoyed a financially carefree life. They had four children, but tragically Margaret Donahue died giving birth to their last child.

Richard Burke married again in 1913 and had another four children, and John Burke, born in September 1926, was the youngest. His father was nearly 70 years old when he was born. His highly intelligent Irish mother, Sheila Geoghegan, was a suffragette who had worked with Emily Pankhurst; she was living in London when she married Richard Burke. Her youngest son was rather doted upon and would sit, as a boy, playing bridge with his father.

John's brother Edward became a chartered accountant and in 2007 was retired in France; his sister Eve married Arthur Goodbody, an academic who inherited a series of businesses. He sold them and bought an Irish estate, where he took up farming. His sister Sheila kept her maiden name by marrying a namesake. After her marriage to Ulick Burke the couple established their own estate, and in 2007 she was training and racing horses in County Tipperary.

John, who was given an excellent education and studied engineering, did not overly concern himself with acquiring a profession. After an exceptional life, in 2007 he was living with his partner Caroline in the mists of Ireland, where we talked for dozens of hours:

'I was always thought of as something of a ne'er-do-well. I loved gambling and I was a good bridge player. I suppose I was a layabout. I was studying engineering but didn't find it that fascinating. The cards were much more intriguing. For me, from early on, it was always about percentages. It rather blinded me to being what people would regard as sensible in terms of career and future.

'I was fooling around in Dublin. I got a job at one point

selling calculators, which I rather enjoyed because I do like numbers – life really is all about odds. Yes, there is luck but it is percentages, often tiny ones, which count most.

'I shared a flat in Dublin with Richard Parkes. He was one of the nicest people I have ever known. He was English but his family lived near Dublin and we were great friends. I played a lot of cards, often at Trinity College, with, among others, two divinity students, who would leave the game on a Saturday night and Sunday morning for about an hour to do God, and then gamble again. I suppose they were hedging their bets.' John Burke's talent at the card table won him a place on the Irish Bridge Team and he represented his country in international matches. Each year there was the opportunity to play at the top level in European capitals. One year, aged 22, he attended a bridge congress in Copenhagen. On the way back to Dublin he stopped off in London. He liked it, and stayed for a week.

Five years later, in 1953, the International Congress was in Finland. On the way home from Helsinki he again stopped in London. 'It turned into a fifty-year holiday . . .'

Today, London society is much changed from the circles he mixed in then, where the characters he met could have been drawn from the novels of Evelyn Waugh and were, in some cases, the inspiration for Waugh and other writers. It was a world inhabited by the gifted and the deluded, the famous and the infamous; where you could be rich one day and poor the next and vice versa: you couldn't bet on it either way. There could never be any odds available. Or much public gambling.

As the nation struggled out of the lingering aura of auster-ity there were no casinos or betting shops (cash betting except at the tracks was illegal); no one-armed bandits, no spread betting or betting exchanges like Betfair (where more than £300 million was wagered via their website on the 2006 World

Cup). Even the housewife's choice, bingo halls, had not yet arrived on a scene governed by gaming laws established more than a century earlier. Under the 1854 Gaming Act groups could gather and play cards, and gamble on anything they liked, but the hosts or organizers of the games could not charge for providing the facilities. That was illegal. Of course, that didn't prevent such enterprises.

For John Burke and Bobby McKew, London in the 1950s was like two cities: there was the rarified world of Belgravia, Mayfair and Chelsea, where the inhabitants had money and glamour and double-barrelled names. Gentlemen were still gentlemen, with their sacred code of honour. A gentleman would always honour a gambling debt, whereas his tailor or wine merchant might have to wait to be paid. Tradesmen were, well, tradesmen. At the same time, the capital was also a city of myriad dark corners and double-barrelled shotguns, of bohemian Soho with its spivs, pubs and clubs and its clip joints where tinsel and morality were casually stripped off. Gangsters would cut, shoot and kill – often each other – for power and profit. Each territory had its own rules and risks. Yet they often made a compatible connection.

That London was a village compared to the sprawling metropolis of the twenty-first century; Hampstead was an out-of-town trip, and there was no congestion on the roads to charge for. Of course, few people had cars. The average price of a house was £2,081. A skilled worker took home about £11 a week – the equivalent in today's money of £161. An income tax rate of 45 per cent did not help. Foreign travel was unheard of for most people. A flight between London and Paris cost £10 – nearly a week's wages. Trains still ran on steam, but a programme of electrification was being introduced.

London had the intrigue of wartime Lisbon and the action of pre-war Berlin. It was a potent mix. It wasn't so much *Who's Who* as Who was Really Who? There was certainly a sense of anything goes, an overspill of the Blitz mentality, of the blackout; for the wide boys, the chancers at every level, there were many opportunities. The cold war was chilling nicely and many ordinary people were still suffering post-war deprivation; food rationing did not end until midnight on 4 July 1954. Yet an extraordinary mix of aristocracy, landowners and villains were rolling in cash.

John Burke, a tall, elegant man who quietly kept his own counsel, found friends in both camps – as did many others. Mark Sykes, a man of aristocratic connections and a leading rascal of the times (he was the inspiration for Robin Cook's landmark 1962 novel, *The Crust on its Uppers*), is certain the connection followed on from the war, where officers and other ranks relied so tremendously on each other.

'It was a very positive thing at that time,' he says today. 'It hadn't happened since the days of William Crockford, since Regency times – and it hasn't happened since. It was a time of toffs and spivs, the other lot didn't matter one bit. The upper classes and the lower classes always get on well because they hate the middle classes. They regarded them as terribly pretentious. Which they are, of course, they are.'

Indeed, 'suburban' appeared to be the dirtiest word of that time; John Osborne's plays, the Northern novels, and real-life dramas of the 1950s and into the 1960s reflected a view that the only lives worth living were ones of privilege or those of the working class. It was working-class lads, actors like Albert Finney (*Saturday Night and Sunday Morning*) and Tom Courtenay (*The Loneliness of the Long Distance Runner*), who brought them to life when they were celebrated in the cinema. It was a time of Shakespeare or the kitchen sink. 'It was an extraordinary time. Fun, always fun, even when things did get a little shaky,' observed the ever-ebullient Sykes.

When he arrived in London, in Belgravia of course, John Burke found life intriguing, although there were to be 'shaky' moments for him too. It was a time of change but also a time where everything appeared to offer a financial opportunity. People were smarter and sharper, and most of all the con men and hustlers, scam artists, the gangsters and the gamblers. It was a time for opportunists, for players.

John met two sets of people: as a professional bridge player he mixed with world-class bridge masters like Boris Shapiro and Terence Reece, and bridge players like Michael Alachouzos, Eric Leigh-Howard, Emilio Schisa, Stephen Raphael, and the Frenchman who ran an illegal poker room at Crockford's (the original Hellfire Club) in Curzon House Terrace. Through his friend Richard Parkes (owner of three dog stadiums), who was also now living in London, he met a racier circle, men like 20-year-old already buccaneering entrepreneur Jimmy Goldsmith, and Peter Sargent, the son of hugely popular conductor Sir Malcolm Sargent. Peter was fond of the horses and was known to the bookies, then and later, as 'the bandleader's boy'.

Parkes' close crowd also included the 26-year-old Ian Maxwell-Scott, a well-connected aristocrat (he called the Duke of Norfolk 'Uncle Bernard'). With the help of a family trust, he would happily gamble around the clock, at the racetrack (horses and dogs) and card tables. The great-great-great-grandson of Sir Walter Scott, he was calm, enervated, ever confident, never fazed by anything, and to John Burke likeable in the extreme. He also liked the more energetic John Aspinall, then aged 27, who was Maxwell-Scott's great friend and fellow gambler at Oxford University. The smart set called him 'Aspers', but he was almost a stranger in this confident crowd of men, people who were rich and connected to the upper classes in a 1950s Britain still ruled by grandees. Aspinall was the new boy on the block; he was an *arriviste*.

He was also the most outré of men, an iconoclast who wanted to join the party, in his case the Establishment, at the same time as he was giving it an enormous thumping. In the military manner, he carried a rolled umbrella with a gold pencil built into it with which he would mark his race card. One day at the races a punter watched him and exclaimed, 'Blimey! The Count of Monte Cristo!' Certainly for Aspinall, as with Dumas's Monte Cristo, there were other people's treasures to be enjoyed.

Aspinall worked at the image. He was tall with blond hair and an athletic figure and cut quite a dash around town. He has been called a maverick but he wasn't: he was a wide boy on the make. He just spoke a little differently from his counterparts on the other side of the game. And, when he wanted to be, he was egocentrically charming, a brilliant and amusing raconteur, which all helped create the myth. John Burke found him splendid company from the moment they first met at the offices of Sydney Summers, who ran an illegal SP (starting price) betting shop from a flat in Jermyn Street.

Sydney Summers was a near-sighted East End Jew who spoke like Henry Kissinger and wore thick glasses which gave him a sinister look at odds with his kindly nature. A master of understatement, he would have squeezed perfectly into a corner booth of a Damon Runyon speakeasy with Harry the Horse and Bookie Bob. He was a character, and he ran a thriving business. Bookmakers had offices, rather drab affairs, where you could ring up and place a bet, and they were 100 per cent legal. But places like Sydney Summers', where you could go and hang about with friends, have drinks and place a cash bet, were not. Of course, they were far more convivial and far more popular.

As always, John Burke was well groomed and smartly dressed – good suit, polished shoes (Fosters of Jermyn Street) – when he first met John Aspinall. He was also with the wealthy Richard Parkes and known as someone who played bridge for high stakes. Aspinall took this to mean that his new acquaintance had money. Of course, he didn't.

Aspinall invited John Burke to lunch at Wheeler's in Knightsbridge. He was not yet the sophisticate he would learn to be but he wanted to impress Burke so when he ordered white wine to go with the fish he picked the most expensive, Chateau d'Yquem. It was a sweet dessert wine. Yet by a remarkable metamorphasis, within two years Aspinall was hosting lavish dinner parties where everything was perfect. He was a quick learner – at everything, including how to cheat at cards.

John Burke found himself enjoying Aspinall's company: 'Occasionally I played poker with him. We used go to the races together or to Sydney Summers' office and then on to tea at the Ritz, which was only a short walk away. Sydney had his marvellous connections; many policemen won on the horses without even placing a bet. There was never any trouble and always lots of fun.'

As the new friends gambled around town, John Burke repeatedly heard stories about an amazing card 'mechanic' called Bruce, an Australian who had displayed his proficiency in London at the start of the decade. As a young man, Bruce had murdered his wife and spent nine years in jail in Tasmania. Every day, all day, in his prison cell he had developed his skill with cards. By the time John Burke arrived in London the card sharp had flown home, but the legend of his expertise remained.

John Aspinall had met Bruce through an agreeable East Ender called Joe Dagle who ran a poker game with Bruce. The Australian could arrange cards in a certain way without being spotted as he shuffled the pack (or, in the case of *chemin de fer*, packs). Bruce taught Aspinall, and presumably others, some simple card tricks. The legend of Bruce would live on in all sorts of establishments, usually of the gambling variety. It moved along like falling dominoes . . .

Dagle lived with Pauline Wallis, who was an appealing,

charismatic lady. She would graduate in the club/gambling trade with some associates at the Mount Street Bridge Club in Mayfair, once a fashionable card club where John Burke played. Her brother Aubrey once acted as a 'runner' for Aspinall and Maxwell-Scott when they ran a short-lived SP office – half a dozen telephones and two rooms – at 33 Dryden Chambers near Oxford Street, an operation financed by Richard Parkes.

The influence of Bruce on Aspinall and subsequent events cannot be stressed too much: he gave him not just the know-how but the intent and the callous application of it. The willingness to take an edge – if not, yet, the big one.

From Bruce, Aspinall learned one simple card trick which, cleverly used in five-card stud poker games, was to separate wealthy young bucks around town from their generous allowances. The poker games, which were not illegal as no charge was made, were staged in hotels and flats in central London locations by Aspinall, though not in any organized way. If he and Ian Maxwell-Scott saw a mug poker player they would get him into a game. An opportunity was an opportunity; it was casual but calculated.

Which is how the great con man George Denison-Webster found himself a little short of readies. Something of a toff, Denison-Webster, at this time in the money, was wandering through the foyer of the Ritz when he was spotted by Aspinall and Maxwell-Scott. Early in the evening they inveigled him into a poker game in their hotel room, the cost of which they almost always recovered. By 5 a.m. the next morning the inevitable had happened – their guest was a huge loser.

Denison-Webster wrote out a big cheque and left. Aspinall spotted that it had been drawn on a bank in his victim's home town of Moreton-in-the-Marsh in Gloucestershire. Aspinall knew that Denison-Webster, although he had money, was highly likely to stop the cheque when he realized what he had done. So he got Maxwell-Scott to drive off in the early hours to be on the doorstep of the Cotswolds bank at 9.30 a.m. with the cheque and to lodge it to Aspinall's bank in London. At 10 a.m. Aspinall instructed his bank to call Moreton-in-the-Marsh and find out if the cheque had been cleared and it had. By then, it could not be stopped by Denison-Webster when he woke up at lunchtime after his costly night.

It was in those early days of their friendship that John Burke identified what the Duke of Devonshire called the 'amoral' aspect of Aspinall's character. 'I reflect now that John Aspinall was pathologically dishonest. I think it was through Bruce that he first "practised to deceive". He certainly defrauded a young man called Rory McKechnie. I witnessed some of the game. John was desperate for money, and Rory had inherited £100,000 or something like that.

'I'd called to visit him and a game of stud poker was in progress. There were four players – Aspinall, Maxwell-Scott, another friend of his and McKechnie. Somewhat to my surprise, I noticed that on one hand when John was the dealer he arranged the cards in such a way that he would win the hand at the expense of McKechnie; in other words, he cheated. His method of doing so was simple. There were four players and the victim was sitting opposite to him. The game was five-card stud, in which the first card each player receives is dealt face down and the remaining four cards are dealt face up. While shuffling the cards before dealing, Aspinall arranged the top eight cards so that the second and sixth cards (McKechnie's hand) would both be kings and that the fourth and eighth cards (his) were aces. Since one ace and one king were hidden and John bet sportingly and freely without even looking at his hole card – good psychology – a large pot built up before the inevitable, though apparently and mathematically improbable, denouement took place when full five-card hands were revealed.'

John Burke's reaction was to be slightly shocked – gentlemen did not cheat at cards! It was beyond the pale. Apart from the drudgery of honest toil there were other methods of keeping the wolf from the door, such as getting very long-term credit from landlords, tradesmen and others, knocking bookmakers, skilful honest card play, being economical with the truth and charming to bank managers and, *in extremis*, bouncing the odd cheque – issuing what Ian Maxwell-Scott called 'nasties'. Now he had seen Aspinall, who had the appearance and manner of a gentleman, behaving like a card sharp – actions condoned by his aristocratic friend Maxwell-Scott.

Burke confronted his friend, asking him what was going on and what he was up to. Aspinall smiled calmly back at him. 'Burkie, it's all just as needs must. A necessity.'

'Necessity?'

'I've written a couple of important cheques and if they turn into nasties I'll be homeless. Didn't want them to bounce, so I had to get the money.'

Burke nodded and said nothing.

Aspinall went on: 'And it's big enough stuff to get me taken to Tattersalls and warned off all racecourses.'

John Burke understood the implications, and also understood that for Aspinall there was an even stronger reason to cheat.

'I've been tipped about an unraced two-year-old which is going to do the business. I needed the money for that.'

'For John this was an extremely plausible explanation,' says Burke, 'to have wind of a pending coup. He wanted, needed, all the financial firepower he could get. It would never have been in his nature not to go after it.

'John's attitude was that he had stolen a few hundred pounds which was nothing to the amount the lad had been gifted. It was not going to damage him financially. That summed up John Aspinall's morality. John was a determined and charismatic character and he made those reasons difficult to argue with. He often talked of his ambition and his perfect evening. He dreamed he was playing poker in a luxurious, upper-class club and saying: "Your monkey, Duke, and up a grand."'

John Burke admits he could have objected to Aspinall's devious methods and simply walked off. He didn't. Instead, he witnessed other victims being taken, including one important company chairman.

Why? Ambitious politicians often find it helpful to their advancement not to be burdened with sincere, rigid principles and beliefs; gamblers and entrepreneurs also find an advantage in having a flexible moral code.

One game led to another, the stakes and, increasingly, the chances taken, ever higher. At the Westbury Hotel, in that affable cul-de-sac off Bond Street, a poker game was taking place in the fourth-floor room of John Burke's good friend Stephen O'Flaherty. The ebullient O'Flaherty was a superb and enormously rich businessman with the Volkswagen and Mercedes car concessions in Ireland and England. At 4 a.m. the management objected to the gambling, rather grossly pointing out that they were acting illegally on the premises. O'Flaherty booked out and never stayed at the hotel again. There were other hotels, and lots and lots of other games.

Mark Sykes attended many of them and ran some himself. He was not an Aspinall fan: 'People always thought he was a tremendous sport because he'd offer to cut the pack at the end of an evening for the total winnings, which could easily be in excess of £1,000 – in the 1950s, quite an amount. The helpful Aspinall was always the first to cut the pack.

'What all these people didn't know is that it's one of the easiest things in the world to win, usually with a card that is a very slightly different shape and in the shuffle put next to an ace. A card player like Aspinall could perform that trick in a second – he didn't need to tamper with the cards before the cut.

'He always sought the upper hand no matter what. He could be very disagreeable. I went out with his half-sister at one time and I don't think she had much time for him. Aspinall was an absolute world-class shit, but he was good company. That's the story, really. He was a world-class shit. A very good phrase which I will always remember in conjunction with Aspinall is, "It's very easy to steal from your friends."'

Unfortunately, even with the card tricks, John Victor Aspinall was not making enough money at poker to satisfy his expectations. As the perceptive John Burke – an eyewitness and primary connection to all that happened – has pointed out, Aspinall was quick to learn the rules and terms of engagement, and to use them fully to his own advantage.

Which he did when he first met the Vicar.

2. PREACHING TO THE CONVERTED

For what we are about to receive,
may the Lord make us truly thankful . . .

TRADITIONAL DINNER GRACE

He was middle aged, middle class, plump from good food and red in the face from the bottle of claret he normally had with dinner. He was tough, told risqué stories, was foul-mouthed in general conversation, and they called him the Vicar in the way that classroom giants are known as Tiny.

Leslie Price, the Vicar, had no illusions about humanity. It was there to be fed off. He had a voice, but not one for sermons. He was a grand storyteller, spouting his tales above a chequered waistcoat bursting with good living. He was also an extremely clever gambler with gangland connections. Indeed, blessed were the strong.

John Aspinall first encountered the Vicar in the early 1950s. It was a 'road to Damascus' moment. They were both on the make, Aspinall with his poker parties and Price running highly lucrative gambling evenings.

Aspinall's connections were immaculate even before he saw the light; he knew people who were happy to gamble and, so much more importantly, reliable in paying up. As well as the trusted Ian Maxwell-Scott, his crowd included people like Anthony Blond of the Marks & Spencer family; Johnnie Holbeach, the future powerhouse of Gordon's Gin; the affable but naughty Peter West; Richard Parkes; Dominick Elwes; newspaper heir Vere Harmsworth; Alan and Colin Clark (sons of Lord *Civilisation* Clark); and wealthy American Gerry Albertini. It was a glamorous set, enlivened by the presence of people like Lady Jane and Lady Annabel Vane-Tempest-Stewart, daughters of the Marquess of Londonderry, and Lady Annabel's future husbands, the tall Old Etonian Mark Birley (first) and Jimmy Goldsmith (second), and Jimmy's brother Teddy. Princess Margaret's crowd hovered and added another cloak of sophistication. When the veneer was stripped away, all that was there was more veneer. For the majority it was all jolly fun; for Aspinall it was a deadly serious business.

Perhaps appropriately, his life up to that point had been something of a lottery. He was born in Delhi on 11 June 1926. His father – or so he believed – was Robert (Robby) Aspinall, a medical officer in the Indian Army. His mother, originally Mary Grace Horn, was the daughter of a civil engineer. Robby and Mary Grace had married just two weeks after they had met on the dance floor where Robby was a star turn. Their first son Robert, always known as 'Chips', was born in 1924.

John, the second son, was very much his mother's favourite. At the age of 6 he was sent with his brother to a boarding school at Eastbourne and the boys saw their parents only once a year for the next half-dozen years. They spent their holidays either with their maternal grandparents or with a local farmer, Jack Pring, who became a surrogate father and taught young John the lore of the countryside.

His parents divorced when John was 12 but it wasn't until he was 26 years old that he discovered one effect of his mother's unhappy marriage and another influential 'Bruce' in his life. He found out that his true father was an Army officer, later Major-General George Bruce, and that he had been conceived under a tamarisk tree beside a lake in Uttar Pradesh after a regimental ball. Mrs Aspinall's extramarital lover had then been a young captain in the infantry with something of a reputation, being apparently a useful swordsman privately as well as professionally.

In 1938, Aspinall's mother had remarried George Osborne, who had beautiful home in Sussex. When her husband inherited a baronetcy, his mother, who could never conceal her delight at such a thing, became Lady Osborne, forever known in the Aspinall circle as Lady O.

Much of John Aspinall's ruthlessness and determination was inherited from his mother; Lady O. was a keen gambler and a remarkable woman. Once she opened a credit account with Charlie Matthews, a well-known Irish gypsy bookmaker who also ran a second-hand car business at Warren Street and a huge tyre business, Matthews of Brixton. Charlie, who bet under the name 'Monk', was himself a dodgy character noted for his 'strokes'. For once, he met his match.

Lady O.'s weekly racing account went the way that such accounts frequently do – she had a sequence of small winning weeks and duly received her modest cheque on the following Tuesday. Then one week everything went wrong; the get-out bets, small at first, got bigger and bigger and all of them lost, right up to the final plunge on Saturday. So, for the first time, in her Ladyship's mail on the Tuesday morning, instead of a cheque from Monk, a large bill arrived. Charlie waited confidently to reclaim everything he had already paid Lady O., plus some more.

John Burke recalls it well: 'Perhaps he waited patiently – knowing Charlie I doubt this – but he certainly waited. After about a week he began to get a trifle worried and so he telephoned Lady O. to ask for his cheque. Charlie's telephone manner was, of course, superficially the most friendly. "'Ow

about a little kite, love – 'ave you forgot?" He was not, however, prepared for the effect that his friendly words had on
Lady O.

'Adopting a majestically haughty tone, the "Lady" verbally
tore a strip off the unfortunate bookie – never before or since
has a message so full of disdainful contempt been carried over
the telephone wires between East Sussex and Brixton.

'"Matthews! How dare you telephone up your social
superiors and ask for money; I will have the law on you!" was
the final outburst before Lady O. slammed down the receiver.
The account remained unpaid, and when we wanted to wind
Matthews up we'd only have to ask, "Have you seen Lady O.
recently?" The air would immediately turn blue.'

The one driving force in her life was the intense devotion
and protective urge she felt for her son, John. The she-tiger
guarding her cubs from danger was as harmless as a teddy
bear compared to Lady O. when she felt that her darling
needed support. John Burke knew her well and was often in
awe at how calculating she could be: 'Though not overly
intelligent, she had a devious, totally crooked mind and was an
accomplished schemer.' The famous Whites Club description
of Lady O. was that she had 'the mind of a Borgia in the body
of a cook'. The remark has been attributed variously to the
Duke of Devonshire, Bernard van Cutsem and Henry Vyner.
Whoever said it was spot on.

However she behaved to others, Lady O. looked after her
youngest son as far as she could. Yet the great influential event
for the teenaged John Aspinall was his reading of H. Rider
Haggard's *Nada the Lily*, the tale of Umslopogaas, illegitimate
son of an admired Zulu king, Shaka. Against all odds, and
standing alone, Umslopogaas becomes a magnificent warrior
and triumphs; the book began for Aspinall a lifelong obsession
with the Zulus and with tribalism.

Many others have tried to explain the psychology and the workings of Aspinall's mind, yet even as they do, it's clear they have never totally grasped it. John Aspinall was a curious, complex character. He firmly believed in the survival of the fittest, that the strong would rule the world, the weak go to the wall. He was an unmatched mixture of good and evil. John Burke saw his man in glory and in desperation, often as startled as a rabbit in the headlights. He explained:

'He had very definite set views about some things. Once he got them into his mind, he would convince himself that he was right, then no power on earth would make him change his mind. I know that he would justify his conduct in his own mind, saying it was like a tiger's entitlement to kill deer.

'Following from that, he was entitled to rob the rich, the decadent, and weak and useless people in order that he had the funds to do what was important in the world. In his eyes. In his eyes alone.'

Lady O. arranged the more secular aspects of her favoured son's upbringing with the help of the always kindly and generous Sir George, who paid for him to go to Rugby. In 1943 the school suggested he did not return for another term. After Rugby, he spent three years in the Royal Marines.

In 1947, aged 21, he went up to Jesus College, Oxford, where the first thing he learned was guilt-free gambling fever. It was there that he established his life-long friendship with Jimmy Goldsmith. They were kindred spirits: Goldsmith had left Eton as a 16-year-old following an extraordinary gambling success, an accumulator bet on three horses, Merry Dance, Bartisan and Your Fancy at Lewes, a roll-up, which netted him £8,000. So when Jimmy Goldsmith turned up at Oxford to visit his brother Teddy and met John Aspinall and his set, he was in financially sharper shape than the others. But it was determination, single-minded attitude and poker playing which made Aspinall warm to him, though Aspinall was seven years older. It was a mutual attraction.

Mirroring his new friend's audacious gambling, Aspinall risked his entire term's grant of £70 on a horse called Palestine in the 2,000 Guineas. It won in a photo finish at 7–2 on, and Aspinall's faith in himself soared – even with short odds.

The winnings were as short-lived as the odds. He was sent down for missing his 1950 finals, feigning illness and slipping away, with the ever-ready Ian Maxwell-Scott, by hired Daimler to Royal Ascot, which had the bad luck to clash with the examinations.

The affable Maxwell-Scott was most certainly a leading star in the gambling set. At Grand National time in May 1956, he and John Burke were staying as house guests of Richard and Angela Parkes at their flat in Wellbeck Street. The two young men were in financially embarrassing circumstances – they were broke.

Maxwell-Scott was a long-odds player at the horses; he always bet on outsiders. For the Grand National he worked out that ESB (Electricity Supply Board in Ireland), quoted at 66–1, represented the best value in this tricky lottery. A borrowed two pounds was his total gambling capital, and he courageously wagered it all on ESB to win. John Burke recounts the story still with some amazement in his voice:

'Two pounds may sound a paltry sum of money. However, fifty years ago and in the prevailing financial climate of the Parkes' house guests, it was far from paltry, in fact, we considered Maxwell to be brave to the point of foolhardiness for betting his all on such a long shot. The race is well documented in the history books. The Queen Mother's horse Devon Loch came over the last jump well in front of all the other horses still remaining in the race and was striding out to win easily, when, just before the winning post, he slipped and slithered down onto his belly.

'This allowed ESB, who was a long way behind in second place, to gallop slowly past the prone Devon Loch and win the Grand National. We were listening to the race; the commentator was Raymond Glendenning. Glendenning pulled out all the oratorical stops in order to describe this royal equine tragedy with due solemnity. In measured funereal tones, his commentary continued:

' "A hushed silence has fallen over this vast crowd, stunned by the enormity of the tragedy they have just witnessed. While all our thoughts, our hearts and our sympathy go out to the most gallant of ladies, our Queen Mother . . ."

'At just about this point, when ESB had safely passed the post and was confirmed as winner, the Parkes' drawing room was shattered by an eruption of raucous laughter. It was Ian braying, in his own inimitable aristocratic tongue.

' "Wup! Wup! Wup Wup!" he thundered. "Fuck the Queen Mother; I had a two-er on ESB!"

'Financial reality totally scuppered Glendenning's eloquent bathos.'

Financial reality was not something which interfered with John Aspinall's lifestyle. He never took to regular employment, despite the efforts of his stepfather Sir George to help him with his 'connections'; instead he spent his days at the racecourses and his evenings, when possible, gambling at cards. He was often lucky at the races and was regarded as a good judge – of rich men as well as of horses.

He became friends with Gerry Albertini, a rainbow of genetics but American by birth and wealthy from his family's clever US business investments with Reynolds/Veitch. 'Gerry was always kind and generous, to all of us, not just John,' remembers John Burke. 'With Gerry's financial help, John had a few spectacular coups at the races. But he would lose just as spectacularly. Gerry or Richard Parkes would usually bail him out but that was not a balance John liked at all.'

What could Aspinall do? The ongoing drawback for a man with irregular income was the lack of regular funds.

'Yet, whenever he had a "sure thing" he was able to get the money to bet; he would never miss an opportunity. It didn't matter who had to lose their money, or how they lost it,' recalls John Burke, who would become a friend of the Vicar.

John Burke would play poker with Leslie Price but was never invited to his professional chemmy games – for the obvious reasons that he was too good and canny a card player and, more importantly, was not rich. With the chemmy games, the Vicar had picked a winner. It made him rich, bought him a spectacular home in Esher. There he had installed a slot machine, a one-armed bandit. It was intended to distract not his card players, but his staff. The gamblers tipped generously and the Vicar calculated, correctly, that he'd get that money too, with the waiters and others playing the machine. He did not miss much.

His success was built not on a grand idea but a clever one: convenience for his clientele. In the late 1940s and early 1950s Britain's wealthy gamblers would fly from Lydd airport in Kent to France, to the casino of Le Touquet, to feed their gambling habit and perhaps play golf during the day. Deauville was also close by. There, of course, the game of choice was chemmy. When he published *Casino Royale* in 1953, Ian Fleming had James Bond gambling in north-eastern France, in the fictional town of Royale-les-Eaux, because that's exactly where the action was at the time the book was set, in 1950.

The Vicar decided, correctly, that if the games were closer to home there would be even more action and, for him, profit. Of that he was certain. For with chemmy there was a crucial advantage to the host – there was a 5 per cent charge, the *cagnotte*, on every winning bank. No matter how the players prospered, with the French rules – that 5 per cent charge on at least 50 per cent of hands – the house always won. In Leslie Price's games, he, the Vicar, was blessed with profit at every evening's gambling.

Still, he made one error. After he had begun running his so highly lucrative chemmy games on a carousel basis at friends' and associates' flats and homes in the West End and Belgravia, he went, as he often did, to the Star Tavern, the fiefdom of the late and lunatic landlord Paddy Kennedy.

The Star stands on a quiet cobbled mews at the end of Belgrave Square. An early nineteenth-century building, it was created to house the servants from the rich homes of Belgravia. When Paddy Kennedy took over the house, the catacomb of domestic rooms had been opened up, with scrubbed pine tables and two fireplaces in the downstairs bar and the kitchen upstairs with another bar. Upstairs was, de facto, private, in that if Kennedy took a dislike to a customer he or she was told to get lost. Indeed, the only thing extraordinary or spectacular about the place was the landlord.

The Star, although a little obscured by the arch framing the northern entrance to Belgrave Mews West, was a magnet for an eclectic cast of characters, many of whom considered luck itself a skill – or maybe an art form. Rather like life. John Burke often played spoof at the bar with the great painter and, as a young man, highly enthusiastic gambler, Lucian Freud. They were regulars, as were Bobby McKew and, in the mid 1950s, John Aspinall. Over time they chatted with glamorous characters like Chelsea-set leader, the well-connected Michael 'Dandy Kim' Caborn-Waterfield, and soon-to-be Great Train Robber Bruce Reynolds. There would be Billy Hill at one end of the bar and Wally Virgo, Commander of Scotland Yard's Serious Crime Squad, at the other, a case in those quiescent days of law and disorder, and vice versa. Between them would be the man all the regulars called 'Boss', once the richest man in the world. The Eton-educated Sandhurst graduate and newly divorced Maharaja of Baroda, Sir Pratap Sinh Gaikwad, enjoyed the cut and thrust of the company.

When he was at Eton he'd been approached by a master and reprimanded for not attending church.

'But why would I?' asked 'Boss'.

'To pray to God,' boomed the pompous master.

'Sir, in my country, I am God.'

He didn't act the part at the Star, however. He was also always happy to buy a round, ordering in his soft, agreeable English–Indian accent, which endeared him even more to the crowd. Eddie Chapman reckoned 'Boss' was the nicest foreign person he ever met.

Paddy Kennedy, the landlord, a biggish, often exhausting man with dark hair, dark humour and either a grin or a scowl on his red Irish face, was as much an attraction as the customers. He was tough, loud, and if anyone – it didn't matter who – upset him, he would physically eject them from the premises. But his bark could be worse than his bite. One evening Eddie Chapman was there with his friend and associate Jim Hunt. Kennedy placed his chin on the bar and challenged Hunt: 'Go on, hit me!'

Hunt's fist moved about three inches; Kennedy was out for twenty minutes.

Kennedy said he wouldn't allow the Kray Twins, then fledgling gangsters, through the door, but the reality was that they would not have tried to drink there because Billy Hill did, and he was the guv'nor. John Burke met one of the Krays one evening when he was at dinner with Kennedy at a nearby restaurant. Not long afterwards at the Star he inquired of Billy

Hill what their status was and got the quiet reply: 'I let them do little jobs for me sometimes.'

Paddy Kennedy always got on well with John Burke, Bobby McKew and the Vicar – as he did with Billy Hill, who used to sit in a corner of the pub playing cards for astronomical stakes with Peter Rachman. Rachman's protégé Raymond Nash, a large, gregarious, clever and colourful Lebanese, would sit watchfully at another table.

Peter Rachman's name cast a notorious shadow over London in the 1950s and early 1960s. Part of his infamous legacy was to the English language. The *Concise Oxford Dictionary* defines Rachmanism as: 'Exploitation of slum tenants by unscrupulous landlords. From P. Rachman, London landlord of the early 1960s.'

'What used to astonish us,' recalls Bobby McKew, 'was that Bill sat with a pack of cards on his lap and openly cheated Rachman. There wasn't much of an attempt to disguise what he was doing. He'd sometimes drop cards, aces and kings, on the floor and pick them up. There was no attempt at subtlety.

'It was all about Rachman not losing face. He didn't want to be known as a man paying protection money, but if you didn't look after Bill, whatever you were up to quickly got shut down. This way Bill got his money and Rachman got to get on with what he was doing.'

It was an eccentric environment. Paddy Kennedy did not let much upset him, perhaps because his own behaviour was not always to order. To get Elizabeth Taylor to move seats, when she was on a visit to London promoting her movie *Beau Brummell*, he ordered: 'Get your fat arse off that stool and let my friend sit down.' She happily obliged.

John Burke recalls the ambassador from an African nation being rather more flummoxed than the Hollywood star by Kennedy. The ambassador and his retinue had arrived for lunch. It was busy. He enquired several times what the always short-fused Kennedy would recommend from the menu to be finally startled by a bellowed: 'Try the roast missionary, you black heathen bastard!'

The Star was a refuge for many, including genuine refugees. 'Achtung' Alfie was an Austrian Jew who had escaped Hitler's regime, and was well liked. One evening in the Star he went on and on about his brother who had fled to America and made his fortune after the war. 'I should have gone to America,' moaned Achtung. Kennedy was getting irritated, but still Achtung whinged on: 'I should never have bothered with bloody London, a waste of time.'

That did it. Kennedy cracked down a pint glass on the bar and turned on Achtung Alfie: 'You snivelling bastard – you should have stayed in Germany: you'd 've been a grand lampshade.'

'There's no doubt what Paddy was,' says John Burke. 'An argumentative, intolerant, racist, sexist chauvinist. He was also the kindest and most generous man I've ever had the pleasure to get drunk with.'

Kennedy employed a superb barman who called his boss 'Sir' and gave the customers their titles and due reverence. When 'Boss' Baroda saw Kennedy in a dreadfully hungover state he offered to buy him some salvation.

'His Royal Highness would like to buy you a drink, sir.'

'Tell the cannibal to make it a large one.'

Yes, he could be affable when he wanted. Kennedy owned a beautiful Alsatian called Danny who had a famous trick. When the pub was full, the dog would bound down the stairs and Kennedy would command: 'Danny! Show us what girls do to get fur coats.' Danny would roll over on his back with his paws in the air. Danny knew the score, as did the girls in the minks.

It was at the Star that the Vicar met his match, though of

course he didn't realize that he was about to be screwed. He allowed John Aspinall to, as it were, look up his cassock.

'Another drink, Vicar?' asked Aspinall in the upstairs room, nodding for top-up gin and tonics for himself, John Burke and their companion. The Vicar was clearly prospering. On occasion, Burke and Aspinall had met him at the afternoon races, but Leslie Price usually kept vampire hours.

'You're looking in great form,' Aspinall told the Vicar. He then went on to enthuse about Leslie Price's success and his own more precarious gambling life. The Vicar, overcome either by the gin or the charm, quietly explained in the crowded, smoke-filled bar that his upmarket evenings of *chemin de fer* were always odds-on winners.

Then he made his mistake: 'Aspers, why don't you come along one evening. Burkie here is a poker man, but you come, you'll like it.'

The chemmy evening was on the upper floor of a house, since knocked down and redeveloped, off Park Lane. Aspinall pointed it out to John Burke as the place where he hit the jackpot, although his funds were in 'a spot of bother' that first night and he lost.

Aspinall told John Burke he had gone to the game with the casually charming court jester Dominick Elwes who, in company, softened Aspinall's sharper edges. Elwes's girlfriend Sarah Chester-Beatty was there too, and she, as bad luck required, provided the cash to pay off the two men's losses at the Vicar's evening.

Aspinall immediately spotted the secret of the Vicar's affluence – the *cagnotte*, the table slot into which went 5 per cent of every winning bank. The *cagnotte* depended on the bravado and the bankroll of the player who had called 'banco'. As the evening progressed it steadily mounted, shoe after shoe, hour after hour. Some shoes could accrue a *cagnotte* of £100. If you were the host, like the Vicar, then chemmy was that curious and supposed impossibility, a sure thing. With the *cagnotte* in play life was, without any complaint, a cabaret.

John Aspinall grasped the possibilities immediately.

'Come again next week,' said the Vicar. 'Sorry you lost.'

John Burke was told what happened next: 'John rushed away with no intention of ever returning. The Vicar probably reckoned John would be back with more of his friends and boost the profits. Not a bit of it. John was already working out what food to serve at his own chemmy parties. One of his first stopping points was to see Paddy Kennedy who he did a deal with to provide booze on credit for the first parties. Paddy liked John, enjoyed the chancer in him.

'But with these games John played it straight. Why not? Eventually, if the debts were honoured, the money would roll in.'

The Vicar was much greedier and liked more than a little edge with his chemmy. One evening at a pub called the Bunch of Grapes in Knightsbridge he explained to John Burke how that had become a problem at his big Ascot week game:

'The Vicar had just had his big game of the year during that important racing week and quite deadpan he told me his tale of woe. The right sort of people were playing, all right, but the wrong people were winning. People who settled immediately on the dot when they lost were winning and people who were slow payers were losing. House players were getting drunk and making fools of themselves and *banco*-ing when they should be keeping quiet. Everything that could go wrong, went wrong. Leslie Price had one thing in his favour though. He had one line of defence: he employed a very experienced French croupier, a man in his sixties called Louis.

'I knew him, as did others, as "Louis the Rat". He was quite able to arrange the cards to the Vicar's advantage. After one disastrous shoe the Vicar announced, "Well, now we'll go next door and have champagne and caviar and we'll have a little relaxation and then we'll carry on playing the next shoe."

'They left the table and went into the next room to be served with the best-quality champagne and caviar and all the trimmings. One player, Lord Willoughby de Broke, who was extremely rich and the star player of the evening, did not indulge. He just came from the chemmy table for a moment and then he said to Price: "Leslie, that croupier of yours looks very tired, I think I'll give him a hand."

'Price, of course, was horrified. He had to stop this happening. I can still hear him saying: "I tried to explain to His Lordship that the croupier wasn't really tired, it was just the way he happened to look."

'He couldn't stop him and his lordship went back to the table where "Louis the Rat" had already "prepared" quite a lot of the cards. They were stacked up nicely, in every sense. Willoughby de Broke took the cards and thoroughly reshuffled them, to the total horror of the Vicar, who moaned, "All this good work done for nothing!"

Good 'mechanics' could swell the proprietor's profits. Considering that in French casinos chemmy croupiers spend hours every day for years of their lives shuffling cards and putting them into a wooden shoe, it's not difficult to imagine how, with ingenuity and more practice, they can attain quite spectacular skills. Yet, like the fastest guns of the Old West, there is always someone quicker. Or with a better idea.

It most certainly looked as if the Vicar had blessed John Aspinall, who, it appeared, had never had it so good.

3. DUCKING AND DIVING

So we beat on, boats against the current,
borne back ceaselessly into the past.

F. SCOTT FITZGERALD, *THE GREAT GATSBY*, 1925

When he finally got fed up with being a publicity shill for the Rank Organization – he felt confined by the job, the hours and by office life – Bobby McKew found himself being happily drawn into Chapman's inner circle of associates. There was always a scheme, a scam, a way to earn a guinea or two; there was plenty of work outside the nine-to-five parameters, especially in the gambling arenas.

In this world without betting shops, there were the book-makers' allocated spots at the point-to-points and racecourses which offered opportunistic betting, and a shaping of the odds at times; they had long been controlled by 'Italian' Albert Dimes, who had a justifiable reputation as a killer. He was the official minder to Maxie Parker, one of two brothers who bought Ladbrokes from its previous gentlemanly owners. One had to be careful, but the young McKew's new friends were older and more experienced, especially Billy Hill who had overall control. They went where there was money, not trouble. Which included the greyhound tracks, as Bobby McKew recalled:

'At one meeting we doped five of the runners. We used something called Luminol which was hard to detect. What we didn't know was that the trainer, for his own reasons, had doped the sixth dog, the one the bent money was going to be on. All the dogs staggered out of the traps. It wasn't a race but an endurance test.

'Once we went to West Ham where they had a great sweeping racetrack. It was in the middle of winter and one of the dogs was drugged up so much it couldn't take the bend – it went straight into the straw bales at the side of the track. Doping certainly wasn't an art form.'

Nor were his escapades with gelignite: 'Eddie was still blowing safes and I'd go along with him. Just for company, you understand. On one particular safe in a London office I said to Eddie: "Can I do it?"

' "Go on then, have a go," he told me.

'I was very young and silly. It was a small wall safe. I put in far more gelignite than you should, and when we touched it off the door came off and it went through three walls. Each one getting bigger; you could see right outside. And there was all this confetti flying up and down in the air. The money. There was a lot of money in there. We were covered in dust and tiny bits of banknotes and I was upset at making a mess of it, but Eddie just laughed and shrugged: "Don't fuss, there's lots of other safes."

'That was Eddie, a real man.'

Bobby McKew found that Chapman could always surprise him. On a little adventure in Paris he arranged to meet Chapman at Fouquets on the Champs-Elysées. When he arrived Chapman introduced him to his companion: 'Bobby, Otto. Otto, Bobby.'

Otto was Obers-Sturmbannführer Otto Skorzeny, Hitler's favourite commando, and the most colourful and famous Waffen SS commander of the Second World War. His daring at the Battle of the Bulge and missions during the Ardennes Offensive and in Hungary during Operation Panzerfaust had won him a reputation as one of the most dangerous men in Europe.

That other dangerous man of the time, Adolf Hitler, personally ordered Otto Skorzeny to rescue Mussolini, who was being held captive. Skorzeny tracked the Italian dictator halfway across Italy for a month and a half until he finally found him at the Hotel Campo, a resort high in the Gran Sasso mountains. Skorzeny took his troops up in gliders and crashed them on the steep rocky slopes surrounding the hotel. They stormed the hotel, capturing the place without a shot being fired. After finding the room where Mussolini was held prisoner, Skorzeny entered, knocked down the chair of the radio operator, destroyed the transmitting equipment and standing to attention exclaimed: 'Duce, the Führer has sent me to set you free!' Mussolini was promptly loaded onto an aircraft that landed after the assault, and flown to Vienna.

Chapman certainly had contacts.

The idea was that Otto Skorzeny and Bobby McKew would help him rob the Vatican. During his wartime escapades, Eddie Chapman had travelled to Rome and been given a tour of the Eternal City. His eyes had all but popped out as they scanned the riches on offer. He was taken to a basement where he was shown diamonds, paintings and gold. He was overwhelmed by the riches, by the possibilities. He told Bobby McKew: 'The Church have been robbing the world for two thousand years – we should rob them.'

Bobby told him: 'It's impossible – it's better protected than Fort Knox.' But Eddie was deadly serious. 'We'll all be billionaires,' he confidently predicted.

'I'd never heard the word "billionaire" until that time,' Bobby says. 'I must say it had a magical ring to it. Eddie was certainly very excited about it. And determined to do it. He made plans and set about recruiting a "crew" to raid the Vatican with him, and Otto and I were to be in on it.

'We would have been very rich men if we'd got away with it. But where would we have spent the money? Alaska? In an igloo eating lots of salmon? There are lots of Catholics everywhere in the world who would not take kindly to the robbing of the Vatican . . . but Eddie got distracted. He got involved in a huge deal in Ghana.'

Back in London, Bobby McKew found himself kicking his heels. He had become friendly with Billy Hill and helped him with the occasional situation but it was then a casual relationship. Bored and looking for adventure, in the early summer of 1953 he sailed to the Mediterranean on his friend Dennis Ives's yacht *Zura*. They found themselves in Antibes, known for sun, sea, sailing and schemes. He also met his friend from London, Michael 'Dandy Kim' Caborn-Waterfield, one-time actor, entrepreneur and well-known social figure.

Kim was aware of Bobby's abilities. 'Always well-dressed and never short of money, he was something of a mystery man. I had seen him racing with maharajas at Ascot, dining with Errol Flynn and drinking at the Astor through the small hours with the villains who controlled the London underworld. And wherever he was there were invariably beautiful girls, all of whom pulsated with an overt sexuality. Strongly built, with wavy fairish brown hair, Bobby clearly exerted a reciprocal sexual force. He was a happy extrovert, a dedicated satyr and a lot of fun at a party, and though renowned for having a short fuse he forgave as quickly as he hoped to be forgiven.

'I was walking past the Carlton terrace in Antibes when I saw Bobby taking *petit dejeuner* on the terrace with Dennis Ives. Ives looked bemused. He was somewhat older than us, a peripheral figure who was known to specialize in arbitrage and "hot" money laundering. At a glance he could have passed as a small-town estate agent but he had a villa in Le Cannet and a yacht in the harbour. He said very little but missed nothing.'

As Ives stayed quiet, the two friends caught up with each other. Kim was playing games on the Côte d'Azure, where you can lie on the sand and look at the stars, and vice versa. He had romanced Barbara Warner in New York, and in the South of France met up once again with the teenage daughter of omnipotent Hollywood mogul Jack Warner. The strongest currency on the Riviera, outbidding the dollar, the yen and most certainly the euro, is the rich man's whim. It has been that way since the Côte d'Azure became a playground for kings and princes, wet-set hedonists and international society.

The passion for possession trumps prudence every time. Since the days of Scott and Zelda Fitzgerald – Scott the novelist, Zelda the novelty – the place has been a magnet for the creative and self-destructive. Giant figures in twentieth-century art and literature – Picasso and Cole Porter, Stravinsky and Somerset Maugham, Matisse, Rudyard Kipling and Evelyn Waugh – were all awed by the magical enchantment, the magnificent 'silver clarity' of the light.

For Jack L. Warner, one of the four brothers who founded one of the original Hollywood film studios and introduced the 'talkies', his villa on the western coastline was just another accoutrement, one more proof of his power and control. In the 1950s, every movie mogul had to have his waterfront chateau.

The west side of the Cap d'Antibes has always been accepted by the cognoscenti as a richer venue than the east. It has to do with the view towards Cannes and the setting sun. This is what provided extra cachet for Warner's Villa Aujourd'hui, a dominant, gloriously white house on the S-bend of coastline above the rocks and the Lilliputian-style harbour of L'Olivette. It was designed in 1936 by the American Barry Dierks, the fashionable architect of the time. He created floor-length windows throughout so that most of the rooms looked straight out to the Cannes headland and that unique blue sea, all the way to the horizon.

Warner enjoyed showing off this prize. There were huge and often wild parties. The guests were household names: Charlie Chaplin, Marilyn Monroe, Elizabeth Taylor; Frank Sinatra and Mia Farrow spent their honeymoon at Villa Aujourd'hui. Warner, brash and arrogant, lorded over all of it. He would take up residence with his wife Anne and daughter Barbara. Later, he would use it as a getaway to be with his lover, the French singer and actress Juliette Greco.

Kim Caborn-Waterfield was in a situation Jack Warner would never understand – he was low on funds and keen to change that situation. He had bar bills to pay and wanted to ship his car back to London. He told me:

'Jack Warner was away and Barbara said she would get money – money I had loaned her in New York – from her father's safe. It was his casino winnings and she said he had promised her a percentage as she had brought him his good luck. She gave me the cash in big ten-thousand-franc notes.

'That escapade got me the reputation of a Riviera thief. The actuality of it was that I didn't even have to open the safe which earned me that dubious renown. I was charged with stealing a quarter of a million pounds in twenty-first-century money.'

Bobby McKew was also charged.

The story of that evening at the villa on 25 August 1953 changes according to who is telling it. Later, Barbara Warner offered her version to a London courtroom: 'At about 9.30 p.m., before dinner, Kim took my arm and led me inside. He said he needed more than 100,000 francs to pay his hotel bill. He asked me if I knew where the key to my father's safe was.

'He searched in my father's bureau for the keys. I did not tell him where they were. I just stayed there. He found the keys and he opened the cupboard and then the safe. Inside he found bundles of banknotes and a travelling bag. Kim took them out. I noticed he counted the bundles to a total of 2,000,000 francs. They were in 10,000-franc notes.

'He opened the bag and went into raptures about the contents. He was going to take everything, but I resisted that. I took the bag from him and he took the bundles of notes. He said he was going to take more than the 100,000 francs. He could have taken 300,000 to 400,000 francs. He then took out a handkerchief and carefully wiped the walls and the safe to remove the prints.

'He put the money in his pocket, and when we got downstairs he told another man about the contents of the safe. His exact words were: "Do you know there is a safe with a great deal of money in it?"

'The other man was agreeably surprised. He turned to me and said: "Can anybody take it?" '

The other man was presumably Bobby McKew. There was, says Bobby, much 'ducking and diving' following the villa robbery: 'The French authorities wanted me to appear in court but I refused. At the time I just pissed off and tried to stay out of trouble and out of France. That Dennis Ives had some of our money and he might have half grassed. All the time they were saying they wanted to interview me, but I've never wanted to be interviewed. I never made a statement then. I won't make one now. I never make a statement.

'Once I was on the boat scrubbing the deck and they came down looking for "Mr McKew". I looked like a tramp and said he wasn't there and they went away. I was the only person who never made a statement.

'The money? Oh, it went to some interesting places, and people. There was strict currency control at the time, so having that sort of cash in your pocket was useful.'

There was an intriguing aftermath to the Riviera robbery when Bobby McKew returned to London, reflecting the power of the then 42-year-old Billy Hill. The Duke and Duchess of Windsor were visiting, staying in the English countryside. And the Duke of Windsor had been robbed. It was something that has never been reported, but what concerned the Duke most was his missing diary; it was a five-year day-at-a-time diary which detailed his movements and meetings, his opinions of the Royal Family and of politicians. It was crackerjack material. Bobby McKew remembered:

'I was out on the Thames with Eddie Chapman and Jimmy Hunt. We were just messing about, trying this boat out, and when we came back to the dock a couple of police squad cars appeared. It was Fabian [the famed Superintendent Robert Fabian, on whose career a popular 1950s television series was based], and he wanted to know if Eddie could help with the return of the Duke's diary. It seemingly had lots of delicate material, who he was seeing, talking to, who, or possibly what, he was screwing, that sort of thing.

'They were quite willing to do a deal. No questions asked. Fabian knew Eddie very well, there was no question about that. As it turned out, Eddie couldn't help. But someone must have, for nothing was ever heard about the diary – and no one was nicked.'

This sort of approach was not unique, says Bobby McKew, even if, in the Duke of Windsor's case, it was extremely discreet. When Gordon Richards, the only jockey to be knighted, was robbed of the golden spurs presented to him by the present Queen's father, King George VI, the higher echelons of Scotland Yard were in something of a frenzy. 'One of the senior coppers was friendly with Billy. Bill had some very heavy contacts there. One day he came off the phone and said, "I've just been talking to ___ _____ and they want a favour."

'Bill got the gold spurs back for Gordon Richards. I don't know how, but I do know he never got a note of thanks from that man Richards who knew what had happened. Every time Richards' name came up Bill would mutter, "That fucking pygmy."'

By now Bobby McKew had a strong association with Billy Hill but was also close to an Indian princess whom he had met through 'Boss' Baroda. One evening the princess introduced him to her friend Shiv Kapoor, partner of fraudster Emil Savundra who, when he arrived in London from India, opened a travel agency in Victoria. He was an enterprising chap and that enterprise took Bobby McKew on the road to Morocco, or rather to the seas off Tangier where he went to work as a smuggler. It was a clever operation, much like a VAT fraud today, where goods were smuggled into Morocco and then came out, officially stamped, as genuine Moroccan-made. It gave Bobby McKew a taste for smuggling, and he began his own operations.

The whole idea of devilry on the high seas and the centre, Tangier, has a romantic ring to it. As Bobby McKew discovered, the reality was more mundane: spark plugs, nylons (the dodgy salesman's best-seller throughout Europe, particularly England), booze and cigarettes, Les Blondes for the light-coloured American tobacco. But he liked the life, the adventure. He sailed with an assortment of crews, mostly contacts from London, around from Tangier to Gibraltar, and along the Spanish coast from Marbella. In 2007 the locations have not changed, just the contraband. Bobby McKew shakes his head, recalling his innocence.

'I remember another smuggler asking me, "When are you going over to Spain?"

' "On Friday."

' "Would you take a couple of suitcases for me?"

' "What's in them?"

' "Hash."

'I thought: "How dare you!" Hash! Drugs! I was very priggish about it. I don't know how many months later I woke up at four in the morning and thought: "Oh God, what I am being such an idiot for?"

'In those days dope just didn't enter our minds. We were getting gin and Scotch out of bond at six shillings a bottle and selling it on for a couple of quid a bottle. But we were really into cigarettes, which is where the big profit was. We put them into Spain and sometimes on long hauls to Italy. We worked all around the Mediterranean. There were quite a few Brits. One smuggling boat captain was "Skip" Edwards, the brother of the comedian Jimmy Edwards who was a big radio star as Pa Glum on *Take It From Here*.

'Lots of different sorts of people love it out there.'

Bobby McKew was commuting between London and Morocco. He was socially adept, a businessman with interests abroad. He was now seeing Anna Gerber, a waterski champion and the daughter of South African multimillionaire 'Lucky' Jack Gerber. His friend Billy Hill, although he did not divorce his wife Aggie, had become enamoured of 'Gypsy' Riley, who as Phyllis Riley had left East London, taken up with 'road' people and then been recruited by Maltese pimps. Then, to all purposes, she became Mrs Billy Hill. The two couples would often go out for an evening together.

And with Billy Hill interested in the action in Morocco and financing some of the operations, they all went to Tangier. Bobby McKew already had accommodation, but Anna Gerber found a flat for Billy Hill. In 1954 it cost £4 a week and in 2007 it was still in Hill's name.

Billy Hill liked the Mediterranean too. And Tangier. 'Tricky Tangier, lovely little spot,' he called it. The city is on the North African coast at the western entrance to the Strait of Gibraltar, where the Mediterranean meets the Atlantic Ocean off Cap Spartel. For opportunists it was all about location, location, location.

The smuggling was good, regular if not spectacular business. Nonetheless, as well as the irritation of customs boats there were the hazards of French gangsters and the power of the Union Corse, the criminal organization which originated in Corsica but was now a highly corporate underworld operation run out of Marseilles. Billy Hill had connections with its leader, Marcel Francisi. That link, similar to but stronger than those he had with the American Mafia, allowed him to take out some insurance on his and Bobby McKew's enterprises. In return the Union Corse needed Hill's backup for any operation in London. Foreign travel was good for Billy Hill's mind. And, in time, very profitable.

Bobby McKew is admiring of the Union Corse. 'Much more powerful than most people ever realized – tougher than tough, more so than the Italian or American Mafia.'

Somehow Hill, whose seventeen years behind bars had left him with a lifelong penchant for prison food, especially corned beef and potatoes, connected with the world of couscous. 'I ate food I had never heard of, met people who were actually kind as well as educated, who were friendly although they were loaded with gelt,' is how he described this particular 'abroad'.

That was his publicity statement. Privately, Billy Hill imported his own food: corned beef, sides of meat, tomatoes and eggs. Bobby says, 'He used to go to a restaurant called the Nautilus in Tangier and give them the food. Then at night he'd come and order dinner and he'd pay for his own food. He was unusual.'

Hill was more than unusual. He had been involved in scores of gang fights, and cut and punched his way out of trouble. His reputation was fearsome, giving him an iron grip on his crime empire. He stood for no nonsense. At an illegal gambling club he ran in Soho a punter, Sammy Naylor, who owed Hill £200, appeared one night to gamble. Naylor wanted to win back his losses. Hill explained that he must pay off his debt first.

'You can't get blood out of stone,' objected Naylor.

Hill gave him a light slap on the face. 'Sammy, who says you're made of stone?'

The debt was paid the next day.

Hill watched over all the details, small debts, big robberies. All the people who worked with or for him, and many of the lawmen, the judiciary and the police who tangled with him, credit him as a criminal mastermind. One of twenty-one children born into a family of criminals in 1911 in Seven Dials, near Leicester Square in London, he was 'at it' from his youth. He became a house burglar in the late 1920s and moved on to specialize in smash-and-grab raids targeting furriers and jewellers in the 1930s. During the Second World War, hc moved into the black market, operating in foods and petrol. He also supplied forged documents for deserting servicemen.

In the later 1940s he was charged with burgling a warehouse and fled to South Africa, where he took over illegal activities at a string of Johannesburg nightclubs. After being arrested for assault, he was extradited to Britain, where he was convicted and jailed for the warehouse robbery. It didn't deter him. Prison never had, just as it never seemed to bother 'Mad' Frankie Fraser, who appeared to have no regrets about spending much of his life in jail when I met him in July 2006. He didn't, they say, get his nickname for nothing. We went for a wander near his home in south London and past a pub called the Stroke of Luck.

Frankie, aged eighty-two, his hair styled like a Brylcreem advertisement and coal black, wearing a blue pinstripe suit, and pristine apart from one spot of blood on the collar of his freshly ironed white shirt where he'd nicked himself shaving, was in lively humour. Brighter and louder than a brass band, he bubbled down Browning Street ('after the fuckin' poet, don't you know?'). He looked over at what had once been white and brown paint, now peeling in faded shreds from the pub: 'Stroke of Luck? – fucking place has been closed down. We'll go round the corner.'

The landlord and the scattering of lunchtime customers greeted him like a returning war hero. We sat in the corner where he nursed a vodka and tonic. Yes, Billy Hill, whom he worked for most of his life, when not in jail, was a mastermind who ran London's crime scene like a chess game.

'Bill didn't know the meaning of the word fear. That's why he was special. If fear had come anywhere near him, he would already be plotting how to go around it. Or he'd get in first and wipe them out before they could have him. At certain times, he knew every cop that mattered in London. He could pick up the phone to the top men. I reckon at one time he had a hotline to the Commissioner. They knew they could trust him. There has never been another man like him before or since. If you wanted to pull a bank job, rob a post office, or make chalk drawings on the pavements of London, you had to have Bill's OK.

'I first met him when I was very young and getting a name for myself – not Bill's standards, but always in plenty of trouble in prison. Your name went around. I done a call for Bert Rogers, him and his brother. They were in Chelmsford Prison with Bill before the war, when Chelmsford Prison was a Young Penal Service institution for those around 21 to about 28. Bert Rogers knew Bill well and he introduced us to him.

'Some years later, 1947 or beginning of 1948, I was in Wandsworth Prison with Bert Rogers and who come on the exercise but Billy Hill. He had just got three years for a warehouse job. Bill didn't want to hang around that long. That's when he tapped up Jack Rose. Jack Rose had the cats [whipped by the cat-o'-nine-tails] done three times, he'd been birched for punching screws and he wasn't getting out early.

'Bill said to me: "Do you think he'd stand for it?"'

'I said: "What do you mean, Bill?"'

'"Well, get him to attack a screw – he's lost all his remission; I jump up and save the screw . . . Do you think he'd stand for it?"'

'I said: "Provided he's going to get some dough out of it, of course he would, Bill. He'd love it."'

'We approached Jack and he did love it. He got a monkey (£500), which was a lot of money in 1947. A lot of money. A day or two later, all of a sudden, Jack jumped up and shouted at a particular screw: "What do you keep looking at me for, you bastard?"'

'The screw hadn't looked at him at all! But Jack goes for him, starts attacking him. Bill's rushed in there and pulled Jack off the screw and calmed it all down. For his good deed Bill got a few extra months on remission. Everybody was happy. Including the screw. What I didn't know then is that Bill had the screw in his pocket 'n' all! Bill always covered all the angles.

'I go way back to when Bill was a kid and I would put Billy above everyone else. In our life, our world, I would put him above everyone. As much as Charlie and Eddie [Richardson], which are two terrific guys, and Italian Albert, terrific guy, nevertheless, I would still put Bill up there. I haven't met another one yet.'

Once out of jail, Hill planned daring 'larks' including a

1952 post office van robbery and a spectacular bullion heist in
Lincoln's Inn Fields in 1954. Ten days before the bullion job
he had announced his retirement, and when the robbery took
place he was giving interviews about his 'retirement' in the
South of France. He was never charged.

Cat burglar George 'Taters' Chatham, who only stole the
very best from the very best of people (he styled himself
'Burglar to the Gentry') found himself in deep difficulties after
the post office robbery. Chatham liked to think of himself as a
Raffles figure. He wore Savile Row suits, drove a drophead
Mercedes, and in his long career as a gentleman thief (much
of it spent in jail) stole an estimated £100 million worth of
treasures.

He was on the Hill team for what was then Britain's biggest
armed robbery. The gang pretended to be a film crew working
near the post office depot by St Paul's Cathedral. Chatham
disconnected the alarm system on the mail van and Hill's mob
moved in and hijacked it. The take was £287,000. Of that,
£15,000 went to Chatham – who immediately gambled it
away at Billy Hill's gaming tables. Chatham then attempted to
'retrieve' his share from Hill's safe but was caught. Hill did
not punish him – he would get even more money from
the gambling cat burglar after his next job. It was a mature,
pragmatic move.

Hill was forty-three then, a snappy dresser in his handmade
suits and a fedora with the brim neatly snapped forward. His
hair was carefully dyed and slicked back with Morgan's
Pomade. By then he had proved himself as a fighter: now he
saw himself more as a businessman, someone to gain advantage from every opportunity. He had no intention of ever
going back to jail. There were escape routes mapped out for
every hint of trouble. Hill was not a literate man but he was
numerate. You could tell him the income and outgoings of the

Star Tavern and he would give you the percentage profit in seconds. The point was that Billy Hill was only interested in profit, and in opportunities for making it.

His passion for moneymaking was illustrated after Bobby McKew and another of Hill's henchmen, the engaging gambler, club owner and smuggler Patsy Murphy, got into trouble at a London club popular with lesbians.

'Patsy had started out doing photographs of tourists in Trafalgar Square – Bill had given him permission to do that for a few bob in return. Much like these street folk in Soho now have to pay over a backhander if they want peace,' says Bobby.

'One night we went out to the Star. Afterwards, we all went round to this lesbian club we'd heard of. Some tart asked Patsy's wife, who looked about seventeen, to dance.

'They danced, and the next thing a butch one came along and said that Patsy's wife was dancing with her girlfriend. Before we knew it, they were on the floor. I said to Patsy, "That's your old woman under there." Patsy pulled her to the top and pulled her over. The next thing mayhem broke out.

'I never knew lesbians could fight like that. There was blood everywhere and I got hit in the chin. It was a terrific bump, a Sonny Liston with a bit of Ali spin on it. I happened to be standing about a foot from the wall. I hit the wall but if I hadn't, I would have gone down.

'I remember hitting someone over the head with a bottle. Gave someone a good bash.

'But everyone was at it, all over the place; I don't think they'd had such fun for a long time. Anyway, there were bodies everywhere and we left.

'The police came but we managed to get out. About two or three days later, and it shows what Billy was like, I got the command performance. "Come round, have a cup of tea."

'I went round and he said in that quiet, drawling voice of his: "Here, what was all that commotion in that club the other night?"

'I told him. He said that he wanted me to do him a favour. He had his dead eyes on: "Look, I'll give you a monkey and you take a monkey up to Murphy but you must promise me one thing – you don't go in there any more. Ever, ever."

'For a monkey you could buy a car!

'I remember going up to Murphy who lived up in Maida Vale. He shouted: "Oh, God, a monkey. We'll never go in there again."

'We didn't, thank God.

'It wasn't until about a year or two later that we found out that the owner of the club had gone to Bill and she said, "I want that McKew and Murphy killed." Bill said: "It will cost you ten grand."

'He got the ten grand and gave us a monkey each! That was Bill. But we got on well. That was just a little bit of business. But if I hadn't kept my word and stayed away from the club I suppose he would have had to enforce his contract.

'Ain't life grand – or nine grand, as Billy would have seen it.'

Indeed, Billy Hill considered himself a winner. He was in profit. Which was perfect.

There are hosts of stories of Hill taking money to 'sort out' problems, of everything from 'cuttings' to contract killings. There are stories of bodies being burned. How true are they?

Hill, in his memoirs, *Boss of Britain's Underworld*, suggests that all he did was stop people doing 'foolish things'. He and his team solved problems. There is one ominous note about this enterprise: the name he gave it, saying: 'During 1952 to 1953 we undertook three hundred missions on our Murder Inc. business.'

Bobby McKew remembered one 1950s gangland get-together, a show of support for a nightclub owner: 'One night at the Pigalle there was a charity evening and a row broke; the police arrived in a rush of cars. They leaped out and asked the doorman, "Who's in there?"

'He told them. There was Billy and us at one table. At the next table was Albert Dimes and his crowd. Beside him was the Twins' table. Billy Hill, Albert and the Krays. The police wouldn't come in. If they had everybody would have united, for the police were the police, so they never came in.

'Mind you, it wasn't a terrible row. It was only that fellow Tony Mellor who got killed afterwards in Soho. I think he got shot. Or maybe he had his throat cut. Can't remember.'

The nightclub 'row' at Al Burnett's club in Swallow Street had begun when Mellor, who was into girls and pornography, upset Billy Hill. Hill made no fuss, just got up and hit Mellor over the head with a big glass carafe of water, knocked him clean out and then poured the chilled water over him.

Bobby McKew said: 'He made his own rules and stuck to them. Always. He had an illegal club in Gerrard Street. He wouldn't go into it. It was a gambling club where all the waiters and all the ponces and pimps went in those days, because it was Soho. Billy wouldn't go in. On Saturday nights, late, at 2 a.m. or 3 a.m. Sunday morning, I'd drop him at home and go down and pick up the money. He didn't want to say "hello" and didn't want to talk to ponces. He just wouldn't go in.

'I knew a chap who was an actor and he did quite well; one day Billy asked me in a quiet voice if I was friendly with this actor.

'I said: "Yes."

'He said: "He's a ponce."

'I said: "Don't be silly."

' "He's a friend of Carol Reed's. I see him all the time at the clubs, at parties. His old woman's at it."

' "Oh, Billy," I said.

'A couple of weeks went by and I'm sitting in this cafe in Denman Street and suddenly Bobby Warren came in: he was the boxing promoter Frank Warren's uncle. He said that Billy wanted me. I went outside and Bill was there and said, "Come on, I want to show you something."

'We drove all the way down around Piccadilly, came up by Duke of York Street, St James's. He stopped the car and he said, "Who's that standing at the corner there hustling?"

'It was this actor's missus. I couldn't talk to him again. Bill wouldn't have stood for it: he paid the money, made the rules. In those days you had to be aware all the time that things and people were not always as they seemed.'

That other quiet and clever survivor, south London gang boss Charles Richardson, gave Hill respect. Over lunch at the Savoy in November 2006, he explained: 'Bill survived for such a long time because he was clever and careful and not greedy. He also looked after the people who worked for him. They were loyal and that's important.'

The Krays, who craved his empire, deferred to him. The brothers, although so much has been made of them, were but schoolboy thugs compared to Hill. There was no animosity between them. In a bedside interview in September 2000, when he was dying in a Norwich hospital, Reg Kray told me: 'With Bill the only clever thing to do was listen. He knew what and how to make everything work. I'd never known anyone make trouble go away as easily as him. He was a one-off, nobody ever like him. It was like he could see into the future. He was a businessman, lovely man – if you stayed in line.'

Billy Hill was a different breed, possibly because he came from an even tougher time and background. His chief opponents were from his own time and place, and his rival was Jack Spot. They had fallen out over who would control the London underworld, which led to a nasty fight between Spot and 'Italian' Albert Dimes on the corner of Frith Street and Old Compton Street on 12 August 1955. Dimes was working for Billy Hill and, rather to his surprise, came out top in the fight after he almost severed Spot's arm. From that point onwards, no one disputed Billy's ascendancy.

Spot and Dimes were arrested for assault. In September 1955, Spot was defended at the Old Bailey by the talented Rose Heilbron, the first woman to become a QC and the second to be appointed to the bench. She was supported in the Spot case by Sebag Shaw, a clever advocate and enthusiastic gambler from the same East End street as Sydney Summers. Sebag Shaw, who in his youth haunted spielers and card clubs, would go on, like his leader in the Spot case, to become a judge and to play his role in gambling history. And, inadvertently, to help Billy Hill.

4. GAME PIE, GEMS AND GREYHOUNDS

Mae West: Is poker a game of chance?
W.C. Fields: Not the way I play it.

MY LITTLE CHICKADEE, 1940

The genial John Burke is not a man, or gambler, to be flustered. He doesn't believe in luck. His investment is in odds, in numbers. He is a man whose practicality is probability. Yet his beliefs were to be tested as his London life raced ahead.

It seemed as if the world had suddenly woken up. So much was happening. And, seemingly, so quickly. John Burke had arrived in London in time for the Queen's coronation on 2 June 1953. He was there when Edmund Hillary and Tenzing Norgay conquered Mount Everest the following month.

The lust was for post-war sophistication: as the decade rolled on, London's bleak 'cafe society' with its old, dark-wood tables and bar, its net curtains and bentwood chairs, was replaced by coffee bars with horseshoe-shaped counters, jammed jukeboxes, painted metal chairs, high bar-stools, line drawings on the walls and striped curtains. At the fancily named coffee bars – the Mocamba, Moka-Ris, La Ronde, El Cubano, Negresco, Il Latino, Sphinx, Aloha and Las Vegas – top table was reserved for the whistling, steaming Gaggia espresso machine. For all that window-dressing, it was at the more blandly named Coffee Inn, an establishment in Park Lane where the discriminating customers were cared for and

the ladies elegantly kissed on the hand by the Polish owner
Teddy Knight, that society's various desperadoes congregated.

The grand society story of the day involved Jimmy Goldsmith. After two years of national service, on coronation night,
in Paris, he fell in love with Isabel Patino, daughter of Antinor
Patino, a Bolivian tin millionaire who objected to the love
affair. The story goes that Patino said to Goldsmith, 'It is not
the habit of our family to marry Jews.' To which Goldsmith
retorted, 'It is not our habit to marry Red Indians.'

Isabel Patino was several months pregnant when the couple
eloped and, after a legal battle with her father, married in
Edinburgh. In May 1954, Isabel Patino died giving birth to
their daughter Isabel. Her father never got over it. The events,
of course, made headlines, something Jimmy Goldsmith would
do for the rest of his life.

It was the heyday of soccer stars like Tom Finney and
Stanley Matthews. Brylcreem cricketer Dennis Compton
helped England to the Ashes at the Oval in August 1953,
and Roger Bannister ran the mile in 3 minutes 59.4 seconds
on 6 May 1954.

Then, in 1955, the Goons were on the radio, Teddy Boys
were hanging around jukeboxes in the newfangled espresso
bars and Bill Haley and the Comets were in the hit parade.
More than half the decade had gone when, on 28 July 1956,
Egypt's President Nasser nationalized the Suez Canal. Prime
Minister Anthony Eden weeks later ordered an abortive
invasion. A rising against communist repression was brutally
crushed in Hungary. On 19 April 1956, Hollywood actress
Grace Kelly became a Princess in Monaco. Elvis Presley
pumped his pelvis in the interests of rock 'n' roll.

In the village which was London at that time, where
people, places and deals appeared to be interconnected,
Tommy Steele, hired by Raymond Nash, was getting £10 a
week appearing at the Condor Club above the Gaggia-gushing

and popular Sabrina coffee bar in Soho. Aspinall's world, and the real world, were changing.

By 1957, Harold 'You've never had it so good' Macmillan had ousted Anthony Eden from 10 Downing Street. As the months went by, the Broadway musical *My Fair Lady* would open for its first night in London, to a rapturous reception. The event, at the Drury Lane Theatre, was stellar: Ingrid Bergman, Dirk Bogarde, Terence Rattigan and John Strachey arrived at the theatre to be cheered by huge crowds. Yet the intriguing connection, to many observers, of Rex Harrison and Julie Andrews, of the odd couple, of two worlds intermingling, the East and West End of Eliza Doolittle and Professor Higgins, also brought into play a new phenomenon – the ticket touts. For the first time in London's theatreland there were black-market tickets selling for as much as £5 – almost five times their original price. Oh, what a lovely scam.

But not as good as chemmy. Aspinall was doing all he could to prove that, as far as his own life went, Harold Macmillan was accurate.

From the moment John Aspinall realized what a jackpot the Vicar's games could be, how they could be boosted both in grandeur and in cash with the right settings, accoutrements and players, he attacked the idea with the enthusiasm of one pursuing his first love. Which, at that time, it most certainly was.

There were gangland gambling spielers, but the only real rival for John Aspinall's enterprise was the Vicar. And he did not have the correct vowels or connections or the secret weapon of Lady O.'s game pie, which, like all her cooking, was by all accounts far more pleasant than she was.

Lady O. was an anomaly and a fixture at the games. And, surprise, she usually won – in her own enterprising way. At her son's chemmy evenings she'd provide encouragement to the players, often having a bet herself on the back of a young man's gamble; she would take her share of a win but happily forget to pay up if it was a losing hand. Her 'pocket money' often amounted to hundreds of pounds in an evening. She found pleasure in that system, and since her bets were small in comparison to their wagers, the other players were willing to regard it as 'tips'. Five-star 'tips', nevertheless.

Lady Annabel Goldsmith and Mark Birley, who had worked for the pioneer advertising agency J. Walter Thompson after leaving Oxford, before establishing the Hermès franchise in Jermyn Street, were among the usual suspects at the games, along with prominent players like Lucian Freud, Johnnie Holbeach, Dickie Muir, Nick Ackroyd, Richard Parkes and Gerry Albertini.

Aspinall – flush one day, broke the next – borrowed and cadged what he needed. He rented a good address in Mayfair, on Upper Brook Street, a short walk from Claridge's, and talked his way into getting free and good art for the walls and polished furnishings – the sort you'd inherit – for his punters to relax around. From Sussex and her Aga came Lady O.'s home cooking, from Paddy Kennedy's Star the potent but discounted booze.

And so the chemmy games began. Half a dozen or so went by and, as expected, with reliable players and the *cagnotte* all but winking its cheering connivance from the end of the table, they were extremely profitable. Aspinall used the profits to upgrade the surroundings constantly and tempt more and more high-stakes players. Like all good managers, he ploughed the profits back into the business. A great advantage for Aspinall, then and even more so later, was that the people attending his chemmy games were 'straight', in that their cheques would always be honoured at some point. This might have contributed to the error of judgement he was about to make.

Always dancing attendance was the man regarded as the

best 'house' player of the era: the urbane, intelligent, charming Peter West. He was the son of a Victoria Cross-winning First World War Air Commodore (the RAF had a fly-past over London when he died) and had 'honest' blue eyes (Aspinall called them 'VC blue eyes') that told the world he could never tell a lie. He was married to and divorced from the aristocratic Davina Portman. 'Westie' lived on his wits. His father had flown the skies over the English Channel – his son flew 'kites', naughty cheques. He was a master of it, as were many of his circle.

Forget credit cards and debit cards; the money-go-round then was all about pieces of paper. John Burke told me how the banking business worked then, something that now seems extraordinary: 'We used blank cheques, pieces of paper on which you just wrote the name and address of your bank and signed it. In the old days of the gambling clubs, they were very generally used. Also, of course, cash cheques were very much involved then; you make a cheque payable to "cash" and the person can go to the bank with it, and provided you know them, the banker would pay the cash over the counter, if you had the money to cover it.

'Peter West was a master of the system of getting cash you never had to pay back. He explained this to me once in detail. Apparently, every bank manager had a limit up to which he could lend money without reference to head office. Say the manager had a £5,000 limit; Peter discovered this. He would then go in to the bank manager and get to know him and have a chat, and open an account. Peter had superb manners and was always beautifully dressed, and there was always a reference in conversation to his father being the Air Attaché at the Embassy in Paris, and his father's VC, and all that sort of thing. He'd been married to a very rich girl.

'Having established himself with the bank, he would open an account with an agreed overdraft limit. Peter would use the account, and the overdraft would go up slowly and eventually get up to about £4,000, and then he would stop using the account and nothing much would happen for a while, and he would get the odd polite letter from the bank suggesting he pay it off or that sort of thing. Perhaps, after a while, slightly ruder letters.

'By this time it was more than likely he was living somewhere else. What did the bank manager do? He has now got this debt which he realizes is a probably a bad debt, and if he goes to head office and tells them what has happened, he'll be in trouble himself. The manager is probably going to retire in a couple of years anyway, and he didn't want aggravation, so he would do what was simplest for him. He would sweep the debt under the carpet. With the big turnover of the bank, it would get covered up some way or other. He would keep it showing in the balance of debts or whatever. Eventually he would retire.'

But 'Westie' wasn't the only master at this. Aubrey Wallis was a skillful practioner too.

'Aubrey was rather naughty, but charming,' says John Burke. 'Aubrey and I once fancied the same horse in the Cambridgeshire Handicap and both had a good bet on it; we were flying together from Heathrow to Limerick on the afternoon of the race, which was on the BBC. The next thing I knew, it was coming through the Aer Lingus broadcast system. Aubrey had had a word with the captain.

'He always liked to "have a word". He was particularly good with bank managers.'

Once, when he needed a new bank account, Aubrey made an appointment to see a West End branch manager. He arrived armed with a cheque for £1,000 that he had got from a friend, and he chatted up the manager in marvellous style. The manager opened the account on the spot.

A couple of glasses of Tio Pepe later (it was a civilized

era), Aubrey was given a chequebook – twenty-five cheques – having lodged his cheque for £1,000. John Burke explained, 'Aubrey tended to treat chequebooks in a rather cavalier fashion and he soon got writing and paid one or two tradesmen's bills; looked after a couple of bookmakers; gave a couple of dinner parties; paid by cheque. He cashed cheques and generally behaved in the way men tended to do in those happier, more casual far-off days.

'There was one major snag. The cheque for £1,000 which Aubrey had lodged was a dud. It bounced. That meant, of course, that Aubrey at no time really had any money in his account, and his cheques, as they came into the bank, also bounced and were sent back "refer to drawer". Aubrey went through the entire chequebook, and every single cheque came back. They all bounced. Zero cheques paid. It was quite a performance, and surely worthy of mention in the *Guinness Book of Records*.'

Wallis was certainly a legend in his own chequebooks; he had been nicknamed 'Educated Aub, the Downside Dude' by East End bookmaker Eddie Fleischer, but now he needed a new name under which to operate. John Burke and Richard Parkes suggested Major Jamieson; it had the right sort of sound, and rank ('Captain' was too golf-club secretary, 'Colonel' too old), to impress potential landlords and bank managers. And it did, oh, it did.

There were several variations, in these supposedly 'casual' times, of financial endeavour.

'Kiting was a very important activity in those days,' said John Burke. 'Other than "Westie", the greatest exponent of kiting I ever came across was Ian Maxwell-Scott. It was a marvellous activity – if you had the nerve.

'Kiting is very simple. If you cash a cheque on Tuesday evening at the pub/restaurant, they would lodge it on Wednesday and it will get to your bank on Friday. You have two and a half days to put in the money to cover it. Of course, if you cash a cheque on, say, Friday, after the bank closed, it would be lodged on the Monday and see your bank on the Wednesday, so you got five days to clear it. Ian would write cheques like that. When the two days were up he would have written other cheques; on the next day he would have to cash cheques and put in the cash to cover the cheques which were the first to be done.

'He was well known in the pubs all around Belgravia, and he'd go in and start off in the morning having found out from the bank how much was needed. The first call in the morning for all of us was always to the bank, and, for most of us, to Martin's Bank in Sloane Street.'

A moment from Sloane Square, Martin's Bank at 153 Sloane Street, is, alas, no more. Forget the call centres so popular with today's banks. The only numbers Martin's Bank knew in Bombay belonged to maharajas. Through their doors some of the era's most talented exponents of these extra-special social and financial skills had wandered confidently – including Leslie Price, who deposited his chemmy cheques there and issued winning payout cheques. He signed all the paperwork 'the Vicar', which the bank found quite acceptable.

Maxwell-Scott, when he knew the exact jeopardy of his finances after his morning phone call, would go on his rounds, as John Burke recalls. 'Ian would raise enough cash to cover the day's cheques. The next day he'd repeat the performance to cover the cheques two days previously. If he were lucky at the races or the tables he'd clear the thing off, and start again.

'The staff at Martin's Bank were very pleasant. I was there one day when Ian Maxwell-Scott arrived, and it was quite late. Banks shut at 3.00 p.m. in those days. It must have been about a quarter to three and he arrived with a bundle of cash he'd achieved at some of the local pubs. He was in high spirits.

'The cashier, Jim Gore – a clever, marvellous man – produced all the cheques he had that were to be paid by 3 p.m. Ian didn't have enough cash to cover all of them. One or two had to be dropped. Had to go RD – refer to drawer. But Ian had a system – he would chose the right ones to have the RD on. There might be some cheque to the bookmaker and he would say "I've to pay him." On the other hand there might be some cheque for laundry and he would say "Oh well, so what." And so on. He'd get to the end of the pile of cheques and there were two or three that were not going to be paid.

'At this point the manager came in – he'd been out for quite an alcoholic lunch – and Gore explained about the bunch of cheques and that Maxwell-Scott was putting in cash to cover all these cheques. The manager said, "Well done, well done." Then he noticed a couple of other cheques and asked, "What are these?"

'Ian, rather shamefaced, said, "Well, you see, those are the nasties."

'There was a tremendous roar of laughter and we all went off to a drinking club where Ian cashed another cheque. But not before Ian told the bank staff to "have a bit each way on Blue Nile in the 4.30".'

Ian Maxwell-Scott, Aspinall's close and trusted confidant, was still an important friend but began to fade from the scene. Aspinall had 'dropped' people like Aubrey Wallis, as they did not fit with the image he was trying to acquire. Many of those he left behind were remarkably like him, eager to make money and make their way. Maybe he didn't like the mirror image they presented.

Maxwell-Scott was a different matter altogether. He had become involved with and married Susan Clark, the daughter of legal titan Sir Andrew Clark. As Susan Maxwell-Scott she was much admired as a strong-minded supportive woman, and as a gambler. After their wedding at a Catholic church in Chelsea, in the tradition of the day, congratulatory telegrams were read out. One was from Lady O. She expressed fulsome wishes for their happiness and future. And, she added, the bridegroom still owed her 'a pony' she had loaned him.

Soon afterwards Lady O.'s mailbag began to feature strange cheques from odd places around the world, made out from the 'Dodder Bank'. One was signed 'Aly Khan but Maxwell can't'. Another was signed 'Inspector Rogers'. It was the work of Paddy Kennedy and his Australian film-maker friend 'Bluey' Hill. Lady O., it seems, was oblivious to the prank and kept going on about 'Ian's pony'.

Aspinall did not attend his friend's wedding. No explanation has ever been given, but there was word that he had a good tip at a race meeting the same day. Whatever went on around it, the marriage of Ian and Susan Maxwell-Scott was a long and glorious union. Both were devoted to each other and to gambling – and they were loyal, always, to their friends.

Susan Maxwell-Scott's family, especially her father, were not so keen on her choice of husband. 'They didn't like Ian's lifestyle and they were particularly uncomfortable with his association with John Aspinall. Also, he was a Catholic,' said John Burke, who retains fond memories of the couple as people he knew well and really liked. 'That's why Ian wasn't around in the early games. It was only later that he rejoined the team, as it were. Dominick Elwes wasn't involved, either. He was only ever there to laugh at John's jokes and take free food and drink. John was left to his own devices, which was not always a good thing.'

Tipping his hat to the glory Regency days of William Crockford, Aspinall created an aristocratic atmosphere at his chemmy games; no longer did the gamblers feel they were men behaving badly. Aspinall laughed with them, not at them. He entertained them with his stories. And the stories about Aspinall's chemmy parties were getting around in 1955, especially from Ludgate Circus to the Strand, along Fleet Street. As a result, Aspinall received a serious knock – and a lesson.

The *Sunday People*, then arguably Fleet Street's premier muckracker (and, apparently, the Billy Hill house journal because of the work of crime journalist Duncan Webb, who exhaustively detailed his exploits), had somehow got wind of one of the Aspinall high-flying gambling evenings. It was at the Grosvenor House Hotel, where Aspinall was staying, and with the gentlemen gamblers turned up the gentlemen of the press. It was a big story and big headlines, and bad luck for Aspinall who had to stop the games for some months. It taught him a lesson – to keep the venues and all that went with the games a secret, and not to let journalists anywhere near the premises.

In spite of the publicity, the resilient Aspinall managed to retain his extraordinary circle of friends. It appeared that he could talk himself out of anything. 'John,' said John Burke, 'could switch topics and tales to suit every punter. He was masterful with the words. When he was in the room or at the table no one was going to be bored. He saw to that.'

Lady Annabel Goldsmith said in an interview with *The Times* in 2000: 'I will never forget the first time I clapped eyes on "Aspers". It was 1954, I was 19 and married to my first husband, Mark Birley. We were supposed to go out for dinner, but he started to tell a story . . . It lasted two hours. "Aspers" was the most incredible raconteur.' In 2006, Mark Birley gave John Burke and myself lunch at his Mark's Club in London. He said: 'It was fun with "Burkie" and the crowd when it all began. The world will never see such people again, they were an extravagant and extraordinary mixture.'

And one of the most colourful, then or at any time, was Nancy Gillespie, girl-about-Mayfair. She moved in similar circles to John Burke and John Aspinall and knew everybody. It was a tremendous asset, for she was also 'Ephraim Hardcastle', one of a team of reporters on the *Sunday Express* gossip column. Today, she is as alert and amusing as the young girl from the Scottish mining village of Patna, Ayrshire, who entranced 1950s London society, European and Arabian royalty and Hollywood movie stars. And her employer, Lord Beaverbrook.

She also impressed John Aspinall. It wasn't mutual, although she happily recalled one evening out with him: 'Greyhound racing was not the sport I'd expected to be popular with that crowd. "The dogs" were supposed by Mayfair to be for the common people. So I was rather surprised when John Aspinall invited me to go with him to the White City. Ian Maxwell-Scott was in the party, and Gerry Albertini. All top-drawer chaps.

'But it seemed that they were not snobbish about greyhound racing. Or any form of racing. Or any form of gambling, for that matter. We did rather well at the White City meeting. And we were just about to leave when Aspinall called out to the other two, "A tenner for the winner. Once round the circuit."

'Before I realized what was happening, Ian and Gerry were over the rails and haring around as if they were greyhounds themselves! Thousands of spectators making for the turnstiles stopped to watch the fun. Some bookmakers even started to make bets on the result. Ian romped home first – he was a lean, lanky man – with Gerry a length behind. Ian got his tenner immediately.

'John Aspinall was a wonderful talker. When he began to have games in private houses he would get people to lend him things – he could talk them into giving him everything from antique lamps to big cheques. When I was having a fling with Gerry (Albertini), he was always after something.

'I knew them all, but I couldn't write about the games. I went to lots of games, but never to Aspinall's or the ones he ran with John Burke. Two more different men you couldn't meet. John Burke is a kind person. The worst man I ever met was John Aspinall. He was a rotten man. And his mother – Lady Osborne. Lady bloody O. She was a bitch. Lady Macbeth was an angel next to her. But Aspinall could turn on the charm like a tap. It was the cold tap for me, but not for many others.'

His magic certainly worked with Jane Gordon-Hastings, who would become one of Aspinall's grandest assets in those early days: a hostess with, according to every eyewitness, the mostest. Aspinall met Jane Gordon-Hastings in the early 1950s, and, much to his friends' surprise, married her in February 1956 at Caxton Hall, in London. The two-night 'honeymoon' at the Connaught Hotel and the Dorchester wedding reception were paid for by a £500 wedding-gift cheque from Gerry Albertini. The groom was all but penniless, but the event was billed as 'the wedding of the year'.

As with almost everything Aspinall touched or talked about, Jane Hastings was not quite what he said she was. Aspinall created much myth about the early romance, and how he first saw the fresh-faced Scottish beauty at a fashion show one afternoon at Fortnum & Mason in Piccadilly.

What, most people who really knew Aspinall ask, would he be doing at a fashion show on a weekday afternoon? It was not possible – nothing could keep Aspinall from the races.

In reality the future Mr and Mrs Aspinall properly connected thanks to Bobby Buchanan-Michaelson, known to his friends as 'Buck-Mick'.

Buck-Mick had been a young man 'doing the Season' in

the immediate post-war days, from 1946 onwards, when society was picking up the pre-war pieces. Stretching from late spring, after the Chelsea Flower Show, through the Epsom and Derby race meetings, until the King and Queen left for their annual summer break at Balmoral, the Season enabled the aristocracy's ingénue debutante daughters to meet eligible young men at a series of dinners and dances and be presented at Court. There were five such events in London each week, often attended by the King and Queen and the young Princess Elizabeth. At one of them young Buchanan-Michaelson asked the princess if, suitably chaperoned, she would like to join a small group of his friends, including Princess Marina, Duchess of Kent, and Prince John of Luxembourg, for a theatre show, followed by a restaurant dinner and ending with dancing at a night club. It was probably her first such experience.

Now, seven or eight years later, he asked Aspinall to come in for drinks at his flat, or 'set', in Albany – a quiet, exclusive eighteenth-century building of bachelor apartments off Piccadilly, where the residents later included Tony Armstrong-Jones (Lord Snowdon), who married Princess Margaret, and Britain's one-time prime minister Ted Heath. Buck-Mick had met Jane Hastings in Fortnum's as she modelled the store's dresses through its always full lunch and tea restaurants and also asked her to come across the road after work.

Subsequently a man of great achievement who went on to become a property tycoon, racing driver and Formula 1 British Offshore Racing Champion, Buck-Mick fondly remembered this socially new beautiful model and reflecting in 2007 said: 'I invited Jane to come over for a drink after work. I'd asked Aspers and some other friends to pop over too.' Bobby was delayed and a little late arriving: when he got to Albany he discovered his friends already waiting, apart from Aspinall and

Jane. Since meeting Jane, Aspinall had lost no time in persuading her to leave with him – and without Buck-Mick – for a jaunt to White City greyhound track.

'She just had that look that could capture kings and emperors,' said Nancy Gillespie. 'She had imperial looks – and that, of course, is what Aspinall went for.'

John Burke was awed by Mrs Aspinall. 'To say that Jane was beautiful is an understatement – she was stunning!' As a gambling promoter who aimed to make his fortune from the higher echelons of society, Aspinall instinctively understood what an asset a glamorous hostess would be. It was never apparent that she understood that.

Still, his future wife learned some things from him, and quickly. She swiftly became adept at creating what Aspinall regarded as an acceptable social image. Not that she was ever a plain Jane to begin with. She was christened Naomi Jane Hastings and brought up in Tomintoul, a small village near Aviemore. As a young woman she made what was only pocket money as a beater on shoots in the area; her life was remote and very different from the social gadabouts of London. Yet she was special, a head turner, and a Londoner on a shoot encouraged her to travel south and try modelling.

An instant success in her new career, she helped ease her way into society by changing her name to Jane Gordon-Hastings, a combination that rang the correct tones in her new world. It was also a name that complemented her looks and personality: tall, elegant and possessed of inherent good taste and manner.

Early in their marriage they were invited to Highclere Castle, the home of the Earl of Carnarvon. 'Porchy' Carnarvon, whose mother was a Rothschild and whose father had discovered the tomb of Tutankhamun, was entranced (as so many men were) by the extraordinarily attractive Mrs Aspinall.

Right.
The Wild Bunch:
Hollywood legend
William Holden shows
gambler Ray Ryan
how far to set his
sights in Kenya.

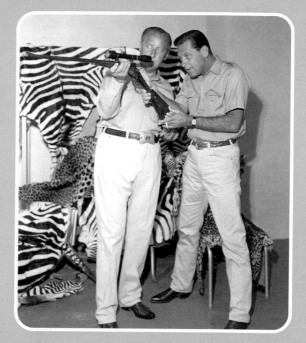

Below.
The debonair
safecracker
Eddie Chapman (right)
outside court with
Wilfred MacCartney
in 1946.

Left. The Maharaja of Baroda, and a female friend. Eddie Chapman considered 'Boss' the nicest foreign person he knew.

Right. Dressed to kill: the suede shoes, the trilby, the double-breasted suit and ever present cigarette, Billy Hill in full gangster chic.

Right.
Bobby McKew and bandleader Paul Adams (left) relaxing in Tangiers.

Below.
Billy Hill in holiday mode, as he and Gypsy Riley soak up the sun in Tangiers.

Above. Nancy Gillespie (right) on the town in 1954 with Michael Heseltine and Lord and Lady Docker.

Left. Claus von Bülow, pictured in 1985, after being acquitted of the attempted murder of his wife. He was often at the chemmy games in the early days.

'Burkie' – John Burke in 1958.

Not a man to be crossed: the young and very determined James Goldsmith.

Always happy to oblige,
the great friend and middleman
Peter West in 1961.

The man with
no luck: the tragic
Dominic Elwes and
his runaway bride the
heiress Tessa Kennedy,
in Havana, February
1958.

Today a successful publisher, this is Mark Sykes dressed for a touch of cold weather in the Swingin' Sixties.

The keepers of many secrets: happy-go-lucky Ian Maxwell-Scott and wife Susan, still keeping her hat on events, in the summer of 1976.

John Aspinall, wife Jane and capuchin monkey Dead Loss at
93 Eaton Place, in 1958.

Aspinall believed that Carnarvon could advance his standing; this invitation was the first move into the highest echelons of society and created great excitement.

By then Aspinall had his black Rolls-Royce and Jim, the driver. Jane Aspinall, as enthusiastic as her husband about the Highclere excursion, packed four trunks of clothes, giving her a dozen changes of outfit. Aspinall's twin ambitions were to make money and to move up the social ladder. The weekend in Berkshire would pay social though not financial dividends, as Carnarvon was never a gambler. In time, though, he would become useful in that area too.

Jane Aspinall was also the ideal hostess for Aspinall's high-class gaming parties. Aspinall cast her in that role, and, no matter what the circumstances, did not waiver. 'When John Aspinall made up his mind about something, nothing in the world would make him change it,' said Bobby Buchanan-Michaelson.

John Burke was fond of the future Mrs Aspinall. 'They seemed to be happy in the beginning but, like his cards, you could never really read what was in John's mind. He was an illusionist.'

The grand magician did not explain to his beautiful wife, who quickly became a Mayfair favourite and known as 'the Spirit of Park Lane', that she was entering a superficial sphere, which for all its glamorous froth had a hard, cynical core. It was a Jekyll and Hyde environment where decency had nothing to do with social status, either earned or inherited. Aspinall cynically encouraged her to flirt with his punters like Sunny Blandford, the Marquis of Blandford (in 2007 the Duke of Marlborough), and other high-stakes players. It must have been difficult for her to accept that while flirting with the rich heir to a stately pile was a highly praiseworthy activity in her husband's eyes, dalliance with a young man she liked, but

who was not a commercial asset to the chemmy games, was
an unforgivable sin.

An encounter with an exotic woman and her lover saw
Aspinall again making headlines in August 1956. In 1943,
John Burke and Bobby McKew's drinking pal at the Star,
'Boss', the Maharaja of Baroda, Sir Pratap Sinh Gaikwad,
had married an extraordinary beauty called Sita Devi, who
became his second maharani. By the time Aspinall's chemmy
games were becoming more and more popular, the couple
were divorced, which was no surprise to anybody given
Boss's proclivity for young and statuesque girls. Yet it had
been Boss who had brought divorce proceedings, citing Neville
Clark, the former racing manager of the Maharani of Baroda,
as co-respondent.

Sita Devi had an extraordinary reputation. When Bobby
McKew attended the 1957 wedding of the Maharaja's son,
she, as the queen, was present: 'She wore a suite of jewellery.
It was all the good stuff, the crown jewels. As was traditional,
the happy couple went off on elephants to parade among the
crowds. Before the elephants returned, Sita was off, on her
way home to Monte Carlo. So was the jewellery.'

Which was where for many years one of the most priceless
Indian treasures, the pearl carpet once owned by the Maharaja
of Baroda, which ranks with the Mughal Peacock Throne as a
symbol of India, was rumoured to be. Sita Devi supposedly
kept the pearl carpet, the 'Moonstone' of its time. It's impossible to estimate its worth. Bobby McKew believes it to be in
the palace of an oil-rich nation, but he is at great pains to
point out that he does not know for sure.

Bobby McKew would often be seen on the town with Boss
and saw at first hand how much he enjoyed the company of
the most attractive and desirable women. 'I don't know where

Boss found the girls, but they were always marvellous. I must say, I looked very good in such company. Too good, as it turned out. This prominent businessman, a very rich man who ran a huge car franchise, and I won't embarrass him by giving his name, approached me and asked, "Bobby, where do you get the girls for the Maharaja? I'd like to meet them very much."

'He thought I was a ponce! I was furious but I didn't show it. I said the girls all came from a good contact, a Wilhelmina Hill. I gave him the phone number, Bayswater 7338, and told him to call. I said, "If a man answers, don't worry about it. He's the caretaker."

'So this guy starts ringing Billy Hill and asking about the girls. About a week later, he came up to me and apologized. He said he knew who he had been telephoning. He never asked about girls again.'

But this well-connected businessman did meet the exotic Sita Devi. It was at a dinner party, and the two of them talked about Aspinall's chemmy games. Sita Devi was intrigued, but rather than attending one of the games herself, she sent Neville Clark.

Sita Devi could not have foreseen that entering Aspinall's orbit, even indirectly, was to result in her name being splashed over the newspapers again. It seems that Aspinall took against Neville Clark and at their next encounter provoked an argument that provided the press with a delightful tale of high society scandal. 'Film Stars See Row in Mayfair Night Club' ran the headline in the *Daily Mail*.

It was on 8 August 1956, and the magnums of champagne were exploding at London's most fashionable nightclub, Les Ambassadeurs (£7 a year subscription). Situated off Park Lane, it was run by the clever former boxer and Polish immigrant John Mills. He was on a winner that evening, hosting the post-premiere party of *The Iron Petticoat*, a

British-financed romantic comedy starring Bob Hope and Katharine Hepburn.

The film's stars were absent but there was still much glamour, with Hollywood actor Robert Mitchum at one table and the British star, the elegant Laurence Harvey, with his actress wife Margaret Leighton, at another. Across the room sat Sharman Douglas, daughter of the former US Ambassador. Next to her was the legendary bandleader Jack Hylton. All around them were the socially keen and accepted.

At one table was Nancy Gillespie, in her 'Ephraim Hardcastle' role, with Peter West. They spotted Neville Clark and the Maharani of Baroda enjoying themselves at a central table with another couple.

John and Jane Aspinall were at home at their rented flat in Upper Brook Street, entertaining Mark Birley and Lady Annabel. It was to there that Peter West telephoned and gave Aspinall the news about the presence of Neville Clark and the Maharani.

Both couples walked down to Les Ambassadeurs. Aspinall went over to Neville Clark and the Maharani: they needed to talk. 'After dinner,' said Clark.

Aspinall joined Mark Birley and the others at the bar. As the orchestra played softly, Aspinall stood there working himself up. He approached the table again. It was 10.45 p.m. They had to talk, he said – immediately.

'You bother me,' said Clark. And Aspinall did. He went berserk, grabbed Clark's hair and pulled him off his chair. The table's contents went crashing to the floor. Guests looked around at the sound of smashing glass. A couple of punches were exchanged and the two men rolled on the floor.

The Maharani shouted that she was pregnant. That was the cue for hip-led Robert Mitchum, certified movie tough guy, to move in. He took a couple of punches at Aspinall. At which point Jane Aspinall entered the fray, armed with her handbag. Fists and handbags flew.

It was a few moments of mayhem. There were gasps and a couple of screams from nearby tables and then the head waiter, William, and a couple of others moved in and separated Aspinall and Clark.

Intriguingly, the society crowd and movie stars were loath to talk about the incident. As he left Les Ambassadeurs that night, Robert Mitchum said, 'Fight? I heard a glass fall. It was all over in a flash. I wish there'd been more to it.'

Laurence Harvey was equally reticent: 'I was eating sole when I heard the din. It wasn't much. Then I heard something smash to the ground. I got on with my sole. It was delicious.'

Nancy Gillespie recalled: 'It all got calmed down quite quickly, champagne on the management, that sort of thing. They had quite a set-to. Aspinall put on a brave face – his crowd all thought it was a "lark", made for an entertaining evening.'

In spite of the titillating headlines, business continued as usual for Aspinall until, in 1957, John Burke 'joined the firm'. The close racing friends partnered up in a lucrative endeavour, Sky Masterson and Nathan Detroit to the gentry, with Aspinall as the owner and chairman of 'the Firm' and John Burke as the finance director.

For them, this was an exciting page-turning period, for not only was there the glory of the gambling, the naughty glamour of the parties that ran in tandem with the gaming; for these young men there was also the devilment of flouting the law of the land. 'Ian Maxwell-Scott wasn't around and John knew he needed someone he could trust to "manage" the games: look after the money, pay out and get in the cheques,' John Burke remembered. 'It was detail he didn't want to bother with. He wanted the grand scheme of things. I, as "Burkie", became the financial director of the operation. John was the chairman and managing director. I learned to be a croupier and from then on John never employed professional croupiers, either he crouped himself or I did.

'Our private chemmy parties attracted a financially solid, honourable clientele. They were men of value, who paid their debts and could afford to wait for payment themselves. Aspinall once got into a difficult situation when a loser's cheque bounced and he couldn't afford to pay the winners from that evening's party. It could have been the end for him, but it wasn't. The players to whom Aspinall owed money were important and reliable men. A few grand floating around between friends was not a problem for them. It could be shrugged off, and was, as fast as they would enjoy a plate of scrambled eggs, a touch of smoked salmon and wild mushrooms. Aspinall was lucky.

'You have to understand the sort of people involved – they don't exist any more. To someone like James Goldsmith, his winnings, a few thousands pounds – enormous amount in those days – was still nothing to him. He'd rather wait for his money, or not have it at all, than fall out with friends.

'John was also close to Richard Parkes and Gerry Albertini and they bailed him out – in their terms it cost them little. It was money they would themselves have casually lost at chemmy.'

I brought along Steve O'Flaherty to our games, which was a very popular move – he would have been the richest player in the early days. The games were not attended by many rich aristocrats or men of national importance. It's easy to understand why. Would a government minister, or a steward of the Jockey Club, or a prominent merchant banker, or the chairman of a large public company risk the glare of media publicity were he to face in open court this charge of "frequenting a common gaming house"?

'Nonetheless, our profit was impressive. There was the *cagnotte*, the losers paid their debts: we couldn't lose. There was no point in "bent" games with the stakes on our table. It was profit, profit, profit and no tax to pay.'

5. THROUGH THE LOOKING GLASS

> Most of our people have never had it so good. Go around
> the country, go to the industrial towns, go to the farms, and
> you will see a state of prosperity such as we have never had
> in my lifetime, nor indeed ever in the history of this country.
> What is worrying some of us is, 'Is it too good to be true?'
> or perhaps I should say, 'Is it too good to last?'
>
> **HAROLD 'SUPERMAC' MACMILLAN, JULY 20 1957**

With his enticing dark-haired wife as a siren at the card
evenings, in 1957 John Aspinall was back in very serious
moneymaking business and John Burke found himself almost
constantly whistling the song 'The Man who Broke the Bank
in Monte Carlo'.

The chemmy games, following the caution brought on by
the bad luck of an exotic cheque and the press invasion,
returned to a reliable routine. The 5 per cent charge, or
cagnotte, raked off by Aspinall and 'Burkie' on the bank's
winning bets provided steady, tax-free income, as much as
£3,000 to £4,000 on a good evening.

John Burke explained: 'In France, chemmy, from the
point of view of the proprietor, was a brilliant game. It is a
one-against-one game and probably takes about thirty seconds,
and the outcome is that there is one winner and one loser. The
winner, if the bank wins the coup, pays the 5 per cent tax on
what he wins, and so you can imagine the profits rolling in.

For us there was only one possible snag. In France, gambling was legal, and if you lost money you could be sued. Gambling debts had to be honoured, legally honoured, whereas in England of course they weren't.

'If you lost money gambling and told the other person to get lost, there was nothing that they could do about it. Even if they were given a cheque, the person who wrote it could plead the Gaming Act and dishonour it. There was no legal redress, which made it none too attractive in England, unless you were dealing with people who would actually pay. And that was our secret weapon. Our players played and paid.'

Towards the end of 1956, John and Jane Aspinall had moved into 93 Eaton Place. Their landlord, the Old Harrovian property developer Douglas Wilson, accepted from them a good rent of £50 a week. They were joined by Bob, the butler, and, later, a capuchin monkey called 'Dead Loss'. For a time, Aspinall kept a bear in a cage at the back of the flat; one winter he took the bear to St Moritz in a trailer behind his chauffeur-driven Rolls. 'It got him noticed,' said John Burke.

Within a couple of years, the animals had all but taken over at Eaton Place. There was Tara, a tigress; and two Himalayan bears, Esay and Ayesha. The Aspinalls' friends were wary of visiting, the neighbours fretful for their safety. Aspinall knew he needed somewhere in the country. After a wonderful, lucky bet at the Newmarket races, he was able to buy Howletts, an eighteenth-century Palladian house set in thirty-nine acres of parkland, near Canterbury in Kent. He founded his first zoo there in 1958 and from then on met its huge and seemingly always rising maintenance costs.

'In fact, "Aspers" far preferred animals to humans; he regarded them as equals, loved them like his friends,' Lady Annabel Goldsmith told *The Times* after Aspinall's death on 29 June 2000.

As it turned out, the monkey, the first member of what

became Aspinall's part-famous and part-notorious wild animal collection, was to be less trouble in the early years than another new friend.

To escape press attention after the debacle at Les Ambassadeurs, Aspinall had taken his wife to the South of France. There, in the casinos, they had met the American Eddie Gilbert, a rather mysterious entrepreneur labelled 'The Boy Wonder of Wall Street' by *Time* magazine.

Gilbert was aggressive and arrogant, and laughed at John Aspinall's stories. A long association of mutual hero-worship began, one that would have long-lasting and remarkable repercussions. The American, even if he did not quite 'belong', became one of the set, someone who was promoted and helped by Aspinall as introductions were made during chemmy evenings at 93 Eaton Place. John Burke had rented a flat (for £60 a week) at 60 Eaton Place from the Egyptian Madame Zulificar. He told her the extra large, elegant drawing room was ideal for his needs, for his nocturnal work table which happily seated nine.

They used other venues apart from the Eaton Place apartments to keep the gambling evenings 'nomadic' and so somewhat within the 1854 Gaming Act. John Burke says that, despite supposedly 'authoritative' reports, they had no 'arrangement' with the Mayfair police.

In this way, a steady business built up, around which an eclectic bunch of those given to risk and chance gathered. Mark Sykes shakes his head at the memories. 'I look back and I'm astonished at what went on. You forget the unbelievable change in lives and the way we lived in forty and fifty years. It was an insane but marvellous time, never been anything like it.'

The pace of life in London, though still snail-like compared with the supermotion of the twenty-first century, was gathering an uneasy momentum, a stretching of the muscles. Almost everyone wanted action, a chance at the jackpot, the bullseye. At Eaton Place, normally at number 93, chemmy for the smart set was quietly fashionable: the gambling was very hush-hush; the atmosphere always convivial. There were girls willing to thrill and be thrilled, the best food – caviar and French pâté and that day's seafood specialities – plus fine wine, and, of course, there was the gambling. Since it was illegal, there was the delicious frisson of risk.

Lucian Freud; Claus von Bülow; Mark Birley and his good friend Geoffrey Keating; Clive Graham; Yorkshire landowner Henry Vyner; Kosoro Ghasghai, a Persian prince who flew from Munich – where he lived in a penthouse hotel suite – for the games; the well-off avant-garde as well as renowned gamblers like Stephen O'Flaherty; all became regulars. It was rare to see the players' spouses at the games, but Janet Mercedes Bryce, who would later marry the Duke of Edinburgh's cousin David Mountbatten, Marquess of Milford Haven, attended on 17 November 1960. Why not? It was fun.

The beautiful debutante Theresa Follet used to drive John Bingham, the future Lord Lucan, to the games in her second-hand green Ford Popular. She talked at her home in Switzerland in December 2006 about her gambling evenings: 'He was not a boyfriend. He lived with his mother in St John's Wood High Street and I lived with my mother in St John's Wood. I had a car and he didn't, so I used to take him. I used to go and pick him up from some awful Victorian building.

'I found him an extremely nice person and a good friend. I went with him many times to the games when it was all highly illegal. I enjoyed it. I like gambling but I didn't have the big money to gamble, I just did even-money things but it meant I could play through the evening at Aspinall's parties. If I won I put a little bit more on, but I had to be careful. One evening I was the only winner in our group, I've no idea how, but I remember everyone being cross that I was the winner and everybody else lost. Including John Bingham, who I don't remember being a very good gambler.

'I think it probably was considered very racy for me to go gambling, but it was good fun. There was good champagne and food and it made for a lovely evening. It was a very small circle in those days. A lot of my friends at that time wouldn't have dreamed of going to Aspinall's. They would rather have died.'

The champagne and the deb delights – equally bubbly – were sideshows, more for hangers-on than the real gamblers. Mark Sykes, who would later run his own games in partnership with Peter Scaramanga, shrewdly pointed out: 'The reason why people gamble is for utter escape from reality. More than sex, more than booze, more than heroin, it is a complete, utter escape from reality. It takes over. Gambling is as addictive as any drug.

'Playing all night was normal, but the concentration on the gambling was go great it was as though the players had snoozed the hours away. They'd thought of nothing but the gambling. All their other senses were resting.That's why you'd often see at eight o'clock or nine o'clock in the morning, after whole nights of gambling, people as fresh as though they'd all slept all night. That's why.

'Many people would go straight to their office. There were lots of City folk – stockbrokers were making huge amounts of money in those days. All crooks, of course. But they gambled and they paid up.'

So Aspinall and Burke were on to something which, in their world, supposedly did not exist – a sure thing. And, of course, it didn't. Well, not exactly. Or, more precisely, not yet.

John Burke, who has seen more millions won and lost than most, has thought much about the motivation of gamblers: 'Is it excitement, greed, sheer pleasure, showing-off or masochism? Gambling is generally asexual. I have seen several masochistic gamblers. Class, the English obsession, is part of the equation. The English upper classes have a strong gambling tradition and the working class enjoy their punting. It is only in some sections of the middle or lower-middle class where there is a puritanical disapproval of gambling, a feeling I believe to be stronger in America than in the UK.

'Of course, as Damon Runyon so wisely said, "All life is six to five against."'

Off Sloane Square, it was difficult to calculate the odds. The cavalcade of con men passing through the doors of Martin's Bank on Sloane Street was not an unusual sight during the summer of 1957, a time of regular and impressive takings for Aspinall and Burke. Yet, despite appearances, the bank did not have such clientele exclusively.

The discreet charm of the confidence man was in the air; it perfumed post-war society. One early afternoon Nancy Gillespie was walking towards Martin's Bank when a familiar, smiling face appeared. It was the Ceylon-born Charles De Silva, dressed at his sharpest. They chatted amicably for a few minutes and then said goodbye, agreeing to have a drink later. De Silva walked down the steps from the bank to a dark-blue Rolls-Royce, where an equally immaculate chauffeur (both hired for the day) held the passenger door open. The Rolls drove him off at a purr.

As she entered the bank the manager came over and after greeting her said, 'I see you know the Maharaja?'

'Charles was a genius,' recalls Nancy Gillespie, of one of the great con men of the era. 'Mind you, the manager's approach was tricky. On one hand I didn't want to grass on Charlie, but I didn't want to claim a great friendship either. Because, whatever Charlie was doing there, it was unlikely to be for the good of the shareholders of Martin's Bank.

'I said, "Oh, I met him at a drinks party at the French Embassy."

'He seemed genuinely pleased at that. Certainly, they cashed my cheque without any trouble, and my solvency wasn't always a guaranteed sort of thing.'

De Silva was a swindler of the highest order. He worked, mostly, on 'commission'; he'd put deals together, everything from 'establishing' chinchilla farms in Ceylon to selling a (young) women's reform home on the outskirts of London to Huntington Hartford, then one of the world's richest men; Hartford had so much money he could, and usually did, buy anything he wanted.

Hartford spent his time with heiresses – Doris Duke and Barbara Hutton; and movie stars – Marilyn Monroe ('too pushy, like a high-class hooker', he told *Vanity Fair* magazine in December 2004) and Lana Turner ('way past her prime', in the same interview). The second of his four wives was Marjorie Steele, an aspiring actress. When they married she was 18 years old. Charles De Silva always did his homework. Bobby McKew relates the story:

'Charlie had got himself into the good graces of the governor of this girls' reform school. Then he arranged to have Huntington Hartford come along for tea. He told him there was an "investment opportunity", but not to mention to the old bird running the place anything about buying it. Anyhow, they turn up there and have tea and buns.

'Charlie could see that Hartford needed encouragement and he wandered over to the window, which he had previously found looked out over a tennis court. There were these attractive birds in their tennis skirts skipping around the place. "Oh, do have a look at the property," Charlie said to his man.

'Huntington Hartford took a look, finished his tea, left the governor's office and before they got to the car Charlie had a cheque for a great big deposit on the place. Charlie sold him the reform school – it was astonishing.'

De Silva was so good at his game that he was entertained at 10 Downing Street by Dorothy Macmillan, wife of Prime Minister Harold Macmillan. In those aspiring post-war days it wasn't six; but arguably three, degrees of separation. Dorothy Macmillan was sleeping with Lord 'Bob' Boothby, who was sleeping with the same boys as Ronnie Kray, possibly a ménage too far. Too rich, certainly, for the always cautious Billy Hill, who detested a fuss.

Once, when Bobby McKew had treated himself to a new sports car, the two were driving from London to Maidenhead, to a club which Hill owned and McKew ran. The driver was showing off his car:

'Bobby, why are you going over the speed limit? It just gives them a chance to pull you over and then they'll want to search your flat. Are we in a hurry?'

Charlie De Silva always was. He never met a person who wasn't a 'mark'. There is a story about the dinner where De Silva met the prime minister's wife. It was a charity affair, and he told Mrs Macmillan, 'My mother died of cancer. May I give you a cheque for the charity?'

'You must come and have tea one afternoon,' she said. He followed through and took a guest, a rich Chinese businessman to whom he later sold the Ark Royal after talking at some length about 'my friend the prime minister'.

But Charles De Silva could not fool Billy Hill. He tried, and tripped up, as so many did, by being a little too greedy – the mistake of almost all of history's players of the confidence trick.

De Silva and Hill set out to swindle a couple of chinchilla breeders in Yorkshire. They were told that the government in Ceylon (now Sri Lanka) was willing to invest £200,000 in chinchilla farms. They, in turn, would hand over cash to De Silva for investment in shipping contracts and other aspects of the hustle, such as moving surplus US Forces cameras from Germany to Switzerland.

It all went wrong. De Silva then involved Billy Hill in a paint-buying scheme – and was found out. Somewhere, £80,000, which Billy Hill believed belonged to him, was missing. Correctly, he blamed De Silva. De Silva said he had given the money to his friend Mark Sykes, and about three weeks later there was an interesting encounter over the matter.

Mark Sykes was enjoying a midmorning cup of coffee outside the Carlton Hotel in Cannes when he saw Billy Hill get out of a cab with Gypsy and go into the hotel. Sykes wondered at the chance of it but did not run over and say 'hello'. Billy Hill didn't like surprises. Instead, Mark Sykes allowed Hill half an hour to settle in and then telephoned from a coin box.

'Could I please speak to Mr Hill?'

'Who is calling, sir?'

'Mark Sykes.'

'Hello.'

'Oh, Mr Hill. I just happened to be in town and saw you going through the door of the Carlton Hotel. I rang on the chance you were staying there.'

'Oh.' A pause. 'You'd better come round.'

Billy gave Mark a warm welcome. His voice stayed at an even level, but gradually his guest realized that something was seriously wrong.

'I'm told you have some money for me.'

'Money?'

'I'm told by Charlie De Silva that you've got eighty grand for me.'

'What!'

Mark explained that he knew nothing about it. Hill did not

seem surprised. This had happened before with Charlie De Silva.

'I thought if you did have it, it was unlikely you'd be phoning me from a call box and coming over,' Hill said. He was playing games.

Mark Sykes said: 'He had a sort of macabre sense of humour, Bill. You'd never at first sight take him for what he was. He had flat, black hair in an old-fashioned way. You would think he was probably a bookmaker or a garage owner, someone like that. With me and the De Silva thing he knew the score from the start, but took his time in sorting it out. I stayed for lunch and then we went to the casino with Gypsy.

'She was a character. She wore a ring, a sort of diamond-as-big-as-the-Ritz affair. Enormous. Her hands looked like jewellery boxes. There was an argument and she cuffed some chap and the man's ear came adrift. She cut his ear off. It was colourful. It was all colourful.'

'She was a tough one,' said Frankie Fraser, 'but I think that's why Bill liked her.'

Billy Hill and Gypsy's home in Moscow Road was an expensive flat, filled with the best of everything. There were chandeliers in every room – even the loo.

'Bill had the money to spend and bought the best of everything. The problem was, nothing matched,' said Bobby McKew. 'It was a nightmare of a place, like the aftermath of one of those dreadful television makeovers that go wrong. Carpeting on the toilet seat, that sort of thing. Billy and Gypsy thought it was smarter than Buckingham Palace.'

One of the great haunts of the 1950s was the Milroy Club, which sat almost next door to the Hamilton Bridge Club on Park Lane. The ground floor was a splendid reception, bar and dining room, with dancing on the first floor. In charge of the music was the bandleader Paul Adam, who was Princess Margaret's favourite. She would send on requests ahead of her arrival. The band played, as it were, by royal command.

Adam was a charming man, a diplomat with his crowd, and would always play special sequences of music to announce the arrival of a regular. Generally, he was known to be discreet. One evening he and Bobby McKew were driving off from the Milroy and stopped in at Moscow Road.

'We walked in and sat down and I watched Paul's face light up in amazement. He eyed the walls, the decor of flocked wallpaper and all the terrible, terrible rest.

'He looked over at Bill and said, "I've never seen anything like . . ."

'I grabbed his arm and pressed on it ever so tightly. He smiled just as tightly and managed, ". . . like a place like this."

'Billy said to Gypsy: "See, darlin', Paul likes it and he knows all about decorations."

'I got Paul out of there as fast as I could.'

Billy Hill was not a gadabout. He could sit in Moscow Road and ponder for two, three and four weeks at a time, rarely stepping outside his front door. He liked his associates to visit him at his home, which was a four-minute walk or so from Bayswater Tube.

One afternoon Bobby McKew was driving his E-type Jaguar to Moscow Road: 'I saw Peter West rushing into the Underground. I was parking the car, and then there he was again, rushing out carrying a couple of bags. I thought he'd done a robbery! When I got to Billy's flat I told him what I'd seen, and he said in his slow drawl:

'"Yeah, he's got a deal going with these stations. He's buying sixpences off them."

'Well, work that out.

'In those days you paid cash for the Tube, and there was a lot of change around. Peter West toured the Underground twice a week and bought up the sprats [sixpences], giving them the equivalent money. He didn't cheat. If there was £500 of sixpences he handed that amount of money over. The point was that the silver in the coins was worth *more* than £500. It was so profitable, it was worth all that trouble – it was worth between 10 and 20 per cent more, melted down. And there was nothing illegal about it – although I don't suppose you were meant to melt down the Queen's currency.

'Bill said to me: "He's collecting for me." He knew all about it.

'Peter West was a very pleasant fellow. He was best friends with Jimmy Goldsmith and he used to go out with birds for Jimmy, one bird in particular. She went to hotels with Peter and people thought she was screwing him. But no, she was screwing Goldsmith.

'That arrangement, or others like it, went on for years, until Jimmy Goldsmith died. Not much was as it seemed.'

6. THE LONG LEGS OF THE LAW

When in doubt, have a man come through the door with
a gun in his hand.

RAYMOND CHANDLER, 1952

The private chemmy parties attracted a financially solid crowd,
but many rich aristocrats and men of national importance still
remained shy. It was, as John Burke remarked, too dangerous
for any high-profile person to risk the publicity were he to find
himself in court.

'The thing was to be careful, not to draw attention to
ourselves,' said John Burke. 'We had a very successful business
going on and it appeared it would go on for ever. There was
no reason to think otherwise.'

Happenstance intervened – spectacularly.

During one gambling evening, John Aspinall and John
Burke were discussing the need to move the chemmy games
around to prevent the police deciding they were involved in a
'habitual' gambling operation. John Burke recalled:

'We decided we couldn't stay in the same place all the time
because it was too dangerous. At this point, what we were
doing was clearly one hundred per cent illegal, there was no
doubt about that. It was done very quietly, all kept very secret,
but we had to be even more careful. It was a moneymaker and
we didn't want to spoil it. We talked about getting another
flat.'

One player, a young man about town, said that his aunt wanted to let a flat in Hyde Park Street, Hyde Park Square. There was one great problem with that: 1 Hyde Park Street was to the north, at the 'wrong' end of the park. But the flat had a grand reception room for gambling and an equally generously sized kitchen for catering. Suitability triumphed over snobbery even with Aspinall, to whom Burke had to explain the advantages.

John Burke did the paperwork for a three-month lease which, for reasons of discretion, was taken in the name of Lady Mary Grace Osborne.

'We went ahead there from 5 December 1957, in just the same way we operated in Eaton Place. I have notes of the *cagnotte* at the games that month and they ranged from £1,100 to £3,000 and £4,300.'

The original, historic account books also show that in that first month Prince Kosoro Ghasghai won £1,854 on 12 December, won another £5,935 on 17 December and lost exactly £9,000 on 19 December. The fanciful Aspinall amused dinner-party guests by telling the story that the prince went everywhere with an armed manservant who stood behind him at the chemmy table to prevent his being assassinated.

The prince missed the excitement on 10 January 1958. That was when an event occurred which was considered unremarkable at the time, but which would change the face of gambling in Britain and rapidly turn London into the gambling capital of the world.

As we know, John Aspinall and John Burke had no arrangement with the Mayfair police. The gambling had gone on; most people were aware of it; but by going 'door to door' (hosting 'floating' games at different addresses), it had stayed safe from interference by the law.

As the Sixties came closer, the ancient gambling laws were regarded as out of touch and contravening them was not a serious crime: nearly half a century on from 'The Night They Raided Hyde Park Square', a suitable analogy might be the smoking, if not the distribution, of marijuana.

The Paddington police were, perhaps, not as sophisticated as their Mayfair counterparts. The 'gambling den' in Hyde Park Square had supposedly been 'observed', to use the police term, for some time. In fact, the chemmy evening of 10 January 1958 was, because of the Christmas holidays, only the fifth game at Hyde Park Square.

It was another pleasant evening. Lady O.'s game pie was as perfect as ever, the champagne chilled, the conversation warm. Just before 11 p.m. the players sat down at the green-cloth-covered gaming table subdivided by chalk marks into units of ten. At number ten sat John Aspinall, as the croupier. In front of him was a wooden box with seventy-seven units in it. Aspinall broke the seal on the required six packs of cards and shuffled them in preparation for the next shoe. Players were sitting at all the marked positions, and most had chips in front of them.

Unknown to the gamblers, one of Paddington's finest, Inspector Samuel Herbert, had shinned up a drainpipe and was now, as he later said in court, 'hanging by his eyebrows' from the edge of the fire escape. Inelegantly perched there, he peered through chinks in the red velvet curtains. He watched the cards being dealt. He saw the chips slide across the table, even if he was not close enough to catch the glint in the players' eyes.

Inspector Herbert breathlessly left his observation post and scrambled down the drainpipe from the fire escape. Waiting in the rain for him was the man in charge, Chief Superintendent Richard Rogers. With this eyewitness account, the Gaming Act of 1845 (not the later 1854 one) allowed the police team to raid the flat and proceed with their inquiries. At 12.45 a.m., Chief Superintendent Rogers blew, as it were, the whistle. He knocked heavily on the door of 1 Hyde Park Street.

Accounts of the evening are legendary and varied. Which waiter was it? Was it Bert Payne or Bob Richardson who opened the door in white tie and tails to find Chief Superintendent Rogers, Inspector Herbert and their uniformed team calling? The truth was far more prosaic. It was a rather flustered washing-up lad who performed that chore, and the police duly marched in. Bob and Bert, both in their smart waiters' gear, rushed over to try and prevent the intrusion but the detectives could not be stopped. They were determined to make their arrests.

There was a cry of 'Hello, hello, hello, what have we here?' as Aspinall barked at Chief Superintendent Rogers, 'What right have you to come breaking in here and searching people?'

'You are breaking the law, sir. This is a common gaming house.'

'I dispute that. These people are all intimate friends of mine and have been invited here.'

Lady O. piped up, 'Anybody would think we were a crowd of criminals. Why don't you catch some real criminals; there are plenty!'

Her intervention allowed the alert John Burke to bundle off with the *cagnotte* and hurriedly stow it in a corner of the room.

'Well done, Burkie,' John Aspinall said with a grin, as Chief Superintendent Rogers asked him and the other players, 'What game were you playing?'

'You know what it is,' replied Aspinall.

'What is going on?'

'My guests are just having a spot of after-dinner fun.'

'What is the bank worth, and the chips?'

Aspinall initially refused to answer the policeman. He paused for a few moments and then said, 'The bank is worth £500.'

Jane Aspinall looked a detective constable straight in the eye when asked her profession, and stated, 'Housewife'.

The startled guests watched and listened in silence. Man about town Lord Timothy Willoughby D'Eresby, Michael Alachouzos and Dougie Gordon shrugged with mild amusement. Bill and Bridget Mond also thought it all hugely amusing.

Lady O. was horrified at it all. She watched her son stand by the chemmy table as Superintendent Rogers, still in his raincoat, formally charged him with 'common gaming house' offences. Next, the policeman charged John Burke. Then it was Lady O.'s turn. Seeming to swell to twice her normal size, she boomed at Superintendent Rogers, 'This is absurd. All these people are friends of ours. And none of them is common. Young man, there was nothing common here until you walked in.' Or at least, that was the after-dinner story Aspinall loved to tell.

But common or not, London's good, great and not-so-great were marched out to Black Marias and driven the short distance to Paddington Green nick. John Burke recalls it all with some whimsy:

'It was all quite civilized. The police are awful snobs, so they treated these people with the right accents in a very nice way, cups of tea and that sort of thing. Of course, half of them were pissed and found it all a great joke. It wasn't a joke for John and me, of course, for it looked like the end of an especially good way of making a living. God's revenge for going to the wrong side of the park. But the police were polite enough, it had the flavour of an Ealing comedy that evening.'

Theresa Follet was there with John Bingham and somewhat alarmed. 'My mother nearly had a heart attack, for my uncle [Sir Alvery Gascoigne] was an ambassador in the Foreign Office and she was terrified it was going to come out. Yet Johnnie and I were the only ones they didn't mention in the *Evening Standard* the next day.'

Mark Birley said that he recalled being bundled off to

Paddington police station. Peter West gave his name as 'Peter Wales' and claimed that he lived at the Ritz.

Nancy Gillespie, banned from the games as a member of the much feared press, nevertheless caught up with events. She said: 'John thought it was very funny. Peter West and Lady Jane Willoughby were at the game when the police arrived, and got arrested. The next night, the two of them went to Le Club. It was past closing time but, of course, they ordered a drink. The next thing the police ran in, and they got arrested again! For drinking after hours. It was quite something to be arrested twice in forty-eight hours.'

Officially, Aspinall, Burke and Lady O. were charged with keeping a common gaming house, while the others were charged with simply being on the premises, 'frequenting a common gaming house'.

But farcical as it may all appear so many years later, the events were absolutely crucial to the future of the UK's millions of gamblers. They were vital in other matters, too, but overall, the Big Casino landscape of twenty-first-century Britain began when the Paddington police raided that spacious rented flat which had the temerity to be on the wrong side of the Park.

And all because John Aspinall and John Burke were bloody-minded.

7. LOADSAMONEY

Your pony, Pony.

SYDNEY SUMMERS, 1958

The Hyde Park Street affair could have been over without much fuss. The three accused of running a 'common gaming house': Lady O., her son and John Burke, could have pleaded guilty at a magistrates' court. Aspinall and Burke, both 31, were accused of using the flat for unlawful gaming; Lady O., as the tenant, for permitting them to do that. The fine would have been something around £100.

'We would then have had to decide whether to continue giving chemmy games while being extremely cautious and security-conscious, as a second offence would probably jeopardize the whole operation, or whether to abandon the scheme,' said John Burke. 'This latter option was clearly one to avoid if possible. It portended the unpleasant possibility of having to work for a living.'

The other option was to fight the charges when they appeared at Bow Street Magistrates' Court.

Aspinall and Burke sought the advice of Sydney Summers, who had, as we know, marvellous police contacts. It was part of the gambling business, a small piece of profit-sharing as it were. He gave Burke and Aspinall a secret weapon in their little bit of difficulty with the law. Publicly, their big gun was a brilliant advocate called Gilbert Beyfus, who would, after an initial hearing at Bow Street, defend them before a judge and jury at the London Sessions on 17, 18 and 19 March 1958 – as it turned out, some of the most memorable dates in the history of gaming. For John Burke, for gamblers worldwide, it was to turn out to be some St Patrick's Day.

Clever as Beyfus was, he was aided by the scheming of his clients and the connections of Sydney Summers, who arranged for Aspinall and Burke to meet a senior police officer who, he felt, might be able to help. How right he was.

The policeman was nicknamed 'Pony', which referred to the gambling sum of £25 that he was prepared to accept for meeting and perhaps giving advice to a 'client'. A 'result' would, of course, call for a larger contribution, possibly a posse of ponies.

John Burke drove Aspinall's black Rolls-Royce (Aspinall never learned to drive) to Sydney Summers' flat in Barons Keep for their important rendezvous. They arrived before the policeman, a tall middle-aged man, who blustered in shortly after them. First, there were the formalities: Summers extended in his nicotine-stained fingers five crisp £5 notes (they were the largest banknotes at the time), and said without a smile, 'That horse you had a tenner on, Pony, won at five to two. Here are your winnings.'

Later, when they were all more familiar with each other, Summers abandoned the charade and at the start of a meeting would hand over £25 with, 'Your pony, Pony.'

John Burke connected well with 'Pony', who was an intelligent man with charm and a sense of humour. He officially earned around £1,750 per annum; nevertheless, his sons all went to public school, at a cost then running at around £600 a year for each schoolboy. Pony, it seemed, had ways of earning lots of ponies.

The chief inspector, always smiling, always happy, was not involved in the case of *Regina* v. *Aspinall, Burke & Osborne* himself, but he was sufficiently high ranking to have access to all the police papers related to it. He supplied the inside story of the prosecution; of their plans, legal tactics and witnesses. Burke and Aspinall then formally passed on the information to Beyfus, quite properly and with no hint of where it had come from, in the presence of their well-known and equally innocent solicitor, Eric Leigh-Howard.

Beyfus used the inside knowledge with deadly skill. Because few people in court, including the jury, had any knowledge of *chemin de fer*, the police had to put an expert witness on the stand to explain how the game was played. This was a Frenchman, Mr Maurice Pomerand, who after working as a croupier in Paris and Monte Carlo for fifteen years now lived in Jermyn Street in the West End and worked at the very proper Crockford's Club.

Across Court No. 4 from Beyfus, his adversary was Mr Sebag Shaw, an eminent QC, and the man who had valiantly but vainly defended Ruth Ellis, who on 13 July 1955 became the last woman hanged in Britain. He helped defend Jack Spot in the same year.

On 18 March 1958, prosecution counsel Mr Sebag Shaw called his expert to the witness box. He adjusted his wig with one hand, and with the other handed Mr Pomerand a wooden card shoe containing cards, telling him, 'I want to play, as though we were at the table.'

It caught the court's interest, and peering over the public gallery was David Mountbatten, Marquess of Milford Haven, who watched Sebag Shaw hitch his gown over his shoulders and say, 'Imagine yourself to be the banker. You are now going to deal the cards. What happens?'

'I put a certain stake, say £100, in the middle of the table, and the croupier announces what the bank is.'

Mr Pomerand then dealt out four cards from the shoe and

neatly placed them on the edge of the witness box. Sebag
Shaw got a king of diamonds and a five of spades. Mr
Pomerand had served himself a queen of hearts and a six of
clubs. Mr Shaw gave his witness a look which was taken as a
question.

'If we were gamblers you would take another card . . . and
perhaps I would also.'

'Let's be gamblers, then,' replied the QC.

There was a shuffle of bodies in the courtroom, people
peering for a look, as Mr Pomerand flicked a card from the
shoe. Jane Aspinall's white flowerpot hat almost fell off. He
held up the cards for everyone to see. A seven of spades for
Sebag Shaw, a queen of diamonds for himself. The player:
two. The bank: six. Wildly, with a big smile, Mr Pomerand
threw his arms in the air and gleefully shouted, 'I win.'

He didn't. Officially, he was the 'catering manager' of
Crockford's Club. Beyfus, however, with Pony Moore's inside
information, knew that Mr Pomerand ran the poker room at
Crockford's Club.

Crockford's was the bridge club and home to MPs and
Conservative Cabinet ministers, where membership had the
benefit of agreeably priced food and drinks. John Burke often
played bridge there, sometimes with Selwyn Lloyd, Eden's
Foreign Secretary during the Suez crisis and Harold Macmillan's
Chancellor for two years from 1960. Sadly, despite the
eminence of its members, it was not financially viable for Crockford's
to maintain its high standards on the revenue derived
from bridge players. To remedy this shortfall, Crockfords,
through Mr Pomerand, ran a poker room open seven days a
week with a table charge for all players. This was illegal.

Whether Crockfords enjoyed an unofficial licence to break
the law because of its elite membership or whether it had a
deal with the local police, has never been disclosed. In either

case, they could not refuse a police request to supply an expert witness for the prosecution in the case of *Regina v. Aspinall, Burke & Osborne*. So, when Gilbert Beyfus cross-examined the unfortunate Maurice Pomerand, in charge of a non-stop illegal gaming operation, it was excruciatingly embarrassing for the gentlemen of Crockford's Committee Room.

John Burke sat in court listening to all the evidence. 'It was a tricky case from the point of view that in order to convict us the prosecution would have to prove that there was profit. There's nothing illegal about friends sitting down and playing cards with you, but if somebody is taking money out of it or a *cagnotte* on every pot, as they do in France, that is another matter. There were some lovely arguments about the Gaming Acts.

'But what really turned the case was that the prosecution needed their expert witness. They were describing *chemin de fer* to the judge. I don't know if he understood it, but the jury certainly didn't. Pomerand had worked in one of the big casinos in Monte Carlo and knew the game inside out.

'Beyfus was brilliant. He wanted to know Pomerand's occupation at that exact moment and exactly where he worked and what he did. The man did not commit perjury. So you had this expert witness in a prosecution admitting he was running an illegal gambling operation at Crockford's!'

After four hours of discussion about the gaming laws (even Henry VIII got a mention), and with the jury absent, Beyfus QC told the court, 'Every single club in St James's with a bridge table is a common gaming house, although the police prefer not to prosecute. In my submission the prosecution have failed to prove that in this case it was a common gaming house. There is no evidence of any illegality at all. If there were, there is no evidence that my clients are guilty of the particular charges that are made against them.

'Our gaming laws are a complete jungle and it is always difficult to draw a straight and easy path through them.'

Sebag Shaw, who shared the same roots as Sydney Summers, was himself a gambling man. His heart did not appear to be in this particular prosecution. Possibly, he thought that the 1854 Gaming Act was inappropriate for the time, for a changing London. He certainly did not press his case aggressively. If he had called the players present that evening to give evidence, and they had told the truth, he surely would have won the case. He decided, for his own reasons, not to do that.

Which allowed Beyfus and his junior counsel, Billy Rees-Davies – a former MP who had lost an arm in the Second World War and was known as 'the one-armed bandit' – after the long legal submissions, to persuade Frank Cassel, the deputy chairman of the London Sessions, to shut down the prosecution with: 'I do not think there was sufficient evidence of unlawful gaming and that is the end of the matter.'

The dismissal of the charges was a virtual acknowledgement that private gambling would be sanctioned. It was a cork-popping moment. There is a grand photograph of a quietly smiling John Burke and a super-confident John Aspinall, rolled umbrella in hand and having a Count of Monte Cristo moment, striding triumphantly out of court. And others of Aspinall and his wife driving off.

They went on to Aspinall's flat at 93 Eaton Place for a celebration. There, Lady O. held court in the olive-green-wallpapered dining room and said without a trace of irony, 'It's a poor thing if you can't have a private party in a private flat without the police coming.'

John Burke recalls Aspinall being asked what odds he would have given on the outcome of the case and him saying in a rather foolhardy way: 'It was a bit of a certainty.' Without

Pony's help, John Burke reckoned the odds against them winning were a 'double carpet', 33–1.

Best, thought John Burke, simply to enjoy the moment. He was certainly going to. He had a goblet of champagne with Gilbert Beyfus and a long talk with Jane Aspinall, who had to keep excusing herself to be presented with bunches and bunches of congratulatory flowers. One punter arrived with a dozen deep-red roses.

John Burke did not stay for more champagne and Lady O.'s reputedly remarkable curry. He had to leave. He had a dinner date at the Brompton Grill with the increasingly popular elegant model Sandra Paul, now a novelist and Mrs Michael Howard, one-time First Lady of the Conservative Party.

Pony was the recipient of £1,000, what is technically known as 'a drink' – and a 'long one' at that. It must have sweetened his retirement. John was sorry to learn some years later, from Sydney Summers, that Pony had died.

Supermodels, champagne, carte blanche; Burke and Aspinall were in open season. The failure to prosecute them resulted in a bonanza.

Newspaper editorials thundered on about the anomalies of the gaming laws. The *Sunday Dispatch*, on 23 March 1958, asked: 'Why are the odds so uneven?' Their leading article said:

'The whole ragbag of our betting, gaming, and lottery laws is chaotic to the point of nonsense. Legislation still in force includes an Act of Henry VIII which was passed to prevent Henry's gambling citizens from being "distracted from the practice of archery". Now is the time to introduce legislation that will clear up the mess. Mr Aspinall's victory cannot fail to inspire the gambling classes to breathe new life into the business. When the law's an ass – and when it is proved to be an ass in public – the time has come for action.'

How true.

The legal triumph was to herald the cry of '*Banco!*' and '*Suivi!*' and the sudden movement of many more thick chips, monetary and aristocratic, around the smart set. Belgravia boomed, as did the profits for John Aspinall and his financial director. The chemmy began again only six days after the case, on 25 March 1958, at 93 Eaton Place, with a *cagnotte* of £1,295. For Aspinall and Burke the purpose was to make their mark, and it was a small game with Gerry Albertini, Richard Parkes and Henry Vyner as the biggest players.

It was now accepted that it was legal to have *chemin de fer* parties. Word was going around that there would be no more police raids, no more fuss and that at any moment Macmillan's government would – as they did – announce new gaming laws.

Others would also benefit, as the Vicar and his many converts held their own gambling evenings. John Burke said: 'One of the instant effects of the case was that every young man in Chelsea who had a flat started a chemmy game and invited his friends to play. There were hosts of chemmy games all over London and other parts of the country. Most of them failed as they ran into one major snag: unless the losers paid it was no good. There was no way you could make them pay. We aimed for the top. The only people we had were people who actually paid.'

Impressive players entered this new, tacitly legal, world of chemmy. Aspinall and Burke hosted games all over London, including one long evening at Pelham Cottage, the family home of Mark Birley. After the case, to be invited to one of their floating society *chemin de fer* games was an honour; it meant you were 'in'. The invitation cards had a gloss of importance about them. They were delivered by hand and with no RSVP; more got delivered to Whites than anywhere else. The venue was handwritten at the last moment to keep the games safe from newspaper intrusion – like today's rave parties, that knowledge enhancing the edgy credibility of the enterprise. And like the raves, they were an endorsement of someone's social acceptability. And wealth – only those with money to lose were invited.

Out of the woodwork, or rather out of Debrett's, Britain and Ireland's stately homes, and the City, came the gamblers. They were hugely wealthy, and the stakes went higher and higher at the lavish and exclusive gaming evenings. Whereas the *cagnotte* had previously been £2,000, £3,000 or £4,000 in an evening, the takings were soon regularly in double figures. Aspinall and Burke were sitting on a gold mine. The figures tell the story. John Burke's records of the games in early April 1958, a couple of weeks after the case, show the 'purses' steadily spiralling upwards. At a game on 23 April 1958 the *cagnotte* was £9,529. That same evening, John Pelham, Lord Worsley and later the Earl of Yarborough, an enthusiastic, even reckless gambler, appeared for the first time. He lost £28,044.

The men now playing knew each other socially. Many were members of Whites. Others were respected figures in the City and there were the smart racecourse owners. But there was an enormous snobbery: 'No jockeys, footballers, book-makers or such like.'

Lord Boothby ('for his assignations with Lady Dorothy, Boothby used to call ahead to Number Ten and say he was arriving to "fix the boiler",' said John Burke) was another jovial new face. He had reason to be even happier: he won £2,160 on 23 April. That evening was also good to Henry Vyner, who won £6,000. Then there was Major Billy Straker-Smith, a director of the Warburg bank, who went home with

£1,323. And for every winning bank, Aspinall and Burke took their tax-free percentage . . .

Another winner that evening was Claus von Bülow, the agreeable man about town who then worked with John Paul Getty. The affable von Bülow was a great friend to the gamblers. He said at his home in Chelsea on 26 September 2006: 'John held one of the first games at my flat because they had to move the games around and that was within the law. Then he had a dance there for Eddie Gilbert, but that had nothing to do with the gambling parties. He staged a ball at my flat and it was an event which attracted a great deal of publicity.'

Of course, the ball, written up as the event of 1959, was a massive and expensive – £15,000 – exercise in public relations. There were fine wines, a lavish dinner, an orchestra and 'minders' to make sure that no one who wasn't wanted came in. The departing coup was the revealing of a huge pack of playing cards. As they left, each guest watched as Aspinall cut the cards and dealt them one. It was the contact for the next chemmy evening.

Claus von Bülow's Belgrave Square flat, despite not being a regular venue, played a pivotal role: it was there that the Duke of Devonshire first appeared at a game. With him was the respected horse-breeder the Honourable Monica Sheriff. John Burke recalled, 'We were told she was his aunt – certainly her treatment of Andrew Devonshire had moments of P.G. Wodehouse, of Aunt Agatha:

'"Go *banco*, Andrew.

'"Now, *suivi* . . . bad luck.

'"*Suivi* again . . . bad luck again! Burkie, another two grand for the Duke!"'

Aspinall could operate in any environment; he was wonderful at working the room. The regular Eaton Place waiters,

Bob and Bert, circulated with the the beluga, foie gras, vintage Cristal and Delamain cognac, and the players would gamble, gamble, gamble. John Burke recalls, 'We were very much still with Martin's Bank in Sloane Street – Tim Holland Martin came to the games – and our cheques were blank cheques which we used to supply to the customers. The customer's name didn't appear on it. It just needed a signature, and often just one name, like Faversham, Derby, Suffolk, Devonshire, whatever.

'One of the Martin's cashiers asked me: "Why don't people use their Christian name as well?"

'He didn't quite understand titles. A great many people who played with us banked with Hoare's, which seemed to be the popular bank for gamblers. Often some punter would have a couple of losing *suivis* and then say, with cheerful laughter: "Quinny Hoare [a bank partner] won't like this." Then they'd play on, true gamblers.'

With John Burke in control behind the scenes, Aspinall was the circus ringmaster of the show: he'd '*banco*' and '*suivi*' with his lunatic punters, calling out 'Napoleon' for a natural nine, or any one of his marshals for a natural eight; his favourite was Marshal Ney, just as Ney was to the Emperor. Aspinall would always turn his 'Napoleon' over with a wonderful flourish. There was something of P.T. Barnum, as well as something of the night, about him.

But the cavalier gambling was an act. Aspinall might lose £1,000 for the house, but so what? It was simply the catalyst to get others betting and so boosting that ever-greedy *cagnotte*. 'John Aspinall was a fine actor in the Tony Blair mould of acting. He emoted. Separating fools from their money is, of course, an essential part of the gambling promoter's trade,' points out John Burke.

'The General' arrived on 7 May 1958 for his first game.

The Sandhurst-educated, socially well-connected General J. E. Spencer Smith had a senior post with NATO in Germany. He was deep in John Le Carré country; the cold war was at its most delicate, but still he flew to London for the chemmy. It used to make the organizers shudder at the thought of the press discovering this particular soldier's tactics.

John Burke liked the General: 'It used to be a standing joke that when the Russians were going to invade, they'd pick a night we had a chemmy game. The General would be absent from his post and his mind would be on much more important things than defending Western Europe from Bolshevism. It would be on the cards.

'Jerry Spencer Smith always said when he was given a card, irrespective of whether it was a good card, bad card or indifferent card: "Quelle jolie carte."'

It was certainly a jolly evening later that month when the big breakthrough happened and the cash began to pour in, like an endless waterfall. With chemmy the rage, they got a multimillion-pound endorsement; after the Derby Dinner on 29 May 1958, a couple of the top people's top people announced they could take a crowd to a card game where the champagne and fun would be flowing. And into Burke and Aspinall's chemmy game walked a history of bulging bank balances led by the Queen's friend, the horse-trainer Bernard van Cutsem, who also became godfather to John Burke's daughter.

'It was a bonanza from then on,' recalls John Burke. 'Not only were these people with money, they were people willing to lose money – and pay up. It was cashier's cheques all round; a wonderful time.'

The 'A' team turned out for the game: names like Derby and Devonshire and Faversham. John Burke said: 'The Derby Club Dinner was a very smart affair at White's, a grand event, and they all came on from it and from the clubs, many pissed members from White's looking for more fun. They were there on the recommendation of my good friend Bernard van Cutsem, who also introduced Andrew Devonshire, whose horses he trained.

'Ackroyd (stockbroking), Gerry Albertini, Jocelyn Hambro [head of the Hambro's Bank] and Major Billy Straker-Smith, Bingham [Lord Lucan], Major Nicoll Collin, Peter Lloyd (property), Dickie Muir and John Ambler, two big, rich gamblers, Tim Willoughby [Lord Timothy Willoughby D'Eresby] – he won £30 – and Colonel Bill Stirling who won ten grand that night. Billy Straker-Smith had a good win and Lord Worsley won a bit.

'But the king of the gamblers, John, the Earl of Derby, lost £24,500. John Derby's young brother, the Hon. Richard Stanley MP, who was a junior minister for Macmillan, appeared for the first time at that game.

'The *cagnotte* that night was £19,401, and as the records show, the house players were, on balance, winners. In 2007 money this might be presented as a tax-free half million pounds' earnings for one night's work.

'Of course the takings weren't always as much as that. Jane Aspinall, playing for the house, lost £700, Peter West lost £1,100; on the plus side Lady O. won £1,800, I won £200, so the house players showed a tiny profit; yet, generally speaking, house players showed a loss, especially when Aspers played himself.

'By being intelligent, and understanding gambling and gambling psychology, John recognized the advantage of displaying himself as an open, free-betting generous gambler, rather than as a calculating promoter. This usually meant losing, but he was only giving back a small part of the profit, and might be described as the sprat to catch the mackerel.

'It is rather ironic to discover from the books that the

person who brought this flock of potential golden-egg-laying geese to our door was my friend Bernard van Cutsem. He was one of the big losers of the evening. He dropped £19,700. As Oscar Wilde said, "No good turn ever goes unpunished."'

8. MASTERMIND

Ah, Mr Hill, murdered anyone recently?

JACK GERBER

By the late 1950s, Billy Hill was extremely comfortable and satisfied, an established, savvy criminal player, yet still aspiring to even more lucrative endeavours. He saw opportunities everywhere. His reputation was now so entrenched in the national psyche that he even 'appeared' in the movies. In John Boulting's 1959 film *Carlton-Browne of the FO*, a vehicle for Terry-Thomas and Peter Sellers, Ian Bannen appears, strangely cast, as the king of some obscure and mythical European nation. The king takes a date to a nightclub, where it's pointed out that he is not wearing the requisite black tie. The management want him ejected, until a waiter pipes up: 'He's royalty.'

'I don't care if he's Billy Hill,' says the manager. There's a pause, and then: 'Don't take a cheque.'

Hill, of course, dealt in cash – usually other people's. Bobby McKew was still flitting between Tangier and London, and avoiding France, where there remained difficulties following on from the robbery of Jack Warner's safe. Now aged 33, McKew had an eclectic collection of contacts, many from his now fixed association with Billy Hill; others from his film company days and many now socially far grander.

In April 1958, he had married Anna Gerber. The quiet ceremony was at Hampstead register office. His brother-in-law was Robin Gerber, who had gone to Eton with John Bingham; his father-in-law was 'Lucky' Jack Gerber, a multi-millionaire and an enthusiastic racehorse owner and gambler. They would often go to the racetrack together. Jack Gerber knew horses and would bet heavily, often winning at good odds. He would not bet against Bobby McKew, whom he believed had 'an edge'. Which, in a sense, he always had, for McKew would not bet on anything unless he knew he would win.

Socially, Jack Gerber was a jovial character, though not a man of great tact. One day at the races, he and his son-in-law encountered Billy Hill and some of his associates, including Hill's now ever-present 'minder' George Walker, brother of the useful heavyweight Billy Walker. Bobby McKew and Hill were talking when a jovial Jack Gerber appeared, and with a smile said, 'Ah, Mr Hill, murdered anyone recently?'

It was a freeze-frame moment broken by Bobby McKew turning to Hill and asking: 'Had any winners, Bill?' Hill smiled and said, 'Not been my lucky day.' He turned and walked off. He never mentioned the incident.

There were other tricky encounters, one with Ronnie Kray in Tangier. Ronnie enjoyed visits there, for Tangier offered lots of chances to indulge his particular sexual tastes. Bobby McKew remembers: 'Ronnie, of course, was the other way. He settled in happily in Tangier.

'Once we were having lunch and there were eight or ten people around the table. A ladyfriend of mine was there, and she leaned over and tapped Ronnie on the tummy:

'"Ronnie, if you put on any more weight, the next time we go out I'm not going to introduce you to any of these good-looking young boys."

'I could feel the sweat running down the back of my neck. But give Ronnie his due. The woman was a *lady*, and he looked over at me and in his quiet voice simpered, "Bobby, tell her to leave me alone."

'Once when he was with us, I said, "Oh, for fuck's sake," in front of a woman, and he went all peculiar. "I don't like you using language like that in front of a lady."

'Ronnie was very like that. With "ladies" he would always lean over and light their cigarettes. Or get up and help them to or from the dinner table. He was very well mannered. Of course, as we know, not to everybody.'

Bobby McKew's circle of acquaintances was growing constantly. At the time he was the director of a West End steel company. His associate, Shiv Kapoor, had been involved with a huge fraud involving the Costa Rican government, a massive and later missing shipment of coffee, and Emil Savundra. Kapoor had gone to jail; Savundra had escaped; but landed in more trouble and a longish term in a Belgian prison for another fraud.

The Ceylon-born Emil Savundra had just arrived in Britain, and kept in touch with Bobby McKew. A remarkable series of coincidences would follow, perhaps not so surprising, since London was a village, and people in certain circles knew, or knew of, each other.

At this time, John Burke was asked by Aspinall to give money – £3,000 in cash – to Tom Corbally, who was familiar with gambling clubs and with the American Embassy in Grosvenor Square. Corbally was a friend of society osteopath Stephen Ward, whose patients included Winston Churchill, and he was linked to several intelligence agencies in Washington and Moscow.

'I have no idea what the money was for. John's story was that he had foolishly joined a poker game, but had soon realized that it was not a game in which he would be allowed to win anything. He had wisely left the table, promising to pay what he had already lost. I've read of Corbally's CIA connections. On much better authority, I've been told that he had stronger Mafia ones.'

Yet it was not an organization but one man, the cool-headed Billy Hill, who still ruled the London underworld. He took much interest in the Aspinall and Burke court case; an intelligent man, a thinker, he believed that the law would change and that he could use it, rather than break it. Meanwhile, following the case, he took an interest in the host of de facto legal games all over the city. John Burke got lucky at one run by Hill's associate, Patsy Murphy:

'Patsy, who was then at the top echelon of the gangster world, and a good friend of Paddy Kennedy, frequently ran a Saturday night chemmy game at a flat in Eaton Place near to me. I had an open invitation to these games, but I did not attend because I'd been told by Sydney Summers that Murphy's game, like many others, was not always dependent on chance. Skill sometimes replaced luck, and a lot of games around London at that time were bent.

'But one Saturday night, on my way home, probably not totally sober, I decided to call in at Patsy's flat and found a game in full swing. Paddy Kennedy was playing sitting opposite the croupier, at number five, and the shoe was getting nearer to him, about two places away. Seeing me, Kennedy exclaimed: "Here, Burkie, take my seat. I can't win at this fucking game!"

'He then got up and checked how much money he owed, said goodbye and went out into the night. I accepted Paddy's invitation and sat down in his vacated place. I called "*banco*" to the player on my left. Won the bet, left the money in for my own bank, and this then started a winning run. I left the maximum allowed in the game in the middle every time, and kept on winning. I do not remember how many coups I won, but eventually, when the bank lost, the croupier pushed over about £3,000 in chips to me.

I played on for a couple of shoes, lost some of my winnings and went home with a cheque for about two grand plus in my pocket. This was a pleasant profit.

'When I told Sydney Summers the story I found out what had really happened. Patsy Murphy, who liked Paddy, was owed quite a lot of money by him, gambling losses. So he and his croupier had constructed a "sandwich" – fixed some of the cards in the shoe. It allowed a long run of winning banks to arrive at the number five seat where Paddy Kennedy was sitting. Of course, there was nothing they could do about it when Paddy decided to give up his seat to myself. Patsy Murphy's behaviour was beyond reproach. He did not show the slightest sign of any annoyance or disappointment.

'Another fair-sized chemmy game run in that period was organized by a very personable young man called David Patrick. He and his wife Primrose had a pleasant flat just off Lower Sloane Street, and had a good clientele of punters. It was a very curious game because it was strictly in two halves. From 10 p.m. to midnight, the game was run as a benefit for different parties, namely David Patrick and two Cypriot characters who were bridge players from the Hamilton Club. One was known to most of us as "Crooked Deeds". The fourth person, and the most important, was Louis the Rat, on loan from the Vicar. Louis's skill saw these four profit on the evening, taking the other players to the cleaners in a small way, which was clever. It was lambs to the slaughter, fleecing all the way. Later, the Cypriots and Louis left, and an English croupier took over; by now more and more players were arriving and the game continued probably until breakfast time.

'Now, the only occasion where the game ceased to be totally honest was if anyone was lucky enough, or should I say foolish enough, to win too much money. I went in there once and left with a cheque for £1,900, serious money in those days, and alas, I discovered it was too big an amount to win. I think I still have the bounced cheque somewhere.'

There was, of course, no legal redress. The story emphasizes the value of Aspinall and Burke's players. They had an extraordinary situation. And, possibly because of the status of most of their players, they were not victims of outside influence.

David Patrick was not so lucky. His friend David Pritchett, a tea-broker who returned from India in the 1950s to a career in the City, also ran what was regarded as the only totally honest chemmy game of that era ('I had no private income') and talked to me over lunch in Knightsbridge in August 2006:

'David Patrick was quite a mate of mine. He died young, because one of his games was raided, not by the police, but by a mob. Gangsters came at him. He got set on and was hit across the back with a crowbar. That didn't do his kidneys any good – it damaged them permanently. He died two years later of kidney failure. He was killed, murdered really.

'I suppose David had been asked for protection money and he hadn't paid it. I often wondered if it was a subsidiary mob of Billy Hill's. He and David certainly had dealings. David was partnered up with Jimmy Mellon and Dennis Hamilton, who'd been married to Diana Dors. Hamilton didn't appear at the games, but he was a sinister figure in the background.

'I was running a private game once a week for about

twenty people. I took 5 per cent *cagnotte*, so it was technically illegal. My games were quite small, banks were £10 up to £100. No more than that. Yet people like Billy Rees-Davies, the MP, and David Milford Haven came. It was fun, and you could make some money.

'The first games I gave were in a flat next door to Esmeralda's Barn. I used to wonder why between shoes everybody would dash out. Then I discovered that if you stood on the seat of the lavatory and looked through the window, you could see these girls changing for the cabaret. My punters weren't all true gambling addicts.

'But the money did sometimes get serious. I had a partner, Alan Elliott, and sometimes I would give my games in his great big flat at 26 Belgrave Square. Our arrangement was that I was responsible for my punters and Alan was responsible for his punters. We would take it in turns to take and pay out the cheques.

'I had a punter who was a friend of mine who I unfortunately introduced to David Patrick, and he bounced cheques with him as well as me. When this debt was run up and it didn't look as though it was going to be paid, there was quite a spat between my punter and Hamilton, who wanted his money. He said he was going to get it. He threatened to bring in Billy Hill.

'I went round with David Patrick to Hamilton's to plead with him to drop all the naughty business. Mellon was also there. They seemed to agree they were being too heavy-handed about it.

'Hamilton was a very nasty piece of work. When I got in there, there was this rather sad little girl present. He ordered her: "Go into the bedroom," and he followed her. He was in the bedroom screwing this girl when the telephone rang, and it was Billy Hill for Hamilton. David Patrick took the call and he said: "Mr Hill, sorry to have bothered you, there's been a mistake, a mix-up." I will never forget that.

'It was an intriguing time. If I wasn't giving a game I'd go to others. A wonderful woman, Mrs Emerson Potter, was one of my rivals, but I was very fond of her. She came off her deathbed and gave a game on the night she knew I was giving a game, and, of course, she got the punters. Naughty old girl. She was a widow of a soldier from the First World War and had terrific style and no question of any ill manners – no swearing at her table, or anything like that. When she died all she had were her poker chips, and she left them to me.

'Characters! Tony Psycopolos was a very anglicized Greek. He had been in the Navy in the war and he was a magnificent boxer. He had been to St Paul's public school. Although he was at least twenty stone, when he went out for a meal he would order a main course twice, if not three times. Yet when you watched him dance, he was straight across the floor of the Milroy. Princess Margaret would stare at him. He was sophisticated.

'He had a mistress in those days. Of course, he was foreign. One Guy Fawkes night he was with her in the upstairs bar of the Star and Paddy came up and said: "Get that whore out of here." Tony told Paddy: "You say that again and I'll knock you down the stairs."

'Of course Paddy said it again. Tony knocked him down the stairs. Paddy came up again and Tony knocked him down again. Paddy took him to court. Tony got knocked down for knocking him down the second time. He had a right to knock him down the first time but not the second time.

'On 5 November for the next two or three years, we'd go round to the Star in Tony's large Jaguar with a lot of rockets and fireworks and blow up the place.

'I went to games run by Mark Sykes and Peter Scaramanga but I never went to the Vicar's card parties.

'I was in the illegal gambling business at the same time as Aspinall,' said Mark Sykes, 'but at a smaller level. I like to think we were more charming than Aspinall. He behaved very badly towards his first wife Jane: it is embarrassing to even think about it. I used to get quite a lot of his leavers, his cast-offs. It was a huge business.'

And there were also other sources of 'income', as John Burke recalls. One involved, in this so-circular world, his acquaintance Patsy Murphy. 'There was a burglary at 93 Eaton Place, and Jane's jewellery was stolen. John had been generous in buying his new and beautiful wife jewellery. Of course, he bought most of it from Mr Money, who was a terrific fence. Jane's jewellery was, as they say in the trade, "bent gear" or "dodgy gear". It had been valued for insurance purposes by Armour Winston in Burlington Arcade, who had no idea it wasn't straight. The theft was no tragedy, because they weren't family heirlooms or anything like that, and they were well insured and John stood to collect about ten grand from the insurance company.

'I was in the Star having a drink and Patsy Murphy came to me and said: "John, tell your friend if he wants his jewellery back I know where it is and I'll get it for him. It won't cost him more than two grand, perhaps a bit less."

'I relayed the news back to John, and he was not pleased at all. He said: "Tell them to keep the bloody jewellery." The last thing he wanted was to get it back. He got his ten thousand pounds and the jewellery was never heard of again.'

That wasn't the only time that Aspinall bought jewellery from Mr Money. Bobby McKew had also bought his wife a splendid diamond necklace from Mr Money – made of fake stones from South Africa. He said, 'It cost me £200 and the only way you could tell the stones were not real was because they were so shiny. Anna knew they were not genuine, of course. One evening she met Lady O. at a Mayfair drinks party and Lady O. gushed about the diamonds. She had exactly the same sort. She told Anna, "You must have a wonderful and rich husband. My son John bought me mine, and I know they cost him an absolute fortune." Anna simply smiled and agreed.'

It was a small, if complex, world, full of intriguing people, gambling dens and nightclubs, with social mixtures not seen since, where it seemed most people were welcome to the party. John Burke's good friends included the extremely well-connected Barbara Langrishe and John Aspinall's half-sister Jenny Osborne, later Jenny Little, whose husband Anthony formed the designer wallpaper company Osborne & Little with her brother Sir Peter Osborne, father of the 2007 Conservative shadow chancellor, George Osborne.

For many, social life revolved around clubs, which were popular in the afternoons and when the pubs closed in the evening. 'Oh, yes, there were many, many places to go,' said Mark Sykes. 'The Maisonette was the melting pot, very much so; other than that there were pubs, restaurants, nightclubs.'

'Indeed,' said John Burke, 'there were always places to be, drinking clubs to go to. On an afternoon at the Colony Room in Soho you'd have Muriel Belcher glaring at her customers, and most days they included Francis Bacon and Frank Auerbach. I'd see Lucian Freud there. He'd work all night and would relax there.

'Drinking clubs were popular because the pub, by law, had to shut at 3 p.m. In theory, people who entered the clubs had to be members, and the clubs were supposed to keep proper books and membership details and all that sort of thing. The Maisonette was easily the best of them, run by Ruby Lloyd and her friend and partner Jock Campbell Muir, who was a most delightful character and a friend of mine. He was also a regular player in David Pritchett's chemmy games.

'Ruby was quite class conscious and loved having people of higher social status: nothing pleased her more than to look around and see titles, gentry idling the afternoon away in her club. She had one great advantage: one of her very close friends was Wally Virgo, who was the Commander of Scotland Yard's Serious Crime Squad. With such a friend, Ruby was not troubled by the local police, who would turn a blind eye to any minor infringements of the drinking laws; sometimes she didn't close on time, and on one or two occasions we played cards there all night. That was obviously against the law. The other great advantage that it brought on was that no would-be gangsters or hoodlums tried to have a go at her for protection money. People didn't want to fall foul of the Commander of the Serious Crime Squad.

'Ruby was quite a tough businesslady – she had to be, in that profession – and she didn't cash cheques foolishly like the barman at White's. The only known instance of her catching a large bouncer was one from Eric Steiner, the famous Swedish con man. He was hugely persuasive and talked her into exchanging a monkey for one of his pieces of paper, something she regretted bitterly for a long time. Were Ruby with us today she still wouldn't have forgiven Steiner.'

Steiner, the son of a Swedish clergyman and one-time manager of tennis champion Björn Borg, would later go into the gambling business with Mark Sykes: 'Eric Steiner was a very funny character. He was an absolutely brilliant table tennis player. Brilliant, and very funny. He died in Marbella. I saw him in 1996 about five years or so before he died. He was one of the first people into heavy facelifts and plastic surgery. He looked about 45 when he was 80.'

John Burke said, 'Eric Steiner was very popular in London in the 1950s. People all over the city knew him. When he went to the Milroy, Paul Adam and the band would strike up the appropriate tune, and somebody would sing, "Nothing can be finer than to wake up with Eric Steiner in the morning."'

Or with a showgirl from Murray's Cabaret Club in Beak Street. A short walk up Regent Street from Piccadilly Circus, it was one of the first of London's fashionable nightclubs. The showgirls stood bare-breasted and motionless on the stage (as required by law), and the cleavage-endowed or uplifted hostesses sought 'scalps' in the form of fruit cups. Every sale meant a 'tip'. Princess Margaret, queen of the royal gadabouts, went there, as did Princess Muna (Toni Gardiner), who took many Arabs to the club. King Hussein was a regular. It was where Christine Keeler met Mandy Rice-Davies and Stephen Ward, and the seeds of the Profumo affair were sown.

'I'd be at all these places for the newspaper,' said Nancy Gillespie. 'It was lots of fun, with the gamblers and the characters. You never knew when you'd open a door and walk into a headline.'

Or, in her case, romance. She'd found that in 1956 when she met Gary Cooper by a Riviera swimming pool. 'We started to chat, when a woman at the other side of the pool realized that her husband was engaged in picking me up. Mrs Cooper jumped to her feet, a pair of binoculars to her eyes. "Gosh, I'd better nip off," Gary said out of the corner of his mouth. "Give me your telephone number, will you – please?"

'I knew I shouldn't, but I was dazzled and flattered and thrilled at the thought of Gary Cooper wanting to date me. I gave him the number of my flat in Lowndes Square. Gary swam off. And I only half believed that I would ever hear from him again. At that very moment I was a guest of my old friend the Maharaja of Baroda at his chateau near Cannes. If I was good enough for him and his friends, why not Gary Cooper?

'A few days later I flew home to London. I still had not heard from Gary again. Then, one night, as I was getting ready for bed, I got a personal call from Cannes. "Come and see me, honey," said the unmistakable drawl. "I need you. Get an air ticket right away. I'll be waiting for you."

'I ought to have turned haughty and said "No". But, of course, I did nothing of the sort. I said "Yes" – and a couple of days later I began my one crazy week of fun with Gary Cooper.

'He had packed his wife off back to the United States, so the coast was reasonably clear. Not entirely clear, because Gary was scared of his fans finding out. So I did not stay at his hotel. I was booked in at another hotel three miles away. I occupied the bridal suite. Gary gave me the money – £20 a night. The manager was most surprised that Nancy Gillespie, the "bride" from London, had no bridegroom with her. He became quite suspicious when he found that I hardly ever used my suite, except to sleep there. And I was a very late bird all that week. I used the suite mainly as a dressing room.

'Every morning I changed into a bikini and went to join Gary on the beach. Every night I changed into evening clothes and met Gary at his hotel or at a restaurant. It was our beach outings that I enjoyed most. We would find some remote stretch of sand and sunbathe. And Gary would whisper all sorts of nonsense into my ear.

'At night we went on fantastic binges – well away from the areas favoured by tourists. And the back of Gary's Bentley Continental was stacked with empties. Usually we covered up the bottles with a travelling rug. It would never do for the fans to have spotted them. But one night, as the Bentley pulled up outside Gary's hotel, the pressure of the bottles in the back forced the door open. The whole lot shot out onto the pavement! It was terribly embarrassing for Gary. He whispered to me, "Gee, kid, I hope there are no newspaper people around."

'Those weren't the only bottles that Gary carried around. He was a hopeless hypochondriac, and he never travelled without a large case that contained bottles of medicine, boxes of pills, lotions and ointments to cope with every emergency. He was always talking about illness and forever showing his suspicion of food that was offered to him. One day we had a perfectly delicious lobster for lunch at an expensive restaurant in Monte Carlo. I thought the meal was wonderful. Gary thought it was horrid. He carried out every possible test on his lobster. He sniffed and he peered and he chewed experimental morsels before every mouthful.

'That night we had a date with Prince Rainier and Princess Grace, his *High Noon* co-star. They were throwing a party at the Sporting Club of Monte Carlo. Before it, Gary was sick. I am sure he had imagined himself into being ill. He recovered before the party. But when we arrived at the Club, Gary was still thinking of his sickness.

'Flunkeys bowed us to the regal presence.

'"Glad to see you, Mr Cooper. How are you?" said Prince Rainier.

'"Not so good, your Highness," replied Gary. "I've been throwing up all day all over your kingdom."

'It was unforgivable, of course. And Prince Rainer did not try to hide his annoyance. I loved every dyed hair on Gary's head, but he just did not appreciate how this could shock. He flew back to London with me – and there we parted. He had to return to America.'

Nancy was moping around London when she met the man

whose title would put her on a par with Princess Grace –
though, sadly, without the money. It was an encounter which
would bring her even closer to the gamblers of London.

'I was dining alone, and rather miserably, at a Polish
restaurant in Soho. I knew the proprietor, who came to my
table. "Miss Gillespie, may I introduce to you an old friend of
mine, Prince George Sapieha?"

'I looked up at the tall, handsome figure by his side.
Somehow I managed to smile. I gave him permission to sit
with me at my table. There was charm in every word he spoke.
I was grateful for his company. We agreed to meet the next
evening. He took me to dinner. When the time came for him
to see me home I knew I was in love.

This was something different. Or so I imagined. Never
before had I felt so stricken with helplessness. Every touch,
every gesture, every word told me this was the man I would
marry. George told me he loved me too. And within a month
we were making arrangements to marry.

'But George's parents disapproved. He was not quite 21. I
was five years older. So we decided to elope. Without a word
to anybody, we packed two suitcases and went to Scotland. At
Glasgow we gave notice at the register office. Then for three
weeks we hid at a small hotel.

'On the eve of the ceremony, I could contain myself no
longer. I phoned my best friend, Sarah Rothschild, the daughter of Lord Rothschild, and straight away she caught the night
train from London to Glasgow in time for the ceremony. I had
never been happier. I was in love with the most wonderful
man in the world. I was now Her Serene Highness Princess
Sapieha. I was a member of one of the most noble families in
the world. George's ancestors included a Tsar of Russia, a
cardinal, and an ambassador to the Court of St James. Their
vast estates spread throughout Poland to the Lithuanian bor-

der. Then the Germans invaded in 1939, and George's family became refugees.

'George himself was almost penniless. He had nothing apart from the few pounds a week he was earning as an advertising representative. By that time I was expecting a child. I had to get some money from somewhere. So I decided on the easiest way of making a living I knew – gambling.'

From then on she witnessed the action at illegal games all over the capital, but not at Eaton Place or at any of the accommodations (like interior decorator David Hicks' apartments) taken for the evening by John Aspinall. She was very close to John Burke but, as a journalist and, worse, provider of high and low society gossip to 'Ephraim Hardcastle', there was no way that she could attend his games.

The press were the enemy. John Burke: 'In Dublin I had been very friendly with Paddy Campbell, who was a writer and also heir to his father Lord Glenavy, the then Governor of the Bank of Ireland. Paddy was now living in London and writing for the *Sunday Times*. He told me he enjoyed a flutter and, therefore, would like to come to some of our games. Having discussed this request with John, with some embarrassment – I had to say no. It was not that we did not trust him implicitly, but that some of the players, knowing that Paddy worked in Fleet Street, might be worried by seeing him at the chemmy table; such was our anti-publicity phobia.'

Still, while John Burke and John Aspinall attracted the top end of the money, Nancy Gillespie had other contacts: 'Some of the Society people who ran private gambling parties were my friends. I knew that they would willingly pay if I brought along clients to their parties. For this service I was never actually paid in cash. I was usually given a certain amount of credit at the tables. Once it was as much as £100 for introducing two millionaires and an industrial magnate on the same night.

'Sometimes I hired out my own flat in Lowndes Square for chemmy parties. That was worth £60 a night to me. But mostly it was at other people's houses that I did my gambling.

'On occasion I could afford to risk as much as £2,450 on the turn of a card or a spin of the wheel. My winnings were tax free. So I was in clover. And I might have gone on being a gambling agent and hostess if it hadn't been for a couple of nasty experiences. I do like my gambling to be above board. And I struck a couple of rigged games in one of the most fashionable homes of Mayfair.

'At one of them I saw an Old Etonian, with a terribly upper-class background, take a dear old millionaire for a £2,000 ride. From the start the millionaire forced the pace. His winnings rocketed. Inside two hours he was £500 to the good. The others seemed almost happy at the millionaire's run of luck. Then I became suspicious. I noticed a girl standing behind the lucky winner. She was looking at the cards he held in his hand. First she raised her right hand and touched her nose with two fingers. Then she touched her hips with her left hand. Glancing to my right, I saw her signals were being received by another player.

'It was the end of the millionaire's winning streak. From then on he began to lose heavily. First one pretty girl, then another, would sidle up to his side with a word of sympathy. They then would take it in turns to stand behind him to continue the tic-tac. He had obviously been specially invited to be "skinned".

'The riggers were my friends. But how I hated them at that moment! I wanted to cry out a word of warning but I knew that I dare not. I was forced to sit in silence and watch helplessly. Like a sportsman, the victim wrote a cheque for that amount and handed it over to his principal opponent. With a cheerful goodnight, he put on his coat and left.

'I confronted my friends, and the truth came out. Several people at the party openly admitted the game had been rigged. My Old Etonian friend had agreed to split his "winnings" 50–50 with his helpers. But then the rumpus started. The millionaire's opponent, who was a little drunk, refused to hand over the cheque. He yelled: "I did all the dirty work – now I'm sticking to the profits."

'One of his opponents sprang forward to snatch the cheque. In the scuffle which followed, it fluttered to the floor in two pieces. There was a ghastly silence. Calamity – cheques from gaming parties were bank expressed. That meant that the winners asked their banks to rush the cheques though for immediate payment – before the losers changed their minds. Here was a case where the loser had to be asked for his cheque again!

'The task was delegated to a young blade, who called on the millionaire next morning. After a sociable drink or two, he gave the millionaire some highly suspect answers to some pointed questions. So he was told to get out – without a penny.

'Sometimes real tragedy followed gambling parties where I was a guest. Johnny Levy, son of the proprietor of a fleet of taxis, sat opposite me one night. He was, I knew, in the middle of a losing streak. At this party, too, he kept on losing. By the end of the evening he was £500 down, bringing his total losses for the month to several thousands. He was ruined. He went home that night and gassed himself. It would have been easy for him to have welshed, but back then doing that was looked on in some circles as worse than death.

'It was horrid. A reminder, if I'm not being too Calvinistic, that retribution exists. Yet such things happened and the gambling went on – even more so. The stakes got higher. In every sense.'

Which is why some of the most famous names in the world

wanted to be playing chemmy. With the threat of prosecution gone, in 1958 they all but paraded along a remarkable rainbow to what had become the most socially acceptable, upmarket games in town. John Aspinall and John Burke simply held out the pot of gold for their punters to fill, in a series of spectacular days and nights of feverish chemmy.

9. LA DOLCE VITA

Who Dares Wins.

SAS MOTTO

Of all the fearless, fanatical gamblers who provided style, dignity and impeccable good manners to Aspinall and Burke's upmarket private chemmy games, John Burke singles out one man as a giant. Indeed, he sounds like someone from the pages of John Buchan.

Funded by ancestral wealth, Scottish landowner Colonel William Stirling was larger than life. He had two younger brothers. Peter Stirling was a diplomat, working mostly in the Middle East. David Stirling was the famous 'Phantom Major' of the Second World War; the founder of the Long Range Desert Groups which became the SAS Regiment. Churchill called him 'the bravest man I have ever known'. He was promoted to the rank of Colonel after the war.

John Burke said: 'He was a charming, modest man. Once, before I knew him well, I introduced him to some other player whom he did not know as "Colonel Stirling"; afterwards he told me gently: "I am not Colonel now, Burkie, I am David." He was always a gentleman. He never wanted to make a fuss – and he was arguably one of the greatest heroes of the twentieth century. Fascinating, all those Stirlings were.

'It's strange, because I watch television and I see Colonel Bill Stirling's granddaughter Rachael, from his son Archie's marriage to Diana Rigg, and I can see the similarities. His like is not to be seen today in any of London's pseudo-smart gambling clubs. A proud bunch, the Stirlings – every reason to be.'

Colonel Bill Stirling was very special. The gambling duo had rented a house in Ascot for Royal Ascot week in 1959. At about eleven o'clock on the morning of 19 June, the all-night chemmy game finally came to a halt. The financial records tell an amazing story. The dubious Eddie Gilbert won £60,000, which was fortunate for all concerned; had he lost an amount like that, the chances of his paying it, even had he wished to do so, would have been rather worse than negligible. Gilbert was a sinking ship who got lucky that night. Most of the players did well.

Bill Stirling was the biggest loser. He lost £174,500, which is more than £4 million in 2007 values. Four million pounds gone – on one night of chemmy. Stirling went into the drawing room of the house, and John Burke joined him with his account book. Stirling signed an IOU in the account book, which John Burke still has. When he had signed off on the money, the Colonel waved to a waiter and quietly asked for a plate of scrambled eggs. There was no sign of distress, and he ate his eggs quite quickly. He had to be off – he had a busy day.

That afternoon at Ascot, in the royal enclosure, Bill Stirling did not appear to recall the loss. He went about the racing as if all was as it should be. He cleared his debt in a few weeks, and his big loss did not divert him from the chemmy tables – or his own rules.

The multi-Oscar-winning Sam Spiegel was an extraordinary character: he began life as a penniless refugee, became a specialist in 'kiting' cheques and went on to produce some of the most renowned films of the twentieth century: *On the Waterfront*, *The African Queen* and *The Bridge on the River*

Kwai. His financial dealings were often questioned, and writer-director Billy Wilder described him as 'a modern-day Robin Hood, who steals from the rich and steals from the poor'.

Spiegel turned up at the home of Lord Timothy Willoughby D'Erersby, who had given his house over for the gamblers to host a chemmy evening. Tim Willoughby was a genuinely well liked and trusted man about town, heir to Astor money and the vast Ancaster estates, and was soon to play an important role in the lives of John Aspinall and John Burke. Sam Spiegel was then very much in the public eye. He was currently in London to work on *Lawrence of Arabia* with director David Lean, and was gambling on an unknown actor called Peter O'Toole in the title role.

There had been a lot of coverage of the film in the newspapers, but Bill Stirling was not a reader of the popular press, the red tops of the day. The fortunes of film personalities were not something to trouble or intrigue him. He was probably one of the few people in the country who knew nothing of Sam Spiegel.

At that time John Burke had his shoes made by Fosters of Jermyn Street; Sam Spiegel was also a patron. One of their designs was a comfortable dark-blue suede shoe. At Tim Willoughby's, John Burke was wearing these shoes with a dark suit. He admits it was bad taste, maybe rather vulgar: gentlemen wore black shoes with laces in the evening. Then came the Elvis moment. Spiegel arrived wearing identical shoes. He, however, was dressed in a dinner jacket, so suede shoes were definitely 'not on'; wearing them was a sartorial solecism.

Suddenly, between chemmy shoes, Bill Stirling took John Burke aside and, indicating Spiegel, asked: 'Burkie, who is that Yid wearing blue suede shoes?' John Burke hastily shuffled his feet under a chair as he explained Spiegel's status in the world of film, a world light years away from the Stirling family.

Spiegel was a sensible chemmy player, if anyone can be

described that way. Sometimes he won, sometimes he lost; never vast amounts either way – merely plus or minus a few thousand. He did employ a strategy, however, that, while not affecting his winnings, nullified his losses. He wisely did not stay at the table all night, and when he left, if he were a winner he would leave with a cheque payable to himself in his pocket, while if a loser he would agree the sum with John Burke and then ask him to go to his office later that day to collect it.

Waiting at the Spiegel office in Dover Street would be a cheque payable to John Burke: 'This was quite normal; many gamblers did not wish their bank managers to see the name Aspinall on large cheques. Yet, while Spiegel's winnings were paid to him personally, his losing cheques were always drawn on a production or film company; successful financiers are ever loath to waste their own money. It's interesting to think, historically speaking, that *Lawrence of Arabia* may have paid John Burke several thousand pounds. Possibly tens of thousands. I can't recall it all.'

For the promoters, one of the most important games, the smartest and, they hoped, the most financially rewarding of their season, was the private game staged during Derby week. In 1959 it was on Thursday in John Burke's flat at 60 Eaton Place, in the drawing room, which was ideal for their nocturnal activities. It was a jovial scene, and most of the gambling was going well.

But outside, danger was lurking. News of the game had reached Fleet Street, and the street outside the front door was alive with newspaper reporters, scenting a front-page scoop. The threat of police action had been replaced by an even more deadly and destructive force. Aspinall and Burke did not alert or alarm their players. They prayed that the press would get fed up and leave. But at breakfast they were still there. The resourceful waiter Bob Richardson carried out a reconnaissance of the basement. He discovered that it was possible to gain access, through a window, to a small back courtyard, and from there onto a low flat roof from which it was feasible to get down into a side street. On that Friday morning in June 1959, this route was used by some notable escapees, among whom were the Earl of Derby, his brother the Hon. Richard Stanley, the Duke of Devonshire and Bernard Van Cutsem, who remarked, 'Colditz would have been child's play to Bob.'

Yet not all the players could use Bob's *Great Escape* route. As always, needs must. Lady O. was anxious to go home, and Bob ensured that she was carried out to a waiting van in a laundry basket. When the game eventually ended at lunchtime, the press had decamped. John Burke points out that the pubs had opened.

Super-punter Lord Derby, having lost tens of thousands of pounds, shinned down a drainpipe to escape the press; later that day the very English, pink-faced John Derby looked immaculate in his morning coat and top hat as he chatted to the Queen at Epsom (the Derby was then run on Wednesday and the Oaks on Friday).

Stamina was an essential for the smart-set gambler in the late 1950s. It appears that waiter Bob Richardson had smarts with his stamina. While it is not essential for play to begin that all nine players' seats at the chemmy table be filled, it looks better for the promoter if they are. In those (for Burke and Aspinall) halcyon days, house players played an important role. There were two types: the obvious 'house' player, as in John Aspinall himself, John Burke, Lady O. or Jane Aspinall – or people who were supposedly independent and gambling with their own money.

It was important, if two or three big players arrived early, to fill up the table and keep the action at a high pitch. As more real punters arrived, the house players would drop out.

Yet, towards the end of the night – which could be midmorning and sometimes later – important (as in rich and foolish) players like Lord Derby would want to play on. This happened at Tim Willoughby's house, with Peter West, the ultimate charming house player, betting £1,000 at a time with Derby and Devonshire until the game ended at 2 p.m. the next day. It is understandable how a character like Peter West could confuse fantasy and reality. Moments after the game was over, he had to check on his account at Martin's Bank. He was £50 short, and looked at his friends. John Aspinall, John Burke and Peter West had £10 between them. Bob the waiter, who as usual had enjoyed lavish tips from the gamblers, loaned West the £50 he needed.

'Let me give you a cheque for £60 for that very kind thing you are doing for me,' West said to Bob.

Bob was not a risk-taker: 'No, better if you give me cash at the next game.'

The chemmy gamblers were an extraordinary collection of people. Edward John Stanley, MC, 18th Earl of Derby, had plenty of stamina and was the leader of the pack. John Derby might have been the reincarnation of some legendary eighteenth- or nineteenth-century aristocratic English gambler. One of Derby's ancestors, when heir to the earldom, was offered the throne of Greece, but replied that he preferred to be king of Lancashire.

Indeed, the chemmy-playing Derby owned lots of Liverpool and much of Lancashire. He was a slightly masochistic gambler and had the same penchant in sexual matters, liking to be beaten with shoelaces tied together by a particular lady he knew from Les Ambassadeurs. He was recklessly fearless at the gaming table (one chemmy game lasted for thirty hours), completely honourable and always courteous – but a lunatic gambler nevertheless. John Burke recalled, 'John Derby was a crazy gambler in that he would double up more and more when losing, a disastrous gambling strategy. One night at 93 Eaton Place, playing against house players after everyone had gone home, Derby was losing £300,000.

'John Aspinall thought that this was too much, and he feared – wrongly, as subsequent events were to prove – that when his lordship sobered up next day he would refuse to pay and never return. Therefore in the last shoe it was artificially ensured that Derby won back half of his losses. This decision was a calculated commercial one, in no way quixotic.'

Of course, if you could allow a punter to win you could also make him lose; you could control the play.

The wealth that was squandered in those long evenings and nights remains astonishing, even to those who enjoy gambling. Before his death, Colonel Bill Stirling in 1975 sold thousand of acres; the family home, Keir House and some extraordinary works of art. Archie Stirling told the clan's website in February 2006 that it was not just 'foolish expenditure' which caused this, but also an 'inability to understand cash flow'.

Aspinall and Burke understood cash flow. They seemingly couldn't lose. Yet, for Aspinall, there never seemed to be enough money coming in. His expenses were enormous. Aspinall, a strange, amoral mix, an apparent emotional wasteland, did not appear to understand how to apply the brake. At times John Burke was uneasy about Aspinall's flexible morality. There is the nagging passage in Brian Masters' 1988 biography, *The Passion of John Aspinall*, on which Aspinall cooperated, where the author suggests that the court case discouraged the punters, when in fact it brought more and more powerful players to the games. At the same time, he writes: 'There was never any suggestion that he was less than scrupulously honest, never a hint of suspicion that he would permit cheating; indeed, this was one of the firmest rocks upon which his success so far had been founded as gambling promoters were, on the whole, a thoroughly reprobate lot without a moral between them. One of the reasons the aristocracy went to Aspinall was that they knew they could trust him.'

'Win or Lose, We'll Have More Booze' was the rallying cry of Major Billy Straker-Smith, late of the Brigade of Guards; the banker was the epitome of an English gentleman and had a passion for the game of cricket. As the long gambling nights went on, fuelled by the liquid ministrations of the waiters Bob and Bert, the gallant major would describe each coup of the chemmy game in cricketing parlance. 'Knocked that one into the crowd for six', he would cry, when some lucky punter turned over a nine, while the smaller 'natural' eight was 'stroked it through the covers for four'. When the *banco* caller narrowly beat the bank, he'd offer: 'stole a quick single', or 'nicked one through the slips'. If the coup went the other way, in the bank's favour, it was a case of being 'caught behind the wicket' or, sometimes, 'run out'.

Major Straker-Smith occasionally expressed himself in language that some might consider rude. John Burke says he always did so in a good-humoured fashion, never with even a hint of anger or bad sportsmanship. His great cry, having lost a coup, was 'Fuck my tits, we're cattled!'

Four members of the Macmillan government were regular players at the games: Churchill's son-in-law Christopher Soames, the Duke of Devonshire, Richard Stanley and Bob Boothby. One night in David Pelham's flat, three of them were at the table. At 8 a.m. two of that trio, the Duke and Stanley, were sober and sensible – they were expected at 10 Downing Street to meet the prime minister at 10 a.m. The third minister, Lord Boothby, was exuberant and not totally sober, clearly enjoying himself. When his Cabinet colleagues tried to induce him to come away with them, he banged the table and shouted: 'Fuck the Cabinet. Fuck Macmillan. I want to play chemmy – *Banco!*'

'It was a strange thing, the language,' said John Burke. 'Nancy Mitford had brought out her book about what was "U" and "non-U". There were words that were unbelievably, terribly "non-U", like "toilet" and "pardon". These were words which a lady or gentleman could never use. Quite acceptable to say "fuck", of course.

'One night Lord Stanley of Aldernay was playing, and his wife Kitty, who didn't often come to the games, was there. Ed Stanley was cursing like the best of them. "Oh, darling, watch what you're saying," said his wife.

'He turned on her: "I'll stop saying fuck . . ." – there was a pause – "if you stop saying pardon."'

One great exception to the press ban at the games was Clive Graham, the racing correspondent 'Scout' of the *Daily Express* in its heyday. He and his wife were well known socially, but Mrs Graham was sometimes protected from knowledge of her husband's gambling. One evening when Clive Graham was playing, Bob the waiter went outside to get a breath of fresh air and saw, coming along the pavement, Mrs Graham with her two little dogs.

'I see you've got a game in John's flat. Can I come in and have a drink?'

Bob, unaware of the instructions to keep her in the dark about her husband's gambling, invited her in. Graham recognized her voice and dived under the table. Mrs Graham went into the game, where one seat was vacant, and Bob poured a drink for her. She would have simply had her drink and gone home none the wiser, if it hadn't been for the dogs. They sniffed around and, as is the way with dogs, they sniffed out their owner. They ran under the table barking, and Clive Graham was flushed out of his hiding place. 'I don't think there were any serious consequences,' says John Burke. 'Mrs Graham had a good sense of humour.'

Not all that happened was amusing. One chemmy evening at 93 Eaton Place, Billy Straker-Smith was a heavy loser: he got up from the table having lost £50,000 and having behaved impeccably throughout the game. Although it was nowhere near the biggest loss that a player had suffered at Aspinall and Burke's tables, it was still the equivalent of around £1 million in 2007 money. It was a great deal to lose in a friendly card game, especially for someone who honourably intended to pay up without much delay.

Straker-Smith was a rich man, but he was not in the same financial league as some of the other players like Devonshire and Derby who had won from him. He put on a brave face, but behind that iron facade he must have been feeling sick. As Straker-Smith was about to leave, having agreed his account with John Burke, 'Aspers' went over and put his hand on his shoulder. Aspinall adopted the most genuine manner he could muster. He nodded at his victim, smiled charmingly, rubbed Straker-Smith's shoulder and then said sympathetically, 'Hard luck, Billy. You played a great game.'

The gallant major drew himself up to his full height, shoulders back, head erect, took a firm grip on his perfectly rolled umbrella and replied in his military voice, 'Yes, John, straight back to the bowler, straight back to the bowler.'

Billy Straker-Smith, soldier and gentleman, then stepped firmly out into the Belgravia dawn.

It was also at dawn that one of the most phenomenal chemmy encounters to take place at 93 Eaton Place finally concluded. In 1960, European playboy Gianni Agnelli was the uncrowned king of Italy. Lord Derby was royalty at the chemmy tables. What luck it seemed that they were both staying in London on 28 June 1960. It was an opportunity, a gift, for John Aspinall, who a year earlier had met the Fiat heir at a Monte Carlo casino.

This fabulously wealthy legendary lover of the good life was on Aspinall's list of the 'Top Ten Most Wanted Gamblers'. Agnelli – suave, sophisticated, a picture of good taste and breeding (his mother was a Bourbon princess) – was regarded as one of the richest men in the world. In 2000, three years before his death at the age of 81, his family fortune was estimated at $5 billion. He was a superb catch for the gambling promoters.

Aspinall and John Burke quickly arranged to have a game that evening at Aspinall's flat. Lady Annabel Birley was recruited to socially impress the Italian. The wine was chosen more carefully than ever, the food presented more lavishly. Extra flowers had been bought. Aspinall wanted the perfect ambience.

Agnelli, who had chased around the world with his friend Prince Rainier of Monaco, dated Rita Hayworth and Anita Ekberg, and escorted Jackie Kennedy Onassis, both before and after President JFK's assassination, now turned his charms on John Burke's Italian girlfriend and future wife, the great beauty Liliana Livon.The two Italians chatted amicably between the chemmy shoes and then the Earl of Derby arrived and the action really got started.

The game was organized so quickly that Aspinall could not contact other big players. The 'A' team was absent. At the table were Michael Alachouzos, Henry Vyner, Peter (Lord) St Just, an American businessman called Ted Bassett and, for the house, Peter West and John Burke.

Aspinall was the croupier. He took the job in order to avoid being caught in a betting crossfire between Derby and Agnelli, where he might have been forced for reasons of prestige to bet large amounts foolishly.

The game had got under way after dinner and a few hours later it had reached, at least for the hosts, a truly happy state, better than they could ever have hoped for. The limit on an opening bank was £10,000 – a large white chip and an astonishing amount of money at the time, the equivalent of more than a quarter of a million pounds at 2007 values.

Agnelli was losing £200,000, and announced that he was not going to play on. That meant a huge payout. There were two big winners, Derby and the house. John Derby was a consistent loser in the games and was, at that time, heavily 'on the books' – that is, owing vast sums to Aspinall. He would therefore collect only part of his winnings. Agnelli, of course, would pay his losses in full and probably quite promptly.

The winners were desperately trying to appear cool. They had won an absolute fortune. How could they spend it? What wishful thinking.

Lord Derby, tall, thin, bespectacled and unprepossessing in looks but not attitude, had other ideas. He wanted the game to continue, and, after much cajoling, he eventually persuaded Agnelli, albeit reluctantly, to sit down again at the table.

In the middle of the shoe, Agnelli opened a bank with a £5,000 blue chip. Derby instantly called '*banco.*' He wanted action. He'd take the bet, all of the £5,000.

The Italian – tanned, neat – stretched out his arm, revealing his watch worn over his shirt-cuff, and picked up his cards. Agnelli's luck was about to change.

Derby lost, an eight to a four. The bank was now £10,000. Derby promptly called, in his thin voice, '*Suivi.*' And lost.

Now, there was £20,000 in the bank. Without a moment's hesitation, the agitated Derby called out again, '*Suivi.*'

The bank was at double the evening's limit. Everyone at the table saw that Agnelli was anxious. Any sane person would be. It was the equivalent in 2007 of about half a million pounds sterling resting on the turn of a card – a gamble played and over quicker than any adrenaline rush.

Agnelli, through either pride or foolishness, accepted the challenge. He dealt the four cards from the shoe. He had a natural nine, Derby a seven. As the hosts watched despairingly, the inevitable happened. With four £10,000 white chips sitting in the centre of the table – say, £1 million pounds – his Lordship eagerly spoke the dreaded word. He squeaked, '*Suivi.*'

This time Agnelli not only demurred, he insisted that he would garage £20,000, leaving £20,000 – still double the limit – to be won or lost in the next coup. Derby argued with Agnelli, a Renaissance man often called 'Prince' in Italy. He pleaded with him not to garage, but the banker was adamant.

It was at this point that John Derby turned to John Burke and asked: 'Tell me, Burkie, who is that foreign chap? He won't have a decent punt.'

Agnelli might have been the richest man in Europe, but to Lord Derby, who was unlikely ever to have travelled in a Fiat, he was simply a foreigner who had made his fortune in trade. Yet the tradesman was the victor.

Derby lost another £20,000. And also the next coup. It was only on his next coup that this particular run of Agnelli's luck stopped. But the game did not. When luck, that fickle thing, turned on him, Derby hit a losing streak. When, because of Derby's obstinacy, the cash situation had turned turtle on the hosts, Aspinall decided to play himself and John Burke became the croupier. It didn't help.

Aspinall lost £20,000, twenty long ones. So, to the hosts' discomfort, did Michael Alachouzos. Alachouzos was playing on the books, so his loss did not help the cashflow. Gianni Agnelli was no longer £200,000 in the red as the game went on; indeed, he was close to profit.

Arguably, if Agnelli had accepted the £40,000 coup with Derby, it could have gone on and on, up to £80,000 and so ad infinitum. When, later, it was John Derby's bank, Agnelli would be morally bound to *banco* any amount, however large, that Derby chose to open for, and to continue in the same vein as his opponent. The situation could have got to the point where the entire Fiat empire was wagered against the vast Stanley estates, including much of Liverpool. All on the turn of a card in a chemmy game.

The end result was that Derby retained a fraction of his earlier winnings, and instead of paying out £200,000, the Italian tycoon left 93 Eaton Place with a cheque for £22,400. John Burke was philosophical: 'His sense of relief must have contrasted vividly with our sense of gloom. For us to have collected £200,000 – £5 million or so in today's money – would truly have ranked as a very pleasant outcome of a friendly card game! As they say: "Win some, lose some."'

Liliana told John Burke that although Agnelli put on a superb, gentlemanly, unemotional facade, he had confided in her that he was genuinely nervous. He had played in Europe's major casinos and gambled for heavy amounts of money: but he had never before encountered anybody like John Derby.

Aspinall and Burke did not run the Agnelli evening in their normal manner: there was no *cagnotte*. They saw the evening as an introduction for Agnelli to their games, and hoped that he would enjoy himself and become a regular player – after all he was only a short private-jet ride away in Turin.

But Agnelli never returned to the London chemmy tables. Perhaps he had nightmares in which the Earl of Derby, in his slight voice, kept calling: '*Suivi*.'

10. MAKING A MINT

To be alive at all involves some risk.

PRIME MINISTER HAROLD MACMILLAN, 1956

For many, of course, including John Aspinall and John Burke, the Earl of Derby was a dream. Aspinall certainly regarded him as something of a private bank, a branch of Martin's, maybe, and he didn't like anyone else making or trying to make a withdrawal there.

At this time an intriguing man called Peter Scott was making many unauthorized withdrawals. Not Scott of the Antarctic, but the one known to regulars of the Star as 'Scott of the Drainpipe'. In 1958 he had officially, in underworld circles, taken over from George Chatham as king of the cat burglars. An eloquent character from Northern Ireland, he was, like Chatham, an inveterate gambler. Maybe it was something to do with heights.

John Burke recalls being at the Star one summer evening when Scott arrived driving a convertible chocolate-brown Bentley. 'In that Belfast accent of his he announced: "Sophia Loren has given me a little present." Of course, he'd robbed the poor girl.'

Or rather, rich girl. Scott knew his targets. The Italian actress was in London filming *The Millionairess*, and trying to keep her distance from her co-star, Peter Sellers. She was staying in the Norwegian Barn at the Edgewarebury Country

Club. Scott, with a stolen Jaguar and an expensively acquired green Metropolitan Police press card, drove into the area and was told where Loren's rooms were. He was in and out before you could say 'Mamma mia!' and departed with a briefcase packed with cash and jewels, valued for insurance purposes at £200,000.

Scott had a drink with his friends at the Star and told John Burke that he was looking forward to the Goodwood Races. Unfortunately for him, Sophia Loren appeared on television and put a gypsy curse on whoever had stolen from her. The cat burglar – who once described himself as 'only a dishonest window cleaner' – lost the lot at Goodwood. Not long afterwards, a well-known bookmaker was seen driving around in a very nice open-top Bentley.

The times were changing for all gamblers. The ill-fated prosecution of Aspinall, Lady O. and John Burke had persuaded the government to tackle the laws on gambling. On 16 November 1959, Home Secretary Rab Butler introduced the Betting and Gaming Bill to the House of Commons. The Lords got it six months later. There were lobbyists both for and against the changes to the law, representing all kinds of interests, including those of slum landlord Peter Rachman. He was a keen gambler and owned clubs with Raymond Nash where illegal games were played. Rachman always aspired to attend John Aspinall's games, but was never allowed.

'There's no way we could have had Rachman at our games,' explains John Burke. 'Yes, OK, there was some snobbery, but it was a matter of business. We had the Duke of Devonshire and the Earl of Derby playing with us, and the press were always a fear. Imagine Rachman at the table with people who'd been on television earlier in the evening meeting the Queen? It wasn't logical.'

Yet it was to Peter Rachman. Up to his early death, aged 42, in November 1962, he never gave up trying to join the games. Raymond Nash told me in Marbella in May 2006 that Rachman had asked him to approach John Burke. 'Peter wanted the best of everything. It was because of his background. We were very close. When he was told by the doctor that he had a heart condition which could kill him, he told me and he said: "What do you think I should do?" I said: "Have the best time of your life. Enjoy every second and do the best for yourself, because you have enough money. Anything you want you should buy, you can have."

What Rachman wanted was the beautiful sixteen-year-old Christine Keeler, then a showgirl at Murray's Club. Nash observed: 'Peter had always had an eye for her. He would undress her with his eyes as she walked by. She became his girlfriend and he bought her everything: high fashion, furs, nightgowns and jewels.'

As well as Raymond Nash, one of Rachman's aides was another East Ender, Tommy Yeardye, the co-founder of the Vidal Sassoon empire. In the twenty-first century he was chairman of the Jimmy Choo shoe company. His daughter Tamara Mellon, glossy magazine favourite and friend of Goldsmith's daughter Jemima Khan and Hugh Grant, was president in 2007.

Yeardye was amiable and well liked and also tried to help get Rachman into the Aspinall and Burke chemmy games, but to no avail.

When Yeardye died in April 2004, newspaper obituaries wondered at the source of his fortune, and the *Guardian* reported: 'The origins of Yeardye's enormous wealth have never been fully explained.' The old stories surfaced again; that he stole from his former fiancée, Diana Dors, that he'd worked with the Krays. Yet Yeardye was indeed loaded. Bobby McKew, in October 2006, offered the real and more prosaic story:

'I knew Tommy well. He asked me around for drinks not long before he died. He was an Irishman. He was adopted and Yeardye was not his real name. His money? He worked for Peter Rachman, like Raymond did. After the war there were houses all over London going for very little money, properties in Bayswater which would be in the millions today. Rachman bought them up in other people's names. He got about ten houses in Tommy's name, and then Tommy pissed off to America. By the time he came back the prices of the houses had soared, and he built on it from there. I don't think he gave Mrs Rachman any of the money after her husband died.'

And Mrs Rachman wasn't familiar with Bryanston Mews, the lavish apartment her husband had bought for his girl-friends after the death of Diana Dors' former husband, Dennis Hamilton.

Hamilton had supplied girls and sex orgies at the grand house he shared with Diana Dors in Maidenhead. He took films and recorded – on a system linked to loudspeakers – familiar names in unfamiliar positions. Rachman went for the high-stakes gambling sessions – and the anonymous sex. He never talked to his sexual partners there.

A relentless voyeur, Dennis Hamilton had a two-way mirror at the house; it was installed in the ceiling. Guests were diverted to watch the action. After his marriage to the tragic Diana Dors ended Hamilton moved the ornate mirror to Bryanston Mews. He died not long afterwards from compli-cations brought on by venereal disease – the Al Capone curse.

Rachman got the flat, and the mirror. Christine Keeler lived there with the model Sherry Danton, who became Ray-mond Nash's girlfriend. Later, when Christine Keeler had left Rachman, her friend from Murray's, Mandy Rice-Davies, moved in. Rachman gave her £80 a week and bought her an Arab stallion. Mandy enjoyed the good life, and her taste would be indulged by Bobby McKew's business acquaintance, Emil Savundra.

Nash, who in 2007 was 75 and married to a Korean princess, was the only man that Rachman allowed at the flat. Together they owned the Condor Club, where Michael Caine and Terence Stamp would become regulars, but Rachman was very much the silent partner. Rock star Marty Wilde, earning £1 a night plus a bowl of spaghetti, was talent-spotted there by the all-powerful entertainment agent of the day, Larry Parnes.

Raymond Nash said: 'Peter was very good friends with Diana Dors and Dennis Hamilton, and went to their house a lot. He liked the fucking there. When Peter started spending all his time fucking and gambling, he more or less gave me the Condor Club.

'Aspinall's sister Jenny Osborne worked for me at the Condor. She worked there for quite a long time. She was one of my trusted cashiers and waitresses.

'I was the one who gave Tommy Steele a job. We had cabaret at the Condor. I paid him £10 or £20 a week. I can't remember exactly, but I gave Matt Monro the same deal. Later, the Rolling Stones worked for me for a little while. The Beatles? They wanted six hundred a week. I said they would never make it. I said that nobody was worth that much in the world!

'The club was a huge success. And my property business was booming. I used to buy twenty properties at a time. I had nearly as many properties as Peter at that time. He was my Godfather, he was the guy who taught me how to borrow 110 per cent from banks, and buy and buy. He was a very kind and gentle man, contrary to what everybody thought – that he was ill-treating tenants and all that. But his reputation was terrible. After Peter died, my lawyers said I should make a statement. I distanced myself from him because his name had become so bad. So many things happened.

'I was running chemmy games. By then they were only semi-illegal but they were quite low class. I used to hire apartments for the games. I started that at a very low level, almost playing on the floor! But people took to it – they loved it. It was chemmy, chemmy, chemmy. Instant gratification. Win or lose, it was over in seconds.

'We had tables where fifty people could go around it. The croupiers were in the centre, and they played with actual coins. We were just one of many games around town – some people got very smart and started importing chemmy tables from Caro in Paris. But people lost money on other tables just as easily.'

Nash and Rachman wanted the new gaming legislation to favour their plans for chemmy games in a string of nightclubs they hoped to open. Raymond Nash told me: 'Peter Rachman and I employed Billy Rees-Davies – we called him the one-armed bandit – to put through the Gaming Act. As a lawyer and an MP, he cleverly talked it up in the Commons. We also used the Labour MP Tom Driberg, who was a fairly nasty queer; people were always trying to beat him up and he didn't always like it. But he did the job for us.'

The new law didn't help Aspinall and Burke, because now the *cagnotte* was banned – whoever won a coup or a hand of cards had, by law, to receive all the winnings. And if the games were held in a club and the players were members, there could only be a set table charge, plus, perhaps, a membership fee. So the incredible profits to be made from taking 5 per cent of every winning bank, tens of thousands of pounds at a time, were over – by Act of Parliament on 29 July 1960, one month after the Agnelli–Derby encounter.

The carousel chemmy games were no longer such a sure

thing; all over London entrepreneurs looked at the odds, and there were strong advantages in opening clubs. One of the first to open, in 1961, was Les Ambassadeurs, where John Mills moved the nightclub, the Garrison, to the basement, and started government-approved gaming. It was there that Derby gambled away a huge sum in just one evening. Much has been written about that event, but John Burke played in the early stages of the game: 'I won a couple of thousand pounds and a little later Mariani, who was then the *chef de partie* in Les Ambassadeurs, said to me, "You look tired, Mr Burke, perhaps you ought to go home." He was giving me a hint that something odd was going to happen later on. Which it did, of course. John Derby lost £165,000.

'John Aspinall was absolutely furious when he heard about this, because by now he believed he was the senior partner in raiding the Stanley fortune. And now somebody else comes along stealing his money, more or less! He felt that John Mills had set the whole thing up.

'We both knew Mills quite well in the old days, because he ran the Milroy where we all went. I don't personally believe that Mills did set this game up. Although it was certainly a crooked game. There was a character there who posed as a rich Greek shipowner, yet none of the upper-class Greek shipowners who I knew had any knowledge of him. It was said that he was a big-time casino crook and he had one or two of Mills' croupiers bent, and they set up a game and the Greek guy was the big winner – he took all this money from Derby.

'I knew John Mills fairly well and liked him. By this time, he was successful and quite rich, and earlier he had made the Milroy a huge success, and the Les A. gambling club was doing extremely well. He had no need for stunts like that. Whatever the truth, naturally, he was an enemy of John Aspinall for ever more.'

Aspinall also fell out with Michael Alachouzos over the same subject – John Derby's money. Alachouzos was Greek – his family were sponge harvesters and merchants, but he was born in the Eastern Mediterranean, in Italian territory, and interned as an enemy alien on the Isle of Man during the Second World War. When the conflict ended, he was befriended by the Marquess of Milford Haven. Liberty ships had been mass produced during the war for badly needed transport, but afterwards they were sold off at cut prices. Through his contact with Milford Haven, Alachouzos bought a Liberty ship very cheaply. He called it the *Medina Princess* – 'Earl of Medina' was one of the Milford Haven titles.

It was a lucky move, because on the outbreak of the Korean War cargo shipping rates soared, and Alachouzos made money. He married an Englishwoman, Josie, and set up home with her – and with June, his mistress, the divorced second wife of Randolph Churchill. It was that rare thing, a happy *ménage à trois*.

A keen social climber, Alachouzos benefited from June's former social position. He was friendly with Aspinall and John Burke, as Burke explained: 'He came to all the private games; sometimes he played for himself and sometimes it was special arrangements. In fact, he became more or less one of the family. He had a great deal of charm and was undoubtedly an intelligent man. The real Greek shipowners who played in the games, people like John Goulandris, regarded Michael with amusement, but they did not dislike him.

'He got on extraordinarily well with the English toffs, especially with John Derby, who took a real shine to him and referred to him as "that splendid Greek". Sometimes Derby invited him to White's to play bridge. Once he invited him to Knowsley, the family seat. Alachouzos used our parties, and in turn, he was an asset to us, which was a happy two-way deal.'

Above. John Aspinall with the most important woman in his life, his mother Lady O., and his first wife, Jane, outside the flat in Eaton Place.

Right. John Burke strides triumphantly out of court with John Aspinall, equipped with his trademark brolly, following their landmark legal victory.

Overleaf.
Pages from John Burke's account book, showing the money won and lost at a single game of chemmy on 29 May 1958.

29-5-'58

W.

████████████	420
Ackroyd	102
████████	1,023
Ambler	4,885
Brigham	450
Cundell	150
Chips	95
Gordon	761
Lloyd	1,070
Lady O.	1,870
Muir	5,840
W. Stirling	10,625
Worsley	1,400
Willoughby	30
Strohr - Smith	12,235
████████	230
J.B.	226
	41,412

L.

Jone	700
Collin	6,490
Devly	24,500
Hombro	3,750
Aspers	700
Men - Kenpon	1,200
Stanley	3,373
Van Cutson	19,700
West	400
	60,813
	41,412
	19,401

Left. They'd never had such a good day out: the legendary gambler the Duke of Devonshire, with the duchess and Prime Minister Harold Macmillan.

Below. Reckless gambler Lord Derby, seen here with Princess Margaret in July 1954.

Above.
The Clermont Club.

Right.
The Star Tavern
in Belgravia.

Above, left. The nightclub maestro: the always impeccable Mark Birley dressed to charm in February 1965.

Above, right. Fraudster Emil Savundra reveals his attitude to the law and 'the peasants'.

Left. They seek him here, they seek him there. A man for all conspiracies, the missing Lord 'Lucky' Lucan, photographed here at his wedding.

Right. Bobby McKew with his friend Richard Harris at the opening night of *Camelot.*

Below. Bobby McKew with Eddie Chapman (right) and producer Dermot Harris (left).

You can almost hear them calling 'suivi' – chemmy at the
River Club, London 1962.

Alachouzos was ambitious. In early 1961, he invited Derby to invest £1 million in creating a fleet of cargo ships. He would organize further financial backing from the City. His approach to Derby was made without the knowledge of Aspinall or John Burke, who said: 'When Derby came to John to ask his advice before committing himself, Aspers was absolutely, totally furious. He didn't explode in front of Derby. He persuaded him not to do it and then he confronted Michael Alachouzos and vented his wrath in no uncertain terms. He was absolutely red faced with fury. He saw Derby as his pigeon and his alone. The idea of another operator, who had actually met his Lordship through him, trying to hone in on the Stanley fortune, was an unforgivable transgression. A diabolical liberty. John and Michael fell out totally.'

Alachouzos also fell out of favour with the insurance companies. The *Medina Princess* had been a great success, but by 1961 she was a liability. On one voyage she encountered extremely rough weather, and, but for the skill and dedication of her English captain, might have gone down. John Burke was with his friend when this was going on: 'I remember Alachouzos pacing up and down in his Mayfair drawing room muttering: "Why doesn't the bloody fool abandon ship?" The *Medina Princess* carried plenty of insurance. Not too long afterwards, with a more compliant master, the ship went down in East African waters; where, although there was no danger of the crew not being rescued, there were no modern facilities for refloating the vessel.'

Insurance companies, wise to the effects of the long and serious slump in shipping rates, were cynical about such events. Alachouzos's insurers refused to pay out. He sued. His barrister was the eminent QC, Sir Andrew Clark, Ian Maxwell-Scott's father-in-law. Sir Andrew lived up to his reputation, and the insurance company coughed up.

Meanwhile, John Burke and other friends of John Aspinall

witnessed Aspinall's keen and rather startling social and financial promotion of Eddie Gilbert, which they viewed with some
suspicion. Aspinall, although he would drop and cut people
on a whim or at any imagined slight, could also be extraordinarily generous, loyal and kind, as he was to Eddie Gilbert.
Gilbert was supposed to have financed him and kept him
going in difficult times, but in fact it was the other way around.
Aspinall treated Gilbert like a debutante, introducing him into
London society whenever he could, as in his grand party at
Claus von Bülow's Belgrave Square home. He did everything
in his power to help his American friend.

He suggested to several people that they should invest in
Gilbert's company, the Empire Millwork Corporation, which
in turn invested in several American businesses. One person
he approached, naturally, was John Derby. In a letter to
Aspinall from the family seat at Knowsley, Derby wrote that
the investment 'does look rather a good thing'. This is followed, from Stanley House, Newmarket, by another undated
letter revealing he has invested £20,000 with Gilbert.

Aspinall himself invested seven times more than Derby's
£20,000 in his friend Eddie Gilbert's stock dealings. However,
just as the real social ritual had done in 1958, Gilbert's
debutante season was about to end for ever. Reality would
soon catch up with him.

The consequences of the robbery of Jack Warner's safe finally
caught up with Bobby McKew in the summer of 1959, and
landed him in Tangier's Kasbah jail.

The Moroccan and French authorities then played ping-
pong with him, as legal arguments over his extradition were
also bounced around. He was moved to another prison in the
Moroccan capital, Rabat, and then, finally, on 22 November,

he was flown to Toulouse. From there he was driven on to Aix-en-Provence, where eighteen months earlier an appeal court had added two years to his three-year prison sentence. His next stop was Les Baumettes prison in Marseilles, that colourful city which was then, and is still, the headquarters of the Union Corse.

At Les Baumettes, Bobby McKew was given library duties, which improved his mind and his prospects: 'I'd go through with the books and that way I met the other prisoners. They were mostly French, so there wasn't much conversation. But one guy, André Marcel, spoke English, and we used to have long talks on Saturdays. We got on well. He was a bright boy. He knew a lot of people.'

It was the summer of 1961 before he was moved from Marseilles to Fresnes prison, about ten miles from Paris, where he was reunited with 'Dandy Kim' Caborn-Waterfield. In 1960, after much British legal wrangling and the Home Secretary getting involved, 'Dandy Kim' was extradited and jailed in France for five to seven years. Kim's prison life began in solitary confinement in cell 140. Then events took over. Jack Warner's lawyer was informed about sensitive documents that had disappeared along with the cash from the safe in the Villa Aujourd'hui. So politically explosive were the documents that pressure was applied at the highest level and bargaining began for the freedom of Prisoner No. 6544.

With just twelve months of his sentence served, Kim was freed and the order for him to repay the 'stolen' money was rescinded. Jack Warner had told Maitre Suzanne Blum, the most highly regarded lawyer in France and Kim's prosecutor, that he had been advised of delicate matters he had been unaware of when he made his accusations of theft. Blum's most famous clients were the Duke and Duchess of Windsor. In 1960, Dandy Kim was freed on his undertaking that he reveal nothing of what he found in the safe until the twenty-first century. He was still keeping silent when he spoke to me in 2007, saying merely: 'I was happy to make that pledge. I was thirty years old with a life to live – and God, how I wanted to live it!'

The arrangement did not give 'Dandy Kim' and Bobby McKew much time to catch up because, of course, it benefited them both. French lawyers had told Bobby McKew's friends that if he paid over the cost of his extradition from North Africa – £1,100 – he was all but on his way home to the new gambling capital of London, having served half his sentence. His wife was living in South Africa and not immediately contactable, so to speed up the process, Paddy Kennedy raised the money at the Star from John Burke and several of Bobby McKew's other friends (all of whom he later repaid in full).

'There was no fuss, and I didn't want any. I went to see the governor of the prison and said I did not want any publicity, my picture in the newspapers. Kim was doing prison interviews and such before he was released, but that wasn't for me. They agreed that if I did just that, kept quiet, they would take me to Paris by ambulance and I could then fly to London. The problem was, the ambulance took me to a hospital, there was a paperwork mix-up, and I ended up in a padded cell. They thought I was some lunatic! It took hours to sort it out, but I was finally on my way.

'At Heathrow nobody noticed me. The press knew I was flying in, but maybe they were looking for someone with a broken nose or something. I got back with no fuss, which was perfect.

'I was glad to be out of jail, back in London. I didn't want any more nonsense. The prisons weren't health farms. Morocco was just very primitive. There were no beds or bunks there; you slept on a mattress on the floor. When you could sleep. There were always a dozen of you or so in a room with one little pisshole. It wasn't the Ritz.

'Les Baumettes in Marseilles had a reputation as the toughest prison in Europe. They still had the guillotine, and in the first few months I was there they guillotined eight men. The stricter prisons are the best prisons. The rules are there and that's the end of it. You get into a routine and you get on with it.'

Which is what he did on his return to London. He now linked up on a more formal basis with Billy Hill. After the Aspinall and Burke court victory, Billy Hill had continued to run gambling dens (spielers), but now he began his own gambling evenings. He operated around London and had one high-rollers game in Eaton Square. He also ran a betting–gambling den near Smithfield Market with Lady's O.'s one-time bookie Charlie Matthews. Hill's wife Aggie had a club in Gerrard Street, Le Cabinet, and he ran games in the basement there.

With the new Gaming Act in force, gambling in clubs was now legal, and Billy Hill took every opportunity to make money. He was 'interested' in other clubs and casinos, but he also started his own. He opened a club at 3 Green Street in Mayfair, and also the Wentworth Country Club at Virginia Water in Surrey. Bobby McKew was the manager there. Bobby was not a gambler, but luck had nothing to do with the profits he made at that grand-sounding country club.

The enterprising pair had some help from their French friends, their connections from the Union Corse – something that gave them an edge. Bobby McKew said, 'They had vast experience in gambling, and their croupiers were the most reliable in the business. They did what was wanted without ever a word. Talk about *omertà*!

'When new people came to London they got an introduction to Billy, because in those days you didn't do anything in London without Billy. We were out with the top guy from the Union Corse and he rather liked me. He'd asked me where I was in prison in France and asked, "Did you ever meet André Marcel?"

'I said: "Yes, I knew him very well."

'He said: "Really. How?"

'"Well, he spoke English." I explained about the books and the library, and then suddenly he leaned over and kissed me on each cheek.

'The result was one night he turned around, he took me out and said: "How you doing? How many girls have you got?"

'I said, "One."

'"No, how many working for you?"

'So I said, "None."

'He said, "I'll give you a job. Come work for me and I'll start you out with pretty girls."

'It wasn't a tempting thought. Billy would have lost it over something like that.'

There was another more tempting prospect. Emil Savundra.

Michael Marion Emil Anacletus Pierre Savundranayagam was a giant fraudster, but was flawed by his own pomposity and self-regard. In Ceylon – Sri Lanka – he had learned the ropes with strange arms deals and stranger shipping movements. He was jailed in Belgium over a cargo of rice for which he was paid, but which never found its way to Antwerp. Then he turned up in Ghana, around the time Eddie Chapman was there, as some sort of 'economic adviser' to the poor. Apparently his advice was not appreciated, for he was deported. He moved on to India, China and, with Shiv Kapoor, the coffee bean swindle in Costa Rica. By the time he got to London, Bobby McKew was back, and he introduced his old acquaintance to Stephen Ward, who was also close to John Burke's friend, David Milford Haven.

As a portrait painter, Ward had sketched, amongst others, the Duke of Edinburgh, Princess Margaret, Princess Alexandra and the Duke and Duchess of Windsor, as well as Christine Keeler who, with Mandy Rice-Davies, had lived with him at times at 17 Wimpole Mews, London W1.

It was an introduction that was to have spectacular repercussions. The sex-mad Savundra was 'the Indian doctor' who had sex at £20 a time with Mandy Rice-Davies at Wimpole Mews. When Ward went on trial at the Old Bailey on 22 July 1963 for living off immoral earnings, Rice-Davies testified that she had taken money from Savundra after sex. It was a tipping point of the case against Ward, the Establishment's scapegoat for the Profumo affair, who was found guilty but committed suicide before he could be sentenced.

Still, Savundra will arguably always be more infamous as a fraudster and for the disastrous crash of his Fire, Auto & Marine Insurance Company (FAM). In the early Sixties, car insurance was a booming business, with more cars and improved roads, including motorways. By law, all drivers need minimum insurance, but even that expense was too high for many. Cleverly, Savundra offered low, low policies which, in reality, were worthless. He did not have the resources to meet the claims. But thousands of new drivers wanted to drive, and the little pieces of paper from FAM allowed them to do that. They did not realize or want to know about possible consequences. It was another of those gold mines dug from people's aspirations and dreams.

As a printer, Bobby McKew did a great deal of work for Savundra, and McKew made some investments in the business. Initially, they had a reasonable relationship, but as business boomed: 'The money went to Savundra's head. He was running a Rolls-Royce and a Hillman, and spending more than ten grand a year at Harrods. He had a house in Hampstead, was gambling, into offshore yacht racing and was screwing everything he could.

'At the same time he was holier than thou. He was a good Catholic. He gave ten per cent of what he stole to the Church. When he was in jail in Belgium, the Catholic Church put so much pressure on the Belgian government that they released him. He looked after the Church; they looked after him. He originally started off doing the money for a cardinal who became the Pope. I don't remember, but you're talking about whoever was the Pope forty-five years ago.

'He took me out to dinner at the Savoy and told me he was having three red cardinals to dinner later in the week. He was all airs and graces by then. He said to me: "I don't think you should come along, Bobby." Because I'd been in prison he didn't want me getting any redemption, I suppose. No, he turned into an awful snob. He didn't want anyone reminding him he was a jailbird too.

'I was doing a great deal of print work for him at the Dulwich Press and it was profitable. But he'd ask me to do special jobs, including Mass cards; they're a piece of paper like a bookmark, with a prayer on it and a picture of Christ. I fell out with him when the money went completely to his head, so when he asked me to do 240 Mass cards I made special arrangements. When the cards were delivered he went into shock. Where the picture of Christ should have been was something completely different. It was a photo graph of me. They said I gave Emil his first heart attack.'

Heart attacks were a Savundra speciality. He sold his FAM shares in 1966, and the company rapidly collapsed, leaving its clients uninsured. Around 400,000 motorists were left with worthless insurance policies. There were nearly 50,000 unpaid claims. Savundra fled to Switzerland, but a year later he inexplicably returned to Britain to be quizzed by David Frost, in his finest hour, on live television.

The audience was packed with widows who had lost their husbands in car accidents and received not one penny in compensation. When he was quizzed by the widows, Savundra replied: 'I am not going to cross swords with the peasants.' It was a few words too many.

Then, after Savundra stated that he felt no moral responsibility, Frost looked at the camera, apologized, and marched out in anger and disbelief. Savundra was taken by stretcher from the television studios. He had the symptoms of a heart attack. He got eight years in jail, spent in a prison hospital, and died in 1976.

11. CLICKETY-CLICK!

The scent and smoke and sweat of a casino are nauseating at three in the morning.

THE FIRST LINE OF IAN FLEMING'S *CASINO ROYALE*, 1953

By spearheading the change in the law, John Aspinall and John Burke had in fact sent society off in a new direction. Their court case was of monumental importance, both social and financial. The Gaming Act had ushered in the start of Britain's gaming bonanza, estimated in 2007 to have an annual turnover of £70 billion. It was suddenly open season for bingo halls and clubs. For the first time, betting shops were seen in Britain, and within a year of the law being changed, several thousand had opened. It is difficult nowadays, when it seems you can bet on the time of day, to imagine the colossal change in attitude and the monsoon of cash involved. 'Having a bet' was no longer a naughty, side-street indulgence. It was legal. There was no government health warning. The general view that gambling was bad had been countered by the fact that the government had made it so much easier to gratify the habit.

With hindsight, it seems little thought was given to the other vices which gather where luck and chance can be the difference between fortune and ruin. The government, with its post-war mindset, did not seem to anticipate that the criminal fraternity would recognize the possibilities offered by the change in the law. Perhaps it was felt that the British would not be corrupted like their American cousins in Las Vegas, where money-laundering and prostitution were part of the package.

After the success of gambling at Les Ambassadeurs, other clubs, including Crockford's, began lavish gaming house operations. The attraction of the around-the-town chemmy games was swiftly fading, and with the *cagnotte* outlawed, Aspinall found his income swiftly diminishing while his outgoings remained vast. Extremely reluctantly, Aspinall and Burke realized that they had to expand their premises and their horizons; their own and their friends' apartments were no longer able to provide the frills, the upmarket dining and wining, to accompany the gambling. More importantly, there was the law to consider, and the competition. Aspinall told John Burke that he would open his own club. It was the only answer. But it had to be top of the tree, the market leader, a venue where millions could happily be lost in the most stylish surroundings. He outlined his plans to create Europe's grandest gambling den.

'It was a difficult decision,' said John Burke, 'because at those rather more informal games the rules were easier – we set them. With a more formal set-up, there had to be more regulation. Or appear to be.'

As early as the winter of 1960, he and Aspinall had talked about opening a club. There was some interest in Crockford's in Carlton House Terrace, which was said to be for sale, but nothing came of that. The two gamblers sat back as Les Ambassadeurs and then Crockford's itself went legitimate with gambling.

They organized a few chemmy evenings, but nothing to cover Aspinall's spiralling costs. 'We were a little bit late at the starting gate,' said John Burke. 'We hesitated. I think it was because it couldn't possibly be the same bonanza that we'd had since the court case.'

Aspinall finally decided to take the plunge and open his own club, and John Burke found himself looking forward to it with much anticipation. He, understandably, felt that there were good omens. In 1961, he had married Liliana Livon at the Catholic church on St Stephen's Green in Dublin. In September 1962, his sister Edith Carroll's horse 'Arctic Storm' won the Champion Stakes at Newmarket and his daughter Daniela was born. It was a happy time. He was also successfully investing through Rudolf Wolff, the most prestigious commodities broker in London, using his contacts and his talent for mathematics to play the market. And in only a few weeks, his and John Aspinall's greatest adventure would begin.

They were both determined that they still had to attract aristocratic gamblers, not just for their titles (although that helped business), but because they honoured their cheques. That meant luxury and location, location, location. It was Aspinall who discovered what he regarded as the perfect venue, in the bullseye of Mayfair.

It was a town house at 44 Berkeley Square, created in 1742 by William Kent, the most prestigious architect of his era. Now, with the skills of interior decorator John Fowler, the building could rise from dereliction and dust to become, for Aspinall and his customers, the most prestigious venue for gambling, where people could surely enjoy losing money. To achieve this, Aspinall had to find money. Where could he go?

'John's image was of this immensely rich man who gambled thousands on games of cards, ran a large home and zoo, and was written up in the newspapers in that way,' said John Burke. 'In truth, he was practically broke. He had assets, but no cash. He couldn't be seen to go around asking for financial guarantees. It would have damaged his wealthy cavalier reputation, and he'd worked hard at establishing that. He asked me to keep the facade intact.'

The Palladian mansion which was about to become the

Clermont Club was owned by Samuel Properties, a company headed by Charles Clore and Lord Samuel, who have said they 'missed' its development potential. They agreed to lease it to Aspinall for £12,500 a year over two decades. 'But they wanted guarantees,' said John Burke. 'They weren't keen on us being a gambling operation. They thought we'd go bankrupt in a couple of months and wouldn't be able to pay the rent.'

Finally, they made the unusual request for three guarantors. Aspinall asked John Burke to arrange it. Burke approached Tim Willoughby, Bernard van Cutsem and Richard Parkes, and they all agreed immediately. In return each of them received £1,000 in shares in the Clermont to be bought at face value. Yet much more money was needed to allow the skills of John Fowler, with the help of architect Philip Jebb, who'd been brought into the work through Dominick Elwes, to recreate the house's long-lost splendour. Aspinall planned to reinvent the spirit and sparkle of the Grand Salon and Club Room, and completely refurbish the house's interiors and the always admired, seemingly endless staircase.

'It had gone to rack and ruin,' said John Burke, 'and it cost a bloody fortune to return it to the very beautiful house which it was. To finance the whole thing, people were invited to lend £10,000, and for that they got the chance to buy £1,000 in ordinary shares.'

Investors included the Duke of Atholl, Jocelyn Hambro, Simon Fraser and many others. It was all officially registered at Companies House as a limited liability company. Yet, publicly, it appeared that Aspinall had created the Clermont Club. The reality was that this empire was built on credit, or, in the parlance of the tallymen of the time, on the never-never. It really was live or, rather, play now, pay later.

Aspinall was superb at what he did. John Burke says the king, who now had his castle, played a masterstroke: 'He lured

over Pearson, the head doorman at White's. It was a touch of
genius. All the big gamblers, the socially acceptable ones
anyway, were members of White's.

'Pearson had worked at White's for several years,'
explained John. 'He was well liked by the members and their
guests, and, needless to say, he knew everybody who mattered
as far as we were concerned in the social world of the capital.
Somehow Pearson's presence inside the elegant front door of
44 Berkeley Square hinted at a connection between the Clermont and White's, and provided members with a sense of
continuity. In terms of prestige, the Clermont Club now owed
something to White's, while in return members of White's who
gambled there frequently owed something to the Clermont.

'Then Mariani approached me. He wasn't very happy at
Les Ambassadeurs and became our *chef de partie*. It is a most
important job in a casino. He was in charge of the croupiers,
of the gambling, and of talking to and looking after the
customers, like a maître d'. Mariani was a great success –
without a shadow of a doubt, the best *chef de partie* in London.'

Aspinall then had another moment of genius. He persuaded Jim Gore, the intelligent and popular head cashier
of Martin's Bank, the con man's Coutts, to transfer to a
similar responsible position at the Clermont. The man from
Lower Sloane Street would be helped on busy evenings by
Mr Money. Aspinall had known Mr Money for some years
and was aware of his talents in getting around the foreign
exchange regulations. He also knew that Mr Money fenced
stolen jewellery, although he never spoke openly about it.
Neither he nor John Burke was aware of his other underworld
connections. Aspinall regarded Mr Money's foreign connections as another attraction for the Clermont, since their members often played the casinos of Europe.

Out of the recent past emerged Ian Maxwell-Scott, who
became number three to Aspinall and Burke in the Clermont

Club Ltd. The fine dining and even finer wine at the Clermont was credited to Maxwell-Scott. And some of the better jokes. 'He told me that he felt he had gone back home when he went to the Clermont,' his daughter Cathy Maxwell-Scott, one of his six children, told me in February 2006. 'He was very happy there.'

The company secretary was the always affable chartered accountant Eddie Thomas. From a smart bridge club where he held the same position, Herbert Pretyman was appointed club secretary, and later a director. He was soon to be looking after close to 700 members. If anyone wanted a shopping list of the good and the great and the gamblers of Britain, then H.E. Pretyman had it. And the club president, the Earl of Carnarvon, tried to control it. 'Porchy' Carnarvon still delighted in seeing Jane Aspinall. For Aspinall, he added social cachet.

In the middle of all these handsome arrangements, a fiscal hand grenade was chucked at Aspinall. All his investment with Eddie Gilbert, around £150,000, had been wiped out by a calamity on Wall Street. Aspinall never complained, but it was a huge blow. He just accepted it, said John Burke. 'Gilbert had a company which boosted the value of the shares; it was a house of cards and it had to collapse sometime. It went sour and he got into all sorts of trouble.'

In fact, it got Gilbert into New York's notorious Sing Sing prison. John Burke recalls, 'John tried to help him whenever in every conceivable way. If John really liked somebody he could be a fantastically good friend. But why Eddie Gilbert? Some friends of John Aspinall expressed surprise at the fact that he had adopted Eddie Gilbert as one of his very closest friends. In private John would become, or used to pretend to become, extremely anti-Semitic; he'd say how much he admired Hitler and hated the Jews: there was something to be said, he felt, for Hitler's ideas about eugenics. "Broadly speaking, the high income groups tend to have a better genetic inheritance."

'It's amazing how much he owed to Jimmy Goldsmith and people like Sydney Summer. Eddie Gilbert, of course, was a Jew. I don't think John really meant it at all. It was probably more of an act to impress people, to startle people. John was a superb actor, a great performer. So was Gilbert, unflappable, like Savundra.

'Gilbert approached John Derby to take a bigger piece of the action after he got his first £20,000, but even Derby had his suspicions. Derby didn't do it. He didn't fall for Gilbert, or he, too, would have lost everything he put in. John Aspinall was blind to Gilbert for some reason.'

But it can't have mattered. Surely Aspinall and Burke were sitting on another gold mine? Far from it, said John Burke: 'Our games provided a financial bonanza from 1958 to 1961. An absurd amount of tax-free money rolled in, especially to John Aspinall. I, too, received and wasted plenty. John was a really big spender: he kept two houses with their resident staff; he had started to build up his collection of wild animals; he had an expensive wife and some impecunious, greedy relations and he enjoyed buying valuable antiques. When we were forced to give up the private games and start the Clermont, his income was seriously diminished – my gosh, it even became taxable!'

It was a very different world for the gamblers. The overheads of running the club were vastly more than those of staging private games once a week. The club games were legal, but Aspinall and Burke could only make a 'table charge' that produced a much smaller revenue for the house. Also, the Clermont did not enjoy a monopoly of A-list gamblers. It didn't have the proper cash reserve that a business like that should have had. On the other hand, it was building up very big assets in money owed, for in 1962 gambling clubs were allowed to give credit. The club was owed substantial sums, by people who were good for it. Yet none of these debts were legally collectable.

'The bank was rather rigid about the situation,' said John Burke. 'We didn't have the sort of overdraft facilities that we needed. In that set-up it's important to have a financial back-up, because something can suddenly go wrong, and if you haven't got the cash to cover it you are in dead trouble. Yet, on a day-to-day basis, things were excellent. The club had a good membership, and the membership was growing, and growing the right way, with the right sort of people joining.'

The Clermont Club was patronized by men who thought they were going to transform Britain, rousing it back to colonial greatness from its post-war socialist torpor. It was a lair for aristocrats, players like Ian Fleming and was to become popular with a disaffected gang of right-wingers like Jimmy Goldsmith, Tiny Rowlands, Jim Slater and the Stirling brothers. All the names from the chemmy games – Derby, Devonshire, and the rest – became regulars. They now had a permanent and sumptuous home in Berkeley Square. At huge cost, Aspinall had created a comfort zone where his guests could waste their money and gamble themselves, as Tacitus said, into captivity. It was a social – and scientific – negative, albeit a fabulously luxurious one.

Indeed, despite being recently married, it became just like home for Lord Bingham, who would become the 7th Earl of Lucan in 1964. From the beginning he was as much part of the furniture as the luxurious armchairs and sofas that John Fowler had found and placed.

'Lucan had that awful thing, he had one little touch when he started the game,' said Mark Sykes. 'He had a huge win at the tables. Lucky? After that, gambling destroyed him. He was very good-looking. He was perfect in that period way. He was perfectly pleasant and agreeable for a long time, and had enormous stamina for drink. He was incredibly stupid. He was as thick as two short planks. He really was, didn't know what was going on.

'I would always see him there; I went for free meals with Jenny, Aspinall's half-sister. She was a charming girl. It was a rather pleasing atmosphere at the Clermont; almost everybody was in black tie and it attracted a social set, debutantes and the like.

'The amount of money that moved across the tables at the Clermont; in terms of money today, it would be millions and millions and millions a bloody day.'

Some of the members had an extravagant 'talent' for gambling and enjoyed doing so wildly in the gracious surroundings. Jane Aspinall would encourage attention, and gambling. According to a young socialite, Una Mary Parker, a few years later the Clermont acquired a reputation as a fast and louche 'alternative court', where young tycoons and ageing aristocrats were gathered.

What 44 Berkeley Square also had to offer was a basement. John Burke says that he and Aspinall had no use for it. There had never been any talk of using it for anything but storage until Mark Birley approached them.

There were some plush nightclubs in London, but they were mostly threadbare affairs where often the piano-players seemed to believe the black and white keys had been switched around; Mark Birley, who would prove to be a genius at style and marketing, wanted to create something which would match the pleasurable ostentation of the Clermont. 'It has to have exclusivity,' he told John Burke.

A hands-on perfectionist, he got the mix precisely. He turned the basement into an English country gentleman's home – with added accoutrements. The bar could be a Chelsea drawing room, the panelled walls a clutter of cartoons, etchings and paintings. There were pictures of dogs everywhere:

spaniels, Jack Russells and whippets. Until he died in 2002, it was the job of one man to polish the club's brass pillars. He was known as 'Mr Brass'. In 2007, no one could recollect his real name.

A huge oil painting of Mark Birley's father, Sir Oswald Birley, watched over the guests as they sat on the red velvet sofas, gossiping and sipping champagne by candlelight. The Marquess of Londonderry had apparently not approved of his son-in-law's parents. His daughter, Lady Annabel, quotes him in her memoir as saying: 'His father was a bounder and his mother a whore.' His daughter responds in the book: 'This assessment was both monstrously untrue and unfair. Oswald Birley had been one of the most respected society portrait painters of the century and Rhoda was a well-known if somewhat Bohemian hostess.'

Birley named the club 'Annabel's' after his wife, Lady Annabel Vane-Tempest-Stewart. It was an inspired choice. It gave the club the required aristocratic touch, like the linen from Ireland, the teaspoons from Denmark, the strict dress code and the accents as cut-glass as the decanters. Lady Annabel herself was a class-perfect asset in person as well as in name. The guests went all the way from A to Q, from the Aga Khan to Mary Quant, and every other Sixties name in the books; the Beatles met their first maharaja there, the Maharaja of Jaipur. Their friends included people like Harry, Viscount Hambleden, and Annabel and Simon Elliot, the sister and brother-in-law of Camilla Shand (later to become Duchess of Cornwall). 'Celebrities' at Annabel's were connected people – those like Princess Lee Radziwill, sister of Jackie Kennedy Onassis. The more the toffs turned out, the more people wanted to get into Mark Birley's hot new club and look at them, even dance with them, as the club had music – a newfangled idea called a discotheque – and plenty of girls.

Mark Birley's club complemented the Clermont, as

music and unaccompanied girls were not allowed in casinos. There was an internal spiral staircase which linked the clubs. There was no need to venture out beneath the striped canopy and up the precarious outside staircase into the dark, dangerous London night, risking more than your money. So, while the world glared bug-eyed at the goings-on of the rich and famous, and the newspapers reported the glitter and the gossip, the gambling went on.

'It was the perfect match for us,' said John Burke. 'People would come and play, go to Annabel's, and then, later, come back to gamble more. We had the best of both worlds.'

In *Annabel: An Unconventional Life*, Lady Annabel wrote that on her wedding night, in Paris, with Mark Birley, she found out about his quick temper. She asked him back to their room while he was gambling at Le Cercle: 'I learned you never interrupt a man who is running a winning bank.'

Yet John Burke, who for five guineas became, along with 699 others, a founder member of Annabel's (in 2006 there were 171 left), says Mark Birley was not a huge gambler in comparison to the Clermont regulars. Indeed, Mark Birley said, with a sly smile, on 3 August 2006, that he did not care to gamble at the Clermont. Why? 'I didn't trust it.'

Still, the gaming and dining club and the nightclub became the essential double for the cognoscenti of the Sixties. Annabel's and the Clermont were kept as exclusive as possible to heighten the appeal to those who could afford to play and pay. Membership procedure was the same as for gentlemen's clubs: candidates needed a proposer, a seconder and would then be passed by the club committee, but not automatically.

Peter Rachman could not get membership. Raymond Nash told me: 'Up until he died he wanted to join. He died before it officially opened, but he asked me to approach them about membership. They were very nice about it, but it was a "no".'

In practice, a rich aristocrat could walk through the door

with ease, and most people with the money to play just as easily. Money was almost always welcome at the Clermont – and always needed.

It was certainly needed at one point by Peter West, when strict currency control was still the law. He took all his money out to the casinos in Cannes, and lost the lot. He also hadn't paid his Carlton Hotel bill. He appealed to Jimmy Goldsmith to send funds. Mark Sykes recalled, 'Jimmy Goldsmith and Aspinall got £3,000, which was an absolutely colossal amount of money, over to him.

'The strict instructions were to take the money, go to the cash desk and go back to the hotel, pay the bill and come home. Unfortunately, between the cash desk and the door there were six roulette tables. He put £500 on each of them on even bets. They all lost. Everything.

'There was a very old lady watching all of this in some amazement. She exclaimed, "Nous n'avons pas vu ça depuis les jours des grands ducs russes. Le coup de suicide!" Which means, in case you lost me: "We haven't seen that since the days of the Russian grand dukes. The suicide coup."

'I think even Jimmy Goldsmith gave up on Peter West for a time after that.'

'Oh, "Westie" could be a problem,' said John Burke, 'but he was always a perfect house player for us: charming, urbane, just the right sort. People would want to sit alongside him, just as they did the lords and ladies. It was all part of the attraction. It's like people going to stupidly expensive West End restaurants so they might see celebrities. It was all part of the package.

'Another house player we had in the early days was one of Clive Graham's successors at the *Daily Express*, Charles Benson. He was a round, pink man. Charles loved gambling, but one night Aspinall caught him trying to steal a £1,000 chip, and that was the end of his employment.'

'The amount of money turning over at the Clermont was finite. Large amounts might be won and lost in an evening; nevertheless, because we were running a club, the money was not falling off the trees, not nearly as much as it used to.'

But John Aspinall was in need of even more cheques. John Burke explained the financial turmoil: 'The Clermont had a very exclusive membership. The reason for that, of course, was that to make money Aspinall was very much a hands-on proprietor. He always knew every detail of our cash situation. I was "de facto" financial director.

'The problem was, because of having to keep books and pay taxes, he couldn't skim enough off the top to pay for his lifestyle. He was spending like flowing water, and when you're into that it's not easy to shut the tap off; it's a difficult habit to break.

'Every day John came in and inspected the books and knew exactly who had won and who had lost; how much the table charges amounted to; who had paid, who hadn't. He checked things out very thoroughly. He was there, of course, every evening, himself. He started the game off, cracked a few jokes and then set about, as he had at our chemmy games, getting the action heated up. But no matter how hot that got, John could not make ends meet. His personal expenses or living costs, or however you care to describe them, were running away with him.

'He had to borrow money. He got around $200,000 from Ray Ryan, who was a benevolent man, always willing to help, to be kind.'

Ryan was also a hustler, albeit an extremely top-of-the-line one: he played his life and business extremely close to the edge, but was never malicious. He struck rich in the 1940s in the booming oilfields of southern Indiana, Illinois, and western Kentucky. He went on to become a huge land developer. He had the money to help. But it was a loan.

The money quickly ran out. Aspinall needed more. He borrowed heavily from Max Rayne, later the philanthropist Lord Rayne, who had made his fortune doing business with the Church of England commissioners, buying their property at cheap prices. Max Rayne had married, for the second time, Lady Jane Vane-Tempest-Stewart, a maid of honour at the Queen's wedding, and the other, lively daughter of the Marquess of Londonderry.

It was an intriguing marriage. Rayne was the son of a Russian Jewish immigrant, born in London's East End; his father a tailor, his grandfather a Jewish scholar. He knew Sydney Summers. He knew Billy Hill.

Bobby McKew recalls meeting Max Rayne at Nice Airport with Hill and Gypsy Riley. 'Gypsy couldn't get over the way Max talked, and said to him: "Where'd you get that funny voice from? I can't believe it! You don't sound a bit like yourself – or your brother. What a funny voice you've got now." But Max was fine. He'd had elocution lessons. He knew Billy from the old days, they had been close in their time.'

When he died, aged 85, in 2003, Max Rayne had established himself as an enduring philanthropist. He was a man who made money – and enjoyed giving it away: 'I do not believe there is any merit in amassing huge fortunes. If you've got it, it's very easy to give it away. It costs me more to give my time, and I'm prouder of giving that.'

When John Aspinall needed some help, Max Rayne gave it to him. John Burke said, 'Lord Rayne was very well set up. He had come from nothing in the East End; at that point neither I nor John Aspinall knew of his friendship with Billy Hill. Had he known, John Aspinall might have changed his mind about borrowing from Max.

'Max bought up lots of Church properties at bargain prices. He was cute, clever and, I suppose, a little guilty, which is why he kept giving his money away. Max Rayne loaned this money to John Aspinall on basically friendly terms, but being a business deal it was in a written agreement. Max held shares in the Clermont as security. It was rather pointless, because if things went well the written agreement would have ensured that he got his money back, but if things went badly the shares would have been totally valueless.'

Max Rayne's old friend Billy Hill knew about the whole operation; he knew what was going on in every casino in London. Indeed, Hill was operating, with an edge, in most of them, including the Olympic and the 21. He had even taken profits from Crockford's. He learned this unique form of larceny from his friends in the Union Corse. It was so good that there has never been a hint, until now, of what was going on. When the police, on occasion, did investigate at the big casinos, they could find nothing wrong.

All the time, the Clermont was a menacing glint in Billy Hill's eye. The other casinos were easier to work, for they had several chemmy tables and a socially wider clientele. Nevertheless, the Clermont, small and exclusive as it was, appeared to Hill as the jewel in the con.

Yet Billy Hill was still not entirely cognisant of the extent of John Aspinall's desperation for cash, or the gambler's paranoia that Ray Ryan would call in his loan. There was also the worry of the Clermont's missing guarantor. In August 1963, Tim Willoughby had tragically vanished at sea. All the people I have talked to have only fond memories of him, especially John Burke, who at that time, along with many others, fervently hoped Tim Willoughby would surprise them all and walk through the door having had some great adventure. It was not to be: no trace of him has ever been found.

Aspinall's costs at Howletts were spiralling as he became more involved with his growing animal kingdom. It seemed that his devotion to them was a manic motivation. What had started as something of a gimmick (Aspinall, in his Doctor

Dolittle moments, would bring a pet baby chimpanzee or miniature ponies down to the Clermont Club for the evening) had become an extremely expensive obsession. His wife Jane he left to her own devices. There wasn't time for everything. His expenditure was running at around £3,000 a week – about £4 million a year in 2007 – to fund his lifestyle.

John Burke, as financial director, was well aware of all the money problems, present and pending. He looked on with growing apprehension. 'It was a crazy situation – John was borrowing in one door and it was vanishing out the other. There had to be a day of reckoning. I dealt with the bank and I dealt with the general finances of the company and made sure there was enough money to cover the cheques and so on. But John had complete control. I was very much the number two, and John was the boss, the man in charge.

'The ideal solution would have been if John had agreed to cut back his own expenditure. But he never believed he could be wrong. It was lunatic arrogance. He was spending money at this stage that was not easy getting out of the company. If John had agreed to cut back, perhaps in a year we could have got things on an even keel.'

John Aspinall did no such thing. Instead, arguably his most cynical and sinister malfeasance manifested itself.

12. THE BIG EDGE

It was beautiful and simple as all truly great swindles are.

'THE OCTOPUS MAROONED' BY O. HENRY

'John, steal whatever you want, but don't rob the man who saved your life.'

When Ray Ryan walked out of the rigged game on 20 December 1963, the foundations of John Aspinall's life and aspirations were shakier than they had ever been. To clear up this nasty affair he would have to pay back Ryan in full. And very quickly. He had no idea what Ryan's reaction, on reflection, would be. He must have felt himself in a vacuum.

There was just so much he could take out of the Clermont: he'd tried and tried to skim off more, but his was now a limited company – and there were limits. Which is why he'd had to borrow so much from Ryan in the first place. He was like a cornered tiger. With his psychological make-up, all he could do was attack. For Aspinall, regarded by so many as the fun-loving, eccentric 'Aspers', was an almighty rogue. He created an image of himself, that he won and lost fortunes, that he gambled. He never gambled: he played games of chance. And he almost always hedged his bets.

John Burke had no early warning of Aspinall's plan to cheat Ray Ryan. He was told only a short time before, when arrangements were made for the upstairs game in the Salle Privée. When Aspinall explained that 'needs must', Burke

understood just how panicked the owner of the Clermont
Club had become. And he went along with it.

Mr Money witnessed all the events of that December
evening knowing exactly who would be intrigued, delighted,
to hear of them. The next morning at Moscow Road he
eagerly divulged all his information to Billy Hill, who now
became fully aware of Aspinall's desperation and of his failed
scheme to avoid paying back Ryan.

That afternoon, Billy Hill and Bobby McKew had a talk at
Moscow Road. Hill was quiet, but adamant that his number
two should contact John Burke. Aspinall, he said, was now
ready for the 'Big Edge'. Bobby McKew was still not certain
about John Burke's reaction, but he could tell how serious Hill
was about getting into the Clermont. He wasn't going to sit
still.

'Billy had simply bided his time,' said Bobby McKew.
'From the moment Mr Money gave us the word about the
Ryan fuck-up, he knew Aspinall would go for it. He'd have
probably gone for it anyway, he was a greedy bastard.'

Still, Bobby McKew did not think John Burke would agree.
Billy Hill asked him to arrange a meeting, and Bobby argued
that his friend would not go for it, or recommend it to Aspinall.
Billy just said, 'Do it anyway.'

There was no chance that Bobby McKew would not follow Billy Hill's instruction. The two Irishmen met at the Star,
where John Burke had often sat in a corner having a drink
while Billy Hill sipped his tea. The taciturn and careful
McKew said only that he had 'some business' with Billy Hill
and that he thought John should have a meeting with the
crime boss. It would be of mutual benefit, he promised. It
was a shock to John Burke, who knew that Bobby and Billy
were friends but wisely had never inquired further: 'I found
out for the first time that my old friend Bobby McKew not
only worked for Billy Hill, but that he was a key figure in

the proposed scam. It was important, because I trusted Bobby.'

Of course, for John Burke it was one thing to have a drink with the gangster; quite another to go into business with him. Burke was living in an elegant Mayfair town house, 4 Aldford Street, that had been the London pied-à-terre of the Aga Khan. His son Prince Aly Khan during his romantic excursions had entertained his conquests there (he said of society Englishmen: 'They call me a nigger and I sleep with their wives.') There was a secret panel where Aly Khan hid his drinks when his parents visited.

Tempted as he was to have a drink, John Burke wanted to keep a cool head for his visitor. He did not know what to think, or, indeed, what to say, to Hill. Bobby McKew had made him somewhat aware of the deal, but it sounded full of risks and dangers. Going bankrupt at the Clermont was one thing; going crooked a much more frightening prospect.

Billy Hill arrived dressed in a smart blue suit. He had a smile on his face as he handed John Burke his hat. Tea, he said, would be very pleasant. John Burke made a pot and brought it into the drawing room of his small but elegant house. The two men sat back in their armchairs. They could have been about to discuss the football results. They had a gossip, but the pleasantries ended quite quickly.

The conversation moved on to Ray Ryan. What a mess. Billy Hill did not think much of Signor Biondi as a card sharp. Indeed, he had arranged for Bobby McKew to drive one of his lads, Bobby Warren, over to Chelsea Reach to have a quiet word with him. Biondi, he said, would now leave the country.

The Italian had been a worrying embarrassment, but his most serious mistake had been not to ask Hill's permission for his misdeeds. Hill had interests in several casinos and did not want attention drawn to his activities. Indeed, if Aspinall wanted to make money, he was going about it all the wrong way. Hill got to the point: 'You are very foolish. If you want a job done properly, I'll do it for you.'

John Burke explained that he could not speak for his boss on this issue. He would tell Aspinall of their conversation, and, if necessary, arrange another meeting. There was cautious delight in Aspinall's eyes when he heard of Hill's approach. But he thought about it long and hard before making a move. If it went wrong, he'd be ruined. His business and social life would end. Howletts would have to be closed down. Yet if he didn't get more money quickly, his hopes and ambitions would be quashed.

Finally he agreed to go to John Burke's home for a meeting with Billy Hill and Bobby McKew. Again John Burke made tea for Hill, and opened his drinks cabinet. The discussion didn't take long; about half an hour. The conversation was amicable and did not dwell on the technicalities. Hill and Bobby McKew would deal with those. Aspinall simply had to go along with their plans and make himself lots and lots of money.

Desperate as he was, Aspinall was still circumspect before finalizing an arrangement with a powerful man renowned for violence and for keeping everything under his control. Aspinall contacted Sydney Summers, who, as we know, had been of great assistance in the past to him and John Burke. Aspinall, a dreadful snob who would never have entertained Sydney at his own home, respected his intelligence and his contacts, especially those in the police hierarchy.

They had a conversation about the Billy Hill proposal, somewhat absurd in a way, but which was to have dramatic financial consequences for many of the rich and famous. Yes, said Sydney Summers, Billy Hill was a scary man of violence, a tough character, possibly one of the most dangerous men around. But the wonderful paradox was that he was straight in his own particular way, even in his errant dealings. Everybody liked Billy, even some of the people he murdered.

'Is it something that will work for me, Sydney?' asked an increasingly anxious Aspinall.

Summers peered through milk-bottle lenses and nodded wisely. In his thick accent, he gave Billy Hill a glowing reference, 'Oh, yes. If he says he will do it and makes a deal, he will stick with it. Billy Hill is an honest crook.'

'After that,' said Bobby McKew, 'Aspinall grabbed at it with both hands; he was dishonest to his roots, so there was no trouble with his conscience.'

Or with his business expertise. He was no rollover on the percentages; everywhere else the deal with Billy Hill was 50–50, but Aspinall persuaded his new associate that with the amounts of money involved it should be 60–40 in Aspinall's favour. He was the one supplying the big golden pigeons. Billy Hill accepted this: 40 per cent of the riches was far better than nothing at all. It was agreed on a handshake at 4 Aldford Street.

The 'Big Edge' was brilliantly designed. John Burke regards it as 'psychologically and mathematically brilliant', and says in some wonder: 'Einstein would have been proud of it.'

Aspinall, no stranger to wagering with advantages, was in for one of gambling's most secret and sensational scams. He wanted the profit, but also wanted to minimize his personal risk, to distance himself from it, as John Burke explained: 'I put John and Hill together because I didn't want to be stuck in the middle of the bloody thing. John had said: "Burkie, I want you to deal with Hill, and here are my conditions . . ." I argued that I could do no such thing; how could I make deals if Hill responded with his conditions?

'John was the boss, and for many years I had always done what he'd asked. For the first time I didn't do exactly what he wanted; I didn't want to be in between two such dangerous men. John didn't like that at all.

'But in time, of course, I was the link. John never wanted

to meet Hill if he could possibly avoid it, so I used to go and see him. I was the intermediary. There was never any problem. We'd have a chat. It was happily easy for me to deal with him, but rumour had it that he was not always so polite.

'I don't altogether blame John Aspinall when he had been for years spending money like water, because money was coming in like water. It's hard to curtail. So when John did eventually decide to do business with Billy Hill, I acquiesced with these decisions. It would be hypocritical to say that I didn't.

'Obviously, morally, I should have taken a stand and perhaps even resigned. I saw that it meant financing John Aspinall's lifestyle through cheating rather than through stealing money from the Clermont – money that belonged to the shareholders and the taxman – in order to pay his bills. A choice between Scylla and Charybdis.

'Enough time has gone by to tell the truth. It is the whole truth and nothing but the truth. Clearly, when Billy Hill was alive and when Gypsy was still around, this would not have been a sensible enterprise. I got on well with Billy Hill at our meetings and I wouldn't have wanted to embarrass him with murder, especially my own. Seriously, it would have been a life and death matter. Now, I believe it is a part of history that should be shared. So, here goes.'

And a nightingale sang about Berkeley Square.

'I'm not suggesting I've grown a halo. I do this with no malice, but just to correct so many, many errors that have been put forward over the years. Not because people wanted to mislead, but because they did not have access to the true facts.

'They had John's stories, but that's what they were – stories. This is how it was. He was a very curious character, neither a saint nor a demon. In his own mind, he was entitled to rob in order to have the funds to do what was important in the world. That was what he believed.

'The Clermont, the glittering jewel of clubs, magnet for all the big names in the gambling world, took for a ride just about everybody who was unlucky enough to walk through its doors on the evenings when the financial outcome of the gambling was not determined by luck. It was grand larceny. But very clever.'

As the Christmas and New Year holidays ended in 1963–1964, preparations went forward to introduce the 'Big Edge' to the Clermont Club. There were clubs where the 'Big Edge' could operate every night, but the Clermont had a tight circle, an exclusive membership watched over by the careful 'Porchy' Carnarvon. Aspinall was intelligent and knew the risks involved. He allowed Billy Hill's boys to 'perform' once a week, at the most. He would brief them before every evening of cheating the Clermont members.

'It was so simple it was brilliant,' said Bobby McKew, who still shakes his head at the wonder of it. 'No one ever had an inkling.'

Aspinall had always been subtly manipulative about soaking, like a vampire, the wealth of all those he lured into his gambling dens. John Burke said, 'Aspers didn't care whose money he took. The psychology behind the cheating was twisting all the rules of fraud – you couldn't see the swindle for looking at it, hearing it almost. It was advertised, but all these aristocrats and tycoons, powerful men and women, would not believe what was happening. It was like stealing a wallet, snatching a handbag, but it was as though Fagin was in charge – they didn't feel a thing.'

The details of the method by which players were cheated have remained an underworld and gambling secret until now.

The normal method of cheating at chemmy was for the proprietor to employ a clever croupier like Louis the Rat who could do things with the cards, like arranging for a big winning bank to arrive at a fixed place, when the cards had been shuffled between each shoe. This was the simplest part of his legerdemain; a house player would win four, five, six, eight, ten coups the first time he got the bank.

Sometimes the cards were pre-prepared, known as 'the sandwich', and they were just inserted by sleight of hand into the pack and either the proprietor or one of his house players had a long bank and won a nice bit of money. That had problems, as John Burke explained: 'The main snag about that is that if it happens regularly, and people at the table are not complete idiots, the players want to know what's going on. They get suspicious.

'If it was going to work, which it did, it had to be smarter. And then the psychology was brought in. In brains versus greed there is no contest. All true gamblers, and even non-gamblers with a modicum of self-confidence, believe that a slightly uphill struggle as exemplified by fractional odds against can, by means of skill or even a little luck, be transformed into slight odds-on. And given the opportunity to bet at even money on a proposition that is mathematically odds-on, surely no proper man with red blood – or blue – in his veins would refuse to have a go.

'Betting with the odds in your favour is technically known as "value". I have always supported the idea that value ought to be taught as a separate school subject, or, at least, as a recognized brand of mathematics. The laws of probability and chance have a much stronger bearing on our affairs than any algebraic equation.

'Value is an essential component of risk assessment, which plays a vital role in our everyday life. The obvious examples of businesses that are dependent on understanding risk assessment and using it intelligently are insurance and book-making.

'But what if you take away most of the risk? What I am going to explain has never been described before. It is unique.

It is a system of cheating that is technically ingenious and extremely clever, both psychologically and mathematically.

'In gambling there are two types of people – winners and losers. An easy example – bookmaking. People backing horses. The bookmakers are risk assessors and make odds accordingly, in such a way that there is a percentage in their favour; assuming the money they take in is evenly distributed, for every £110 they take in they pay out £100. The bookmakers, who often have a bigger edge, win, and the punters lose.

'Poker is a good example. There are two kinds of players at poker. The player who plays to the odds; careful, tight play. He only risks his money when he thinks his hand is worth it. Then there's the open player who likes to play at every hand and bet freely, and comes in all the time even with a pair of twos, and might even play and draw four to an ace in old-fashioned draw poker. Of course, such a player, provided he pays his debts, is always extremely welcome. He's the guy you want in the game. He may have a lucky night, but on balance he's going to be a loser.

'At chemmy you have the same thing. This is universal to gambling. In chemmy it's not quite so obvious to see it, but it is very much there. I should know. I have been somewhat involved in the game. Each coup, each hand, is a contest between two parties. The bank, who has a shoe and deals the cards, and the person who goes *banco* and plays the hand against the bank. It's a straightforward contest.

'The bank has a built-in advantage. And that's official. After a long evening at Annabel's in 1963 with Basil de Ferranti, who headed his family's huge wireless and electronics company, I had the game analysed and computer-programmed by Professor Nigel Foster at the London School of Economics.

'Basil de Ferranti put the results through his company computers and they concluded that in chemmy, the bank's built-in advantage is roughly 1.78 per cent. Call it 1.8 per cent – the person calling *banco* has that shade of odds against him.

'The bank has that advantage because when the player who called *banco* asks for a third card, it is dealt face up. Depending on his hand, that gives the bank a small or big advantage because the bank now knows, mathematically, whether to rest or draw a card himself. During a playing session, this translates into 1.8 per cent in the bank's favour.

'The *cagnotte*, of course, has no effect on the mathematical odds of each coup. However, it means that because 5 per cent of the profit is deducted when the bank wins a coup, financially speaking, the bank is no longer a winner – all players now contribute to the house.

'However, with the *cagnotte* gone, the bank was always going have the edge.

'Or was it? There's always been a feeling among chemmy players that the person who just ran his bank and did nothing else was a mean player and was rather despised, whereas the open player who called *banco* all the time and bet freely, the Lord Derby figure, was the hero. He was the man every careful player and gambling promoter wanted in the game.

'The psychology behind the cheating was inspired. When the law changed and a table charge was substituted for the *cagnotte*, it meant everyone sat down and paid a certain amount for the privilege of playing a shoe of chemmy; the table charge was the same for all players. Whether you did nothing but wait for your bank and run your bank, or whether you bet freely, it cost the same amount to play in the shoe. This accentuated the difference between the careful player and the betting player. And, forcefully, the advantage of the bank.

'Mathematically speaking, the optimum procedure would be to sit quietly and when your bank came to you, run your bank and then sit quietly until it came around the next time. Like waiting for a train, *chemin de fer*, going around the railway:

deadly boring but mathematically correct. It's like someone today playing poker on computer against an anonymous somebody in Australia; it's not much fun. People who followed this rule, of course, were very unpopular and considered mean. Especially in the Clermont sort of games, where confident, outgoing people are there for fun, at a table chatting and drinking and trying to impress each other.

'The cavalier gambler's flourishes encouraged other people to bet freely. And the constant *banco* and *suivi* were music to the ear. The punter could have been shouting "lose" and "lose", because the statistical chance was that he would.

'As I said, prior to the "Big Edge" there was basically one form of cheating at chemmy: that was to give a good winning bank to somebody representing the house, the proprietor or one of the house players – the artificial banks known as a "sandwich" or a "sausage". Strange, then, if the proprietor or his friend or a house player had a winning bank every time. Even idiots would think there was something fishy about this. And the croupier was in on the cheating, and they had to trust the croupier not to talk, and it also lent itself to suspicion. Both were disadvantages.

'Is there a way of getting around it? Well, there is one way, but it sounds impossible.

'Could the winning be done by the person who goes *banco*? What if you turned the odds around? What if you could make the person calling *banco* odds-on? Apparently, the guy who is betting against the odds? Could he be created the winner by any manner of means?

'Eventually some genius, it must have been a genius, came up with a scheme to do it. That was the scam. That was the "Big Edge". A genius worked out a method whereby it wasn't the bank who won the money, it was the punter. It was the lunatic punter who everyone dreamed of having in the game and who was sure to lose; he was the person who won. That was the genius of the psychological end of it, and the mathematics of it are equally fascinating. God knows, whoever invented it had a special forte, something like the man who broke the Enigma code. It has never been discovered although thousands of people sat down at the tables and played with these cards for tens of thousands of hours. Nobody saw because it was so extremely subtle and so cleverly done.

'Now, the technicalities: in chemmy the cards are put in a wooden container known as a shoe, and they fit in exactly. The shoe is sloped and the cards come out through a brass mesh at the end, and behind the cards there is a heavy weight.

'The cards are held in tightly, with the heavy weight behind them and the brass mesh in front of them which they are pulled through one at a time; you can only get one card at a time. The effect of pulling cards through like this puts a slight curvature on the card.

'If you look at a pack of cards when people are playing bridge or poker, normally the cards are absolutely flat. Some people do have a habit of shuffling in such a way that the cards acquire a curvature. Yet there is no design to it. It is happenstance, what happens to the cards. But in chemmy a slight curvature is normal. You don't expect the cards to be absolutely flat, because they are not. That helps to explain how this whole thing can be done. Think of it like pulling a file from a rigidly packed filing cabinet. There will be a very, very slight bend to the file. Has to be.

'Our mastermind worked out a system whereby the cards could be distinguished. He discovered that there were only three possible changes in the cards. One, is that they came out exactly as normal, with that slight curvature from the shoe.

'Two, is that there is a slight adjustment made to the two diagonally opposite corners, right and left.

'Three, there is a slight adjustment made to the two diagonally opposite corners, left and right.

'That way you had three slightly different-shaped cards. When I say slightly, I mean extremely slight. So slight that none of the people playing the game for hundreds and thousands of hours would spot it.

'Except for the "readers", Billy Hill's people, who had perfect eyesight and were trained, practised for hours and hours at the cards coming out of the shoe. Instantly, and I saw them do it often enough, they could "read" the cards. They couldn't "read" the exact card and call the king of hearts or something, but they knew enough to have the edge. They could pick up the differences. They could put each card into one of three categories.

'What cards should you put in each category? There are ten values of cards, thirteen cards with four of them having a value of zero. King, queen, jack and ten are each a value of zero. The other nine are between one and nine. What way should they be apportioned into three? The answer they came up with, and somebody must have spent a lot of time working it out, was very clever.

'If we say A, B and C. A was a high card – nine, eight, seven. B were the lower cards – six, five, four, three, two. C were the zero cards and the ace.

'You have two cards, each of which has three possible clarifications – and, therefore, six possible combinations. In order of merit:

1: A and C, the best possible.
2: B and B, the second best.
3: A and A, third best.
4: B and C, fourth best.
5: A and B, fifth best.
6: C and C, worst.

'Clearly, an A and a C was the best hand, if the closest to nine is the winner. But an A and an A was not, as one might think, the second-best hand. The maximum would be an eight: two nines, eighteen, counted as eight happening one time in nine.

'Better off with a B and a B, which gives you twenty-five combinations, nine of which give you a nine or an eight. There are four chances at a nine, five at an eight. The odds are 16–9 against getting a "natural".

'The bank's hand and the punter's hand are classified in exactly the same way. What is important to know now is which is the better hand. Which is, mathematically, the best combination to hold in order to win the coup from the *banco*ing point of view. It's not difficult to work out that the best is a high card with a zero. So an A and a C is obviously the best hand. The "reader" knows the combination – it's like Eddie Chapman and the combination to a safe. If he gets it right, he's in the money.

'The well-trained "reader" reads each of the two pairs of cards as they come out of the shoe. He now knows who has the better chance of winning the coup – bank or caller – and therefore he can adopt the mathematically optimum strategy, either calling a bet or keeping quiet. Statistically, the bank will have the better hand five times out of twelve, likewise his opponent, while in one coup in six their cards will have the same rank. There would be situations when a canny reader might call *banco* with the inferior hand, hoping to lose for appearance's sake.

'The "reader" did not need to see the cards dealt on the table – he could "read" them as they came out of the shoe. That meant that if the *banco* was on his right, he had the option of going "*banco* prime", (taking the bank first) or, indeed, if the *banco* was on his left and likely to win, he could say in a friendly way to the caller, "a hundred with you for luck".

'Yet, and here is the brilliance of it, the "reader" knows which hand is more likely to win; he does not know which hand will win. If he did, it could be very suspicious. That's why it's so clever. The "reader" backs plenty of losers because things don't always work out, but he is betting with the odds in his favour.

'If the odds are in the favour of the *banco* he would go *banco*. If the odds were in favour of the bank he would keep quiet. In the course of a game of one hundred bets he will win, say, 60–40. That's profit. Perhaps he might win sixty-five and lose thirty-five. Maybe only win fifty-seven and lose forty-three. He would always have the edge.

'A simple way to look at it, as a non-gambler? There are two possibilities. One is mathematically more probable than the other, and you can back either of them at even money – so which one do you back?

'To put it another way, if you like, if it is mathematically 6:4 on (4–6) that a certain event will happen as opposed to not happening, and you can back it happening at even money, you would want to have a bet, wouldn't you?

'Now the character crying *banco*, the mad player, the lunatic if you like, is the winner. At the end of the game, of course, it needn't be obvious how much he's winning, because he doesn't win any big amount in one go and he can always put some of his chips in his pocket. He is the winner and anyone thinking about it would say: "Lucky bugger. Next time he plays he'll lose twice as much."

'There were ways of handling this situation intelligently. If it was spotted that somebody was winning consistently, a losing night or nights might be arranged. Someone else would do the winning, so that neither the house nor Billy Hill lost.

'It was the psychology of it that was so good. Punters wanted the daft guy going *banco* and *suivi* all the time to win. They knew he'd get his comeuppance, but it was great to see him win big coups. It was exciting, it turned them on. And that was good for business too.

'It was a superb concept, and Billy Hill was not just in at the Clermont, he was in many other clubs. That's the beauty of this thing. Billy Hill's man maybe has a hundred bets. Loses forty and wins sixty. It's so much better that way.'

'By God, the inventor of this scam had a clear brain when it came to cheating the punters and gamblers who knew the system, pumped it like a money well. Psychologically, mathematically brilliant – can't say that enough times. They made millions.

'Mr Money, who acted as the money go-between for Billy Hill and Aspinall, took huge sums of money to Switzerland and turned them into numbered accounts at the Banca del Gottardo in Lugano.

'Millions.'

13. NEW CARDS, PLEASE

The reason he is called Sky is because he will bet all he has, and nobody can bet more than this.

'THE IDYLL OF MISS SARAH BROWN', DAMON RUNYON

While the scam was exceptional in its circumspect simplicity, it still required a skilled operator to oversee the mechanics. Bobby McKew was the man. A year after he returned to London from his French imprisonment he bought a printing company, the Dulwich Press in Herne Hill, and that had become part of Billy Hill's grand casino larceny. The main operational centre was a rented flat in Maitland Court, only a moment away from Bobby McKew's flat.

The 'Big Edge' relied upon the Clermont's customized cards being available for treatment before the night they were to be used. The cards were kept in a locked cupboard at the Clermont, and Aspinall would give several sets at a time to Mr Money to take to Billy Hill. Hill had a team of men on £200 a day.

'It was very good money for two reasons: it kept them at it and it kept them quiet,' said Bobby McKew. 'Billy knew when to work with expenses. He was never cheap, and no one complained. Or talked.'

At Maitland Court, the cards were given the 'Big Edge' treatment. In a room filled with cigarette smoke and activity, the smart Caro cards were put through a device like a small clothes mangle which an engineer had created for the sole purpose of 'customizing' them, giving the cards a unique 'look'. It was nothing sophisticated. Bobby McKew still smiles at the thought of it. 'You could have bought the machine in Hamley's, the toy shop in Regent Street – one of those children's mangles – and adapted it. But we had the machine specially made. It was a steel cylinder with thin tyre rubber around it. It was adjusted until eventually they got it just right. When it was right, it wasn't touched. That was the "Big Edge".

'It "marked" the cards in this special way. You couldn't tell anything had been done to them. You could fly them to the moon and back, and no scientist in the world could tell.

'When the cards came in they were wrapped in cellophane, and the packet was carefully cut with a razor blade. We'd take the cards out, put them in the roller and a seven would come out with that ever-so-slight curve and a two with an ever-so-slight curve the other way. And so on, throughout every pack.

'You had to go through each packet and be very careful to put them back in the correct order. It was a lot of work to make sure they were one, two, three, four and the rest of it: when the croupier opened the pack of cards – "new cards, please" – he would spread them out so that everyone could see. One mistake, and that's it. Somebody would notice.

'Mind you, there again, maybe not. The great thing about gambling people is that nobody watches anybody else's bets, they are only watching their own. It's a selfish business, gamblers are the most self-obsessed of people, up their own arses; their eyes are only on themselves. Nobody is going to look. People would get up and go and get a drink. They'd be talking to each other. Would they notice?

'But we never made mistakes. Every pack of cards was checked and rechecked. The cellophane, the seal, were put back on perfectly, using a cellophane machine I had at the Dulwich Press.

'It's just that the cards had gone through the machine, and the "readers" could spot a face card from a high card and a low card, and so on. The odds were irrevocably changed. The cards were bent. So to speak.'

It was a superbly clever operation, but the Clermont was an extremely difficult club for Billy Hill to work: there were only a small number of players, an exclusive bunch. A great deal of care was taken, and Billy Hill was highly intelligent about getting people into the Clermont – but only with John Aspinall's clearance and help.

Hill had many players 'on the books', some of whom had long hours of training as 'readers'; others who were sent in as back up. Yet not all were suitable for the Clermont; they operated at the bigger casinos where it was easier because people could walk in off the street. The Clermont 'readers' were hand-picked, and cover stories were developed for them. Mr Money established overseas bank accounts for them, and acquired glowing references. Billy Hill opened similar accounts for the Clermont 'players' in London. It was all for safety, for insurance against discovery, to show they had the money to play, but the references were never needed. They played on their good credit, 'staked', on paper, by Billy Hill. There were always two: one to play, one to watch and assist, on any evening.

The only exception to this rule was the Clermont. What Aspinall had insisted upon at the start was that he must meet, agree to and guide Hill's players and they must work alone. The first one he 'cleared' was a man called Bata – by lucky coincidence this was a name which suggested money, as Bata was a successful European shoe company, the Nike of its day. Bata was an expert, with experience of the top French casinos, especially the Aviation Club de France on the Champs-Elysées. It was there, six years earlier, on a trip to Paris with John Burke, that an audacious Aspinall had taken the bank at baccarat and had been wiped out for around £5,000. The gambler was now interested in much larger sums of cash.

Aspinall met Bata for a drink, introduced him to other members, and then proposed the newcomer for Clermont membership. In the middle of January 1964, the 'Big Edge' went into the Clermont. Or, rather, Bata did on his own. He was so good that he did not need an assistant.

The grand Clermont host, Aspinall briefed him on what table to choose, who to 'take', and whom to avoid cheating – usually a player in debt to the Clermont. But Bill Stirling and others like him were 'good targets'. Aspinall suggested Bata might 'try for ten grand'.

Aspinall wandered over to the cashier's office, where Mr Money was helping out that evening. John Burke was there, too. They were all apprehensive, first-night nerves.

They watched as Bata took his seat and a shoe began. Immediately, he had a run of the cards and the chips stacked up in front of him. Aspinall whispered to John Burke that it was going too fast. None of the other players, however, seemed in the least disturbed by this winning streak.

The pattern went on from that evening. Bata won more than £10,000 – but it didn't look like it, for much of the loot, as chips, was in his dinner jacket pocket.

When two of Hill's men played, chips were secretly exchanged between them. The non-player went to the cashier's office and cashed in the chips, always trying to get cash rather than a cheque in return. Still, if it was a large amount, it was always met by a Clermont cheque made out in the name of Hill's operative. The cashier would know exactly what had been cashed; and therefore so would Aspinall. If Mr Money was on duty, there was an added witness to the sums involved, should Billy require it. It was only a precaution, for nobody was inclined to skim off money from Billy Hill.

At the end of that first evening's play, Bata cashed in and

got a Clermont cheque in his name. He'd won a little less than £6,000. Or so it seemed to any casual onlooker. In fact, with the chips already cashed, the winnings were closer to £14,000.

The cheques went directly to Maitland Court, where they endorsed them for payment to the special account Mr Money had set up, with Billy Hill as a co-signatory.

Predictably, it was Mr Money who returned the next day with Aspinall's 60 per cent, £8,400 – enough cash to meet his expenditure for a couple of weeks or so. Aspinall, who was always paid off in cash, attempted to be nonchalant, but could barely conceal his excitement from John Burke.

From then on Aspinall enthusiastically played the ringmaster of the 'Big Edge'. Mr Money would usually deliver Aspinall's share. Once, John Burke returned to 4 Aldford Street to discover that a thick package had been shoved through his door. It was a wedge of Scottish £100 notes (a total of £4,800), proceeds from the 'Big Edge' performing in Glasgow, being used to give Aspinall his cash share from the Clermont scam. John Burke received irregular payments from the 'Big Edge', and says that if he had insisted on a fixed percentage, Aspinall could hardly have refused. 'But I didn't need the money – John Aspinall did.'

As a director of the Clermont, John Burke was paid £10,000 a year – the equivalent of £200,000 in 2007, had the use of a chauffeured car, and signed bills at the Mirabelle, Annabel's and other fashionable restaurants and clubs, all of which were met by the Clermont. 'I was condoning the cheating but not getting a great profit from it. Maybe I was uneasy, but that said, if I had really needed the money I would probably have asked John Aspinall for a set cut.'

With the initial success, John Burke said the confident Aspinall was superb in introducing Billy Hill's gambling troops: 'John was a master of the art. He would say: "We've got this chap who has just inherited twenty million from his uncle . . ." – all this bullshit. "This is my friend who's just flown in from a big corporate deal in America / Hong Kong / China . . ." – John would just fill in the blanks.'

The scam had begun, big time. There were no slip-ups, except for one evening when the wrong cards were used instead of those treated by the 'Big Edge'. Nevertheless, even then the 'reader', a highly intelligent player, had a good evening and won a few thousand pounds.

But Aspinall did not warm to all of his new business partner's associates. One evening a supposed barrister turned up (wearing a dinner jacket in the early evening!), and was greeted by Aspinall. But this 'reader' was told to get lost. Aspinall thought him thoroughly unsuitable, especially because of 'the dodgy vowels'.

A bigger problem was Billy Hill's mistress Gypsy, who wanted to gamble at the Clermont. Aspinall went purple in the face at the thought of it. Bobby McKew recalls, 'She had a twenty-grand ring on her finger but she didn't fit the place. She was attractive and looked good, but there was something about her. People realized it. She wanted so badly to mix with those rich gamblers.

'If Gypsy had sat down and started her antics, the other players would have wondered what was going on. And her picture had been in the newspapers with Bill. She wasn't a lady. There was no way she could get into the Clermont in the middle of the scam and play.'

Still, she did make it into the downstairs bar for one drink, and that alone, said John Burke, all but gave Aspinall a nervous breakdown. Bobby McKew said wryly, 'But Gypsy got her money anyway. Billy would be splitting up the cash and he'd say: "I'm taking this £1,200 for Gypsy."

'I said: "What does she get for making the tea?"

'That didn't win me many points. I remember once Bill said: "Do you know, she's got fifty grand in Switzerland." I couldn't believe it. That amount of money! But, of course, she had. That was her bonus, bigger than any City bonus today. But Bill was raking it in, and so was Aspinall.'

So the scam continued at full pace every week at the Clermont, and never was there a hint of upset or disquiet from any of the members or their guests. Lord Derby would line up and shout his string of *bancos* and *suivis*, as would the Goldsmiths, the Stirlings, government ministers, European ambassadors, and other prestigious gamblers. They were totally unaware of the 'Big Edge'.

Not even James Bond knew what was going on. Bond's creator, Ian Fleming, cut a suave, stylish figure at the Clermont. John Burke liked him, despite 007's strange gambling habits: 'Bond's gambling is portrayed very poorly. Fleming lost a lot of money to us – he should have known better. But he liked the atmosphere and the girls, the edge to it all, so maybe he wasn't watching the cards. There are always people who are trying to lose money, and there are people who are there for the fun.

'One night when Fleming was playing at the big table in the Clermont, the club president, the Earl of Carnarvon, who, without understanding too much of our business, took a keen interest in the financial affairs of the club, advised me in his best stage whisper: "Give you a tip, Burkie, specially clear that fellow Fleming's cheque; he's got a dicky heart, might drop dead any moment."

'A few weeks later Ian Fleming had a fatal heart attack. "Porchy" Carnarvon was subsequently pleased to learn that all cheques paid to the Clermont by Fleming had been safely cleared in time.'

Which was the spectacular spin to the 'Big Edge': the heavy losers were always good for the money. If they lodged a cheque with the cashier, it would be honoured. It was a marvellous moneypot of ill-gotten gains, and Billy Hill was stirring it.

At the top tables with the toffs – those described by author Brian Masters in *The Passion of John Aspinall* as 'the best roll-call of rich and exclusive London society of the 1960s' – were the players from Maitland Court. It was a smooth operation, and Bobby McKew said: 'There was never a problem with the cheating at the Clermont because Aspinall was clever and did not let it be overdone, but sometimes there was trouble at other clubs with the scam. Once at the 21, the police got involved. The owner, Meadows, wasn't in on it, but the cashier and a couple of croupiers were. The police knew something was going on, because Billy played there. Even I did, a couple of times, and I never gambled unless it was crooked and I knew it.

'Some of the top people from the Yard came in and took all the cards away in a bag; they were going to get forensic experts to have a look. They came back and said: "Nothing wrong with these." That was in the 21, using the same card scam as at the Clermont and elsewhere.

'If cards were "clocked" – with a certain dot that indicates it's a six or a king – you can tell what it is. There are infrared methods, too; if you wore dark glasses you could read the cards coming out. But these cards weren't marked. That was another wonder of it.

'At the Clermont nobody noticed. They seemed to love losing money. Gamblers are like that. I told a friend of my wife's about a bent game. He'd lost £15,000.

'I said to him: "It's crooked. Don't go gambling there again."

'He nodded. The following week he went in and did about another ten, twelve grand. I don't suppose he believed me. Or just didn't want to. Gamblers!

'Some gamblers go in knowing they are going to lose. Billy Hill went in knowing he was going to win. Couldn't fail. The Union Corse, through his old friend Marcel Francisi (he was shot dead some years later, eight or nine bullets, think it was a machine gun), had brought the system to him, and he played it to the full. He worked it in every other major gambling club in England. Took a fortune.

'From the Aspinall deal and all that Clermont Club affair, Billy must have taken his share of what today would be at least £10 million. It was like robbing Fort Knox or the Bank of England. Just a lot easier. It was sweet. And not one of the victims ever knew what was going on. No one did. Millions and millions, tax free, into numbered accounts, Gypsy's purse and God knows where else, no questions asked.'

Aspinall never showed any concern for those he was mercilessly ripping off. For John Burke, there were moments of disquiet: 'I remember having a pang of conscience on hearing Aspers explain to the night's "reader" before a big game that he was to sit to the left of Major Derek Wigan, who had been having a good run, and concentrate on making him a big loser. I did not know Derek Wigan well, but I always saw him as a considerate, courteous gentleman, and hearing Aspinall describe him to his stooge as "detestable" forty-odd years ago is something that I cannot, but wish I could, forget. Perhaps that incident helped to give me a slight nudge in the right direction . . .'

14. COPPER-BOTTOMED

Que sera, sera – Whatever will be, will be.

DORIS DAY'S HIT SONG, 1956

As the 'Big Edge' settled into a reliable routine, John Aspinall began to spend the money as swiftly as Billy Hill delivered the cash to him. He had the upkeep of zoos and his town house in Lyall Street, Belgravia, to pay for, and his financial needs seemed to grow by the day. While Aspinall showed no qualms about cheating his members and his supposed friends, John Burke, although he insists on his culpability in the scheme, suffered disquiet. He also got lucky: his conscience was aided by a massive coup on the London metal market.

He'd gambled in copper on the London commodities market with the help of his friend Geoffrey Marriott. He'd met Marriott, by all accounts a dashing, charming man, in Dublin in the late 1940s, and they became great friends. After the war Marriott married Maura Ryan, the sister of Eddie Chapman's lover, the film star Kathleen Ryan, but it had a tragic conclusion when, driven by alcohol and drug addictions, she killed herself.

When the two old friends met again in London in 1960, Marriott was married to Anne from Amsterdam: 'They were good friends of Liliana and me. Geoffrey's job was copper buyer for Pirelli Tyres, when copper was a very important component in the manufacture of tyres. He was also a close personal friend of Sir Ronald Prain, who was the chairman of the Rhodesian Selection Trust which controlled the Rhodesian copper mines; he was the number one man in the world of copper, and his inside knowledge was invaluable.'

All the financial news said that there was overproduction of copper and that the price would drop. It did, but then the copper producers said they would not sell copper any cheaper. Still the financial pundits insisted that there was too much copper, not enough buyers and too many sellers, and the price would collapse.

Sir Ronald Prain told Geoffrey Marriott, and therefore John Burke, that the copper producers would make a stand and hold the price. But because of all the doom reports about the price, copper could be bought forward on the commodity market cheaper than the cash price. It is known as backwardation. It was very unusual: normally when you buy a commodity – gold, silver, copper – six months forward, the price is higher, if only to factor in the effect of inflation.

In the summer of 1964, John Burke, who had huge credit with Rudolf Wolff, was able to buy forward, on paper with no money exchanged, 1,500 tons of copper at a few pounds less per ton than the cash price. He had done this before, and he and Geoffrey Marriott had made steady profits, every three months turning over a few thousand pounds.

Suddenly, the situation changed. There were problems in America, a big strike in Chile. Instead of there being a surplus of copper, there was a shortage. Many speculators who had sold short heavily on the London Metal Exchange now had to buy back quickly in a market controlled by sellers. The price of copper exploded. It went up and up and up. John Burke was astonished, and remains so.

'We thought we were going to turn over a few thousand; instead we turned in a massive profit. After a few other profitable speculations, I walked away with somewhere between

£300,000 and £400,000, which was a nice amount. Quite a few millions, in today's money. Mr Money introduced me to the Banca del Gottardo in Lugano, where I opened an account. My one-time seven-figure Swiss franc account has, alas, dissolved into thin air.

'My relations with John Aspinall were not brilliant at this stage and I was also a bit worried. We were in this ridiculous situation with Billy Hill, and if it ever came out we would be in serious trouble. It was a highly criminal operation.'

This was forcibly brought home to Burkie in late 1964, when he had a nervous few days after he was approached by a friend, a highly placed lawyer and member of the club. He told him the authorities were investigating the Clermont. John Burke's informant was connected enough to know about such matters, but too discreet to pass on all the details. John thought it might be to do with government officials' habits – something MI5 took an interest in, or, more probably, currency exchange schemes – what would be called money laundering today. He never found out. He told Aspinall, and the investigation went away: 'John had the sort of friends who could do that.' Even so, for John Burke it was the final push he needed.

He sought out John Aspinall and told him: 'John, I wish you the best of luck but I feel I must bow out.'

Aspinall was furious. He felt betrayed. 'Burkie! You can't go!'

'I must.'

'Well, don't go now, stay till the end of the year.'

John Burke agreed to stay on for that time. Ian Maxwell-Scott heard of John Burke's decision to leave, and sought out his friend. They went for a drink at the Star, and Maxwell-Scott said that he, too, wanted to leave Aspinall. He, too, found the situation intolerable. He asked John Burke's advice: should he resign?

Ian Maxwell-Scott was on a generous income from the

Clermont, but also had a large family and the upkeep of Grants Hill House in Uckfield, Sussex. Without the job, the gambler would find it difficult to make ends meet.

John Burke, who talked Ian Maxwell-Scott out of leaving, himself got out of the Clermont about twelve months after the 'Big Edge' went in at the club.

'I officially resigned as director of the Clermont and moved on. I hadn't grown a halo. I said nothing about the "Big Edge". If I had, there would have been a huge scandal; the Clermont would have gone bust; the shareholders, many of them friends of mine, would have lost all their investments; and the directors, of whom I was one, would probably have been in for some heavy flak.'

As far as John Aspinall was concerned, the until-then always supportive and loyal John Burke was the forgotten man. He might as well have been dead. Aspinall ruthlessly wrote his friend out of his life:

'In John Aspinall's eyes, I had done something unforgivable. I was an outcast. I was a traitor. I had walked away and deserted him in his hour of need. I'd behaved in a despicable way. No Zulu warrior would dare to behave like that towards his great hero, the Zulu leader Shaka. The unfortunate warrior would have been banished to the most inhospitable corner of the kingdom. John never changed his mind. Once the idea was there, he wouldn't ever think back and rethink it.

'There were rumours that all was not above board in London gambling clubs, and no wonder, considering how much money was changing hands. I never made an effort to re-establish the friendship with Aspinall, because he told a couple of people that "One or two things strange happened when that fellow Burke was here, as he was friendly with gangsters."

'It was a rather rotten thing for Aspinall to say about his ex-friend and partner, but I suppose he saw it as his way of getting out of a tricky situation. He couldn't say it to too many people, of course, because anybody who understood anything about the running of a gambling club would realize that for anyone to infiltrate the Clermont Club from the outside and take a lot of money without the proprietor knowing would be not only impossible, but utterly ludicrous.'

Ironically, a few months later John Aspinall used John Burke's departure as the opportunity to cut his links with Billy Hill. He decided that he need not give away 40 per cent of his dubious earnings. He sent word to the gangster through Mr Money that he believed things were becoming too difficult for the 'Big Edge' to continue at the Clermont. Hill was practical about it. Without Aspinall's connivance with the 'readers', the scam could not operate. He'd got into the Clermont and taken a fortune from it. There were other casinos to rip off. Why try and pressure Aspinall, who was not an easy knockover? Why make a noise?

Yet Aspinall's financial needs, as ever, were still growing. The 'Big Edge' might have left the Grand Salon, but in its place he introduced another scheme. John Burke said, 'John simply began another scam to make money directly for himself. It was devilish and cunning; he employed a really first-class "mechanic" croupier, somebody who was streets ahead of even Louis the Rat, but almost in the same class as Bruce the Australian.

'There was a lot of money owed to the company; many members had lost vast sums of money, largely because of the Hill activities. If a recognized player had gone too far, got in too deep and reached the limit of his credit, he might want to withdraw from the game for a while. He'd plan to clear it all off; it might take a year or so, but before he did, John would go to him and say: "Hey, this is what we'll do – you can continue to play, but play for me. You enjoy playing. You're popular at the table, people like to see you sitting down there, and you lend an atmosphere to the place . . ." All that sort of bullshit.

'The deal was that if the player won he took 10 per cent, and if he lost it cost him nothing. It looked like a very good deal, and John would present it extremely well to people like Lucan who were on the books owing the Clermont a lot of money. The player would agree, and John would say: "Well, there's a big party next Wednesday, why don't you come Wednesday night." He would make one condition. He would say: "By the way, the only thing I would say is don't go calling *banco* all the time, just have the occasional bet. But run your banks for the maximum all the time."

'Apart from anything else, this was the right strategy because now we were not taking the *cagnotte*. There was a table charge, which is the same for every player at the table. So the odds were in favour of the bank and against the punter. It was the correct mathematical strategy to run your bank and bet as little as possible.

'What happened during the game would be that, at the right moment, the person who was playing for Aspinall would get a massive bank, a run of ten or twelve winning coups. It would happen perhaps twice in an evening. This croupier was a genius. But the person with the lucky bank was a regular player – not a "house" player – so there were no questions about it. In the Clermont, the big winner was someone of unquestioned integrity.

'John's man would be a big winner at the end of the night; say he won fifty grand, John would say, "Take £5,000 for yourself," and the person would very probably say: "Oh no, knock that off what I owe the company." Of the fifty grand, forty-five would go directly into John's pocket and the other five grand would go to the club.

'Good business all round. And of course, there's no danger of exposure, because neither party would talk about it and admit that was the way it was happening. And John's player thought it was just a behind-the-scenes deal with him; only John knew about the mechanic sending the winning banks to the correct seat.

'It would all go unnoticed, and John could use it to his advantage, saying: "How lucky so-and-so was with his win last night. Good player." It was clever!'

With the gaming laws of the UK changed in 2007 and Britain starting to look like one great casino, John Burke is a more than interested observer:

'It's as though we were going back to the gambling fever of Regency days, although today gambling is democratic and much of it is run by computers, not croupiers. There's a great history to upper-class gambling in England, and there's also, of course, the English working man who would go into the pub and play darts for a pint of beer and later visit the betting shop. Then there's that bunch of people who think gambling is wicked. And another bunch who want to take the gamblers for a ride, make money, lots of it, out of them.

'There is no question that a gambling bonanza is happening in Britain, with the online betting – I use Betfair – and the casinos. The casinos will be like corner shops in no time.

'The future of gambling? I have not gambled in a casino in London for twenty years. I would charitably assume that everything is now completely above board and that the people who are running the industry are men of undoubted integrity.'

He paused, thought for a moment, and with a smile added, 'Although it might be wise not to ignore, or indeed forget, the time-honoured proverb concerning the leopard and his spots . . .'

15. THE RETURN OF BRUCE

Never give a sucker an even break.

W.C. FIELDS, 1941

In 1972, Bruce returned to London.

Mark Sykes believes Lord Derby had won huge amounts of money at the Clermont, or that was what he was told. John Burke believes that it was a hugely successful businessman who had been a big winner. It is not very important who is correct. What is more disquieting is that the big winner became an even bigger loser, thanks to Bruce the marvellous card mechanic; the man who could work magic with any pack of cards.

The winner – whether it was Derby or another man – enraged John Aspinall. His run of luck had gone on all evening and into the early hours of the next day. There was no mechanic at play for Aspinall, just the house players, who, like the members, were getting their cards by chance, not by sleight of hand or direction from the croupier.

Aspinall wanted his money back. Badly. He said to the winner: 'How about a private poker game?'

It was agreed that a game would be arranged in two weeks' time at Aspinall's house in Lyall Street. Aspinall was so desperate for the return of the money that he wanted the best mechanic he could get, and someone who would be unknown to the membership of the Clermont.

Mark Sykes received a telephone call from Peter West. West asked if he knew someone who was absolutely top quality, an international card sharp, to come and play poker for the house. It was urgent. The game was in two weeks, very short notice.

Mark Sykes told West that he knew the perfect player: Bruce the Australian. He was really good. But he was in Tasmania.

'We'll pay all his costs,' said Peter West, adding: 'He's just got to get here for this game. It's vital.'

Mark Sykes called Bruce on that faraway island to tell him that his talents were urgently required for a special game. The money for a first-class air fare and expenses would be wired to him. Over thirty years ago, it took Bruce three days to get to London. On arrival, he went to stay at a little hotel in South Kensington. It was there that Mark Sykes introduced Bruce to Peter West and their arrangements were made. Mark Sykes 'was very well looked after'. Bruce was to be paid £25,000 for his help: there was, it seemed, never any question that the big winner was going to go down.

Indeed, Bruce won all the money back for Aspinall. The details of the game were kept quiet. All those involved were absolutely discreet and never told the exact details: whether it was one session, or over one day and into the next.

And there could have been more than one victim at the table. Aspinall would not have been keen to have their names known, because no possible good could come of it. It might do him serious damage or hamper future operations.

Aspinall said to Bruce: 'By the way, don't ever mention the names of the people who subscribed so generously to us.'

Bruce played his part, which is why he may have dissembled, telling a white lie to his good friend Mark Sykes and naming John Derby as the big winner, and subsequently big loser.

It completed the circle.

Bruce stayed around for a week and played cards with his friends, including Mark Sykes, who recalled that Bruce had a problem; he used to drink. 'Even when he was ripped he could make the cards do whatever he wanted. That is the most unbelievably, incredibly difficult thing even to think about doing. You've got to know where every single card in the pack is. You've got to try and remember. It's an astonishing feat.'

John Burke recalls that it was Bruce who taught John Aspinall one or two simple tricks of the trade at poker; how to arrange the cards in such a way as to take off some gullible young man. Not much had changed since his first encounter with John Aspinall in the Jermyn Street offices of the entertaining master of the understatement, Sydney Summers. Yes, Aspinall was good with the cards, John Burke confirmed.

'But Bruce was spectacular. You want four aces? You want a straight flush? Anything you want, you got it. Even following Mr Dooley's advice about always cutting the cards doesn't help in those circumstances.

'Cheats, as Sydney said, have the "Big Edge".'

POSTSCRIPT: GUYS AND DOLLS

Nobody's perfect.

JOE E. BROWN, THE LAST LINE OF *SOME LIKE IT HOT*, 1959

Lord Lucan has had a bad press. In contrast to what has
become the established view, many people liked him and
enjoyed his company. It was only later, when his marriage was
in tatters and he lost custody of his children, that drink and
his sorrows made him difficult and obsessive. But friends,
especially the Clermont set, he had. One of the most loyal
was Ian Maxwell-Scott. Lucan had become a house player
for Aspinall – a titled shill at the Clermont Club, a man
of unquestioned integrity. Just the sort of player Aspinall
required.

Lucan may not have been the most intelligent of men, but
he was not a complete fool. He knew cards: he'd played bridge
at the Hamilton Club with Stephen Raphael, and was an
experienced gambler. He had played at the Clermont almost
constantly from the opening night. Instinctively, he knew
something was wrong with the gambling at the Clermont: the
constant run of coups, the big winners. It's not clear whether
he confronted Aspinall about it, but Ian Maxwell-Scott told
John Burke, with whom he remained close friends all his life,
that Lucan had approached him. Maxwell-Scott said Lucan
was distressed by the cheating and 'had a lot of problems
with it'.

John Burke said: 'In the 1950s, John Bingham had a dead-end job in banking, but he loved gambling. He lost money, but he became one of the Clermont's house players in the late 1960s.

'What helped send him off his head was the ongoing despair when he found out about the mechanics, the bent croupier, the cheating scheme. Bingham was an honourable man – cheating at cards! My God, to him, it was despicable. When he discovered what was going on he was terribly troubled by it. It only messed up his confused mind even more.

The madness took over totally on 7 November 1974, when Sandra Rivett, the nanny to Lucan's three children, was killed.

Lucan had quietly entered the five-storey mews house, opening the door to 46 Lower Belgrave Street with his latchkey. His wife Veronica and his children were upstairs, watching *The Six Million Dollar Man* on, television. After the programme Lucan knew his wife would send the children off to bed and then go to the kitchen in the basement to make tea. On the stairway to the basement, he took the light bulb out of the socket. Then he went down the stairs to the darkness of the kitchen and waited.

True to form, after the TV show, 'Lady Lucan' walked down the stairs, having tried but failed to turn the light on. At the bottom of the stairs, her estranged husband hit her over the head with a ten-inch-long piece of pipe. She fell to her knees and was bashed on the head again and again. Lucan had planned the murder, his alibi and the disposal of Lady Lucan's body. But then he heard her voice from the top of the stairs, saying, 'Sandra, Sandra.'

Nanny Sandra Rivett, like her employer just five feet two inches tall, had changed her night off so that she could see a boyfriend later in the week. Fate had dealt Lucan a joker, a case of mistaken identity. He had killed the wrong woman.

Shocked, enraged, bewildered, he went up the stairs at a pace and began to attack his real target: his wife. He hit her with the pipe, tried to strangle her and stuck gloved fingers into her throat and eyes. Lady Lucan fought back, grabbed him between the legs and squeezed hard. She then managed to quieten Lucan and, moments later, when he was distracted by the appearance of his daughter Lady Frances, she escaped and ran down Lower Belgrave Street to raise the alarm at a pub called the Plumber's Arms. From there the Lucan saga unfolded.

Mark Sykes told me: 'I can well imagine him murdering the wrong woman by mistake; it was just the sort of thing he would do.'

It now seems that the Lucan mystery may never be solved. The 3rd Earl of Lucan, John Bingham's great-great-grandfather, directed and was disgraced by the disastrous charge of the Light Brigade, which resulted in massacre in the Valley of Death at Balaclava, during the Crimean War. Infamy and many questions still surround the 7th Earl of Lucan.

What we can clear up here is that Lucan did borrow £10,000 before the killing. It was not from Jimmy Goldsmith or Aspinall, or any of their so-called 'set'. It was from a group of moneylenders in Mount Street, near the formerly intimidating premises of the Mount Street Bridge Club. When Lucan vanished after the murder of Sandra Rivett, the guarantor of the loan, John Burke's good friend Richard Parkes, had to pay over the £10,000. John Burke recalls:

'He did so without a quibble. Richard was such a man that he never said a public word about it. He knew the pressures that were on Lucan. He thought he could use the money to pay debts and sort himself out.'

In 2005 it was suggested in print that a certain 'Mr X', a 'secret' man with a facility for international money dealings, especially in Switzerland, had arranged for Lucan to escape from Britain and then, some time later, had him killed. The theory was built around an interview with the late Susan Maxwell-Scott. Her daughter Cathy said in 2006: 'My mother did talk to the writer, but she was very ill. I don't think anything that was suggested was true, and I've grown up with the whole Lucan business.'

An underworld figure who was said to have facilitated the murder of Lucan said in January 2007: 'I never met Lucan, which means I never murdered Lucan.'

Yet Susan Maxwell-Scott was the last person to see Lucan alive. Her husband was staying at the Clermont when Lucan, only a few hours after the killing of Sandra Rivett, appeared at Grants Hill House in Uckfield. He was distraught. He wrote some letters. He babbled. He left.

Not too long afterwards, Susan Maxwell-Scott, a devout Catholic who took such things more than seriously, had a Mass said for Lucan. John Burke said: 'As far as she and Ian were concerned, Lucan was dead then. Mass was not a trivial thing for them, not some token gesture. They knew he had gone. They would never have had a Mass otherwise.

'Did he kill himself? Was he killed? I don't know how he died, but I believe he did. Susie wouldn't have done that unless she knew for certain he was dead. Ian always said Lucan was dead.

'Lucan was a friend of mine. He was also an unlucky gambler. In every sense.'

Aspinall played on the Lucan mystery from the beginning. On 8 November 1974, the day after Sandra Rivett's murder, Aspinall's friends (but not, expensively for *Private Eye*, Jimmy Goldsmith) gathered for lunch. The *Eye*, under the editor of the time, Richard Ingrams, stated that Goldsmith had been present at the lunch. Goldsmith took it as an accusation that the lunch meeting was to talk about helping Lucan escape, and that the magazine was implying he had therefore conspired to obstruct the cause of justice. He went on to issue sixty-three writs against the satirical magazine, which launched the 'Goldenballs' fund to defend itself against Goldsmith's legal onslaught.

The day after Aspinall's lunch, newspapers suggested the implausible, the impossible and the incredible, including the theory that Lucan had begged Aspinall to feed him to his tigers. Aspinall, who went to great lengths to promote a conspiracy theory and to imply that he had been an integral part of it, was interviewed on television and said that if Lucan showed up he would embrace him; this was tribal loyalty, the Zulu rules which he insisted upon from his friends. Aspinall was asked if he was proud to be the friend of a man who had murdered a woman and attempted to kill his wife. Aspinall said: 'If she'd been my wife, I'd have bashed her to death five years before, and so would you.'

The Clermont set had their fun at the expense of the police investigation. Detectives got short shrift when they tried to quiz members at the Clermont and Annabel's. Lady O. was reported to have ended a telephone conversation with the police: 'Got to go and give Lucky his food. He's down under the tiger cage.'

Another story – but remember Aspinall's imagination – goes that when the police arrived at Howletts' they were told by the butler: 'I'm sorry, Mr Aspinall is having dinner.'

'But we're the police.'

'I'm terribly sorry. I've been told not to disturb Mr Aspinall.'

'We have to see him now.'

Eventually, they were led into the dining room. Seated at the table were John Aspinall, his wife, Lady O., and a gorilla.

There were many strange events and stories following the

murder of Sandra Rivett. One involved the American who had
introduced Signor Biondi to Aspinall. He knew Lucan and
played backgammon with him. The day before the murder,
Lucan had sent the man a cheque to pay a backgammon debt.
When a writer expressed surprise at such a detail, he was told:
'Those gamblers. Their sense of integrity is devoted more to
each other than even to their families, particularly the ones
who are addicted.'

Loyalty was essential. Those like Dominick Elwes, who
supposedly broke the code, were ostracized. Elwes, the court
jester of the crowd, made the mistake of selling a painting
he'd done of the 'Clermont set' to the *Sunday Times* colour
magazine. It was published in the inside pages to illustrate a
superb investigative article by James (*White Mischief*) Fox.
The picture depicted Lord Lucan, John Aspinall, James Goldsmith, Charles Benson, Stephen Raphael, the Earl of Suffolk,
Peter West, and Nicholas Soames, the grandson of Winston
Churchill.

On the cover was a photograph taken twenty months
earlier in Mexico of Lucan, and, next to him, Lady Annabel,
the lover of James Goldsmith and mother of his two children.
Goldsmith lost the plot. He went crazy with rage. Elwes was
'out' of the crowd. Mark Sykes told me what happened next:

'When he found himself cut off from the company that
he adored, my poor, sad cousin committed suicide. He was
my fourth cousin. He was a depressive, but one of the reasons
why he killed himself was that he had been thrown out of
the Clermont lot and told to "piss off" by Goldsmith and the
others. Basically, they gave him the boot. They thought he
had given a story or something to the *Sunday Times* and been
paid a lot of money. They were all in it, and they thought it
was disgraceful.

'They didn't think that the poor bugger had to get a few
quid together. I saw him on the evening he topped himself.

At his funeral, Aspinall had the nerve to make a sententious speech. Dominick and I shared a little squat, rugby-playing Welsh cousin called Tremayne Rodd who is now Lord Rodd. He went up and gave Aspinall the most useful punch in the face you have ever seen in your life. Aspinall sat down in the road. He did. Aspinall had the grace to say: "None of my gorillas have ever done that to me!" It was brilliant.'

After he died, it was revealed that Dominick Elwes, although short of money, did not sell the photographs to the *Sunday Times*. It was Lady Lucan who made that arrangement.

Another suicide victim was the brewery heir Mark Watney. In the early days of the Clermont, he had an affair with Jane Aspinall. 'The Spirit of Park Lane' had been encouraged by Aspinall to flirt with his customers, but it seems she did more than flirt. Aspinall did not openly berate her about the affairs, one said to have been with an animal-keeper at Howletts, another with a well-known aristocrat.

Jane and John Aspinall were estranged by 1964 and divorced in 1966. In their bitter divorce Aspinall retained custody of the children, and Jane Aspinall was all but banned from contact with them.

Aspinall did not forget what he saw as her betrayal. Some years later, Mark Watney bounced a cheque for £1,000 with the Clermont. Aspinall had him 'posted', disgraced, as his bad debt had been made public. In reality, it was a trifling sum to Aspinall, and the cheque would have been honoured by the Watney family, if not, later, by Mark Watney himself.

Watney, who had other personal problems, found it all too much. He killed himself, shooting himself in the head, at the Star in Belgravia. The apocryphal story says that Watney had a gentleman's manners, and pulled a plastic bag over his head before pulling the trigger.

For Paddy Kennedy it meant there was less mopping up.

After Watney's death, the publican checked his credit book and saw that Watney owed £200. 'What the hell,' he told his customers, 'we might as well wipe that out and let him go with a clean slate.' He opened a bottle of the house champagne, Krug, and toasted the beer heir's departure in what he always called a 'glass of Krugelberry wine'.

After the divorce, Jane Aspinall pawned some jewellery at Sutton's in Victoria. It was found to be stolen, and the police began inquiries. They could not locate her, but it was easy to find John Aspinall. When quizzed he quickly replied: 'Lord Timothy Willoughby gave my wife a present of some jewellery.'

Of course, Tim Willoughby, a man of good name who had guaranteed Aspinall's lease on the Clermont, was dead. In that, he served John Aspinall's purpose. It was a cynical ploy: Tim Willoughby was not a dealer in stolen goods, nor did he have an affair with Jane Aspinall, which was the implication of Aspinall's remark to the police.

Until the upset of the Salle Privée, Ray Ryan had also served Aspinall's purpose. He had been repaid with interest by John Aspinall, and Ryan added the funds to the already considerable investment he had in the Mount Kenya Safari Club – the 1,256-acre game ranch he created with the Hollywood actor William Holden, a little more than one hundred miles from Nairobi.

John Burke met up again with Ray Ryan in 1967. 'I assumed that Ryan would very much give me the cold shoulder. On the contrary, he was extremely friendly. He'd made his own inquiries about what had happened at the Clermont, and he knew that it wasn't my idea. I wasn't even consulted about it, and I had nothing whatsoever to do with Signor Biondi. Ryan even invited me and Liliana and our daughter Daniela to be his guests in Kenya in the first week of of 1968. It was a wonderful holiday. Magnificent chalet.

I remember going to the races in Nairobi, and we saw the Kenya Derby.'

He never saw Ray Ryan again. On 18 October 1977, Ryan went to a health club in his home town of Watertown, Wisconsin, as he often did. When he finished his workout, the 73-year-old Ryan walked outside to his new Lincoln Mark V coupé.

A bomb was linked to the ignition of the car. Ryan turned the key and the car exploded. The blast killed him instantly. It took two days to locate and collect all of the pieces of his body and the car – one piece was found 377 feet from the scene.

In 2007, three decades after the killing, the murder has still not been solved. Clearly Ryan upset the wrong person or people at the wrong time.

The Mafia have often been mentioned in connection both with Ryan's death, and with gambling in London. Ryan had been subjected to a US Government Internal Revenue Service (IRS) investigation before his death. There was a suggestion that the Mob bosses believed he might have said too much.

In the mid 1960s they were taking an interest in Billy Hill's gambling territory. By then the Clermont had established itself as the Beautiful People's gambling mecca. The Mafia wanted their own establishments, and that's when Bobby McKew again met some men with vowels at the end of their names. At the time he had an interest in a couple of London clubs, including one of the first discotheques:

'I met them with Billy because they couldn't really do anything in London without his cooperation. They wanted someone to run their club, the Colony. I was talking to Billy and I said that the ideal person would be Paul Adam. He'd be a marvellous "front" because he was Princess Margaret's favourite bandleader, played in the Milroy and was the housewife's choice. He was tall, handsome, a very good-looking man.

'The Americans, two men who never gave their names – dark suits, white shirts, very smart-looking men, with beady eyes – were staying in a hotel off Conduit Street and came over to see us. The oldest had close-set eyes. He looked at you and he could freeze you just by doing that.

'I asked them: "Drink?"

'They both growled: "Club orange."

'Paul was there and had had a few and he was pissed, and he kept pulling up a girl's skirt. The Yanks were annoyed, and the next day when we met they said: "He drinks. He's not for us."

'Which was when Billy told them: "You need an Englishman. You've got to realize the Mafia here is the police. If you haven't got an Englishman who can deal with them, it won't work."

'The Mafia guys were from the Midwest, tough guys, and didn't quite believe all this, and they said: "We'll put our guy in, there's no question about that."

'Bill said: "They won't reign long there."

'He was right. They put in George Raft. Raft lasted about six months, if that, at the Colony. They had an interest in a few other places, including the Mount Street Bridge Club, the one where Jack Buggy was carpeted. Raft was provided with a chauffeured Rolls-Royce and a Mayfair penthouse for his time at the Colony.'

In 1978 I spoke several times with George Raft, who, trying to live up to the part, wore a corset under his dinner jacket at the Colony. His last big movie had been, yet again, playing a gangster in *Some Like It Hot*, Billy Wilder's superb 1959 confection with Marilyn Monroe, Jack Lemmon and Tony Curtis. Now aged 83, Raft was once again in the gambling business.

Every morning at 10 a.m. he turned up at the offices of the Riviera Hotel-Casino on Wilshire Boulevard in Beverly Hills. His job was to promote the casino and help lure gamblers to Las Vegas. It was all rather sad. He'd stare out from beneath his silver toupee and wave to passers-by who peered in the windows at him. He was the $500-a-week 'ambassador of goodwill', a role like the hosting work he performed at the Colony Club.

He'd never talked in detail about the Colony Club, the Kray twins, or his lifetime ban from Britain (then Home Secretary Roy Jenkins had banned him for life in 1967). Along with eight other Americans – men with those vowels at the end of their names – he was considered to be someone 'whose continued presence in the United Kingdom would not be conducive to the public good'.

'What did I do?' he asked me. 'I'm still very hurt, very bitter. What was my crime? I'm not a member of the Mob, never was. Rocky Marciano had organized the whole thing. He picked me up at my hotel in London one Sunday afternoon and said we were going to meet some poor kids in the East End of London. So, I met the Kray twins. I had my picture taken with them, but I didn't know who they were. No, no, they didn't look like poor kids. No, sure they didn't.

'I admit I was wrong, but I couldn't get any work after the London business. I liked to gamble, I once had twenty racehorses and I still go to the races, to Hollywood Park and Santa Anita. I lost a fortune. But it was that club in London that finished me off. They just wouldn't let me do that job. I'd hardly got to London and they kicked me out.'

Bobby McKew simply nods at the story: 'We never fell out with the Mafia over the Colony. In fact, they paid more attention to us over other matters. They understood we knew what we were talking about. We had even more clout.

'The next ones who did come in were the Playboy Club, Hugh Hefner, who had Victor Lownes running it. I went up there once or twice and in the lounge there were half a dozen people, all drinking, and they were all policemen. Plain clothes.

'They were American, which just shows you that you could get around it. I don't know how they managed it, but they did it anyway. That was the late 1960s, and they were more relaxed about the gambling.'

And there were more clubs. Mark Sykes and Eric Steiner ran the Pair of Shoes at four different London locations. It was a moneymaker, said Mark Sykes. 'Eric organized what he called "junkets" for high rollers from Las Vegas, who were flown over to London and stayed for a week at the Dorchester, all expenses paid. The American gangsters in Las Vegas sent over planeloads of people who would gamble at the Pair of Shoes.

'It was staggering business. It was wonderful. All these people would come over and they took over our casino. These people would open with credit of 250,000 bucks each, and the gangster guy at the other end would guarantee the money. We were paid everything in two weeks. No money changed hands. All markers went into the accounts and within two weeks we had the money. Tremendously efficient, the Americans.'

In the late 1960s, Eric Steiner offered to sell the Pair of Shoes for next to nothing to John Burke, but he turned it down. By 1977, John Burke and Liliana had divorced and he had married again, to Gigi, a Swedish girl: 'I married in a Catholic church on St Stephen's Green in Dublin and in a Lutheran church in Stockholm. Not bad for an agnostic.'

They separated in the mid 1980s and divorced in 1989. With Gigi he had three children, James, Janina and Richard.

In 2007 he had retired to a remote part of Ireland with his partner Caroline Gray.

Nancy Gillespie, who was divorced from Prince George Sapieha in 1960, continued to amuse smart dinner parties with her stories. Now married to Michael Lambton – an early and besotted devotee of Christine Keeler – she was living in London, where we talked many times in 2006. She thought her husband might be in Austria and added, with a wink: 'With a girl, you know. He always liked the girls.'

Her memories of the past are as sharp as ever. 'When I was at the *Express* I was walking into the front hall one day when Beaverbrook walked up to reception. He saw me, but didn't say anything. I went to the editor John Junor's office and said to him: "Do you know where Lord Beaverbrook is?"'

'He said: "Yes, he's in Florida or Jamaica."'

'I said: "No, he's not, he's in the front hall."'

'He said: "Don't be so ridiculous."'

'I protested. I told him what Beaverbrook was wearing. He made sure everybody was at their desk when Beaverbrook did arrive. Beaverbrook gave me a big wink. He hadn't missed a trick. I was a very attractive girl in my youth.

'There were some characters around. I knew Jimmy Goldsmith very well. I once lent him £3. It was at a party in Oxford. He said: "Nancy. Have you got any money on you?"'

'I said: "Who, me? Not much."'

'He only wanted £3 for a taxi to get him back to the Randolph. He was always very grateful. Naturally, I got it back. He, too, was ruthless, but he wasn't like Aspinall.

'I met Ava Gardner, and she became a great friend. My husband Michael Lambton had a flat in Onslow Gardens, and Ava had a flat beneath. That's how I met her. She got ill, and then sicker and sicker. She rang me up in the winter of

1989 and asked if I could come around; she said that she felt
so ill she wanted to go back home to America, and she said:
"You'd better ring Frank and ask him if he can fetch me."

'I said: "Frank?"

'She said: "Frank Sinatra."

'She gave me his number and when I rang up I said: "I'm
ringing for Ava Gardner, she's in a bad way and she would
really like to speak to Mr Sinatra."

'The voice said: "Is she drunk?"

'I said: "No. She's not drunk, she's ill."

'Sinatra said, "I'll send for her straight away."

'He sent a plane for her. It was not many months before
she died, back in London. I think he always loved her dearly.
She was the love of his life.

'Lots of people have gone. John Burke, who was a good
friend of Peter West, and I went to Peter's funeral. Aspinall
was there. He didn't want to be there, but Jimmy Goldsmith
was paying for it all. Peter West adored Jimmy. At the
graveside, Jimmy said: "What do I do now?"

'I said: "Take a handful of earth and throw it on the
coffin."

'He said: "Are you sure?"

'I said: "Yes, I'm sure."

'Aspinall marched up to me: "What did you tell Jimmy to
do?"

'I said nothing; I was very rude to him. And he didn't like
me either.'

John Burke recalls the 1996 funeral: 'Jimmy Goldsmith
and Peter were always close friends; in their last years they
became inseparable. So Westie was able to enjoy the good
things of life, which he appreciated, while Jimmy had an
intelligent, amusing companion who was also a loyal friend.
Jimmy died only a year later.'

Sir James Goldsmith – 'Sir Jams' to *Private Eye*, which

he had sued over the Lucan affair – was 64 when he died on 20 July 1997. He left a fortune. Estimates put it at £1.8 billion, but that was just a guess. As it had to be when Billy Hill died at his Moscow Road flat on New Year's Eve 1983. Frankie Fraser said, walking down Browning Street in 2006, that he knew Hill was 'a goner'. Fraser had been in prison ('when wasn't I?') when Hill had visited him: 'He said the docs had told him he'd die if he didn't give up smoking, in four years, probably two, maybe three. They didn't know for sure, but he was taking a ball of chalk. I told him he should just quit the fags.

'He said: "Frank, I can't do it. I can't do it."

'See, such a tough guy, but he couldn't quit smoking. Says something.'

Ian Maxwell-Scott died from a heart attack in November 1993, and his wife Susan Maxwell-Scott, the last person known to have seen 'Lucky' Lucan, died in September 2004.

In 2007 Michael 'Dandy Kim' Caborn-Waterfield was working on his memoirs. He has quite a story to tell. He met the Kray Twins in Tangier, ran guns to Cuba, upset Joan Collins with a naughty story about her one-time husband Anthony Newley and launched the Miss Topless World beauty contest with Lord Patrick Lichfield as photographer and Earl Alexander as musical director.

He has seen everything and everyone: he evaded a naked Pamela Digby Churchill Hayward Harriman, 'a true redhead, she was aflame, mop, collar and cuffs'. He loved and managed Diana Dors from her teenaged starlet days to her tragic early death from cancer in May 1984. He was the last person to talk to Dors' distraught husband Alan Lake, vainly trying to stop him killing himself. On the way he helped Greg Dyke rescue then struggling TV-am, befriended political Mr Fixit, Lord Goodman, founded the Ann Summers chain of High Street sex shops, wrote a bestselling sex manual, and made movies with Stewart Granger, Anthony Newley and Petula Clark. He only married once, to the beautiful *Vogue* model Penny Brahms by whom he had his daughter, Campbell.

Bobby McKew, like Oscar Wilde, could resist everything but temptation. And boredom.

He was kicking his heels, working the gambling clubs and other schemes with Billy Hill in the 1960s, when towards the end of the decade he linked up with Richard Leigh, the heir to a baronetcy. Neither of them was interested in titles – just money: Swiss francs, and lots of them.

A clever technician, Bobby McKew recruited a team of expert printers and a camera operator. For three weeks they worked to originate the plates to forge Swiss franc notes, each of which carried a face value of around £10. He said: 'They wanted to know how many to print and I thought we might as well go for one million. Should have said ten. Had I been left alone, I would have solved Britain's balance of payments problem.'

And he might have. After the scheme was discovered, Swiss bankers called the forgeries the finest they had ever seen. They were so good that the Swiss government had to change its note-printing methods. It all ended in tears, and jail, because the gang did not have a distribution system as good as the forged notes. And somebody talked, just as the next few millions were being printed.

Interpol worked with Scotland Yard: forgeries were found in Munich; £50,000 worth were used to buy Swiss watches; and thousands more passed to a man, identified in court as 'Syd', to pay off 'Dogs of War' mercenaries in Biafra. The distribution was haphazard and traceable, and led to the Old Bailey in 1970.

Bobby McKew was fined £10,000 and jailed for five years. He served three at Albany on the Isle of Wight. 'I just had to get on with it. There's a great class system inside. If you are "in", you don't get any aggravation from the screws or the other inmates. Most people don't want trouble, especially if you're in there for a long stretch.

'In jail in France, they didn't know what to do with me. For a long time I was the only Englishman in the jail. They treated me fairly. In Albany, which is a much tougher nick than Parkhurst, we sat apart from the petty thieves and the burglars. I'd eat with Charlie Kray and one of the Train Robbers; I can't even recall which one now: there were a lot of them inside at one time or another. There was an upper echelon, and we were left alone.'

While he was in Albany, it became clear that his mother Iris was dying in South Africa, where she had moved to be close to his sisters Joy and Paddy and her grandchildren. He asked to see the governor and requested compassionate parole to visit his mother. The governor looked at his record, told him it read 'like the Debrett's of crime', and denied the request.

Also during his prison term his marriage of fourteen years ended, although in 2007, thirty-five years later, he remains close and friendly with his former wife.

After Albany, he moved to another island, the sunnier one of Ibiza. He did some 'transport work', for which read smuggling, there, but had no intention of going behind bars again: 'I'd much rather be outside prison sweeping the roads than inside with a million waiting for me. Anyone who does something knowing it will get them into prison is an idiot. It's a ridiculous place, a total waste of time.'

He wrote the novel *Death List*, which reads chillingly like reality. He was encouraged to do so by the actor Stanley Baker, to whom the book is dedicated. Baker planned to turn it into a film, but died from cancer before this could happen. His long-time friend Richard Harris's production company took up the option.

Bobby McKew, Harris and his brother Dermot Harris were discussing the project in New York in the mid 1970s when they were invited to dinner with Frank Sinatra. When they sat down to eat it was at Umberto's Clam House in New York's Little Italy, with Sinatra and Mafia boss Joe Pagano. 'They made a point of putting me in this corner seat,' said Bobby McKew. The seat was the one where, on 7 April 1972, Joey 'Crazy Joe' Gallo was gunned down in a Mob hit. 'Sinatra thought it was a huge joke.'

After another meeting in Los Angeles with executives from MGM, Bobby McKew went on to an awards dinner. When the studio bosses realized who he was, he got all but a standing ovation. 'They all hated Jack Warner and wanted to applaud anyone who had ripped him off.'

For all sorts of reasons – Hollywood ones – *Death List* went off the boil, only to be heated up again in 2006 when a studio in Los Angeles optioned it for a six-figure sum. 'It would be nice to see it get made, for Stanley and Richard, for they encouraged me.'

In 2007, he remains close to people from his past, including Charles Richardson. Together with Richard Harris, they were able to help out the House of Windsor and save the Royal Family from embarrassment.

Harris, who had enjoyed romantic encounters with Princess Margaret, learned that actor-gangster John Bindon was offering for sale lurid pictures of the Queen's sister. Bindon had played the villain as something of a violent artful dodger in television series and films. In Chelsea and Caribbean circles he was better known for his ability to hang beer mugs (one to five, depending on who tells the story) from his erect penis.

Bobby McKew is matter-of-fact: 'Bindon was a right prick. A year or so after Richard's affair with Margaret ended, Richard phoned me sounding tense and said he needed to see me urgently. He told me he had just been to see the princess, who'd been told that Bindon was trying to find out how much he could get by selling pictures of them together in compromising situations. All involving Bindon's famous body part.

'She was aware that Richard and Bindon knew each other, and hoped Richard could help. They were embarrassingly explicit photographs taken on Mustique, where she had her Caribbean home, and she was paranoid about them being made public.

'I knew Richard had met Princess Margaret in the 1960s, but I didn't know they had been to bed together until he told me in the early 1980s. They got together again while he was playing King Arthur in *Camelot* in London in 1983. She went backstage to see him and later instructed one of her staff to invite him for tea. They obviously hit it off again, for he was invited back for more tea.

'When the photograph business started Richard could have spoken to Bindon himself, but he'd fallen out with him. He asked me to see Bindon to find out how much he wanted for the pictures. I'd met the guy several times, but I didn't think he would take me seriously. I said: "There's one man Bindon respects and tips his forelock to, and that's Charlie Richardson. Why don't I ask him?"

'I'd introduced Charlie and Richard shortly after Charlie was released from prison in August 1984 [he'd been jailed for twenty-five years in the 1960s 'Torture Trial']. Richard liked anyone with a brain who was worldly and able to converse on several topics, and he found Charlie fascinating, stimulating company.

'"Do you think he'll do it, Bob?" he asked me.

'I said: "I'm sure he will. For two reasons. He loves the Royal Family and hates a bully, which is what Bindon is."

'"Ask him to find out what Bindon wants for the photos and I'll pay it," Richard said. "And tell Charlie I'll pay him for his trouble."

'The next morning I explained everything to Charlie over a cup of tea. He reacted the way I thought he would, and a couple of days later contacted Bindon, who invited him to his flat in Belgravia. Apparently, Bindon was quite lairy, boasting he was going to sell the photos for nothing less than £100,000.

'I don't know everything that was said, but I do know that when he is asked to do something important, Charlie does it. And I know he can be very persuasive. Finally, Bindon agreed to hand over the pictures for £5,000. That evening, Charlie arranged to meet Richard and me and arrived with a sealed brown envelope.

'Richard looked to make sure the pictures were inside, then dropped the package on a fire in the corner of the pub. He gave Charlie an envelope containing £5,000 in notes, and said: "That's for Bindon. Now, what can I pay you for yourself?"

'Charlie shook his head and said: "It's nice of you, Richard, but I don't want anything. You were only doing someone a favour. And I'm happy to have been able to do one for you."'

A close friend of Harris commented: 'When Richard told me about the affair, he said he told Princess Margaret that he was only doing to her what her sister and those before her had been doing to his country for three hundred years. She told him: "But you're doing it much better."'

Bobby McKew said, 'It's weird how Margaret and Richard were linked: she died in February 2002, and then in the October he passed away. Marvellous characters, in their oh-so-different ways.'

John Aspinall had gone before them. At Eaton Place he had given a home to a mini-zoo, before buying Howletts and thirty-eight acres of Kent on which to establish a refuge for hundreds of animals; he opened the collection to the public in 1975. Later he added the nearby estate of Port Lympne and its 275 acres. Both zoos are unorthodox in approach, encouraging close personal relationships between staff and animals, and today are run as a charity by the John Aspinall Foundation.

John Aspinall carried out pioneering work on the preservation of endangered wild mammals, yet his legacy as a zoologist is controversial thanks to his belief in close bonding with the animals. He frequently appeared in public scarred and bruised after being mauled by one pet or another. Five keepers were killed and at least one seriously injured by Aspinall's animals, while a young boy lost an arm to a chimpanzee. Yet John Aspinall, the Zulu warrior, was proud that his zoos had achieved eight elephant births, fourteen black rhinos, seventy-five gorillas, twenty-five leopards and some 400 tigers. He claimed to have more black rhinos than Zambia.

His casino career was also colourful. He sold the Clermont for £700,000, but lost his investments in the 1974 stock market crash. This forced him to start all over again by launching, with financial help from Jimmy Goldsmith, Aspinall's Club in Knightsbridge, which became the Aspinall Curzon in Curzon Street. With Goldsmith's sage advice he made an enormous amount of money – £90 million – when he sold it in 1987. In 1992 he opened yet another gaming club, again called Aspinall's, and in 2007 it was run by his family and was regarded by those who know as the smartest and most socially aware casino in London.

He died from cancer on 29 June 2000. After his ten-year marriage to Jane Hastings ended in 1966, he married Belinda 'Min' Musker, a granddaughter of the 2nd Viscount Daventry; when they divorced in 1972, the same year he took his wedding vows again with Lady Sarah Courage.

The affable Claus von Bülow, who was 80 in 2006, was a

great friend to the gamblers. In 1966, he married the former wife of Prince Alfred von Auersperg, who became Martha von Bülow, known as Sunny. Claus von Bülow was charged with trying to kill her with an insulin overdose in late 1980.

In 1982, he stood trial in Newport, Rhode Island, was found guilty and was jailed for thirty years. Two years later the conviction was reversed on appeal. At a second trial in 1985, a jury found him not guilty on all charges. John Burke sent him a telegram which read: 'Well done on a winning suivi.'

Von Bülow's appeal lawyer, the celebrated American lawyer and lecturer Alan Dershowitz, wrote a book which in 1990 became the movie *Reversal of Fortune*, for which Jeremy Irons won an Oscar as Best Actor, starring as the melodically voiced von Bülow.

Families? What did Philip Larkin say?

A grand character, Mark Birley had three children with his wife: Rupert, Robin and India Jane. Tragically, Rupert vanished while swimming off the coast of West Africa in 1986. Many explanations have been offered over more than twenty years: everything from an accident to the theory that he was a spook and was whisked away to Moscow; that one probably had more to do with the fact that he spoke Russian than with a Soviet ship being seen in the ocean near Togo on the morning of his disappearance.

Robin Birley, tall and charming like his father, immaculately dressed and mannered, was also almost lost to his parents. When he was 12, his mother took him to Howletts, John Aspinall's zoo, where he was mauled by a pregnant tiger. His mother thought him dead, but nine hours of surgery saved him; he endured much reconstructive work to his face.

He and his sister revamped Annabel's on its fortieth anniversary in 2002. They were helped by their half-brothers Ben and Zac Goldsmith and their half-sister Jemima Khan, ex-wife of Pakistan cricket star Imran Khan and, later, companion of actor and Annabel's regular Hugh Grant.

Artist India Jane Birley and her brother were involved with the running and overseeing of most of their father's businesses. In 2003, Robin Birley was put in charge of Annabel's, but in September 2006, then aged 48, the son of the man who created Britain's most exclusive nightclub renounced that role. The gossips went to work.

By October that year, it appeared that father and son had been engaged in an almighty row. One reason, according to gossip, was Mark's disapproval of some of the 'celebrities' the club was attracting. The estrangement got even messier in October 2006, when Mark Birley was absent from Robin's wedding to Lucy Helmore, the former wife of singer Bryan Ferry.

It was reported that Robin's half-brothers Zac and Ben Goldsmith had offered to buy Annabel's and reinstate him: Mark Birley, supposedly, did not want the club run by a Goldsmith. If that was true, he got his way as always. In 2007 all his clubs, including Annabel's which he had obsessively presided over for more than four decades, were sold for £102 million to the fashion tycoon Richard Caring who is also the owner of prominent London restaurants, including The Ivy.

With the family row not resolved, on 24 August 2007, almost exactly a year since John Burke and I had lunch with him at Mark's Club, Mark Birley suffered a massive stroke and died. He was seventy-seven. In his obituary for the *Independent* his friend David Wynne-Morgan, the publicist for Annabel's from the opening night wrote, 'He was one of the stiff-upper-lip brigade. He didn't want to show his emotions and he didn't. I was probably his closest friend and he didn't talk about it – but the family feud must have been a stress and a strain. It wasn't nice for him.'

And David Wynne-Morgan revealed that the evening before his friend's death he gave him a present – this book. 'I did see him the night before he died for a drink and he was in good spirits. He was going away to France. I gave him a book, *The Hustlers*, which he featured in. I said here is some holiday reading and sent him on his way with a smile.'

Like Mark Birley, Paddy Kennedy was a stubborn man. In the end he refused the help of friends, and died in a charity nursing home run by publicans. Even there, he was said to be a rascal.

One big rugby game weekend in 1965 after the Profumo affair, John Burke was with a group of politicians in the horseshoe bar of the grand Shelbourne Hotel on St Stephen's Green in Dublin when Paddy Kennedy arrived with Christine Keeler on his arm, and announced: 'I've brought Christine over to reshuffle the Irish Cabinet.'

The Star Tavern is still there at 6 Belgrave Mews West, and they do a fine pint of Fuller's and decent pub food. It's unlikely that the legendary deals of the past go on there any more.

Deals such as Billy Hill's proposal in the upstairs room to fund the Great Train Robbery, using the proceeds of a bullion raid; yet Bruce Reynolds, who did much of the robbery's planning there, rejected the offer. 'It was simple business,' said Bobby McKew. 'Bill wanted the lion's share of the haul, at least 60 per cent. They didn't go for that. They made other arrangements.'

The Great Train Robbery, a £2.3 million heist, went ahead on 8 August 1963, at Bridego Railway Bridge in Buckinghamshire.

Today, the Star doesn't have that Kennedy edge either; no longer a place where people would drop in just to listen to the landlord swearing. Which he did, to great glee, when the fish in his display tank kept vanishing. Kennedy was convinced that someone was stealing the goldfish that he got from a shop in Kensington High Street. He just kept buying more, and didn't spot that one of his fish was getting fatter. Eddie Chapman had slipped a piranha into the tank.

And piranhas, or perhaps sharks, lead us to the Clermont and Annabel's of 2007, for there's been much frenzied feeding there and elsewhere. Especially by the government. New Labour appeared to be turning the UK into one big casino in 2007, with a new Gambling Act which was to come into force in September of that year. It was claimed that the National Health Service would require more money to treat gambling addiction.

Although gambling is not as socially smart as it was in the 1960s, plans were under consideration for the Millennium Dome to become a gambling temple, and it appeared that just about every town would have its own casino. Also, while the American authorities were all but outlawing online betting, Britain's Department for Culture, Media and Sport (DCMS) was lobbying the Treasury towards the end of 2006 to get a better tax deal for online betting and gambling companies.

That summer Richard Caborn, the Minister then responsible for gambling, visited the headquarters of PartyGaming and 888.com in Gibraltar. At the end of October 2006, Tessa Jowell, then Secretary of State for Culture, hosted an international summit for politicians to talk about gambling regulations. She held it at Ascot racecourse. United Nations and European Commission representatives were invited, along with executives from major credit card companies.

Caborn also had meetings with Mark Davies, the managing director of the punters' much-loved Betfair, the online betting operation. The plan was to establish Britain as the 'world leader in online gaming'. This would, argued the government officials involved, protect the punter. Others, like Mike Atherton in his 2006 book *Gambling*, claimed that the Gambling

Act of 2005 would threaten 'an area of life that has been regulated and crime-free' for decades.

John Burke smiled when he read that. 'Crime-free and gambling is, I think, a superb example of an oxymoron.'

The transformation of Britain into Las Vegas, something begun so long ago with the outcome of *Regina* v. *Aspinall, Burke & Osbourne*, was analysed in the *Evening Standard* on 15 January 2007 by the writer and seasoned gambler Matthew Norman. He suggested that this might well be Tony Blair's legacy. He wrote: 'It is the first government policy in memory, across the developed and democratic world, designed to increase human misery.' He believed it would lead to a rise in poverty, opportunistic crime, domestic violence and 'other life-destroying social ills'.

The Macao-factor in the UK, the deregulation of gambling, was estimated by some to point to the industry doubling in size, and the money involved being close to £100 billion by 2008/2009. Certainly at the end of 2006 the London casinos, fast overtaking Monte Carlo as the most popular in Europe – places like Crockfords on Curzon Street and Park Lane's Les Ambassadeurs (sold in 2006 to Indonesian businessman Putera Sampoerna for more than £100 million) – were vastly popular.

The Clermont was less so, but the signs were that business was improving – which was good news for Quek Leng Chan, a Malaysian lawyer and a billionaire, who in August 2006 bought the club for somewhere around £30 million from Grosvenor Casinos. He clearly likes a gamble. His game is not chemmy but *punto banco*, a variant of chemmy in which everyone can participate in the betting.

He won out over bids from more familiar Clermont surnames. Zac and Ben Goldsmith, the sons of Jimmy Goldsmith from his marriage to Lady Annabel, and their friend and partner Ben Elliot, failed in their attempt. As did

Damian Aspinall, the son of John Aspinall and Jane Hastings. Damian Aspinall has a daughter, Freya, with the MTV and *Big Breakfast* television presenter Donna Air, and runs his father's estate Howletts. The couple met at a dinner with Tara Palmer-Tomkinson in 2001, when she was 21 and he twenty years older. He has two daughters, Tansy, 17 in 2007, and Clary, 14 in 2007, from his marriage to Louise Sebag-Montefiore.

John Aspinall's son was reported to be worth around £42 million in January 2007. As well as the expansive Kent estate, he has a enviable town house in London. He made his takeover bid for the club his father founded with another famous son, Jamie Packer, whose late father was the great gambler and Australian media baron Kerry Packer. Like his own father, Damian Aspinall is a determined man. With Jamie Packer he has opened a casino called 'Aspers' in Newcastle, to great success. The partners plan to launch a chain of 'Aspers' casinos across the UK.

'Aspers' is still gambling.

Bibliography

Allsop, Kenneth. *The Angry Decade*. John Goodchild Publishers, 1984, originally, 1958.

Atherton, Mike. *Gambling, A Story of Triumph & Disaster*. Hodder and Stoughton, 2006.

Blond, Anthony. *Jew Made in England*. Timewell Press, 2004.

Evans, Sir Harold. *Downing Street Diary: The Macmillan Years, 1957 to 1963*. Hodder and Stoughton, 1981.

Fabian, Robert. *Fabian of the Yard*. The Naldrett Press Ltd, 1950.

— *London After Dark*. The Naldrett Press, 1954.

Fallon, Ivan. *Billionaire: The Life and Times of Sir James Goldsmith*. Hutchinson, 1991.

Fleming, Ian. *Casino Royale*. Jonathan Cape, 1953.

Foreman, Freddie, with Lisners, John. *Respect, Autobiography of Feddie Foreman*. Century Books, 1996.

Fraser-Cavassoni, Natasha. *Sam Spiegel, The Biography of a Hollywood Legend*. Little, Brown, 2003.

Goldsmith, Lady Annabel. *Annabel: An Unconventional Life*. Weidenfeld and Nicolson, 2004.

Haggard, H. Rider. *Nada the Lily, A Tale of the Zulus*. Longman, 1892; Wildside Press, 2001.

Henessy, Peter. *Having it so Good, Britain in the Fifties*. Penguin/ Allen Lane, 2006.

Hill, Billy. *Boss of Britain's Underworld*. The Naldrett Press, 1955.

Keeler, Christine, with Thompson, Douglas. *The Truth at Last*. Sidgwick & Jackson, 2001.

Masters, Brian. *The Passion of John Aspinall*. Jonathan Cape, 1988.

Morton, James and Parker, Gerry. *Gangland Bosses, The Lives of Jack Spot and Billy Hill*. Time Warner Books, 2004.

Owen, Frank. *The Eddie Chapman Story.* Allan Wingate Ltd, 1953.

Read, Leonard, with Morton, James. *Nipper Read: The Man Who Nicked the Krays.* Futura Paperbacks, 1992.

Reynolds, Bruce. *The Autobiography of a Thief.* Bantam Press, 1995.

Richardson, Charlie, with Long, Bob. *My Manor.* Sidgwick & Jackson, 1991.

Sandbrook, Dominic. *Never had it so Good: A History of Britain from Suez to the Beatles.* Little, Brown, 2005.

Thomas, Donald. *Villains' Paradise, Britain's Underworld from the Spivs to the Krays.* John Murray, 2005.

Index

Visit **www.panmacmillan.com** to read more about all our books and to buy them. You will also find features, author interviews and news of any author events, and you can sign up for e-newsletters so that you're always first to hear about our new releases.

Also by Marianne Kavanagh

For Once in My Life
Don't Get Me Wrong
Should You Ask Me

Marianne Kavanagh

Disturbance

HODDER

First published in Great Britain in 2019 by Hodder & Stoughton
An Hachette UK company

This paperback edition first published in 2019

1

A CIP catalogue record for this title is
available from the British Library

Paperback ISBN 978 1 473 63940 9
eBook ISBN 978 1 473 63939 3

Typeset in Plantin by Palimpsest Book Production Limited,
Falkirk Stirlingshire

Printed and bound in Great Britain by Clays Ltd, Elcograf S.p.A.

Hodder & Stoughton policy is to use papers that are natural,
renewable and recyclable products and made from wood grown
in sustainable forests. The logging and manufacturing processes
are expected to conform to the environmental regulations
of the country of origin.

Hodder & Stoughton Ltd
Carmelite House
50 Victoria Embankment
London EC4Y 0DZ

www.hodder.co.uk

For Matt

The moment of crisis arrived with no fanfare, no warning, on an ordinary working day at the end of November. It was very cold. Even at ten in the morning, the slate roof of the extension outside her office was still sparkling with frost, a shimmer of silver in the clear light.

She could hear the fear in his voice. 'You'll have to come and get me. I can't move.'

At work, Mike had leaned down to retrieve a file from the bottom drawer of his desk and a kind of electric shock, like a cattle prod in his lower back, had made him cry out.

After she'd ended the call, Sara sat quite still, letting the implications sink in. She'd promised to leave straight away – to go to his office, collect him, and take him to see the GP – but she was frozen to the chair. She must have known, even then, that picking up the car keys and walking out of her safe and predictable job was going to change everything. If she'd stayed put, working three days a week in the wills and probate department, she would have had more objectivity. She might have been able to cope.

Eventually, Sara dragged herself to her feet and went to make her excuses. When she told Jane, the office manager, that she had to go because there had been an accident, Jane put on her sympathetic face, thinking that Sara was talking about a car crash. But then Sara explained about Mike's back,

and having to take him to the doctor, and Jane raised her eyebrows and said, 'Couldn't he get a taxi?' Sara, silenced by the stupidity of the suggestion, just stared. After an awkward pause, Jane swallowed and dropped her eyes to her keyboard, which Sara took to mean that she'd won the argument and had permission to leave.

It was a frustrating, thirty-minute drive through slow traffic. Sara's car – a black second-hand Polo with a reluctant gear stick – shook with elderly nerves each time it stopped at traffic lights.

When she got to the office, Mike was lying on his back on the floor, surrounded by his employees. They stood at a respectful distance, no one daring to acknowledge her arrival, hushed and downcast like mourners round a grave. Mike was very still. She could see from the greyness of his skin that this was much worse than the grumbling pain of the past few months.

He opened his eyes. 'You took your time.'

Four of them helped him to the car. It was clear that every movement hurt, but he didn't say a word, the muscles in his jaw rigid.

As she started the engine, she said, 'Maybe we should . . .?'

He said, 'Don't start. For God's sake, don't start.'

Fear fluttered in her stomach.

In the weeks that followed, Mike worked from home, lying in a state of desperate immobility on one of the big white sofas in the formal living room. Coffee stains appeared on the velvet cushions and office detritus on the silk rug from Marrakech. Crazed by pain, he rumbled with suppressed rage, bellowing out orders, hurling out blame. Sara scurried about like an overworked waitress, trying to cater for his every need but

becoming so muddled and forgetful because of all the shouting that she ended up delivering entirely the wrong things – a charger when he wanted his reading glasses, extra strong mints when he needed his painkillers – so that Mike boiled over with frustration and roared, 'Are you doing this on purpose?'

Her mistakes multiplied. Every time, without fail, she rushed out to fetch his prescription from the chemist at exactly the moment he needed her most. Once, she came back to find him apoplectic because a motorcycle courier had shouted through the letter box that he couldn't leave the documents without a signature and Mike had been in too much pain to hobble to the door.

'You knew he was coming.'

Sara trembled. 'I had no idea.'

'They sent you an email.'

'If they did, I didn't see it.'

His outburst was savage. 'For God's sake, Sara! Fucking concentrate on what you're doing!'

The house quivered with tension. She flinched each time he yelled. She cried when he threw a whisky glass that narrowly missed her head. She was bawled out so often for misunderstanding what he needed that she ended up doubting her ability to make a cup of tea.

The worst of it was trying to get Mike to eat. Normally a man of large appetites, he lost interest in food completely. This worried her. As she kept telling him, he shouldn't be taking painkillers on an empty stomach. One cold winter morning, she spent hours making the kind of chilli-laced soup he would normally have devoured with gusto and carried it through to the living room on a tray, the white bowl nestling on a jaunty red-checked napkin.

Mike looked up from the sofa. 'What's that?'

'Lunch.'

'Take it away.'

She stood there holding it, uncertain what to do. 'Mike—'

'I don't want it.'

'But shouldn't you—'

His flailing arm, dismissing her, caught the edge of the tray. It flipped up, tipping the contents of the bowl on to Sara's front. The soup was hot. She cried out.

He said, 'Just go away and leave me alone.'

By Christmas, the atmosphere was so sharp and jagged you could have cut yourself. Edward shut himself in his room, protected by headphones that blocked out everything but electronica.

James, her elder son, was disgusted. 'Is this what it's going to be like from now on?'

She said, 'He's worried about the business. He doesn't know if they can manage without him.'

James gave her a look that was almost pitying. At eighteen, he forgave his father nothing. 'That doesn't mean he can take it out on us.'

It took its toll in the end. You can only be in crisis mode for so long. When Mike, for the third time that week, woke her at three in the morning demanding painkillers, Sara found herself weeping in the bathroom with the shower full on so that he couldn't hear.

Of course she knew that none of this was Mike's fault.

But it wasn't her fault either, which Mike didn't seem to understand.

*

Early in the New Year, just after the boys had gone back to school, the doorbell rang. For a moment, Sara was tempted to ignore it. Mike was now able to climb the stairs, swearing at the walls, and was upstairs in his study. The moment of calm was precious.

She opened the door to a young woman about the same age as James, with large brown eyes and clear skin, pink from the cold. Everything about her seemed on the brink of unravelling – dark shiny hair falling from a haphazard bun, stray threads trailing from a hem. When she spoke, the warmth of her breath puffed the air into steam. 'Hello. My name's Katie. I live just round the corner, and I wondered if . . .'

Sara frowned, trying not to look too welcoming.

'. . . if you'd like someone to walk your dog.'

For a moment Sara was confused. How did she know about the dog? Then she realised that Bundle's demented barking in the back garden – so much a part of her everyday life that she didn't even notice it any more – was so loud that it could be heard by anyone passing the front gate.

Katie hesitated. 'It might not be a good time.'

There was a vivid sweetness about her, a sheen of health and vitality.

Sara stood back and opened the door wider. 'You'd better come in.'

As Katie passed, her voluminous cloth coat – old and baggy, made for a much larger woman – wafted out cold air.

Sara had forgotten that the house could seem intimidating. She saw Katie's expression of awe as she glanced up at the huge modern chandelier, a cartwheel of crystal that caught the edges of the January light. The hall was double height anyway, with stone stairs and a black iron balustrade curving

up to the gallery above, but the brilliance of the decoration – white walls everywhere – expanded the space still further, turning the Georgian rectory into a palace of ice.

Sara led Katie through the house, all the way to the great glass room at the back. Building the extension had been an indulgence, because no one could pretend that the original layout had been cramped, but the result was worth the expense. Exterior and interior were perfectly united. The working part of the kitchen was right at one end, with ingenious cupboards that hid everything from view. You could sit at the long wooden table overlooking the garden completely shielded from the hum of fridge and dishwasher.

In the early morning, Sara would watch the greyness lift from the yew trees and it felt as if she were outside, on the lawn. At night, she could look up and see the stars.

'Coffee?'

Katie said, breathless with astonishment, 'This is so beautiful.'

Sara allowed herself a smile. 'I know. I love living here.'

At that moment, Bundle, who had been ferreting about in some distant part of the garden, hurtled towards the house. Sara pulled open the sliding doors and he raced inside, claws clacking on the flagstones.

'How old is he?' Katie was hard to hear, caught up in a muddle of woman and dog that seemed to delight them both.

'Two.'

'They're a lot of work, aren't they, springer spaniels? Full of energy.'

Bundle, weaving in and out of Katie's legs, was a blur of black and white. Sara said, 'He's Edward's dog, really. But no one pays him much attention these days.'

Katie looked up. Her eyes held an eagerness to please that was so intense it was almost blinding. 'It's the same with all my clients. They just don't have the time.'

It didn't take much to get Katie to talk. Unlike most people, she didn't bridle at direct questions. As she took off her coat and scarf and Bundle settled at her feet, behaving like the good dog he'd never been, the words spilled out in a rush. Katie had a dear little face, with a kind of startled look, like a kitten. For a moment, the tightness in the house loosened. It felt like a small reprieve from the darkness of recent weeks.

Sara said, 'So how many clients do you have?'

'Three so far. But I've only just started. So that's quite good, isn't it?'

Katie said that her dog walking business was a way of supplementing her student loans, really – she was in her first year of a degree in tourism and hospitality management, and had hoped to cut costs by living at home, but her parents had sold up and moved to Spain. The move had been very sudden – one minute her father had been offered early retirement, the next they'd packed up and left. She'd been really worried about finding somewhere to live within a bus ride of the campus, but she'd met Pete in the pub, and he said that if she wasn't fussy about staying in town and didn't mind going a bit further out into the country, she could live rent-free in the tiny house he'd just bought in the village, tucked into the cul-de-sac át the end of Sara's garden.

Sara looked out of the great glass doors at the back. The trees were far too tall to see anything of the cramped modern estate beyond the fence.

Katie said that Pete didn't want any money from her – the house was in such a bad state. No one had lived there for

years because it was wedged into a damp corner and the windows were too small to let in any light. As soon as he got planning permission from the council, he was going to knock it all down and start again. So it was all a bit grim. Black mould had flowered all over the ceilings and the boiler was on its last legs. The bathroom was a kind of lean-to, added on as an afterthought, and slugs clung to the shower screen as if they'd got confused and thought they were still outside in the garden. But Katie said at least it was a roof over her head, and it was fine until she could afford something better.

When she paused to draw breath, Sara said, 'So how long have you lived round here?'

'Since the summer.'

'Do you like it?'

Katie hesitated. 'It's a bit different. I'm used to having cafés and restaurants and shops and a cinema. I mean, I'm sure I'll get used to it. People like peace and quiet, don't they?'

Katie said it wasn't that easy meeting people in the village, because everyone went off early in the morning and didn't come back until after dark, and so many of the houses were hidden behind walls or shrubs or hedges, so you never saw anyone to say hello. She said it was sad because most of her friends apart from Anna and Baz had moved away, or gone to universities in other parts of the country, and she didn't really feel she'd got to know anyone on her course yet. Her dog walking clients were out at work all day – she had keys to all the houses – so if she was studying at home rather than going in to lectures she could spend a whole day not talking to anyone at all.

Sara saw a shadow behind Katie's eyes, as if the loneliness frightened her. 'I know what you mean. We've been here fourteen years and I still don't feel I've got to know anyone.'

Bundle, sprawled at Katie's feet, gave out a long shuddering sigh.

'Even the village shop's empty,' said Katie, 'during the day.'

'I don't think I've ever been in it.'

Katie was surprised. 'Not even for a pint of milk?'

Sara explained that she was normally out at work herself but had taken unpaid leave for a few months because Mike had hurt his back and needed her to be around to help him. Katie looked sympathetic, but Sara cut her off – any mention of back pain seemed to compel people to come out with pet theories about chiropractic or surgery or acupuncture, as if Sara hadn't heard of any of them or was too stupid to have done any research. She told Katie that the solicitor's office where she worked had been very understanding and were happy for her to take as much time as she needed.

What she didn't say was that no one had been in touch since she'd left. Sometimes it felt as if she'd dived down to the bottom of a pool and the waters had closed over her head, causing her to disappear without trace.

Katie looked impressed. 'It must be really interesting being a lawyer. Hearing people's secrets.'

Sara shook her head. 'Most of the time, I'm just filling in forms.'

But she could tell, from the shining admiration in her eyes, that Katie didn't really believe her.

Sara could have put Katie out of her misery and told her she'd got the job, but there was something so appealing about Katie's openness and honesty – something so unusual about

talking to someone who hung on her every word – that she was reluctant to bring the conversation to a close. 'So how are your parents settling in to life in a new country?'

'They love it, I think.'

'You haven't been out to visit?'

Katie lowered her eyes. 'It's a bit difficult. They've got a spare bedroom, but Dad snores really badly, so Mum needs it to get some peace.'

'That's a shame.'

Katie looked unhappy. 'Mum says I'd be welcome any time. I could sleep on the sofa. But they couldn't put me up for more than a day or two because the flat just isn't big enough. I can see what they mean. We'd all get on top of each other.'

Sara said, 'Which part of Spain is it?'

For the first time since they'd met, Katie seemed lost for words. Sara waited, curious.

Katie said, in a muffled voice, 'I really miss them.'

'Of course you do.'

Katie hung her head.

With a little more prompting – a gentle nudge here and there – the whole story came tumbling out. Katie had just started going out with someone called Danny when the move to Spain was first mooted. Her parents didn't approve. Caught up in the bliss of a new relationship, Katie had ignored them. A rift had opened up. When Katie was offered the small dilapidated house, just weeks before her parents packed up and left, and Danny had moved in, her parents were appalled. The damage seemed irreparable.

'Why didn't they approve?'

'They said he was too old for me.'

'How old?'

'Twenty-four.'

Sara made sure she didn't smile. 'Are you still together?'

Katie shook her head.

'What happened?'

'I don't know.' Katie's expression was bleak.

Sara stayed very still, her eyes on Katie's face.

When Katie spoke again, her voice was shaking. 'I thought it was forever. But then he left me. After he'd gone, everything fell apart. I couldn't get up. I couldn't leave the house. Anna came and dragged me out of bed and took me to the doctor, and he said I was depressed and put me on anti-depressants.'

Bundle, sensing a change in mood, raised his head.

Katie bent down and stroked his silky ears, her cheeks bright red as if someone had slapped her. 'I've said too much, haven't I? You won't want me to walk Bundle now.'

Sara was astonished. 'But I do. Of course I do.'

Katie opened her eyes wide. 'Really?'

'I can see the way you are with him. I'd love you to walk him every day. Twice a day if possible. I should have said so earlier.'

Katie moved to the edge of her chair, eager to make amends. 'I promise I'm reliable.'

'I'm sure you are.'

'I'm getting therapy now. To make sure I don't get depressed again.'

Sara said, 'We all have times when things get too much.'

Katie's mouth trembled. 'You're such a kind person. I'm so glad I've met you.'

Sara smiled.

★

'A dog walker?' James was surprised out of his usual laconic indifference.

'Just for a while. It's one less thing to worry about.'

Bundle was extremely irritating. Inside, he barked to go out. Outside, he barked to come in. She'd bought him for Edward for his twelfth birthday, thinking a dog might provide reassurance and help with his social interaction. But her research was flawed. It turned out that springer spaniels are full of energy and easily bored, which was exactly the wrong sort of dog for a boy who hated surprises.

James leaned back against the wall. Tall and angular, completely different from his father, he looked older than eighteen. In only a few months, he would have finished school altogether. 'You should have asked me.'

Sara shook her head. 'You're much too busy.'

She felt his eyes following her as she cleared the table. The house was unusually quiet. Edward was in his room. Mike was in his study. James said, 'So when does she start?'

'Next Monday.'

Sara didn't tell him all the details – the dilapidated house, the absent parents, the depression.

He said, 'I wouldn't have thought the dog was the problem.'

She looked up. 'What do you mean?'

'You know what I mean.'

Sara's voice was firm. 'In a few months, everything will be back to normal.'

James bent down and picked up his bag, heavy with books. 'I'll be away the whole of the summer. As soon as exams are over.'

'I know.'

'And if I get the grades, I'll be gone for good.'

She said, 'James, you mustn't worry about me. Everything's going to be fine.'

James adjusted the weight of the bag on his shoulder, but still made no move to go. 'He's getting worse.'

'James—'

'You can say what you like. He's getting worse.'

They held each other's eyes.

She took a deep breath. 'He's your father. I don't want you to fall out with him.'

James gave her a look of incredulity. 'It's a bit late for that.'

The following morning Mike was even more irritable than usual. By the time the boys had left for school he had already created a level of noise in the house that was singing inside Sara's head. She felt as if she were standing on an island in the middle of rush hour traffic, or on a runway beneath the belly of a low-flying plane. On her way through the hall, as Mike was dragging himself round the living room haranguing someone on the other end of the phone about deadlines and delivery, she opened the heavy front door on to the gravelled drive just to remind herself that a world existed outside the hell of his temper. The sky was a frozen grey. Sara closed her eyes, trying to blank out sound, concentrating on nothing but breathing in, breathing out, breathing in, breathing out.

A voice said, 'It's all kicking off today.'

In front of her was the postman, wearing his personal all-weather uniform of olive bucket hat, knee-length khaki shorts and brown hiking boots. He was a familiar sight round the village. Sometimes you came across his metal trolley of letters and packages jammed into a hedge, as if it had got tired of waiting and wandered off by itself.

Sara jerked out of her reverie. 'I'm sorry, what did you say?'

The postman nodded towards the house. 'I said, it's all kicking off today.'

Now that her moment of calm had been shattered, she could hear it all over again – the booming percussion of Mike's voice punctuated by the distant cacophony of Bundle's manic barking.

She tried to smile. 'Just one of those mornings.'

The postman scratched his cheek. He had quite a weathered complexion, being out all hours in the wind and the rain. 'Sounds upset.'

What could she say? She didn't want to be disloyal. 'Not really. Not more than usual.'

He looked disbelieving. 'I could hear it all round the cul-de-sac.'

Sara was silenced.

'If I were you, I'd do something about it.' He hoisted his mail bag higher on to his shoulder. 'I couldn't listen to that all day.'

She watched as he trudged across the gravel, muscles bunched in his calves.

Mike expressed no interest in meeting Katie. When Sara first told him about employing a dog walker, he gave her his usual flat stare, as if he thought she was mad but it wasn't worth having an argument.

Sara guessed he was worried about the cost. Since he'd been forced to take time off work, he'd become obsessed with household expenditure. She had her arguments prepared – they

didn't have a cleaner any more, she'd been using the cheap supermarket near the bypass. But Mike didn't raise the subject, so neither did she.

Their first meeting wasn't a great success. Katie had just arrived as Mike was making his way across the hall. He gave her a terse nod and disappeared into the living room.

Sara said, 'He's not a morning person.'

Katie gazed after him with an anxious expression.

Later that week, Katie was putting on her coat in the cavernous hall when a roar of frustration spilled over the black balustrade from the floor above. Katie glanced at Sara, a question in her eyes.

Sara said, 'He hates losing things.'

There was a thud, and then a crash, as if something had been thrown against a wall.

Sara said, 'The stupid thing is, whatever he's looking for is usually right in front of his nose. He just can't see it.'

'That's just like my dad,' said Katie. 'He had us all looking for his glasses once, and it turned out he'd had them in his hand the whole time.'

But mostly the house was silent when Katie brought Bundle home in the afternoons. Mike was always working – propped up on the sofa, or closeted upstairs in his study, staring at several screens – and the boys were making their way home from school. So it became a habit, if they were both free, for Katie to sit in the kitchen having a cup of tea while Sara started preparing the evening meal.

It was Sara's favourite time of day in winter, the half hour before turning on the lamps and drawing the curtains. There was a softness to the dying light, a blurring of edges that encouraged intimacy and confession.

They talked about general subjects at first – how Mike had his own business and was a bit of a workaholic, how James was hoping to study maths at university, how Katie's friend Anna used to be a teaching assistant until the job had been axed, so she now worked in the charity shop and gave Katie first refusal on anything that might be useful.

But as the weeks passed, and conversation moved to more personal matters, Sara found herself shutting the door to the hall to discourage eavesdropping. Bundle was mercifully quiet. Exhausted by racing up and down Ogden Hill or skidding through the icy ruts of Smith's Field, he flopped on to the floor and slept.

Katie said her therapist was called Maxine. She saw patients in the converted garage attached to her house – which was always cold because the heating was turned down so low – and wore bright red lipstick and black knee-length boots that shone under the fluorescent light. She used to be a nanny – which you could tell, because she didn't like being interrupted and believed in setting boundaries – but had recently switched careers. They'd met in the charity shop. Maxine had been searching through the winter coats, lifting each one out on its hanger to search for flaws. Katie had admired her thoroughness.

'Do you like her?'

Katie said she'd only had one session so far, and they'd talked about the importance of self-esteem. Maxine said you couldn't let other people walk all over you, and you had to believe you deserved the best. This meant radical personal transformation and cutting yourself off from negative influences, including people who tried to control you and tell you what to do.

'She says I have to give myself permission to grab hold of what I want, and that it's time to put myself first and be the centre of my own life.'

Sara nodded.

'But she says she can't do it for me. Her job is to nudge me in the right direction, but it's my responsibility to make it happen. I have to give one hundred and ten per cent commitment to personal growth.'

Maxine had explained that she was going to give Katie a series of homework tasks. Some of the assignments might feel quite difficult because Katie would be pushed out of her comfort zone, but change was challenging and there was no gain without pain.

'Have you talked about Danny?'

Katie shook her head. 'Not yet.'

'It will be good when you can. So that you can sort out your feelings a bit more.'

Katie didn't respond straight away. After a while she said that her friends Anna and Baz were so angry with Danny for the way he'd treated her that they'd banned all mention of his name. They thought she'd get better more quickly if she pushed him out of her mind. But it was really hard to do that, because she still didn't really understand why he'd left. It kept going round and round in her head but none of it made sense.

Sara kept her eyes on the task at hand, chopping onions and skinning tomatoes.

Katie stared into space, momentarily silent.

A few days later, Sara came home from shopping to find Katie and Mike sitting together at the kitchen table. This was a shock. Mike looked as if he'd been there for hours,

shirtsleeves rolled up, elbows on the table. Sara was so used to Mike's domineering presence – neck and shoulders like a rugby player, a voice that seemed to boom through a loudhailer – that it took her a while to realise that he was drunk. He'd filled a glass for Katie too, but she hadn't touched it. Sara wondered how long she'd been sitting there, bombarded by words.

Mike leaned forwards, wagging his finger in Katie's face. 'It's what I'm always telling James. You can't sit around waiting for life to give you a break. Make your own luck. Create your own opportunities. So many people want it all on a plate. But it doesn't work like that. You've got to get off your backside and do something.' Mike reached for the whisky bottle. 'I started a cleaning business when I was fourteen. Nothing complicated. But I'd earned enough for a deposit on a flat by the time I was twenty. And do you know why?'

Katie stared back, glassy-eyed.

'I worked out what people wanted, that's why. Thorough, reliable and cheaper than the competition. Not rocket science. Just common sense.'

Sara tried to attract Katie's attention, to communicate somehow that she could leave whenever she wanted to.

Mike poured himself a generous measure. 'There's so much crap talked about enterprise and business these days. But anyone can do it. Anyone can start their own business. You just need focus. Determination. Be willing to get your hands dirty.'

Sara said, 'Katie has started her own business. At the same time as studying for a degree. She's a dog walker.'

Mike took a mouthful of whisky. 'You can't afford to hang about. When you're young, you think you'll go on forever.

But one day you realise it's crept up on you. Old age. Your best years are behind you.'

Sara said, 'I should get on with supper. The boys will be hungry.'

'That's why you can't fuck around. You've got to seize the moment. Decide what you're going to do and do it. Don't waste your life waiting for the right time because there never is a right time. You've just got to get on with it.'

'Mike, maybe Katie—'

'Life happens while you're making other plans. Who said that? It's true. It all goes so fast. I'm going to be fifty in June. God, that's depressing. Beginning of the end.'

Sara said, 'Maybe—'

'You see it all on TV. Dementia and cruises and retirement living. I might as well shoot myself now.'

'Mike, we shouldn't hold Katie up.'

Mike fixed Katie with a heavy-lidded stare. 'So how old are you?'

'Eighteen.'

Mike said, 'You remind me of someone.'

Katie looked panicked.

Mike swivelled round. His eyes were bloodshot and unfocused. 'Don't you think so, Sara? Who does she remind you of?'

'I don't know.'

'Yes, you do. You know exactly who she reminds me of.'

'One of James's friends maybe.'

He mimicked her, making his voice sound unpleasantly high and whiny. 'One of James's friends.'

'It's late, Mike. We mustn't keep her. It's time for Katie to go home.'

There was a small silence. Then Mike threw back his head and laughed. The sound reverberated round the room.

Sara caught up with Katie by the front door. 'Don't take any notice of him.'

'Why was he laughing?'

'I've got no idea. It's what happens when you drink too much.'

Katie nodded but still hesitated.

Sara made her voice calm. 'Don't give it another thought. He was rambling. He'll have forgotten all about it in the morning.'

After Katie had gone, and Sara had rushed round in a whirlwind of activity because everything had been so delayed, they had supper. Mike lapsed into a kind of brooding silence and concentrated on shovelling mashed potato and chicken stew into his mouth. Once, when Sara looked up, she saw James staring at his father with an air of puzzled distaste, as if the family meal had been interrupted by a random stranger who'd wandered in off the street and hadn't yet been asked to leave.

Later that evening, Sara came back into the great glass extension to find Mike sitting at the table in the dark. She felt a small tug of alarm. He had his back to her, a hulk of shadow facing the black void of the garden.

She said, 'Can I put the lights on?'

When he didn't reply, she turned on the lamp by the shelves, a gentle illumination that no one could object to. She tried not to look at him too closely, but she could see that he had slumped forwards and that his hands were still nursing a glass of whisky.

'Do you want a cup of tea?'

Still he said nothing. At the sink, she filled the kettle. The black night pressed down on the glass above, making her feel small and insignificant.

When she couldn't waste any more time wiping clean surfaces and rearranging mugs in the dishwasher, she made the tea and brought it back to the table.

He said, as if they'd been in the middle of a conversation, 'She's pretty, isn't she?'

Her heart sank.

'Trusting. Innocent.'

Sara was unwilling to sit down, but there didn't seem to be any other option. She lowered herself on to the edge of the chair, ready to move quickly if the mood turned ugly.

'Works hard, too. Turns up twice a day, regular as clockwork. Takes the bloody dog out.' His voice was harsh, like iron scraping on stone. 'Reliable, honest, loyal.'

She raised her eyes to his face.

'I give it six months.'

She kept her voice light and casual, as if they were discussing something inconsequential. 'I hope she stays longer than that.'

He gave her a hard stare, as if she were being deliberately stupid. 'You'll tell her to go.'

'Of course I won't.'

'You will. Because that's what you do. You'll pick an argument and say it's her fault.'

It was such a reversal of reality that she was silenced.

Mike looked at her with cold contempt. 'You'll fall out with her. Because you fall out with everyone in the end. No one's ever good enough, are they, Sara? No one ever quite meets your exacting standards.'

For a moment, her head was full of bitter retorts. It was tempting to put the blame where it really belonged.

But looking at the flushed, drunken face of her belligerent husband, she thought it was probably better not to reply.

It was several weeks before Katie told her about Danny.

Katie had been describing her third session of therapy in the cold converted garage attached to Maxine's house. 'She says my fixation with Danny is because I'm clinging to the idea of true love. She says I don't need *Sleeping Beauty* and *Cinderella*, because they're just fairy tales for children, and I have to commit to a completely different way of thinking.'

According to Maxine, the modern trend was about picking up different people for companionship or sex as and when you needed them, a way of life she called random conscious coupling. She said that long-term monogamy was dying a death, a thing of the past, which was perfectly obvious if you looked around you because everybody kept getting divorced.

Katie said, 'It's all about attitude. Being open to change. You have to keep challenging yourself and asking if your needs are being met. If something's not right and you're not satisfied, there's nothing wrong with ditching it and moving on.'

Maxine talked a lot about sex, particularly theories about trust and abandonment, and had an extensive knowledge of fetishes and kinks. Given that the traditional approach had been so disappointing, she thought that Katie would benefit

from widening her horizons and experimenting with different kinds of relationship, and suggested she sign up to a number of dating sites catering for a more adventurous market.

Sara said, 'How do you feel about that?'

Katie said there wasn't much point in paying for therapy if you didn't follow the advice you were given, but the idea still made her nervous. 'I'm not sure I'm ready for it.'

'I can understand that,' said Sara. 'It's not long since you and Danny broke up.'

Katie bit her lip.

'There's no rush. Maybe you need a bit more time.'

When Katie looked up, her eyes were full of tears.

It turned out that everyone knew Danny. He'd grown up in the area and was a long-term regular of the Goat, the cramped Tudor pub on the town's main high street that smelled of fried onion rings, beer-soaked carpet and damp. His nan lived in one of the terraced houses by the railway line, next to the recreation ground – the ones with thick black mortar round the bricks as if they'd been drawn with marker pen. But he was a lot older than all her friends, and he'd been away for a few years, so she hadn't met him until they all went to a house party at the beginning of the summer.

She'd noticed him straight away, leaning against the wall in the kitchen, arms folded, head down. Someone shouted her name and he looked up and gave her an intense, assessing glance. He was very thin. His skin was white, like a musician who never sees daylight. He always wore a long black coat that swung around him as he walked.

She had no idea that he liked her. And then one Saturday night as they all trailed back laughing and shouting through the town past the chicken and kebab shops, he waited until

all the others had gone round the corner and pinned her against the brick wall outside Sainsbury's Local.

They'd been together six months. The whole time, she couldn't believe how lucky she was. She'd wake in the early morning and look at him in the pale yellow light, lying in the bed next to her, and wonder what she'd done to deserve him. Some weekends they never got up at all. Outside it could be raining or snowing, and it just didn't matter – they'd be curled up in the warm like mice in a nest. If he got hungry, he'd kick her out of bed, and she'd run downstairs and make tea and toast. When she got back her feet were like ice, but she'd burrow back under the covers, and he was like a furnace, pushing out heat, even though he was nothing but bones.

He smelled of burnt caramel. She could recognise him instantly, even in the middle of a crowd.

Danny always knew what he wanted. He could have picked anyone. But he picked her.

Sara, listening, kept very still. This was a story she knew well. All those years ago, Mike had done exactly the same thing – ignored the crowd and focused just on her, as if the simple fact of her presence had been so dazzling, so bright, that he couldn't even see the people around her.

For Katie, the end was brutal. One Friday night in the Goat, when the pub was packed with after-work drinkers, Danny said it was over. There had been no preamble, no warning. It was such a shock, she started crying. He pushed back his chair, jogging the table so that beer slopped over the edge of his pint glass, and his voice was angry as if she'd accused him of something he hadn't done. 'I never said I loved you.'

When she got back, she realised the house had been cleared

of everything that belonged to him. He'd packed up before he'd even got to the pub, before he'd even told her it was finished.

A few days later, the spare key arrived through the letter box, like an afterthought.

Katie's voice was thick with tears.

Later, because she had been concentrating so hard, Sara almost felt that she'd been there in the Goat herself the night that Danny said he was leaving. She could smell the old carpet, the frying oil, the sugary yeast of the beer. She could see Danny in front of her, loud with self-justification.

At the end of the afternoon, when Katie finally put on her coat and scarf and they stood in the great hall, the shadows wide on the white walls, Sara said, 'Can I give you a key? Then you can let yourself in whenever you like, whether I'm here or not.'

Katie's eyes were solemn. 'I'll keep it very safe.'

'I know you will.'

Over the next few days, Katie continued to tell Sara about Danny. The stories tumbled out like gas exploding from a bottle. Every so often, she'd stop and look up, hot with humiliation, apologising for the constant stream of words.

Sara said, 'You need to talk.'

'But I'm wasting your time.'

Sara shook her head.

Everything about Danny was perfect – his light blue eyes, his long fingers. He had a way of creating space that belonged only to them, leaning in close to tell her secrets that no one else could hear. She never had to share him with other people – sometimes on Saturdays they went into town to one of the cafés that served all-day breakfasts because Danny was fond

of a fry-up, but he always chose the one behind the car park so they didn't have to talk to anyone they knew. Danny usually ordered everything on the menu, including baked beans and fried bread – but not the mushrooms, because he said they were slimy – and decorated everything with tomato ketchup. He always left the white round the fried egg, though, because he said it turned his stomach.

He laughed at her for getting into debt so that she could study for a degree. That's just playing someone else's game. Use your brains. Work it out for yourself.

Sex had been urgent, immediate, as if they were running out of time. They didn't always make it upstairs – slid from the sofa to the floor in front of the small electric fire that smelled of burning plastic. They did it in the woods once, on the way back from the pub. The grass was wet and the air was rank and rotten. The next morning she had a rash all the way up her legs from her ankles to her groin.

In the beginning, she'd worried all the time that he might leave. But then his toothbrush appeared in the plastic cup on the toilet cistern, and his private stash of beer in the fridge, and he hung up all his work clothes on a black iron rail in the spare bedroom, his shoes in shiny pairs underneath.

He said to everyone in the Goat that he was her lodger. 'I'm renting a room at Katie's.'

Except that he never paid her a penny. And the room was just for his shirts.

He was in sales, Katie said, working on commission. He didn't have to sell the windows, just get people to agree to someone coming round to give them a free quotation. He often got invited in for a chat, especially by the elderly ladies living alone. He could turn on the charm. They wanted to

fatten him up – cake, biscuits, lots of sugar in his tea. He used to say, 'They love me. Can't get enough of me.'

One afternoon, they went to see his nan. She'd smoked for so many years that the skin on her face had dried out like the apple you've forgotten at the bottom of the bowl. Every so often, she'd turn away from the telly and squint at Katie through the yellow fog and fire questions straight out, like a policeman – how old are you, where did you go to school, what job do you do.

Later, Katie said to Danny, 'I don't think she likes me.'

Danny said, 'She doesn't.'

One bright February morning, Sara took her courage in both hands and went to the village shop, just ten minutes' walk from her front gates. It didn't look very inviting – a fixed white portacabin on scuffed grass next to the children's swings. Inside was no better – slippery lino, a sparse stock of packets and tins, and a humming chiller cabinet that smelled of cheese. There was no one there except for a small woman with round glasses standing behind the counter who said, giving Sara her change, that it was lovely to see the crocuses peeping through but there was going to be trouble if the forecast was right and they were in for a fall of snow.

Outside again, turning up her collar against the icy wind, Sara couldn't help feeling disappointed. She had wanted a more significant encounter.

A few days later, hoping for a better outcome, Sara went

back and spent a dispiriting few minutes hunting through the biscuits for anything she might want to buy. The shop was, once again, deserted. Even the small woman with the glasses seemed distracted and unwilling to talk.

On the way out, Sara found her path blocked by a woman with tight grey curls and a waterproof jacket. She had an air of authority. 'I see Katie's working for you.'

Sara stared. She had been expecting an inoffensive remark about the weather, so this rather aggressive observation threw her completely.

'Your dog walker, Katie Franklin. She walks our dog, too. Mary Miller saw her with a springer spaniel in Smith's Field and put two and two together.' Her expression was amused. 'You look shocked.'

Sara found her voice. 'Not really.'

'You can't keep anything secret round here. You knew that, didn't you?'

'I—'

'We all love Katie. Just a bit scatterbrained sometimes. She once took Dexter to Meadow Rise and Lulu back to Bay Tree House. But then she probably has better things to think about.'

The conversation, with its assumption of shared interest, felt like an affront.

Later, when Sara reported the exchange back to Katie – remembering to leave out the comment about being scatterbrained – Katie unravelled the whole thing. She identified the woman as Rachel Reeve, a maths teacher at the local state secondary who lived with her rather stooped and miserable husband and two teenage sons in Bay Tree House. Rachel's dog Dexter, a wiry and intelligent animal with traces of Jack Russell, was known to be very fierce.

'She seemed quite abrupt,' said Sara.

Katie said that Rachel believed in plain speaking, but that was probably because she was used to keeping crowds of children under control. 'I thought your boys might know each other.'

Sara thought it might sound unfriendly if she said that James hated the village and spent as little time there as possible, so just shook her head and said that they all went to different schools.

Lulu turned out to be the red setter belonging to Grace Knight, a beautician who lived in one of the modern detached houses in Meadow Rise at the edge of the village. Grace knew everybody. She even had clients in London. She often called you 'babe' or 'sugar' because she wasn't good at remembering names, which seemed surprising for someone who spent a lot of time up close and personal doing eyebrow threading and bikini waxes, but you could always rely on her for the latest gossip, although it was never usually earth-shattering – more on the lines of where someone was going on holiday or what they were thinking of buying their mum for Christmas.

'She has her own YouTube channel,' said Katie, eyes big with awe, 'with tutorials about skincare and beauty products and how celebrities do their make-up. She's got thousands of followers.'

Sara could hardly keep up. 'I thought you didn't know anyone in the village.'

'It's because of the dogs. You know what it's like. People with dogs always talk to each other.'

Sara tried to think back to the rare occasions when she'd taken Bundle out, but she could remember only rain and mud

and overwhelming irritation because he never came when she called.

Mary Miller, who'd seen Katie walking Bundle in Smith's Field, owned Daisy, a large honey-coloured Labrador, and lived in a small cottage right on the main road. According to Mary, everyone had been curious about Sara and her family for years, because the Old Rectory was by far the biggest house in the village and no one could quite see over the hedges.

Katie said she could hardly get past the church these days without people stopping her to ask questions. It had cheered her up a lot. She felt she was starting to make friends in the village.

'Questions about us?'

Katie nodded.

Sara wasn't sure whether to be flattered or appalled. 'What do they want to know?'

'Everything. What you do as a job, where you shop, what colour the curtains are.'

For a moment, Sara felt frightened. 'What do you say?'

Katie looked serious. 'I tell them I've only been walking Bundle since the New Year and I don't know very much about you.'

Sara was still anxious. 'You wouldn't ever pass on any personal information, would you?'

Katie was shocked. 'Of course not.'

'I wouldn't like to think people were talking about us.'

'It's only gossip. Having a chat and passing the time of day. It doesn't mean anything.'

Later, when Sara thought this over, she came to the rather nervous conclusion that getting to know her neighbours might

mean a level of intrusion she wasn't really used to. It was a strange idea. She had never thought of the village as a community. It was just an address, a place to live. No one could pretend it was pretty – not much more than a string of houses clinging to the main road, surrounded by flat agricultural land under a wide grey sky. Most of the time people drove through it on their way to somewhere more interesting. You only found the Old Rectory if you took a turning just past the garage with its dark and oily interior, and drove up a long spindly lane with overgrown hedges frothy with blackthorn. After a while, if you kept on driving, you found yourself passing an estate that used to belong to the council – brown pebbledash houses ranged round a scrubby square of grass with a climbing frame, rusty swings and the fixed portacabin containing the village shop. Further up the lane was a squat thirteenth-century stone church with a square tower and a stained-glass window of St George and the dragon, glowing scarlet and purple, which most people didn't know about because there was only a Sunday service every other week and the wooden door was usually locked. Beyond the church, past a row of cottages and set well back from the road in a couple of acres of garden, was the Old Rectory with its smooth façade of honey-coloured stone.

It was the isolation that had attracted her. She liked the feeling that you could live your life without the constant interaction that so many people demanded. It felt like a sanctuary.

'You're sure?' Mike had stood in the hall, gazing up at the gallery above, clearly wanting it all so badly that he could hardly breathe. A house like this summed up everything he'd ever worked for – not just wealth but the trappings of wealth, the conspicuous exhibition of success.

The estate agent had taken himself off to a distant part of the house – the scullery, perhaps, or the small whitewashed room just inside the back door with hooks for waxed jackets and wooden shelves for wellington boots. He had recognised their need to be alone. He had already seen the commission from an imminent, indisputable sale.

'Yes,' she said. 'I'm sure.'

In time, the ability to shut herself away saved her sanity. They didn't get the diagnosis until Edward was five. Perhaps they should have done something about it earlier, before his behaviour became quite so marked, but her instinct had been to hide him away and protect him. There were so many things that upset him – loud noises, strong smells, sudden movement. If something pushed him over the edge and he started screaming, there was nothing she could do.

She saw the judgement on people's faces. They thought she was a bad mother who couldn't control her child.

At home, behind the high hedges, they were safe. They were lucky to have so much space. When they first moved in, Mike had persuaded her to employ a gardener. But old Mr Priest kept trimming and pruning and creating neat lines and angles, even though Sara explained again and again that she wanted something less ordered and suburban. Mike had said, in those early days when they still laughed together, that he thought the garden revealed her secret self. He said it showed the fire and passion she preferred to keep hidden.

In the end it was a relief when Mr Priest said it was all getting too much and he'd decided to retire. Sara no longer had to explain her antipathy to blowsy flowers and regimented annuals.

Edward dug in the dark earth next to her, transferring

worms and snails to a wooden trug. Sometimes he'd lie on his stomach, staring through the blades of grass as if his concentration could magnify ants into armies.

At the start, she hid what was happening. The excuse she gave herself was that Mike was working long hours and under a lot of stress. In any case, she didn't want to shatter his illusions. Every evening, coming home for the boys' bedtime, he was so relentlessly positive, so determined to see only the best in his family, that it seemed cruel to disabuse him.

Edward, just out of babyhood, was deaf to his surroundings. Sitting motionless in front of the TV, he stared at the screen as if absorbing every particle of pixelation.

Mike was uneasy. 'Is he all right?'

She made light of it, lying through her teeth. 'He's just tired.'

He deferred to her judgement. He thought she knew what she was doing. So she kept up the pretence that everything was fine and eventually, when this was impossible, that she was coping. The lie exhausted her. She enfolded herself like a live nerve in layers so thick that no feeling was left exposed.

When the boys were small, she and Mike hardly saw each other. As the business grew, he was away for weeks at a time – conferences, sales trips, visits to clients. He wished he could spend more time with them – of course he did. But when you run your own company, every minute is devoted to its survival. Even at weekends, he was upstairs in his study working.

Luckily for Mike, she craved solitude. All day she longed for freedom from small sticky hands, from the physicality of feeding, washing, holding, restraining. At night, in the cool darkness, she had responsibility for no one but herself. She

lay still, listening to his steady breathing, her skin wired like an alarm because one more touch would have made her scream.

When Edward was nearly two, they decided to get an au pair. It was Mike's idea – he thought it might help if there was someone around to share the load. Sara was worried about having a stranger living in the house, but the agency sent Hilda from the Danish Faroe Islands, and Sara liked her immediately. She was small and fine-boned with shoulder-length blonde hair and an air of calm capability. Hilda said she lived in Tórshavn in a red house with a green roof, and had five siblings. In her musical English, the words dancing to a different rhythm, she said that being part of a large family meant that you always had company and someone to talk to, but there was usually a queue for the bathroom and her little sisters stole her clothes. Sara listened entranced to her descriptions of black cliffs, puffins and kittiwakes, feasts of fermented cod, angelica and sorrel.

She said to Mike, 'Can we go there? Can we go to the Faroe Islands?'

But Mike said he didn't have time for holidays.

By the time Hilda arrived, Edward's sensitivity was already very marked – he hated mess of any kind and shrank back with fear if anyone came near him. But Hilda smiled, and said very little, and gradually Edward tolerated less and less distance between them until they were almost sitting side by side on the same sofa. She was very easy to have around. Even Mike liked her. Sometimes Sara would get back from work and Mike would be catching up with paperwork at the kitchen table while Hilda padded round in her dressing gown, blonde hair a mess, obviously relaxed and at home.

When Hilda left, Sara realised she couldn't manage on her own any more. By now Mike was so often travelling for work that he was hardly ever home. By chance she met Amanda at the GP's surgery. It could have gone badly wrong. Even before Sara had sat down on one of the blue plastic chairs, Edward had launched himself full-length on to the floor by Amanda's feet and started untying her shoelaces. But Amanda just glanced down and turned back to her dog-eared magazine as if the whole thing was completely unimportant. When her name was called, she stood up and gently shuffled beyond Edward's grasp.

Sara said, 'I'm so sorry.'

She smiled. 'Little scientist, that's what he is. Trying to find out how things work.'

Amanda was a local childminder. To begin with, Sara left him with her just a few hours a week, precious time that she filled with all the tasks she couldn't manage with Edward in tow. But once he was settled, and Amanda had agreed to take and collect both boys from school, there seemed no reason not to go back to a job she enjoyed and was good at. She chose a local firm that dealt with family law, and was assigned to the wills and probate division.

It wasn't so much work as a chance to breathe.

Amanda turned out to be one of the few people that Edward ever really liked. All the time she looked after him – until a place came up for him at a specialist school nearby with a bus that delivered him almost door to door – she was his champion and defender, determined to see his behaviour as logical rather than strange. She said that Sara mustn't worry about his delayed speech because Einstein didn't say a word until he was six, and that was only because the soup was too cold. Until that moment, he hadn't had cause to complain.

She said, 'It makes sense if you think about it. If there isn't a problem, don't make a fuss.'

After a while, Sara realised this was true.

The black cloud of Mike's fury made the house dark.

His obsession with saving money had intensified. He told Sara they couldn't rely on the kind of income he'd been able to bring in before, and that they'd have to economise in order to reduce overall spending. To Sara, this made no sense. She knew from happier days when Mike had been less secretive that the house was paid off, there were a number of investment accounts and insurance policies, and that Mike had a fully paid-up pension. She couldn't believe that they were in that much financial difficulty.

'He's worried about the business,' she said to James. 'He's had to take a lot of time off.'

The worst of it was that the austerity drive turned into a kind of petty madness that did nothing much to rein in expenditure but greatly increased the general atmosphere of bad temper. Mike switched off all the lights, plunging the house into gloom. He turned down the heating so low that James, studying in his room, had to hunch over his desk in coat and gloves. He scrutinised supermarket bills and vetoed expenditure on anything but own brands so that Edward, faced with unfamiliar packaging, kept going into meltdown.

'I haven't noticed him cutting back on alcohol,' said James, blowing on his hands.

'Don't begrudge him the odd drink.'

'The odd drink? Have you seen the number of bottles in the recycling bin?'

'James, he's going through a really difficult time.'

James looked at her with irritation. 'I've noticed.'

When she could, Sara escaped to the garden. It had always been her refuge in times of stress – a place she loved that rewarded her care and attention. It was the hard physical work she enjoyed most, digging the beds, picking out the stones and old tree roots, freeing up the clay clods into friable, rich-smelling soil. She liked the feeling that she was creating the best possible conditions for the plants to grow. In the February frosts, there wasn't much she could do, but she cut back the lavatera and ceanothus and tidied up the hedges. The air was sharp and clean. Sara turned her face to the sky and willed herself to be positive. Mike had to get better. There must be an end in sight.

One evening, as they were finishing supper, James asked if he could take the car.

Mike looked up with his usual impassive stare. 'Which car?'

'I'm not insured to drive yours.'

'Your mother's car?'

'Yes.'

Mike considered this. 'Why?'

'I want to see a friend.'

'Which friend?'

'You don't know him.'

'I don't know him?'

'No.'

Across the table, Edward echoed, 'No.'

Sara put a warning hand on Edward's arm.

Mike picked up his wine glass and drained it.

Sara said, 'I think your father's wondering whether it's a good idea to go out on a school night.'

James looked at his father with feigned interest, as if keen to understand his views.

There was a taut silence.

Edward started making a sort of anxious humming sound, like someone standing on the edge of the topmost diving board wondering if the whole thing might be a mistake.

Sara took a deep breath. 'Maybe tonight's not a good idea.'

James was still staring at his father.

Sara said, 'Maybe tomorrow would be better.'

Mike reached for the wine bottle.

James stood up and left the room. As Mike filled his glass, Sara heard James walking across the hall, then a kind of scuffle as if he was putting on his shoes. The front door slammed. Moments later, they heard the engine of the Polo and then the crunch of gravel as the car pulled out of the drive.

Edward had stopped humming, but his eyes were on Sara's face, waiting to see how worried he should be.

Mike's words were slurred by wine, 'He's lying.'

Sara said, 'You don't know that.'

Mike laughed.

Sara stood up and started gathering the dirty plates together.

Mike picked up his glass. 'You know what I think? I think he's gone to meet the lovely Katie.'

'If he wanted to meet Katie, he could walk round to her house.'

Mike leaned forward. 'What if they did it here? Under your roof? What would you say to that?'

A knife from the pile of cutlery on the top plate fell on to the table.

Her voice sounded much too loud. 'That's enough.'

Mike looked up, a slow grin spreading across his face.

Thanks to Katie's descriptions, the faceless inhabitants of the village were beginning to become people with names, jobs and families. Katie said that Mary Miller, who had been one of her very first dog walking clients, was the one who'd asked the most questions about Sara, but it was probably just habit because she'd only recently retired as a receptionist in the local health clinic.

'She wanted to know all about Mike's back,' said Katie. 'She said the pain can be excruciating. She remembered a patient at the surgery who was in such agony he wanted to throw himself off a cliff.'

Mary and her Labrador Daisy were both plump, arthritic and permanently out of breath so spent most of their time in Mary's hot little kitchen crammed with dog paraphernalia – Labrador fridge magnets, a 'Puppies of the World' wall calendar and a tapestry cushion of a black Highland terrier in a tartan beret. There was nothing Mary liked more than a long afternoon of gossip over tea and biscuits.

It turned out that she'd somehow got hold of completely the wrong impression about Sara because she'd once seen her waving her arms about and shouting at Mike in the front seat of the BMW, which made her think that Sara had a bad

temper. Katie said that Sara was quiet and kind and never even raised her voice, so what had looked like a row was probably just Sara singing along to the radio. Mary also thought that Sara was unfriendly and kept herself to herself, but Katie explained how busy she was, working and looking after the boys.

Sara said, 'People don't understand what it's like to be shy.'

Katie paused, as if this was a new thought.

'You have everything you want to say in your head, but you don't know how to start, so people think you're cold and reserved. Or you blurt it all out at the wrong time, and everyone thinks you're rude.'

'I've never thought you were rude,' said Katie, her eyes anxious.

'But that's because we've got to know each other.' Sara smiled. 'You know what I'm really like.'

Katie said that Grace Knight had also been very keen to find out more about Sara, but this might have been for business reasons as she was always keen to introduce new clients to her beauty salon on the high street, a little slice of a shop two doors down from the Goat. Everyone loved Grace because she had the knack of making even a small treatment, like a facial or a manicure, feel like a complete makeover. As Katie said, you walked in feeling plain and ordinary, and walked out feeling like someone in a magazine. Naturally enough, both Grace and her red setter Lulu were beautifully groomed. Lulu was so used to being admired that she would stand quite still – staring into the middle distance, the wind ruffling her coat – like a top model posing for a photograph.

'We were talking about Mike,' said Katie, 'and Grace said aromatherapy might help to relax him.'

Sara shook her head. 'He won't consider it. I know he won't. He won't even do the exercises the physio's recommended.'

'What if you bought him a session as a present?'

'There's no point. He won't try anything new. I've spent hours trying to persuade him, but he says it's a waste of time.'

Katie's other main client was Rachel Reeve – the amused maths teacher – but she also occasionally took out Sally Cook's Labradoodle if Sally was down in Cornwall looking after her mother.

'The Cooks live in the thatched cottage overlooking Smith's Field,' said Katie.

Sara nodded, struggling to keep up. Even now, with all Katie's patient explanations, she was easily confused by all the different names.

Katie said it was quite exciting, really, getting to know everyone. According to Mary Miller, the village was a very sociable place to live. Sometimes the gossip seemed a bit relentless, but it was only because it was a small community and people wanted to help out where they could. When Lauren Shipman's husband was laid off and Lauren lost her job at the shoe warehouse, there was a rota of people cooking meals for the children until they got back on their feet, and everyone was always calling in on Sheila Clark, who was ninety-four and pretty much housebound, to check if she needed any shopping done.

Sara looked awkward. 'I would never have known any of this if it hadn't been for you.'

'You were out at work all the time.'

Sara shook her head. 'I should have made more of an effort.'

It felt to Sara as if Katie had woken her from a kind of hopeless inertia, a beige and anodyne life that she'd come to accept because she didn't know that anything else existed. For the first time in months, she looked up and took notice of the world around her. The free newspaper that came through the letter box on Thursdays had always gone straight into the recycling because Sara had dismissed it as nothing but advertising – mobile hairdressers, tree surgeons, minicabs. But now she found herself searching through for local events and snippets of news. She wanted to find out more about her neighbours. She wanted to make up for lost time.

Katie said, 'You could always invite them over.'

Sara looked up, surprised.

'They're dying to see the house. It wouldn't have to be much. You could ask them round for coffee one day.'

There was a small, awkward silence.

Sara said, 'I can't.'

'I could help. I could buy the biscuits and everything.'

Sara shook her head.

Katie said, 'I know you like being private, but—'

'It's not me.' Sara felt the embarrassment tying her up in knots. 'It's Mike.'

'He doesn't like people coming round?'

'No.'

Katie was still confused. 'Ever?'

'Not really. Particularly people he doesn't know.'

Katie thought about this. 'But he's all right with friends?'

Sara didn't want to answer this directly. 'He'd just rather the house was quiet. He doesn't like noise if he's working at home.'

They looked at each other, both acutely aware of the

enormous echoing space around them, the high ceilings, the fact that conversation in the huge glass extension could only be heard by the birds.

Katie said, 'You wouldn't think sound carried much in a house like this.'

'He's very sensitive,' said Sara. 'Very easily distracted.'

Katie's eyes opened wide with alarm. 'What about me? Do I disturb him?'

'No,' said Sara quickly, 'not at all. You make things better. You take Bundle out and stop him barking all the time. Mike loves having you around.'

Katie opened her mouth to speak and shut it again.

'He used to be more sociable,' said Sara, anxious to make Mike sound more reasonable, 'years ago. When I first met him, he loved going to parties. He used to stay up all night. But he's in too much pain these days. He doesn't really feel like seeing anyone.'

They contemplated this with some sadness.

'If you want to find out a bit more,' said Katie, 'about who people are and what they do, you could always go round and see Mary. She knows all the stories. She doesn't get out much, but she picks up every tiny scrap of gossip. Half an hour with her and you'd know everything about everyone.'

Sara was immediately enthusiastic. 'I could take her some flowers.'

'Cake would be better. Or chocolate biscuits. To go with the tea.'

Sara felt a quiver of excitement. Katie was opening up opportunities she'd never even thought of. 'If I make a few visits round the village, people will stop thinking I'm unfriendly. They'll see I'm making an effort.'

'Book yourself in for a facial at the salon,' said Katie, 'and Grace will love you forever.'

They smiled at each other.

'And maybe when Mike goes back to the office,' said Katie, 'when everything's back to normal, maybe we can arrange something then.'

Sara nodded.

'Shall I say that? If anyone asks?'

'Do you think they will?'

'They might,' said Katie, looking uncomfortable.

It was clear that Katie had been under pressure for some time to get Sara to issue an invitation.

'I think it's better not to mention it.' Sara tried to sound neutral. 'It could be months yet before Mike's fit again, and I don't want people to get all excited.'

There was another awkward silence.

'Maybe in the summer,' said Sara, 'when the weather's better.'

It was important to keep things positive. The last thing she wanted was for Katie to report back to the rest of the village that Mike was a bad-tempered bully who refused to let his wife have a few neighbours round for coffee.

A few days later, Sara knocked on the door of Mary Miller's cottage, only a pavement's width from the traffic hurtling along the main road, and was immediately welcomed in.

'Katie said you might call.'

'I'm not disturbing you?' Sara tried not to show how horrified she was by the clutter and stuffiness inside.

'Not at all, dear. It's lovely to meet you after all this time.'

In the hot little kitchen at the back, there was hardly any room to sit down.

'So how's your poor husband?' said Mary. 'I hear he's in terrible pain.'

Sara said he was finding the enforced inactivity very hard. 'He just wants to get back to work full time.'

'Of course he does. What man wouldn't?'

'But he's definitely improving. I can see little changes for the better day by day.'

Mary leaned across the table and patted Sara's hand. 'He's very lucky to have you, dear.'

It turned out that Mary had a soft spot for Mike. She'd once been struggling back from the portacabin with two heavy bags and he'd insisted on taking them from her and walking her all the way to her front door.

Sara was surprised. She'd never heard this story.

Mary said, 'You mustn't worry if he's not quite himself at the moment. I saw so many people with back problems at the surgery and you know it's like Jekyll and Hyde – man to beast in a matter of seconds. They get frightened, you see. They think it's never going to end. And men are never good at talking about their feelings, are they? Just keep their heads down and struggle on.'

Daisy the Labrador, stretched out by the stove, opened her mouth in a huge yawn.

Over a packet of Tunnock's caramel wafers, Mary filled her in on the latest village gossip. Jane Cannon's husband wanted a divorce – it had been on the cards for years, but

he'd waited until their youngest had left for university – and Jane was frightened they'd have to split their assets and sell the house, which would break her heart because she loved it with a passion and never wanted to leave. Sally Cook's son-in-law Omar, who was a web designer, had gone in for a routine check-up and come out with testicular cancer, and Sarinda Nunn's husband had high blood pressure and suspected gout. Rachel's younger son Arthur had a girlfriend his mother knew nothing about, whose sister had got pregnant while still at school and swore blind it wasn't the biology teacher even though everyone knew he had form.

Daisy wheezed and coughed, a honey-coloured balloon.

'So much happening,' said Sara, bewildered by this avalanche of information. 'I had no idea.'

'That's the thing,' said Mary. 'It all looks happy on the surface. But you never really know what's going on behind closed doors. There's a rumour that Malcolm Friar's been renting porn again. Either that or someone's hacked his account.'

'I always thought it was quite a peaceful village.'

Mary nodded in a knowing kind of way. 'Sometimes I look at the headlines and I wonder why they never pay us a visit. You could fill a whole paper with what people get up to round here.'

After two cups of tea, Sara said she ought to be getting back in case Mike needed her, but she'd love to pop in again one day if Mary had the time.

'You're always welcome.' Mary smiled. 'And remember what I said. Don't worry if he's a bit crotchety. Once his back's better, your lovely husband will be back to his old self.'

Sara was suddenly anxious. 'Did Katie say something?'

'About what?'

'About Mike?'

Mary said, 'The only thing that Katie's said is that privacy is very important to you, and I know exactly what you mean. No one wants their secrets plastered all over the neighbourhood for everyone to hear.'

When Sara got back to the house, the light was fading.

Mike met her in the hall. 'Where were you?'

'Why?'

He glowered at her.

She said, in a bright voice, 'Katie will be here in a minute.'

He turned his back and disappeared into the living room.

She found herself standing alone in the great empty space.

Over the next few weeks, her interest piqued by Mary's revelations, Sara began to work out how local gossip worked. The fastest-moving stories were those that incited collective outrage, especially if the perpetrator was rude or unkind. If the guilty party was an outsider – or at least someone that no one in the village knew very well – rumours whipped round like a sharp wind, causing shivers of shocked disbelief.

The whole village stood behind anyone who had been wronged. Judgement was swift, and there were no second chances.

One Thursday afternoon, Katie was taking Dexter, Rachel Reeve's dog, for a walk round Smith's Field when she caught sight of a short middle-aged man with a large bulldog some

way off on the corner near the holly bush. He was wearing an olive-green waxed jacket, knee-length wellingtons and a flat cap, and his shoulders were hunched against the cold. Katie was just wondering who he was, and whether she ought to wave, when the bulldog started to run, bowling towards them with such speed that the distance between them disappeared in seconds. Hurtling into view, he took a flying leap at Katie, steadied himself on his hind legs, and began rhythmically thrusting his willy into her thigh.

Katie, trapped in the icy ruts of mud, looked round in desperation. A few feet away, Dexter was barking at top volume, but the bulldog's owner didn't seem to have noticed. He strode ahead, apparently unperturbed, while the fevered humping went on behind him.

Without warning, the bulldog, a large and muscular animal, adjusted his grip, grabbing Katie so hard that his claws dug into her skin. Katie yelled out in shock. In response, Dexter – who had traces of Jack Russell – threw himself at the bulldog's back leg and bit him.

Katie gasped. She had visions of Dexter being eaten alive.

But the bulldog, with a whelp of pain, let go of Katie's thigh, dropped down on to all fours, and retreated several steps. Breathing heavily, his great tusky teeth pushing up the folds of his jowls, he glared from Dexter to Katie and then – to Katie's great relief – shot off after his owner like a cannonball.

As Katie told Sara later, she was touched by everyone's concern. Rachel Reeve said she was a bit worried that Dexter had gone on the attack, but very glad that Katie wasn't hurt. Grace Knight said she thought it was diabolical the way some owners behaved and she hoped Katie wasn't too upset.

The story shot through the village. All Katie's clients were

outraged. No one could identify the man in the green waxed jacket, and it was universally decided that he must have been a visitor from outside the area.

The following day, Sara bumped into Sally Cook in the portacabin. By this time, she had learned quite a lot about Katie's dog walking clients and was about to say hello, with a degree of confidence that this was the woman with the Cornish mother and the Labradoodle, when Sally launched into a long and complicated story about how she'd been thinking about what had happened to Katie at the exact same moment that her husband started watching one of those dog training programmes on TV. Apparently, according to the voiceover, experts believed that humping was sometimes a display of dominance, but mostly it was just play. It rarely had anything to do with sex.

Unusually, the shop was quite full. A small knot of people had gathered by the counter and Sarinda Nunn was resolutely ignoring those wanting to pay, her whole focus on the discussion in front of her.

Mary Miller drew herself up to her full height. 'I don't care whether it's got anything to do with sex or not. As far as I'm concerned, it's disgusting and that man should be ashamed of himself.'

There were murmurings of approval.

Sara realised, with a shock of excitement, that she was so much a part of the small circle of indignation that it was somehow taken for granted that she agreed with everything her neighbours were saying.

*

Despite being sure it wouldn't do any good because Mike would never listen, Sara decided to find out more about aromatherapy.

Grace's salon was on the town's cobbled high street, tucked into the historic stretch of half-timbered buildings that had been carefully – and incongruously – preserved in the latest round of regeneration. Behind the wattle and daub façade were upmarket estate agents, small boutiques and expensive coffee shops, with the dark and insalubrious Goat leaning out at a drunken angle. Beyond this tantalising glimpse into the past, the cheaper end of the high street was all plate glass and brightly coloured fascias, tailing off into a small muddle of pound shops and vacant premises. Right at the end, next to the keycutter and locksmith's, was the charity shop where Katie's friend Anna worked, its window full of second-hand cookbooks and black high-heeled shoes.

In the salon, the air was thick with a kind of damp warmth smelling of hot wax and essential oils. Grace herself was a work of art – so buffed and polished that everything about her shone like glass.

'Men are funny about aromatherapy.' She gave Sara a knowing look from under her thick black eyelashes. 'They think it's all about scented candles and bath bombs. You might want to call it sports massage instead.'

'Would it be a good idea for someone with a bad back?'

Grace drew back. 'I'm a trained masseuse.'

'I didn't mean you'd do anything that wasn't safe,' said Sara, realising she had somehow got it wrong and caused offence. 'I meant, would it make him feel better?'

Grace seemed mollified. 'He'd still have a bad back, but

he might feel more relaxed. And that's got to help with the pain, hasn't it?'

But as Sara reported back to Katie later, Mike was unimpressed. He said if he wanted to try out a new treatment, he wouldn't ask a fucking beautician.

It was a mistake to repeat it word for word. Katie's eyes widened with surprise.

Sara said quickly, 'It doesn't mean anything. He only swears to let off steam.'

Katie looked doubtful.

'You won't tell Grace, will you? She's been so kind.'

Katie said that of course she wouldn't pass anything on. The last thing she wanted was for Grace to be hurt. It was just really sad that Mike wouldn't at least give aromatherapy a chance, because everyone said Grace was brilliant at massage. 'You wouldn't think it from looking at her, with the eyelashes and extensions and everything, but she's really strong. It must be all the Pilates.'

When Sara next saw Grace for a manicure – she had begun to call into the salon on a weekly basis – she made up an excuse about Mike not being able to come in because he was completely snowed under with work. Grace read between the lines and said Sara wasn't to worry – a lot of men were a bit scared of massages and it took them a while to come round. Her boyfriend Ryan, who worked at the BMW garage just beyond the bypass, was spending his day off keeping Grace company at the salon, bronzed biceps bulging from the sleeves of his white T-shirt. He said he'd been just the same to be honest until he'd had two hours of shiatsu at a local health club. He'd never realised the tension in his neck and shoulders until it wasn't there.

Afterwards, Sara thought about the way Ryan was so loyal and backed Grace up in everything she said. His eyes followed her round the salon, his face tender with pride as she plumped up the pink cushions on the wicker sofa and straightened the bottles of nail polish on the glass shelves. Seeing the way he looked at her, Sara felt a small flash of loss.

'I wish Mike would listen to me,' she said to Katie later. 'But he's so stubborn.'

Katie nodded. 'Anything's got to be better than being in pain all the time.'

'It's so hard not being able to help.' Sara didn't want to be critical, but it was a relief to tell the truth. 'But he doesn't want me to interfere. He keeps telling me to stay out of it.'

Her only function, it seemed, was to absorb his rage and act as some kind of emotional punch-bag.

But she didn't say this to Katie. It would have been too humiliating.

It had been a busy few weeks. When they finally found the time to catch up, Katie brought Sara up to date with her latest sessions of therapy.

'So how's it going?'

'Really well,' said Katie.

She spoke with such conviction that Sara knew something was wrong.

Katie said that she'd been following Maxine's orders and going out with men from various specialist dating sites. This hadn't been altogether successful. Her increasingly strange encounters had included a tussle on a sofa with a large sweaty supply teacher who thought she was into bondage, and a surreal conversation with an insurance broker who was desperate for her to strap on a dildo. One of her dates had

licked her ear and asked if she was into threesomes. Even the silly stuff was creepy, like the time a thin-faced web designer in a tight flowery shirt leaned forward over his triple-cheese pizza and said was she interested in squirty cream because he had a lot of it at home.

Sara listened, trying not to look too appalled.

Katie reached for a biscuit. 'So I asked Maxine if I could go out with people who were a bit more conventional.'

'What did she say?'

'She said, did I mean wine bars with men in shabby suits drinking prosecco and talking about dental work and divorce? And I said, yes. So that's what we're going to do from now on.'

'That doesn't sound very exciting,' said Sara.

Katie looked miserable.

'Are you sure this is working for you?'

Katie bit her lip. 'Maxine says that change is uncomfortable. I don't think I should give up now.'

Sara was doubtful about this but stayed quiet.

Katie said it hadn't all been doom and gloom. A few weeks before, one of her dates hadn't turned up, so she'd been sitting all by herself in the wine bar, trying to look busy by scrolling through the messages on her phone. Al was sitting on the same long wooden bench, but further along, and she realised he must have been stood up, too, because he looked really nervous and worried, chewing his thumbnail and sighing. He was slight and young-looking, with dark skin and brown eyes.

After a while they smiled at each other in a shy kind of way, and Katie said, 'I don't think he's coming, is he?', and he said, 'It looks that way', and they started chatting about general things like forgetting arrangements and the traffic on

the bypass. He was a bit vague about what he did as a job, which was something to do with digital media, but he wanted to know all about the dog walking, and it turned out his mother had a Labrador like Daisy, and his favourite breed was a bichon frise.

They ended up sliding along the bench until they were side by side, and when the waitress came back they ordered the vegetarian special and a bottle of wine, and got on so well that they met up the following week.

Once, as they walked along the high street, Al reached out for her hand and Katie's heart sang.

After a few more dates, she invited him back to the house for Sunday lunch, which wasn't a particularly good idea because she had to rush around tidying up and wiping slug marks off the shower door. Also, because he was vegan, she tried to make hummus, but the chickpeas were like bullets and wouldn't mash. So she ended up boiling some pasta and opening a jar of ready-made tomato sauce, which looked as if she hadn't made any effort at all.

Al arrived on time with a bunch of white carnations, and they watched a film on TV, and ate the pasta, and drank two bottles of beer. Then they both fell silent, because it seemed the moment had come. Al leaned forward and put his cheek next to hers. She tried to hug him, but somehow their bodies didn't fit together, as if their bones were in all the wrong places, and she kept being aware of things that didn't matter, like the roughness of his sleeve and the fact that he smelled of something faintly antiseptic, like mouthwash.

He drew back.

She said, 'What's wrong?'

He swallowed. 'I'm sorry.'

He left soon afterwards. Katie sat there in the damp living room, mulling it all over as it got later and later and colder and colder, and decided in the end that he just didn't fancy her.

'Oh, Katie,' said Sara. 'That's so sad.'

'I really liked him. He was so gentle and kind.' Katie hung her head. 'Maybe we should have just stayed friends.'

Sara hesitated. 'You know, sex isn't everything.'

Katie looked up.

Sara said, 'I've got a friend who hasn't had sex with her husband for years. They got out of the habit after their youngest was born, and they haven't done it since. It's just not part of their relationship.'

Katie stared. 'Really?'

'It doesn't bother her any more. She doesn't even think about it.'

'What about her husband?'

Sara said, 'He had affairs, I think, over the years.'

'Why did they stay together?'

'A compromise. For the children's sake.'

Katie shook her head. 'I couldn't live like that. Can you imagine? It must be so lonely.'

Sara looked out of the big glass doors to the shadows of the trees beyond.

The following Saturday, holding a large pack of toilet rolls, Sara made her way down the treacherous steps of the

portacabin to find herself once again face to face with Rachel Reeve.

Rachel said, 'So what do you think about the therapist?'

Sara, who wished she'd been carrying something less strongly associated with bodily functions, stared back.

'Maxine. Katie's therapist.'

Sara felt a stab of dismay. 'You know about her?'

'Only because I asked. Apparently, she's not even qualified. She's halfway through an online course. It explains why she's offering cut-price sessions.'

Sara had never asked Katie how much she was paying Maxine. 'Should she be charging at all?'

'Well, exactly. It doesn't seem very professional.'

Sara shifted the mega pack in her arms. 'I'm not sure Katie needs therapy anyway.'

'Her GP suggested it. But there was a nine-month wait for counselling. Services are so stretched. She'd probably be waiting until next year for a course of CBT.'

Sara hesitated.

'Cognitive Behavioural Therapy. Changing patterns of thinking so that your mind works in more positive ways.'

'You sound as if you know quite a lot about it.'

Rachel pulled a face. 'Not really. Only the basics. Mental health is quite an issue in schools these days.'

Sara found herself clutching the toilet rolls more tightly.

'I hear your son wants to study maths.'

'If he gets the grades.'

Rachel fixed her with a direct gaze. 'And will he?'

Flustered, Sara said, 'I hope so. Although he seems to be spending more time planning his summer holiday at the moment.'

'Ah yes. Travelling round Europe.'

Sara was astonished. 'How did you know?'

'It's what they all do. Interrailing and music festivals. Arthur did it last year. I wanted to staple a condom to his forehead.'

Sara recoiled.

'Incidentally, did you know that she was a homeopath?'

'Who?'

'Sarinda who owns the shop.' Rachel nodded towards the portacabin. 'She's a registered homeopath. You know, arsenic for depression. That kind of thing. Of course it's sometimes a bit full on. You go in for a packet of tea bags and she's talking about inherited tendencies. But I thought it might be useful for your husband.'

Sara's voice was cold. 'He wouldn't consider something like that. He's not into anything alternative.'

Rachel smiled. 'Neither am I. I just thought I'd mention it.'

Unsettled by the encounter, Sara wandered home in something of a daze. It was only as the Old Rectory came into view that she wondered how Rachel knew about James wanting to study maths.

It might not have been Katie.

It could have been anyone.

Sara crunched over the frozen grass, deep in thought.

Late one afternoon, Katie opened the front door just as Sara rushed into the hall in a panic of distress. As they stood there

staring at each other, Mike's disembodied voice yelled out, 'Why are you so fucking useless?'

Katie looked shocked. Sara worked hard to get her breathing under control, trying not to show how frightened she was.

'How am I supposed to work? How am I supposed to do my job when you're so fucking unreliable?'

The air trembled with emotion.

'His laptop.' Sara's voice was shaking. 'He's shouting at his laptop.'

It wasn't convincing.

There was a thud, and then the musical crash of breaking glass.

Mike shouted, 'Sara! Sara, get in here!'

Katie put her finger to her lips. Then she called out in a clear carrying voice, 'It's me, Mr Parsons. It's Katie. Can I help?'

After a while, sounding infinitely weary, Mike said, 'No, it's nothing. Forget it.'

Katie touched Sara's elbow and the two of them crept across the hall, out of Mike's line of sight. When they reached the kitchen, Sara shut the door and leaned back against it, momentarily shutting her eyes with relief as if they'd only just managed to escape some terrible danger. Before Katie could speak, she said, 'It's a bad day, that's all. A bad day.'

Katie stared back, her expression full of concern.

'I forgot to pass on a message from his PA. It wasn't really important, but it just set him off. He hates inefficiency. He can't bear wasting time.'

Katie said, 'But shouting like that . . .'

Sara took a deep breath. 'It's not him. It's the pain. He keeps trying to manage without the pills.'

'Why? Why would he do that?'

'He doesn't like being dependent on them. It makes him feel weak.'

'But he needs them.'

Sara nodded. 'If he doesn't take them, he's in agony.'

'Can't someone talk to him?'

Sara didn't want to sound defeatist. But she had to be realistic. 'He won't listen to anyone. And especially not to me.'

They stood there, unable to move.

Sara said, 'I don't want you to worry.'

Even to her ears it sounded pathetic.

As time went on, Katie began to admit that Danny had his faults.

She told Sara about a Saturday morning some weeks after he'd come to live with her. They were lying in a mess of crumpled sheets when Danny leaned over to the floor and rummaged around in the pile of clothes by his side. He lay back on the pillows and tossed something on to her stomach. It was an old-fashioned watch with a finely worked bracelet and a small white face.

Katie felt a rush of pleasure. As she explained to Sara, it was the first present he'd ever given her. It wasn't exactly what she would have chosen herself, because it looked like the kind of thing you'd see in a glass cupboard in a junk shop, but she was excited and happy all the same, turning her wrist this way and that to admire it.

Afterwards, she thought her body must have known before her head, because she suddenly felt very tired. When she glanced up, hoping for reassurance, he looked away. So she fiddled with the catch and the two sides of the filigree bracelet fell apart, the watch slithering to the duvet in a small gold heap. Neither of them said anything. She reached for her big baggy T-shirt, got out of bed, and went downstairs to make a cup of tea.

When she got back to the bedroom, the watch had gone.

Sometimes over the next few months, Danny would be in the pub, and slide his hand into his back pocket and pull out a wad of tens and twenties, and she'd wonder if he'd flogged something else he'd nicked from one of the old ladies who invited him in for biscuits and cake and cups of tea. But she didn't say anything, because she didn't want to risk making him angry.

When she'd finished telling this story, Katie looked up, her eyes full of guilt. 'That was wrong, wasn't it?'

Sara chose her words with care. 'You forgive people all sorts of things when you love them. You make excuses for them.'

'But I should have been braver. I should have asked more questions.'

Sara thought about Danny. She thought about his bony fingers, his blue eyes, the long black coat swinging out as he walked. She thought about the dark sweet smell of caramel. 'I don't think it would have made any difference.'

'What do you mean?'

'I think you're right. He would have got angry. And it wouldn't have stopped him. He would have carried on doing it anyway.'

Katie said, in a small voice, 'I don't think he was a bad person.'

'Of course not.' Sara put her hand on Katie's arm, a touch of warmth and reassurance.

Katie looked up. 'Thank you.'

'For what?'

'For helping me sort it out in my head. Maxine says I have to draw a line under it. If I even mention his name, she gets impatient and says I'm dwelling on the past instead of thinking of the future.' Katie took a deep breath. 'I'll never forget him. But it doesn't hurt so much any more. Not now I've been able to talk about it.'

Later, lying next to Mike in a bed so wide that there was never any danger of them rolling into each other, Sara stared into the dark and thought about Danny. She tried to imagine his voice, wondering how that wheedling tone would sound. She thought about the collusion, the way he'd get you to agree to anything because he'd carved out a place that only you fitted into, so exactly tailored to your measurements that it would have been stupid to turn your back and walk away.

She remembered the first time she'd met Mike.

It was a Sunday afternoon. She quite often went to art exhibitions on Sundays when she lived in north London because they were usually free and surrounded you with lots of people without obliging you talk to any of them. Leaning forward to examine a tear in a canvas – it looked intentional, as if the surface had been attacked with a knife – she had felt someone's eyes resting on her face. She turned her back and moved on to the next painting. When she got to the end of the room, she glanced behind her, and a large man with bulky shoulders and a thick neck was gazing at her with an

expression of puzzlement. His face had a kind of unfinished look because his hair was a pale reddish gold and his eyelashes were so fair they were almost non-existent. This was quite arresting. You couldn't help searching his features for what was missing. So they stood there, staring at each other across the gallery. When he started striding towards her, she looked away, because she didn't want to appear to be inviting contact.

'Have we met before?'

Not the most original of opening lines, obviously, but it sounded like a genuine question. She shook her head.

'Are you sure?' He smiled, the edges of his eyes becoming a fanfare of lines that turned his ill-defined face into something altogether more interesting.

'Quite sure.' She knew he was older. She could see that. He was thirty, it turned out. She was twenty-two.

'Do you like them?' He nodded his head towards the paintings.

She didn't want to encourage him, so tried to appear non-committal.

'The blue one at the end,' he said. 'The one with the yellow stripe. My friend Charlie did it.'

She looked round the room in a vague kind of way and then gave him one of those tight, would-you-excuse-me type of pursed-lip smiles and moved away.

Of course, that didn't stop him. He wouldn't let one small brush-off stand in his way. Somehow they ended up together in front of a different painting a few minutes later, and this time he told her about Charlie's scholarship to the Courtauld, and how amazing it was because no one else in Charlie's family could even hold a pencil let alone draw, and it wasn't as if Bletchley, where they'd both lived as teenagers, was a

town with a reputation for fine art. By the time they reached the exit, Mike had formally introduced himself and asked if he could buy her a cup of coffee. Such was the force of his personality that she couldn't think of a good enough reason why not.

London still didn't feel like home. It must have been because of the cloying attentions of her over-protective mother that she'd ended up in a city where she knew no one at all, renting a room in a shared house, eating mainly pasta and washing out her underwear every night in the bathroom sink. But the job was promising. She had managed to get a junior position as a legal assistant, and was working her way up the career ladder quite nicely. The only drawback was her earnest and acne-covered boss who would gaze at her with hungry longing, his skin glowing bright red.

She wasn't happy or unhappy. Her life was neutral. She watched how other people behaved and copied them. She fitted in well enough.

Then Mike appeared.

She didn't know why he wanted her so badly. She gave him very little to go on. Perhaps that was the point.

Sometimes she wondered if it was all a case of mistaken identity. Early on, Mike had decided that her rather cool exterior hid an exciting personality and clung to this misunderstanding even when reality was trying to prove something different. He'd look at her with fondness, his mouth curving into a smile, and say, 'I know what you're thinking', even when she didn't have an opinion one way or the other. He pre-empted her more facile remarks with clever views he was sure she held. He believed her silence spoke volumes.

Mike was very loud, so disagreement would have been

hard – she would have had to shout with considerable force to make herself heard. But it was also true that she quite enjoyed being given a new personality, because her own bored her to tears. It felt as if someone had slipped a very expensive coat on to her shoulders and she was looking in the mirror, twisting this way and that, admiring her reflection and thinking how much it suited her.

Mike even gave her a sense of humour. She'd say something she genuinely believed, like 'Cyclists should be fined for going through red lights,' and he'd throw back his head and roar with laughter, as if was the funniest thing he'd ever heard. She enjoyed that. It made her feel witty and intelligent.

Of course, she should have known better. Of course, she shouldn't have pretended to be someone she wasn't. But in her defence, she was very young. Mike had to take the blame. He can't have been blind to the fact that young people tend to look up to those who are slightly older. Wealth and experience are bewitching to those who have neither, and even then Mike was raking it in. He loved making money. He was a born entrepreneur.

Mike asked her to marry him on their third date. She pulled a face to show she thought he was mad, and he laughed. He said he'd known the first moment he met her, and that she should congratulate him on his patience so far. It became a kind of joke, or perhaps a kind of bullying. On a visit to Sheffield to see Charlie, who seemed as confused and uncomfortable as she was, he introduced her as 'the future Mrs Parsons'. Driving back, he told her he'd already picked out the house they were going to live in, and boasted he'd bought an antique ring with emeralds and diamonds, ready for when she caved in and agreed.

Was this romantic or manipulative? At what point does persuasion become coercion?

Mike kept telling her that she was in charge and that his whole life was in her hands. But it didn't feel like that. She felt like a small child being pulled along by invisible string.

In the end, as is always the way, a random event changed everything. Four months after they first met, Mike turned up at her place of work in the middle of the afternoon. She was astonished and angry to be called down to reception because a Mr Parsons was waiting to see her. She didn't approve of his overbearing style of courtship interrupting her working day – it felt crass and unprofessional. In the lift on the way down, she almost resolved to teach him a lesson and tell him it was over.

In the polished neutrality of the atrium, Mike was sitting on one of the black faux-leather banquettes, his head bowed. When he looked up, his expression was so bleak she felt a rush of fear. His beloved father had just died in hospital. He didn't know where else to go. She sat down next to him and took his hand, and he turned his head into her shoulder and sobbed.

It was this moment that changed her life forever.

By the end of February, as long as he took his strong prescription painkillers – which Sara couldn't always rely on – Mike was beginning to keep his temper under control. Sara allowed herself to feel optimistic. There was no reason why life shouldn't return to normal. Mike always kept his back very

straight, as if he had a broom handle glued to his spine, and there was a new wariness about him as if his confidence had been dented. But he was starting to drive again, lowering himself into the BMW with great care, and went into the office two or three times a week.

Sometimes, when there was no one in the house, Sara lay on her back on the cold stone floor and listened to the silence.

One morning she suggested it was time for her to go back to work.

He looked up from his laptop. 'Not yet.'

'But you're so much better.'

'It's unpredictable.'

Sara nodded, as if this was worth considering. 'As long as you don't push yourself too far, you're fine.'

Mike looked at her as if she were stupid. 'You have no idea, do you?'

Sara opened her mouth to speak but thought better of it.

He said, returning to the screen, 'What's important is the business. Everything I've built up over the years. We have to focus on that or we'll lose it.' He jabbed at a couple of keys. 'It makes more financial sense for you to be on standby.'

'On standby?'

'To help out if I need you.'

She cleared her throat. 'A sort of assistant? Carer, chauffeur, PA?'

He raised his eyes to her face.

She said, 'It doesn't have to be me. Someone else could do that.'

'Help me out of bed, get me dressed, drive me to work?'

'You're past all that now.'

Mike took a deep breath. 'That's my point. We don't know.

I've got a lot of things at a critical stage, and you might have to step in and give me a hand.'

She said, 'I have to tell them something at work. I have to say when I might be able to go back.'

'Tell them you'll ring them in six weeks.'

'They need me.'

He looked tired. 'It's a part-time job helping a bunch of solicitors. Anyone can do it.'

The shock felt like ice.

He said, 'It's not going to be forever. But right now I've got nineteen people depending on me for their jobs and we need to work together.'

'I don't think you're listening to me.'

He exploded, suddenly and with fury. 'For God's sake, Sara! Can't you think of someone else for once?'

It would have been funny if it hadn't been so tragic. Words crowded into her head, jostling for position. 'Have you calculated the impact of my projected loss of earnings?'

'What?'

'We'll be less well off without my salary.'

He gave her his usual flat stare. 'Hardly.'

She shut herself in the downstairs toilet and cried for an hour.

Later, she rang Jane, the office manager, and apologised for what had become a prolonged period of absence. Jane said she wasn't to worry, and these things happened. In fact, they'd recently taken on a new member of staff who could probably take over Sara's role without too much trouble, so she shouldn't feel under any pressure. If at any point in the future she felt she wanted to come back, they'd probably be able to find something for her at roughly the same sort of

level, but there was no hurry, and Sara should take all the time she needed.

When the call was over, Sara sat in the kitchen looking out at the grey garden. Her hands shook. There was a ringing in her ears, and she felt as if she was choking, as if she couldn't breathe.

When they went to bed that night, Sara said, 'I've told the office I'm not coming back.'

Mike turned, his back rigid, to switch off the bedside lamp. 'Good.'

James had always been able to goad his father into violent outbursts of temper. But now, after weeks of practice, he had perfected his technique. Sara watched, powerless to intervene. They were like two rutting stags locking antlers.

As she explained to Katie one afternoon, it was just an unfortunate set of circumstances. In the old days, before the problems with his back, Mike had been away so often that no one in the family had seen him very much. She herself had become so used to his absence that if they came face to face on the stairs unexpectedly, she found herself nodding to him politely, as if they were fellow residents in a block of flats.

Mike had hardly ever been home in time for supper. Sara usually left his plate by the microwave covered in clingfilm.

But now everything had changed. Because of Mike's

enforced move to working from home, father and son had been thrown into each other's company, and there was a simmering tension just under the surface the whole time.

Sara said, 'I keep asking James to be a bit kinder, but he can't resist.'

Mealtimes were full of potential clashes. Sometimes the aggression in the air was so thick that she couldn't swallow. She found herself leaving most of the food on her plate.

'It'll be easier once James has gone to uni,' said Katie.

Sara tried to smile. 'He can't wait to leave. He'd go tomorrow if he could.'

Hostilities between James and Mike soon reached a peak.

A week or so after the discussion about Sara going back to work, Mike's treasured personal possessions began to go missing. The first report he filed with the police was about his antique Rolex watch, which he used to wear all the time – so much so that his wrist looked strange and bare without it. He'd maintained it meticulously over the years, replacing worn parts and getting it cleaned frequently, so it was in perfect working order. There was high drama when he couldn't find it. The whole house was ransacked, wardrobes emptied, sofa cushions hurled across the room. Sara only stopped him turning every single drawer in the kitchen upside-down by pointing out that if the watch was, indeed, hidden among old corkscrews and biodegradable rubbish bags, pitching it on to the hard stone floor would probably jam its tiny cogs and crack its handsome face forever.

James said, 'You're going senile.'

Mike looked up, his eyes full of thunder.

Sara said, 'I don't think that's fair, James. Your father's always very careful with his watch.'

James shrugged. 'Not quite careful enough.'

Mike made a sudden movement towards his son that dissipated into a kind of ineffectual shove against the table.

Sara said, 'He only ever takes it off at night.'

Mike glared at her. 'You must have put it somewhere.'

She stared back, astonished.

James said, 'That's got to be the solution. It's Mum's fault.'

Sara said, 'James—'

Mike shouted, 'It was by the side of the bed!'

Sara struggled to stay calm and rational. 'Would it help if we went back over your movements yesterday and see if anything jogs your memory?'

Mike knocked over a chair and left the room.

Shortly after this, Mike lost his laptop – the light, slim, incredibly expensive laptop he carried with him everywhere. Again, Sara tried to help him run through in his mind when he'd last had it, whether he'd taken it to his most recent meeting, if there was any possibility he could have left it in the BMW or in the office. Mike yelled at her to stop treating him like an idiot.

James said, 'He's losing it. Alzheimer's. Dementia.'

'Don't, James. It doesn't help.'

He raised his eyes to her face. 'What doesn't help is the way he's trying to blame it on you.'

'But you can see it from his point of view. The laptop's his life. It's got everything on it.'

James patiently explained that it wasn't a long-term problem. Everything on the laptop had been backed up two or three times over in different locations and protected by so many anti-hacking and anti-theft encryption programs that there

could be no breach of security. 'It's just an inconvenience.'

Mike was certain the laptop had been stolen. Again, he made a formal notification to the police.

Not long afterwards, Mike lost the keys to the BMW. The air went blue. Edward retreated to his room and didn't come out for hours. When Sara suggested they should sit down and retrace his steps, Mike smashed the large water jug she'd bought in France on their first holiday after James was born, shattering the glass across the flagstones.

She cleared up with enormous care, anxious that the dog she disliked so much would end up with a needle-like splinter in his paw.

But for days afterwards, cooking a meal or clearing the table, Sara would catch sight of something glinting on the floor. When she went over and knelt down, there it would be, hidden in plain sight – another sharp little shard.

A few days later, as rain threw itself against the great glass doors of the extension and the sky turned from a bluish mauve to gunmetal grey, Sara said, 'Grace is taking a lot of trouble with her appearance these days.'

'Is she?' Katie put down her cup of tea.

'You know – spray tan, hair extensions.'

'But she always does, doesn't she?'

Sara nodded, as if Katie was absolutely right.

'She's a walking advert, if you think about it,' said Katie. 'People look at her, and she's so beautiful they start thinking

about having a manicure or a facial. So she has to look perfect all the time.'

'Yes,' said Sara. 'I expect that's what it is.'

Katie was puzzled. 'Do you think there's something else?'

With some reluctance, Sara said she'd been wondering if it was anything to do with Ryan.

'Ryan?'

Sara shook her head and said it was nothing.

Katie persisted.

Sara said it had been a split second, that's all, and who knows what was really going on, but she'd been driving down the high street past Sainsbury's Local and the Goat, and had stopped at the traffic lights, and glanced over to a white van unloading boxes outside the delicatessen, and she thought she saw Ryan, Grace's boyfriend, down at the end of the alleyway by the bins, his whole body wrapped round someone who definitely wasn't Grace.

Katie's mouth dropped open. She said that just wasn't possible – not Ryan, he adored Grace, worshipped the ground she walked on. Sara immediately agreed, and said she must have got it wrong, although Ryan's honed physique was pretty unmistakeable even from a distance. Katie asked what they'd been doing, and Sara made the kind of face that said, use your imagination. After that, they sat in miserable silence. Katie asked Sara what they should do, and Sara said she thought they shouldn't do anything, and Katie nodded and said Sara was right, and with a bit of luck it would all blow over, and Grace would be none the wiser.

Not long after this conversation, Sara bumped into Mary Miller by the post box and asked after Daisy's arthritis. Mary was touched and invited her in for tea so that she could

see for herself. The kitchen at the back of her small cottage smelled of hot pie. Daisy was lolling by the stove like a stranded seal.

Sara was struck all over again by intense claustrophobia. It seemed impossible that anyone could live in such a confined space.

Mary squeezed past, holding a tray perilously laden with crockery and biscuits. 'And how's Edward doing?'

'Let me take that. You sit down.'

'Getting on well at school?'

But Sara was too focused on preventing a crash of china to reply.

Once they were settled at the tiny round table, Mary said she often saw James waiting at the bus stop in the morning and thought he was turning into a very fine young man. 'Any girl would be lucky to have him.'

'I think he's too busy with his exams at the moment,' said Sara.

'I wondered about Katie.' Mary settled herself more comfortably on the wooden chair. 'Pretty little thing.'

'She is, isn't she?' Sara smiled. 'But they're just friends, I think.'

Mary filled her in on Sally Cook's volunteering with the homeless, Sheila Clark's great-nephew's new wife, who came from Bulgaria and was either a psychiatrist or a paediatrician, and how Lauren Shipman's husband had finally got a job at the food-to-go factory, working mainly with wraps and sushi.

Mary glanced behind her as if worried about unseen eaves-droppers, although the only other pair of ears belonged to the dog on the tapestry cushion. 'And of course, you've heard about Ryan?'

Sara shook her head.

Mary said it was very sad, and Grace was devastated, but Ryan had been caught out doing what he shouldn't.

'What happened?'

Mary said that he'd been seen in broad daylight having it off with a strange young woman, Sara's original story now embellished to include extra details about her height and the colour of her hair.

'Who told you?'

Mary shook her head, looking solemn. 'My lips are sealed.'

When Grace confronted him, Ryan had insisted he was innocent, that he'd never even looked at another woman, and Grace was the only one for him. But Grace was having none of it. She had suspected for a long time that Ryan was having affairs on the side. She kicked him out that same night, throwing his sports bag, Lycra shorts and protein shakes into the road outside their house.

Later that day, Sara told Katie what Mary had said, and Katie dropped her eyes and said in a small voice that things like that always got out in the end.

Mary had planted an uncomfortable thought in her mind. Was there a flicker of interest between James and Katie? It was irrational, of course, but Sara didn't like the idea of two such special people in her life being paired up by village gossip. She felt it was somehow disrespectful. No one should be making up stories about James.

There was also something unpleasant about the idea of James being dragged into Katie's personal therapy. As soon as Sara started remembering Katie's descriptions of her recent sexual encounters, she started feeling light-headed and had to sit down. Had Mary been dropping hints? James kept everything so secret. He never talked about his friends or brought them home. Was there something going on?

Sara remembered Mike's horrible suggestion that James might be sneaking off to see Katie late at night. At the time she'd dismissed it as yet another example of Mike's prurient sense of humour, but now she wondered if she were somehow missing the obvious. James kept himself so distant and aloof that it was hard to know what he was feeling about anything. Even the goading of his father seemed to be some kind of game, testing Mike's temper to the point of explosion.

Of course, she respected her son's privacy. She didn't want to pry. But she had to protect him. The last thing you want is to be tied down too early. If you make a mistake when you're young, you can end up saddled with the wrong person for life.

One evening, she asked Katie to stay to supper, claiming she'd cooked far too much and it would never get eaten otherwise. Katie was initially apprehensive but agreed once she found out that Mike wouldn't be there – she was still very nervous in his company and flinched whenever he swore. To begin with Edward was terrified to look up and find Katie sitting opposite him at the long wooden table. But Katie, with great tact, didn't force any kind of interaction. She seemed to understand that Edward just needed to be left alone.

Sara found herself remembering Hilda, their Faroese au pair.

During the meal, Sara watched James closely. Katie prattled away as usual, talking about her friends Anna and Baz, and Friday evening at the Goat, and the modules she'd chosen for the summer term, and James looked at her with the kind of cool indifference that would have made most people dry up and grind to a halt.

By the time Katie left – walking the long way round by the road even though there was only a fence between them – Sara was quite certain that Mary had got carried away, and had seen romantic possibilities where none existed.

It was a huge relief.

The next time Katie stayed to supper, James said very little and went upstairs to his room the minute the meal was over. He seemed to find Katie boring. Sara felt ashamed that she'd ever listened to Mary's insinuations.

Later, James said, 'Why do you like her so much?'

'Who?'

'Your dog walker.'

She smiled – all that worry, and James couldn't even work out why she and Katie were friends. 'I just do.'

He looked at her as if he didn't believe her.

She said, 'What made you ask?'

'You never like anyone. What's different with her?'

It was such a cruel observation. Sara felt suddenly childlike, as if she wanted to cry. For a moment, she was desperate to explain how much it took for her to trust people, to feel happy in their company. She wanted to say that there was nothing wrong with being discriminating, especially when it came to female friendships.

But later she was glad she'd said nothing. James hadn't meant to wound her. It was just a misunderstanding.

*

In March, as the buds on the honeysuckle and climbing roses burst into life, there were ominous signs that Mike's recovery was stalling. The lines on his face deepened as if someone had scored his skin with a Stanley knife.

Sara said, 'Are you remembering to take your pills?'

He shouted at her to stay out of it and leave him alone. The fury in his voice made her heart plummet with fear.

Shortly afterwards, he took himself off to see a private specialist, and there was talk of steroid injections and surgery.

'So what will you do?'

'I don't know.'

He seemed smaller somehow, diminished by pain. She stared at him, wondering at the disappearance of her bombastic, domineering husband.

As the days passed and Mike withdrew into silent introspection, it felt as if his grip on them all had loosened. The house was strangely quiet. He didn't shout at Sara for her lapses of memory or throw recalcitrant objects at the walls. He stopped yelling at Bundle. Even mealtimes were calm, with Mike ignoring – or perhaps not even hearing – James's attempts to nudge him into explosions of temper. Looking at him sitting there, hunched over like an old man, Sara wondered if Mike was finally considering some kind of surgical procedure. He'd always dismissed it before – every operation carries risks, and he'd been told that there were no guarantees and that radical interventions sometimes made the pain even worse. If he was seriously thinking of going into hospital, he must be in agony.

She wanted to ask if she could help him decide, but always managed to stop herself in time. He would only tell her not to interfere.

With his father so preoccupied, James didn't bother asking for permission to use the car. If Sara didn't need it, he drove off on Friday and Saturday nights, often coming back so late that the whole house was asleep by the time he came in. Sara rejoiced in his independence but wished he told her more about where he was going and what he was doing. It felt sometimes as if James had found a magic key and could let himself out while she was still imprisoned until further notice.

Liberated from his father's moods, Edward seemed braver and more resilient. Some of his artistic projects – miniature constructions made from thin cardboard, each piece meticulously cut and folded – left his bedroom and took up residence around the house. One of them grew bit by bit over several days at the end of the long wooden table in the kitchen, so neat and detailed that it looked like an architect's model of some kind of ancient catacomb.

She said, 'Is it a house?'

Edward shook his head.

'A palace?'

Edward frowned.

She didn't understand but admired his creativity.

Sadly, the brief respite from Mike's temper was short-lived. One night, Bundle, excited by something he couldn't quite see, nosed Edward's tiny masterpiece off the table. By the time Edward came down in the morning – the first to arrive in the great glass extension – the intricate structure had been flattened and squashed, chewed into a mess of damp pulp.

Edward's agonised wailing sent Bundle to the opposite corner of the room where he crouched in terror, whining and scrabbling at the floor.

Mike, who had got up early and was working on his laptop in the living room, limped through to the kitchen, disturbed by all the commotion. He was scathing. 'Of course the dog's going to get it if you leave it out like that.'

Sara was near to tears herself. 'I didn't think.'

'Obviously,' said Mike.

She couldn't stop herself. 'You could have moved it! You knew as well as I did how precious it was!'

Mike looked at her with contempt. 'That's right. Blame everyone but yourself.'

'Why is it always my fault?'

He shouted, 'Because the dog is your responsibility!'

'Why? Why is he my responsibility?'

Edward had his arms over his head, trying to block out the noise.

Mike's fury ripped through the air, a jagged dislocation of sound. 'Once, just once, can you keep the fucking noise down so that I can do some work?'

When Sara looked up, Katie was standing in the doorway, her face pinched with shock. The row had been so loud that no one had noticed she'd let herself in.

James appeared beside her, tall and white, naked except for a pair of shorts. His dark hair was sticking up at angles. 'What's going on?'

'I'm going upstairs.' Mike pushed past him, knocking him sideways against Katie.

On the far side of the kitchen, making little keening sounds, Edward was squatting on his heels in a tight protective huddle.

'Mum?' James was still dazed with sleep. 'What's happened?'

Katie lifted the lead from the hook on the wall and made encouraging patting sounds on the pocket of her coat to get

Bundle's attention. The dog struggled to his feet, his rear end buckled under in a kind of squat as if someone had kicked him, and crept after her to the front door.

Later, Sara thanked her for taking Bundle out so quickly.

Katie's eyes were sympathetic. 'I thought Edward needed some space.'

'He did. He can't really cope with arguments.'

'Is he all right now?'

Sara took a deep breath. 'I think so. I got him off to school in the end.'

'Sara,' Katie spoke in a rush, 'are you OK?'

'I'm fine.'

'Are you sure?'

Sara nodded with such finality that Katie couldn't ask any more questions.

Over the next few days, in ways she didn't quite understand, Sara felt as if a grey curtain had fallen over her life. The tension in the house was still there, but she could no longer work up the energy to feel that it mattered. Something inside her had finally been used up and couldn't be replaced. This led to a strange detachment that wasn't altogether welcome, as it wiped out the brisk efficiency of her usual routine. Sometimes she would find herself standing halfway up the stairs, or in the blue-and-white guest room overlooking the garden, wondering where she was going and what she was doing. Lists were half-written. Appointments were forgotten. Her brain felt disconnected, unmoored, floating free in her skull. It was as if all the tiny electrical sparks had stopped firing across its synapses.

When Mike yelled at her because she'd forgotten to pick up a prescription from the chemist, or collect his dry cleaning,

or buy him more whisky, she stared at him blankly, wondering at the redness of his face.

He said, 'Are you ill?'

'Tired.'

He glared at her. 'Go to bed.'

But she didn't want to lie down and stare at the walls.

To Katie, Sara pretended that it was an old problem she'd had before, hinting at low iron levels and anaemia, and Katie insisted she sat down and had a cup of tea while she herself took over chopping up onions and garlic and peeling potatoes as the light faded from the sky. She began to stay for supper more and more often, becoming such a normal part of the evening routine that it seemed strange when she went back to the hovel instead. Edward was no longer worried by her presence. Overall, he was probably much more disturbed by the dog.

Late one evening, when Mike and the boys had disappeared to distant parts of the house, and they were clearing the table in companionable silence, Katie said, 'He never stops, does he?'

'Who?'

'Mike. He's always up there, working away.'

Sara nodded. 'It's his life.'

'You'd think he'd want to take a break and do something relaxing.'

She couldn't hold it back any more. 'Maybe he is.'

Katie looked confused.

Sara's voice was edged with misery. 'All I know is that he doesn't want me to see what he's doing. If I knock on the door, he yells at me to go away.'

Katie opened her mouth to speak but seemed uncertain what to say.

Sara said, 'It's always been like this. Ever since the boys were small. It's his escape. It's more real to him than we are.'

'Work?'

Sara couldn't quite bear to put it into words.

The two of them stared at each other, communicating difficult possibilities.

Katie said, 'A lot of people are addicted to gaming.'

Sara's eyes filled with tears.

'Sit down.' Katie put a hand on her arm. 'I can finish clearing up.'

'It just makes me feel so useless. So tired. That he'd rather do that than . . .' Sara couldn't finish. She stared down at the table, defeated.

There was a small silence.

'Does it run in the family?'

Sara looked up, confused. 'What?'

'The tiredness thing.' Katie picked up Mike's empty wine glass.

'I don't think so.'

Katie said, 'Do you think you should go and see your GP?'

'No.' Sara pulled a face.

'Just for a check-up. To make sure you're all right.'

But she'd spent weeks ferrying Mike to clinics and hospitals. She'd had enough of doctors.

That night, because of Katie's random comment, Sara found herself thinking about her family for the first time in months. It made her uncomfortable. She remembered her mother's hunched shoulders, her shrinking timidity, her belief that her main function in life was to keep her only daughter safely bubble-wrapped from all possible dangers. Lying there in the dark, Sara tried to shut off the memories and think of

something more soothing, but she no longer seemed to have the ability to stop things happening. She floated along like a dead leaf on water, a dried husk carried by the current.

Her father had walked out when she was very small. She could hardly remember him. Her mother said, 'He couldn't face up to his responsibilities,' which made Sara feel as if she'd been something unpleasant, like a debt or a duty.

The final separation had been brutal. By that stage, her mother hardly left the house, a shadow of a woman, listless and defeated. She had tried very hard to stop Sara leaving home, but Sara had ignored her. The minute she finished school, she went to London and spent an eye-opening summer working as a chambermaid in a dirty four-storey hotel in Bloomsbury, wiping shower tiles, polishing mirrors, and wondering at the various manifestations of bodily fluids around and inside sheets, sanitary towels and long, stringy condoms.

At the wedding, her mother had been overwhelmed, twisting a white handkerchief round and round in her hands.

Mike had said, 'She's very emotional, isn't she?'

Sara had allowed herself a tight little smile.

The pictures kept coming. She remembered the narrow suburban street of terraced houses where she'd grown up, the small concrete gardens at the front just big enough for the plastic bins. Two doors down was a girl about her age, with straight red hair and freckles. They used to soak pink rose petals in water and pretend it was perfume. What was her name? Lisa. They played together all the time. Lisa stood in the sunlight, raising her arm to shield her eyes. 'I knew I'd like you because you've got a nice face.'

You treasure compliments. You store them up and keep them safe.

Sara lay still, listening to the grumble of Mike's breathing. She thought about Katie. She remembered the time she'd said, 'You're so wise, Sara,' and hearing it had made her dizzy with pleasure, as if she'd been spun round in a giant teacup or drunk a shot of neat gin. Close female friendships are so important. Of course, Katie hadn't quite got it right. She was too young to understand. It wasn't about wisdom at all. It was knowing how to listen. This was something Sara had worked out years before. Keep eye contact, even if your thoughts are racing ahead. Keep eye contact, but say nothing.

She hadn't always remembered to follow her own rules. In the wills and probate department, faced with those who were lazy or whose work was slipshod, she had sometimes said what she really thought. She had realised her mistake immediately, from the shocked look on their faces, even though everyone knows it's hard to maintain civil communication when people let you down. Your temper can get the better of you. You start shouting, and then the words take over and flood out of their own accord, becoming evil and hard and mean.

Mike knew this.

Sara stared into the darkness, the bulk of her husband in the bed beside her.

One Sunday morning at the beginning of April, Mike looked up from his laptop and said he wanted a party for his fiftieth birthday at the end of June.

Sara stared with astonishment.

'Don't start,' said Mike. 'There's no need to go on and on and try to make me change my mind. It's not worth arguing about.'

'You're not well enough.'

'I said, don't start.'

She persisted. 'What about James's exams?'

'What about them?'

'He needs peace and quiet to study.'

'I checked. They'll be over by then.'

'But what if—'

'Sara, for God's sake. It's just a party. A bit of a celebration.'

It wasn't fair. He was asking too much. 'I thought you didn't want to celebrate. You said you hated getting old. You didn't want to be fifty.'

There was a small silence. The air quivered.

Mike's voice was cold. 'You never want me to enjoy myself, do you? Anything that gives me pleasure, you kill it stone dead.'

This didn't deserve a response.

He said, 'It's a way of thanking everyone.'

'For what?'

'For all their support over the past few months.'

Sara frowned. 'So it's a work party.'

Mike looked at her with irritation. 'A birthday party.'

'How many people?'

'Does it matter?'

Sara caught her breath. 'Of course it matters.'

'Fifty, maybe. A hundred. I don't know. I'll make a list.'

Inside, in her head, a little voice was screaming.

He said, 'It's three months away. All you've got to do is order some wine.'

She looked him directly in the eye. 'Please tell me you're joking.'

He wouldn't back down. 'Nothing formal. Just a nice summer party. Friends, family, people from work, eating

strawberries and drinking champagne. They can all admire the garden.'

'Family?'

'You. The boys.'

The relief was so severe, she couldn't speak.

There was an unpleasant glint in his eyes. 'Did you think I was going to ask Ursula?'

She said, trying to sound offhand, 'I have no idea.'

Mike laughed.

The next day, Sara spilled out the whole story – softening it by saying that Mike didn't really understand how much work was involved, even for something so apparently informal.

Katie was surprised. 'I thought he didn't like having people over.'

Sara said he was making an exception because it was all about public relations and corporate entertainment.

Katie said, 'Not just friends, then?'

This was all getting a bit complicated, so Sara said that it didn't really matter who was coming to the party – she was just dreading the whole thing. Mike said he wanted it to be simple and low-key, but she knew he didn't really mean it. He was expecting a grand occasion, something showy and spectacular, which meant hours of planning and preparation, and she was just so exhausted these days. She could hardly get round the supermarket without feeling drained and befuddled.

Katie leaned forwards. 'You mustn't worry. I'll help.'

'Don't you have exams?'

'Coursework. And I finish in May.'

Sara said, in a rush, 'Only if you let me pay you.'

'But I didn't—'

'By the hour. A proper rate. I insist.'

Katie, pink with a mixture of embarrassment and gratitude, eventually agreed.

When Sara told Mike, he was furious. 'You're making a fuss. It's a few drinks, that's all, not a bloody wedding reception.'

Sara said she'd been thinking about what kind of food to serve at the party, and was wondering whether to stick with a few of his top favourites, like lamb souvlaki followed by chocolate brownies and home-made ice cream.

He shot her a weary look, as if he knew he'd been outmanoeuvred.

A few days later, he emailed her a long list of names. As Sara explained to Katie one afternoon as they sat at the long wooden table having a cup of tea, it was a real mixture of work colleagues, business associates, and people he'd known since childhood. Mike had always been good at keeping hold of contacts who might be useful. He was busy networking before anyone had even heard of it.

She said, sounding flat, 'He wants to be the centre of attention the whole time.'

Katie nodded. 'I can see that. He's that kind of person.'

Sara took a deep breath. 'But he's just so – I don't know, uncritical. He needs an audience he can perform to, but it doesn't matter who it is. Anyone will do.'

Katie looked confused.

Sara said, 'I choose my friends with care. I have to be sure I can trust them, and that they won't let me down. Otherwise, what's the point? You're just going to end up disappointed.'

Katie nodded, in complete agreement. 'So will they be coming?'

'Who?'

'Your friends?'

Sara took a moment to respond. 'It's Mike's party. Not mine.'

'But he wouldn't mind, would he? If you invited a few people?' Katie smiled. 'I'd love to meet your friends. All this time I've known you, and I've never met a single one.'

Sara glanced up at the clock and said she hadn't realised how late it was, and Katie – who was sensitive to small changes in atmosphere – took this as her cue to leave.

Easter came and went. James hardly left his room, conscientiously working his way through his revision timetable.

Mike broke his iPhone by throwing it across the kitchen, narrowly missing the great glass doors.

Katie's unorthodox therapy continued.

'Maxine said you don't get anywhere without ambition, and successful people never settle for second best.'

Sara nodded.

Katie's expression was quite fierce. 'She said it's natural to feel angry that some people are born into lives of wealth and privilege while other people scrabble around in the dirt begging for scraps. It's no good pretending that money isn't important. To get what you need, you have to barge your way to the front of the queue, even if it means trampling over everyone else to get there first. The important thing is being clear and focused about what you want, because you're worth

it, and you deserve it, and you can't let other people take it from under your nose.'

'And what did you say to that?'

Katie's shoulders sagged. 'I said I didn't really like elbowing other people out of the way, and she said that was because I didn't have any goals. She said that if I really knew what I wanted, I wouldn't think twice, because success is all about being ruthless.'

'Single-minded,' said Sara.

Katie looked woebegone. 'She said there are winners and losers, and no one wants to be a loser.'

'I suppose she's right in a way.'

Katie screwed up her face.

Sara said, 'You're not sure?'

'I said it all sounded a bit competitive. She didn't like that very much. She gave me one of her angry looks and said I wasn't trying hard enough.'

Sara thought this sounded like a totally toxic relationship. But she didn't want to hurt Katie's feelings by saying so. 'If you're not getting on with Maxine, you could always try a different therapist.'

Katie opened her eyes wide. 'I couldn't do that. She'd be furious. She demands total commitment from all her clients.'

Later, Sara thought that she should have tried harder to make Katie see sense. But she wasn't thinking as clearly as usual. Most days, she felt she was operating in a kind of fog. Even simple decisions were difficult. Sometimes she tried to think rationally, to work out why she no longer felt in control. But she seemed to have lost her powers of analysis. She felt completely useless, like an empty takeaway carton in a gutter, or a piece of tissue paper on the floor.

Because of this, the prospect of Mike's fiftieth birthday party at the end of June – crowds of people invading her house and garden – made her feel dizzy and afraid. All she'd done so far was send out the invitations. The rest of it – the cleaning, the catering, the organisation – loomed in the distance, becoming ever more impossible to arrange.

She kept this hidden from Katie. She was ashamed of her incapacity. Fortunately, Katie was less aware of undercurrents than usual – she had a series of essay deadlines and kept rushing home to the hovel to work.

More importantly, Sara made sure that none of her anxieties were visible to James. Stress had to be kept to a minimum while he was concentrating on his exams. When study leave started in the middle of May, he would no longer be going into school and it was vital that the house stayed calm and quiet.

To her intense relief, Mike – despite his continuing back pain – was beginning to ease himself back into his usual routine. He seemed to have decided to manage his condition through a combination of painkillers, alcohol and willpower. Work absorbed him, and she could tell from overheard phone calls that he was pushing hard for new contracts. This sudden surge of activity meant that she didn't always know where he was going to be, which led to unpleasant surprises, like finding him in the living room or the kitchen when she thought he was at the office, or hearing his car sweeping into the drive when she'd assumed she was going to have the house to herself. But he was generally around much less, and hardly ever at home in time for the evening meal, which meant that she and the boys could eat in peace.

James, focused on revision, was monosyllabic. Sometimes,

sitting opposite him at the table, Sara felt close to tears. It felt as if he'd already left, as if his head was way beyond his mother and his younger brother. She wanted his success with all her heart. At the same time, brilliant results meant she would lose him to a new and independent life.

One morning, car keys in hand, Sara opened the front door to find herself facing the postman. He was, as usual, dressed in khaki shorts and brown hiking boots, his bucket hat crammed on to his head.

'Shall I take them?' she said, nodding towards the letters in his hand.

He looked down with surprise, as if he hadn't expected to find himself clutching a pile of envelopes.

There was an awkward silence.

'What did you do, then?'

Sara stared. 'What?'

'I wondered if you'd had him put down.'

Sara struggled to understand.

'The dog.' The postman shifted the heavy bag on his shoulder. 'Only I can't hear a thing these days. Nothing but birdsong.'

'Oh,' said Sara, realisation dawning. 'No, he's fine. He's out at the moment. In Smith's Field, probably. Or up Ogden Hill. We've got a dog walker.'

'A dog walker?'

'Yes.'

'Ah,' said the postman. 'That would explain it.'

They stood in the May sunshine.

Sara held out her hand. 'Shall I take the letters?'

'I used to feel really sorry for him, barking away. You could hear him all round the cul-de-sac.'

Sara willed him to leave but couldn't think how to make it happen.

'I thought he might have mental health problems. You know, sudden rages. Unpredictable. Aggressive.'

Sara said, 'I really ought to be going.'

'I'm glad you didn't.'

'Didn't what?'

'Have him put down.'

The grey fog thick in her brain, Sara couldn't think what to say.

'I mean, you wouldn't want to do it, would you? But you can see why it happens, because they're dangerous when they're out of control. You read about it all the time. Turn on their own family sometimes.' The postman looked down at the bundle of letters, secured by an elastic band, and then – as if struck by a novel idea – held it out to her.

Watching him crunch away across the gravel towards the tall wrought-iron gates, Sara slowly exhaled.

For a moment, she felt light-headed, as if she might fall.

At the beginning of June, Mike announced that he was going to a weekend conference in Germany.

Sara decided against asking questions.

He glared at her. 'Nothing to say? No little digs? No barbed remarks?'

'I hope you have a lovely time.'

He looked away, disgusted.

It was bliss. In his absence, they all relaxed. On Saturday, James took a couple of hours off revising for his final exams, and the three of them watched a film on TV. Edward even took off his earphones and hung around in the kitchen while Sara cooked spaghetti.

Bundle, as if sensing a change in atmosphere, seemed much less agitated.

Mike was due back on Monday evening. That afternoon, when Katie was hanging up Bundle's lead on the hook in the kitchen, Sara said, 'It feels like a holiday.'

'Because he's not here?'

Sara looked guilty. 'I shouldn't have said that.'

Katie shook her head. 'You deserve a break. I don't know how you've managed to keep going. Everything would fall apart without you.'

Sara said, with sudden earnestness, 'I wish you'd known us before all this happened. He's a good man, you know. Very driven. Very ambitious. But only because he wants the best for his family. He loves his sons. He'd do anything for them.'

Katie's eyes were full of sympathy.

'I just wish the pain would go away.' Sara knew she sounded desperate. 'He won't even talk about it any more. He won't discuss treatments, or what the consultant says, or whether he's still thinking about surgery.'

'I'm so sorry.'

'He doesn't want me to see what's going on. But I know how stressed he is. It can't be right, can it? Swallowing hand-fuls of pills. Getting drunk every night.' Sara dropped her voice to a whisper. 'I'm really worried, Katie. I don't think he can carry on like this.'

Katie had left by the time Mike came home. The taxi from

the airport crunched over the gravel soon after Edward came back from school. James was upstairs studying. When Sara came into the hall, drawn by the noise of Mike's arrival, she found Edward rooted to the spot, transfixed by his father's sudden reappearance.

Mike looked as if it was only force of will that was keeping him upright. His skin was grey. He seemed to have new lines cut into his face. As he turned to take off his coat, he stepped backwards and stumbled over a pair of shoes that had been left near the front door. He cried out, a kind of guttural roar that flattened the air like a sledgehammer.

Edward flinched.

Mike shouted, 'What the fuck are these doing here?'

Sara rushed over to pick them up.

'How stupid can you get? What are you trying to do – kill me in my own home?'

Crouched on the floor, Sara looked up. 'Mike—'

His eyes were like bullets. 'Don't start.'

Edward, wide-eyed with fear, was swaying like a sapling in a high wind.

'Please, Mike.' Sara was finding it hard to breathe. 'Please leave it now. Come and have a cup of tea. Edward didn't mean any harm. It was just a mistake.'

Mike looked at her with fury. 'I wasn't blaming Edward.'

In the middle of the tirade that followed, as his swearing bounced off the white walls and the air was blasted with abuse, Sara froze. Out of the corner of her eye, she saw James at the top of the stairs, his hand on the black iron balustrade. She took a step forward, trying to stop him. But it was too late. There was a kind of rushing in her ears, a blurring of sound and pressure.

'That's enough!'

His voice echoed through the space.

Mike, mid-bellow, looked up.

The silence fell like a sheet of ice.

All three of them were now staring up at James. His fists were clenched. Sara felt sick. In one blinding moment, she knew for certain that there was going to be physical violence – that everything over the past few months had been leading up to this moment, that it was inevitable that her son and her husband were going to lay into each other, to fight for dominance, to batter each other into submission.

She could see blood.

Mike broke the spell. 'I need a drink.'

As he crashed off towards the kitchen, Sara realised she'd been holding her breath for so long that she felt faint.

James came down the stairs in record time. They gathered as near as they dared to Edward, talking in low voices until he stopped shaking.

After a while, she looked up and met James's eyes.

He said, 'You can't let him get away with it.'

She nodded.

But he hadn't finished. 'I mean it. I'm not going to be around forever. Once I've gone, you and Edward will be on your own.'

'I don't want you to worry.'

'So you keep saying.' James was still staring at her, willing her to focus. 'It can't go on like this. You have to do something. He's got to be stopped before it's too late.'

*

'So did he crawl home in the early hours and throw up in the flower bed?'

Sara, startled out of her thoughts, nearly fell into the cans of baked beans. Rachel, sunglasses balanced on her grey curls, had stuck her head round the carousel of birthday cards.

'Arthur's hangover lasted two days. He tried to pretend it was a migraine.'

Sara said, 'I don't—'

'But I expect James is more sensible, being a mathematician. It's perfectly possible to celebrate the end of exams without giving yourself liver damage.'

Sara wished she was anywhere but the village shop.

Rachel smiled. 'I hear there's a big party tomorrow.'

'I'm sorry?'

'Mike's fiftieth. Lamb on skewers, vegetarian lasagne and home-made ice cream.'

Sara could only stare.

'I think it's very kind of you to give Katie the extra work. Poor girl. She has no support from her parents at all.' Rachel had skirted the end of the aisle and was now standing next to Sara, contemplating the packets of soup. 'I do wonder if it's safe for her to live in that horrible house. She says there's fungus growing out of the skirting boards. Something to do with the heat and the damp. I know she wants to keep costs down, but some of the basic accommodation on campus is quite cheap. I said she should find out what's available for next year. Part of the whole university experience is living with other students.'

Sara felt a familiar tension round her temples, as if she was wearing a hat that was way too tight.

'And she needs to get rid of that therapist. She's not even

reliable. Keeps cancelling at the last minute. You can't do that, can you? Not if you're looking after people with mental health issues.' She gave Sara a sideways glance. 'Katie says you're a keen gardener.'

Sara took a deep breath. 'Yes.'

'You've got green fingers, apparently. A riot of colour.'

'In fact,' said Sara, rapidly deciding she didn't need any milk after all, 'I ought to be getting back. There's still a lot to do.'

'And how is Mike?'

For a split second, Sara wanted to be brusque and rude, to put an end to a meaningless conversation that was making her feel cornered and uncomfortable, but she swallowed the impulse and said, 'Up and down.'

Rachel gave her a shrewd look. 'How brave of him to have a party when he's in so much pain.'

What was that supposed to mean? 'It was his idea.'

'I'm sure it was.'

'He wanted,' said Sara, 'to thank everyone at work for being so supportive over the past few months.'

'As well as celebrating his birthday.'

'Yes.'

There was a hint of a smile playing round Rachel's mouth.

Walking home over the dry, scrubby grass under the midday sun, Sara felt a surge of irritation, more than ever convinced that Rachel was treating her as one big joke.

At the Old Rectory, Katie had polished the great glass doors of the extension to a brilliant shine.

'They'd run out,' said Sara, putting down her shopping basket on the table. 'So we'll have to drink it black.'

Katie's normal air of dishevelment had increased. Damp wisps of hair clung to her forehead. 'What about tomorrow?'

'We can get some in the morning.'

Sara glanced up at the lush green loveliness of the garden, the managed chaos of astrantia and hellebore, silene and aquilegia. The weather forecast was good for the next day – hot sunshine and clear skies – and it would be a perfect June evening. She pictured the long trestle tables set up on the lawn, the salads, the strawberries, the jugs of Pimm's.

They had been hard at work the whole day and the house was poised in a state of readiness. Every room had been dusted and cleaned. Even the small white boot room had been swept. In the old scullery, the huge American-style fridge freezer was full of champagne, white wine and beer. In the kitchen, the fridge was packed with food for the party.

Sara had written a long list and was slowly ticking off the tasks one by one.

Weeks later, when the horror was starting to recede, she realised the list had stayed behind the kettle the whole time, the paper curled and spattered by tea, coffee, brandy.

James had already left for the Isle of Wight. When she asked if he was sure he wanted to miss his father's party, he'd given her a long-suffering look.

'You know the answer.'

She said, flustered, 'I just thought I'd check.'

He shook his head as if she'd lost her mind.

She couldn't bear to watch him leave. It felt like the beginning of the end. She focused on Edward, fussing over him until he got upset and started shaking and she realised he wanted to be left in peace.

Bundle, sensing abandonment, howled.

But it was better once James had gone. Emotional anticipation is always much worse than the event itself. Added to

this, Mike had left for Birmingham early that morning, and wasn't expected back until midnight – he was visiting new clients and taking them out to dinner – so the atmosphere in the house was light and happy. After lunch, Katie started folding cutlery into white napkins and counting out plates while Sara made the vegetarian lasagne and marinated the lamb. Late in the afternoon, when their energy started to flag, Sara suggested that Katie stay for supper, and they ate pizza on their knees while they watched *The Hobbit: An Unexpected Journey*, which Edward knew so well that he quivered with excitement each time Gandalf spoke. After that, because Katie was due to come back in the morning anyway, Sara asked if she'd like to stay the night.

'Can I have a bath?'

'Of course. Help yourself.'

Katie's face lit up like a child at Christmas, and Sara remembered the cold lean-to in the dilapidated hovel, the slugs on the shower door.

It had been a long day. Katie and Edward were already in bed when Mike rang. He said that dinner with the clients had been cancelled and he was on his way back. He was in a lot of pain. He needed to get home and sleep.

As Sara told the police the next day, she couldn't remember hearing Mike's car, or the slam of the front door. She didn't hear him come to bed. Their lives that day had been so separate. It was as if she and Katie had been on one path, and Mike had been on another, and it was complete chance that they'd all ended up in the same place in the early hours as Friday nudged into Saturday.

On the morning of Mike's fiftieth birthday, Sara woke at six – as she always did – and got up as quietly as possible,

paying serious attention to every move so that she didn't disturb him. In the bathroom, she got dressed in the clothes she'd worn the day before, because they were going to end up dirty from cooking anyway, and crept downstairs to let Bundle out into the garden. She stood for a moment looking out at the long sweep of the lawn as the light intensified and the day expanded into heat and wakefulness. Then she reached for her list. There was still a lot to do.

Katie came downstairs at about nine, and they had a cup of tea together before they started preparing the salads.

At around ten o'clock, Sara made Mike a cup of coffee and took it upstairs. He was still as she'd left him, a hump under the bedclothes, turned away towards the wall. The room was already warm, and the light was yellow and creamy. She went to his side of the bed, next to the window, and stood there, looking down at his face.

Two irreconcilable thoughts lurched into her head at the same time: he's dead, he's sleeping.

He was still under the sheet, his head on the pillow, so it seemed logical to think that he might wake up. But another part of her brain could see that he wasn't breathing. He looked different anyway, as if the central part of him – the part that made him a person – had somehow disappeared. She put the coffee on the bedside table and thought, 'He won't be wanting that now,' and stared at it, not sure what to do.

Time became long and stretched out all around her, like old elastic or pulled chewing gum, and she saw that her hands were shaking.

Then came a gap that, thinking back later, could never be filled with memory, however hard she tried, until she was in the kitchen, finding it hard to breathe, and Katie looked at

her face and said, 'Oh God, what's happened?' and somehow knew it was something to do with Mike or Edward and ran out of the room, racing for the stairs. Sara slid out a chair from the table and sat down and remembered at that exact moment that it was ten o'clock on a Saturday morning, and Edward was still asleep, and might wake up at any moment and blunder through the doorway and find his father lying there, lifeless, so she ran upstairs too, and she and Katie met on the landing, crashing into each other just outside the bedroom, and Katie said in a high voice, 'I'll ring for an ambulance,' and disappeared so fast that Sara said to nothingness, to empty air, 'There's no point. It's too late.'

Some time later – seconds or minutes, she didn't know – she found herself in Edward's room, sitting on the end of the bed and staring out of the window at the blue sky. She knew she had to wake him, to prepare him for the strangers who were about to arrive – because random, unplanned events were so frightening for him – but she couldn't bring herself to do it. When he woke, it would be the start of a completely different life. It seemed so momentous, so final, that it felt like standing on the edge of a pit, and looking down into darkness, knowing you were about to fall but being unable to stop yourself.

She put her hand on his leg under the white sheet, feeling the hard bone of his shin. It would be impossible for him to understand. He would be confused and upset.

She thought about the warm light in their bedroom.

She leaned forward and gently shook Edward awake.

It was the paramedics who called the police, after they'd examined Mike's body and failed to find a heartbeat. Katie let them in – two police constables in white shirts and black

boots, radios crackling – and one of them went upstairs with her while the other, PC Bush, who had short grey hair and very blue eyes, took Sara and Edward into the big white living room. Edward was rocking back and forth on the balls of his feet saying, 'Where's Dad? Dad's dead,' over and over again, and Sara explained that he was on the autism spectrum, and wasn't really able to process what had happened, and PC Bush nodded and said that was fine, he didn't need to ask him any questions. They sat down on one of the sofas, and PC Bush asked her to tell him what she knew, and Sara passed on all the dry, useless details, embarrassed by how little there was to say.

When she talked about being careful not to disturb Mike when she first woke up – because the day before had been long and stressful, and he needed as much sleep as possible – she started crying, and Edward became even more distressed. PC Bush asked if he could call someone to look after them, but Sara couldn't think of anyone except for Katie, and she was already there.

PC Bush asked whether Sara had moved anything from the bedroom, or whether she'd left everything just as she'd found it, and she said she hadn't touched anything at all. He wanted to know if Mike had any health problems, and Sara explained he'd had trouble with his back for months, and gave him the name of their GP, but couldn't remember the name of the private consultant. They talked about Mike running his own company, and how the meeting in Birmingham had been important because he'd been hoping for a new contract the business badly needed.

Eventually PC Bush creaked off in his black leather boots to find his colleague upstairs, and Sara took Edward outside

into the garden so that they could watch the sparrows in the birdbath. Bundle stood on the lawn, barking, barking, barking, but in her mind Sara turned the sound down so that it was like watching an old black and white film with the odd crackled flash and spark.

The police stayed for a long time. A police sergeant visited briefly, but didn't ask any questions, and was gone before she could offer him a cup of tea. At one point, PC Bush came out to talk to her again and said they'd bagged up all the medication they'd found. 'Had your husband been drinking, do you know?'

'He drove back from Birmingham. He wouldn't have had anything at all.'

'What about when he got home?'

She tried to picture what had been lying about near the sink when she first got down to the kitchen, but it had all been so automatic, clearing away mugs and plates and bowls and debris from the night before, that she couldn't remember. Had there been an empty whisky glass? She'd already run the dishwasher through and unloaded it all before she'd even taken up the cup of coffee. 'Maybe. I don't know.'

'You didn't hear him come to bed?'

'No.'

'So he might have stayed up late?'

She nodded.

'Watching TV? Working?'

'I think so. I don't know. If he was in his study, he always had the door shut.' Then she said, in a rush, 'But I don't think he would have stayed up last night. He would have been tired. He would have come straight to bed.'

A little later, when she thought PC Bush had gone back

inside to talk to his colleague, she looked up to see both police constables walking along the far boundary of the garden, searching the shrubbery, looking up at the high green hedges.

The police were still there when she rang James. With great care, keeping her voice steady and calm, she said she had some bad news, and he said, 'What's happened?' with a level of anxiety in his voice that made it clear that he knew it was something serious.

Later, he said that his friends took all the decisions about getting him home – finding someone to drive him back from the festival, taking him straight from some tent in a field all the way to their front door. He was home by six. It was when she saw him standing in the hall – her son, her eldest – that she broke down. She hugged him, and he smelt of tobacco and wood smoke and unwashed clothes.

He said, 'Can I see him?'

She went with him upstairs and watched him walk into the room and stand there, looking down at the body of his father.

By the time James arrived home, Katie had already been hard at work for a couple of hours cancelling the party. She had found Sara's master list, neatly subdivided into categories with phone numbers and emails attached, and worked her way through, getting help from shocked friends and colleagues who offered to ring some of the guests themselves – even, in some cases, to go round and break the news in person. The background to the daze of hours was Katie's voice saying, 'Yes, very sudden,' and 'We don't really know, I'm afraid,' and 'Yes, of course we will.'

Sara knew she should be doing more but knew, equally

clearly, that she couldn't do anything at all except sit with Edward while he rocked back and forth on his chair.

At about seven, the undertaker appointed by the police came to take Mike's body. By this time, Edward was in a pretty bad way. He depended on routine – similar things happening at similar times, nothing abrupt or unexpected – and the day of Mike's death had been unpredictable from beginning to end. Sara and Katie stayed with him in the garden while James went to stand in the hall, watching as his father left the house for the last time. The expression on his face when he came outside to join them made her catch her breath, as if she'd been punched in the stomach.

When it was all over, when she couldn't put it off any longer, she went upstairs to Mike's study. There was nothing useful on his laptop and she couldn't get into his phone. But right at the bottom of his desk drawer, under hotel receipts and random letters, she found a business card he must have kept from one of their secret meetings in Hong Kong or Vancouver or Paris – a little square of white card with a work email and two phone numbers.

It must have been some time in the early hours in Sydney when she finally got through.

She said, 'It's Sara.'

There was silence at the other end of the line.

She said, 'I'm so sorry, I've got some bad news.'

Still, there was nothing.

Sara said, 'Mike died this morning.'

At the other end of the line came the sound of a woman crying.

*

Sara could never remember much about the day after Mike's death. To her intense relief, Katie stayed on to help, disappearing only once when she went home to pick up some clean clothes. James, normally so capable, had mentally retreated to a place of isolation that Sara couldn't reach. She hadn't been able to answer any of his questions about Mike's death – why he'd died, when he'd died, how he'd died – and after a while he just sat there, staring into space.

Once, someone rang the doorbell, and Katie leaped to her feet and went out to the hall to deal with it.

Sara turned off her phone. She didn't want to talk to anyone.

The hours passed. James went up to his room. Edward sat on one of the white sofas playing games on his laptop. Bundle padded around the house, nudging cushions and jumping at flies.

Late in the morning, Sara said, suddenly panicked, 'I don't know what to do with all the food. There's so much of it. Enough for eighty people.'

It seemed such a huge and urgent problem.

'We'll think about it tomorrow,' said Katie.

Sara said, 'All the strawberries. All the strawberries you got ready. They'll all go to waste.'

Katie nodded.

They sat looking out at the garden.

It was still hot when Katie took Bundle out for a walk. They were gone a long time. When they got back, Sara hadn't moved from the kitchen table, staring at the sun on the lawn.

Katie hung up the lead on the hook by the door.

Sara said, 'Ursula's coming tomorrow.'

'Who?'

'I ought to check what time she's getting in. Although she said she didn't want me to come and meet her. It's much more stressful getting through immigration if you're worried about delays and people waiting for you.'

'Who's Ursula?'

Sara said, 'Mike's sister. She lives in Australia. I said she could come and stay. I had to, really.'

Bundle, panting because of the heat, stretched himself out by the great glass doors.

'She sounded terrible on the phone.' Sara's voice was very quiet. 'It must have been a horrible shock.'

Katie sat down at the table, her eyes full of sympathy.

'All I could hear was the sound of her crying.'

The air was heavy with sadness.

Sara said, 'It's not going to be easy, having her here. I haven't seen her for years. She's never even met the boys.' She hesitated. 'She doesn't like me very much.'

Katie looked astonished. 'Why?'

Sara didn't answer for a moment. Then she said, 'I don't know. I never really worked it out. I think it's because I married her brother.'

'But that doesn't—'

'It's not rational.' Sara looked up. 'I know that. She isn't a very rational person.'

'But what happened?'

'It's a long story.' Sara stared into the middle distance. 'Do you mind if we don't talk about it now?'

Katie was mortified. 'Of course. I'm sorry, I shouldn't have asked.'

'It's not your fault. It's mine for bringing it up in the first place.'

They often talked like this, each of them apologising to the other, like people arguing over who should go through the door first.

Sara took a deep breath. 'The important thing is that we make her feel welcome. Gather her in and look after her. Now that Mike's gone, we're the only family she has left.'

Despite these brave words, Sara's heart still beat uncomfortably fast the following morning when she answered the front door and found Ursula standing on the stone steps. Time had changed her. She was much thinner than Sara remembered, with long stringy muscles in her arms like a long-distance runner. She wore a sleeveless black dress and a spiky silver necklace that bristled in all directions like an anti-climb security device.

Her face was expressionless. 'So here we are.'

Sara stood back to let her in. Her suitcase was red and shiny, a hard shell on wheels. It rattled along, sounding loud and self-important in the empty hall.

In the kitchen, Ursula took out a packet of cigarettes. Sara slid open the great glass doors, and Bundle raced inside, barking loudly. Ursula stood back as he shot past her and skidded to a halt by the skirting board.

There were silver strands in her hair.

It pained Sara to look at her face and see a family similarity with James.

'Coffee?'

It was so early that the boys were still asleep.

Ursula shook her head and walked out into the garden. Bundle followed her, still barking at top volume. The morning was dewy and calm, with the steady self-confidence of a day that's going to become warmer and more beautiful. Ursula lit her cigarette and stood there smoking, her back to the house, blowing out a cloud of tar and nicotine into the limpid air.

As if summoned by Sara's desperation, Katie appeared beside her in T-shirt and shorts, ruffled and sleepy. She mouthed, 'All right?' and Sara shook her head.

Ursula ground out her cigarette on the lawn and wandered back to the house. She stopped and looked over at Bundle, who was now standing foursquare by the yew tree, barking into the shrubbery.

'There's something wrong with that dog.' Her voice had a slight Australian accent.

Sara said, 'He needs a walk. Katie's going to take him out.'

Katie said, 'I'm sorry about your brother,' but Ursula was busying herself with taking out another cigarette from the packet and didn't appear to have heard.

On their way out, Bundle was so excited he did a kind of sideways jump, like someone sailing off a trampoline, and knocked over Ursula's suitcase.

Once Katie and Bundle had left, the silence was oppressive.

Ursula sat down on one of the garden chairs. Sara felt she had no choice but to join her.

'So what happened?'

Sara started to lay out the little she knew – that it was an unexplained death, so there would have to be a post mortem,

and probably an inquest to look into the results – but Ursula cut across her.

'I know all that.' She flicked ash in the general direction of the lawn. 'Just tell me what happened.'

Sara said, 'But that's the point. I don't know what happened.'

Ursula gave her a hard look.

To her intense irritation, Sara found herself stammering as she repeated everything she'd said on the phone the day before. This time, when she said they'd taken away Mike's medication, Ursula said, 'So they think it's an overdose?'

'They don't know. They have to run tests.'

'It might have been his heart. Dad died of a heart attack.'

Sara nodded, lowering her eyes. Perhaps Ursula hadn't remembered that she'd been at the funeral all those years ago. Sara hadn't wanted to be there – she felt it should be a family affair. But Mike had got his way, as he always did, and Ursula had stared at her the whole way through, angry and resentful at the intrusion.

Ursula said, 'So there's going to be a post mortem?'

'Yes.'

'And when does that happen?'

'Today.'

A shadow passed across her face. 'When do we get the result?'

'In about a month.'

Ursula looked at her with fury.

Sara said with apology, as if the whole thing was her fault, 'Because of the toxicology tests.'

'So what about the funeral?'

'We have to wait for the coroner to release the body.'

'When will that be?'

'We don't know. When they're ready.'

Ursula turned away and looked towards the distant trees at the end of the garden.

Her interrogation continued. Sara knew that it was in her power to stop it at any time – she could say that she was tired, or upset, or needed to lie down. But she felt the justice of Ursula's barbed, aggressive questions. She had loved her brother. She needed to find out everything she could.

At one point she asked if Sara thought Mike might have committed suicide.

Sara shook her head. 'No.'

'But he was in terrible pain. You said so yourself.'

'He wouldn't have killed himself.'

Later Ursula said it might have been murder, and Sara looked at her in bewilderment, because the police had ruled out forced entry, so that left only her, Edward or Katie as possible perpetrators. She opened her mouth to explain this, but Ursula had already rushed on to the next question, as if it had just been a stray thought that she'd immediately dismissed.

They must have been sitting in the garden for at least half an hour when Ursula went right back to the beginning and repeated all her original questions – Mike's usual routine, how much he drank, his state of mind, whether he'd ever been careless about his medication, how often he saw his GP – and Sara finally realised, much too late, that Ursula was still in shock, that none of this was normal or rational, and all these incredibly detailed queries were just automatic, because she didn't know what else to do. Sara looked at Ursula's taut, strained face and felt a great surge of compassion.

She said, 'Let me make you something to eat.'

Ursula shook her head.

'Or maybe you want to rest? You must be tired.'

They sat in silence. The day was filling up with heat. Already Sara could feel the sun pricking the surface of her skin.

They both heard Bundle's distant barking. The walk was over. Katie was bringing him home.

Ursula stood up. 'It's all right if I stay?'

'Of course. I'll show you your room.'

'Just tell me where it is. I'll find it.' Ursula managed to sound both crushing and offhand.

'You're in the room just above here.' Sara gestured up to the window overlooking the garden.

In the doorway, before she stepped into the kitchen, Ursula turned round, a flat expression in her eyes.

'Are you pleased he's dead, Sara?'

It was a shock. She felt she should be outraged, but she was too tired to feel anything at all.

Ursula said, 'You enjoyed it, I could tell. When you rang to tell me he'd gone. I could hear the smile in your voice.'

With a sinking heart, Sara realised that this was only the beginning.

The door to Ursula's room stayed shut all morning. After she and Katie had worked their way through a list of phone calls, and Edward was settled with his laptop at the kitchen table, Sara said she was going upstairs to Mike's study to make a start on the paperwork.

'You don't have to do that now,' said Katie.

Sara took a deep breath. 'I have to do something. I can't just sit around waiting.'

But in the study, sitting at Mike's huge black desk, she found herself staring into space.

Ursula would have been in her mid-twenties when they first met in a bar in north London. Sara was completely overawed. Ursula had the kind of spare, straight figure that looked good in clothes – you felt she didn't have to make any effort because the fabric just sat where it should without being yanked and tweaked. Next to her Sara felt colourless. She wasn't the kind of person who turned heads.

Sara could tell within minutes of meeting her that Ursula had no idea what Mike saw in her. Sara sympathised. She didn't either. At that stage in their relationship, he was obsessed. He stared at her face the whole time, trying to work out if she was happy or sad, too hot, too cold, hungry, thirsty, wanting a change of scene. Sara could see Ursula taking this all in, puzzled, trying to work it out. She kept throwing out questions – 'Where did you meet again?' – as if hoping that some vital piece of information might make things clear.

Looking back on it, this all made perfect sense. Mike and Ursula had always been close. When they were young, the family had moved four times in ten years – some kind of money problems kept secret from the children – and in every new place it had been the two of them against the world. The bond tightened when their mother left. There was an angry divorce. Custody was awarded to their father, and their mother disappeared, never to be seen again. Mike was sixteen and Ursula eleven.

And now here she was, staring at her elder brother, waiting for him to notice her. But he only had eyes for Sara.

She remembered one moment from that first meeting with great clarity. Mike went up to the bar to get drinks, and the minute she judged he was out of earshot Ursula whipped round and hissed, 'Do you love him?'

What a question! Sara wanted to say, 'I have no idea. I hardly know him. I only met him a few weeks ago.' But she could tell from looking at Ursula's face that something so logical wouldn't do. So she said, 'It's happening so fast.'

Ursula looked relieved. 'Don't let him rush you. Be sure it's what you want.'

This sounded like kind advice from an older woman looking out for her welfare. But Sara took it for what it was.

They next met about a month later, just after Mike's father had died. Ursula was hardly ever in the UK – in those days, she was a buyer for a high street fashion company, so was always visiting suppliers in different parts of the world – and had just flown in from somewhere exotic like Mumbai. After the cremation – talking to dusty-looking people with uneven teeth and bad haircuts over cups of tea and ham sandwiches – Sara could feel Ursula's hostility. She was outraged that her brother's new girlfriend had gatecrashed an occasion of such profound importance. Sara came up with some excuse as to why she had to leave early. Mike was torn – should he stay or should he go? – but made the right decision and remained with his sister.

He told her afterwards that they'd been up all night drinking. 'She likes you.'

Sara was surprised. 'Is that what she said?'

Mike looked away. He was never much good at lying to

her face. She often wondered if that's why he became so secretive in the end. It was better that things were hidden away so that she didn't even know they were happening.

But at that stage, right at the beginning, Mike wanted to tell her everything. He hardly allowed a thought to enter his head before he wanted to share it with her. It had promise, this relationship – two people who made a rational decision to be together. She hadn't known him long enough to be sure that she understood everything about him. But she was drawn to his energy and integrity. She knew he wouldn't let her down.

Thinking back, she marvelled at how quickly it was decided. They were never able to spend much time at his flat – large and light, the top half of an Edwardian house – but if she ever stayed overnight, she used to wake up long before he did and wander round half-dressed, looking through the bathroom cabinet and his desk drawers and the pockets of his coat, trying to work out who he was, this man lying naked in the next room.

Sex was pleasurable. She enjoyed it most when he forgot to think about her.

She agreed to marry him on impulse. They were having lunch in a café one day, and he asked her yet again, and she said, 'OK,' and he nearly fell off his chair. He grabbed hold of her so hard it felt as if he were crushing the bones in her fingers. If she'd known his reaction was going to be so painful, she would have sat on her hands.

The wedding was small, expensive and very white. There wasn't really anyone to invite from her side apart from her mother, who spent the whole service sniffing into her handkerchief, and a few people from the law firm where she

worked, who weren't quite sure what they were doing there. She didn't ask any old friends from school. There wasn't any point. She hardly saw them any more.

Charlie the painter was the best man.

Ursula did her best. She tried to put a brave face on it all. She said, 'You're everything I could have wanted for him, Sara,' which was such an obvious lie it was surprising she was able to spit the words out.

They went on honeymoon to one of those exclusive resorts where the room opens straight out on to white sands leading to a clear blue sea.

Mike said, 'We're going to remember this for the rest of our lives.'

He was right, in a way. She often thought back to the great wide bed with the white voile curtains billowing in the breeze, and wondered where it had all gone wrong.

To Sara's intense relief, Katie had temporarily moved in. It would have been impossible to cope without her.

For one thing, Bundle's behaviour had become increasingly bizarre. As usual, he stood by the great glass doors barking until someone let him out, and then stood in the garden, feet planted in the earth, barking until someone let him in. But he also ran around the house picking up random objects in his soft mouth and depositing them with great care in the downstairs toilet, and growled at the kitchen sink with an air of menace whenever the tap ran to more than a dribble. He

even became fussy about his food, picking over his biscuits and whimpering until Katie or a member of the Parsons family came to keep him company and make encouraging noises while he ate.

Because no one was functioning normally, all this strangeness was accepted without comment. Katie even put a footstool next to his dog bowl so that the person on Bundle-calming duty could sit in comfort.

Katie's arrival wasn't without its problems. She made tea, ran errands, and kept visitors at bay. She spent hours sitting with Edward as he cut and folded his tiny constructions, handing him scissors and tweezers like a nurse in an operating theatre, and filled in all the awkward silences at mealtimes when everyone stared down at their plates, their throats too tight to eat. But she was also slapdash and forgetful – cashmere on a boil wash, cardboard in the general rubbish – and spread chaos wherever she went, trailing second-hand clothes and glittery scarves down the stairs and littering all available surfaces with keys, rings, tickets and hair clips. Incense billowed from her room, and strange indefinable marks – mascara? pen? – appeared on towels and cushion covers. Sara tried very hard not to mind. She recognised that her usual military precision wasn't to everyone's taste, and the cold sad days of mourning were lightened by Katie's almost childlike delight in small things – a robin perched on the windowsill, the purples and pinks in a particularly spectacular sunset.

Ursula, on the other hand, seemed to find Katie extremely annoying. She kept asking why Sara needed to employ someone to walk the dog, and more particularly why the dog walker had to live in. Sara couldn't be bothered to explain,

so tried to intimate that this was a particularly British tradition that Ursula had somehow forgotten.

Katie said that Ursula sometimes cornered her and fired out direct questions.

Sara was curious. 'Like what?'

'She wanted to know if I had a boyfriend.'

'What did you say?'

Katie looked miserable. 'I said I did but we'd broken up. And she said that was probably just as well under the circumstances.'

Sara was puzzled. 'What circumstances?'

'I don't know,' said Katie. 'I thought you might know what she meant.'

Sara said, feeling for the right words, 'Don't think too much about what she says. She's a bit strange. And she can be quite cruel if she wants to be.'

Katie said in a rush, as if guilty of telling tales, 'I saw her kick Bundle.'

Sara was shocked. 'When?'

'Yesterday. When he jumped up. He was only playing. He didn't know what he'd done wrong.'

Sara said, 'We'd better try to keep him out of her way.'

A look of collusion flashed between them.

Ursula herself answered questions with staccato monosyllables that killed conversation stone dead. Once, Sara asked if she lived alone, and she said, 'Divorced, no children, no pets,' in a voice so cold that Sara didn't dare say another word.

Sometimes Sara caught her looking at Edward with a thoughtful, analytical expression, like a tourist studying an unusual artefact in an out-of-the-way museum.

One evening over supper, James asked Ursula why they'd never met her before.

'I live in Sydney,' she said.

'But you're here now.'

'Special circumstances.' Ursula stopped poking at the pasta and put down her fork. 'Your father's death.'

She didn't sound like an aunt.

'Didn't you ever want to visit?'

Ursula didn't answer for a moment. Then she said, 'Yes, I did.'

'So why didn't you?'

'Ask your mother.'

James glanced at Sara across the table. Sara pulled a face to show that she didn't know what Ursula meant.

Later, when Ursula had gone upstairs, James said, 'Why's she so angry?'

Sara shook her head. 'I'm not sure. I think it's grief.'

He didn't like this. 'She doesn't need to take it out on us.'

Hours followed hours in a kind of sludge. They knew they wouldn't get the post mortem report for three or four weeks, because the pathologist had to wait for the results of the toxicology tests. But knowing this didn't make life any easier. All the unanswered questions hung in the air like exhaust fumes, foul and poisonous.

Ursula said, 'So when can we have the funeral?'

Sara gave a hopeless little shrug.

Ursula looked at her with scorn. 'Have you thought of asking them?'

But the prospect of ringing the coroner's office terrified her. It felt like stirring up trouble. Not knowing seemed preferable to finding out there were serious reasons for the delay.

When she did eventually make the call, shaking with nerves, she was told there was no news.

'If people ask,' said Katie, 'I'll tell them we're still waiting.'

Ursula was clearly unhappy. Once or twice she borrowed Mike's car and went off for the whole day. Sara assumed she was visiting distant relatives or old friends from her childhood. It would have been helpful if she'd told them where she was going and what time she was expected back, if only so that Sara could plan when to put meals on the table, but she didn't offer information and Sara didn't ask. The whole situation was far too precarious to start making any kind of demands on her. Sara hoped she might realise that it made more sense to go back to Sydney until the coroner released Mike's body. But this didn't seem to occur to her. When Sara asked about work and whether they could spare her – she was still in fashion, but vague about the details – she said, 'I'm freelance. My time's my own.'

That seemed to mean, as Sara said to Katie later, that they were stuck with her.

Letters, cards, emails and texts arrived daily. Sara was taken aback by the outpouring of emotion – *honourable and big-hearted, the kindest man I have ever met, my best and oldest friend, the world will be so much poorer without him.* So many people said she was constantly in their thoughts. She appreciated the sentiment but had no idea how it was supposed to help.

One morning, seeing the expression of despair in Sara's eyes when she opened yet another flowery card expressing heartfelt sympathy, Katie asked if she could give her a hand with the replies. Together they worked out a system of standard templates tailored to all the different groups of people – relatives, work colleagues, schoolfriends, business associates – so that all Sara had to do was sign her name at the bottom.

'I'll send them off,' said Katie. 'You don't have to do anything.'

Sara nodded, unable to speak.

'You don't even have to see them if it's too much.' Katie gathered up the latest batch of envelopes. 'You can look at them all when you're feeling stronger.'

So many people, thought Sara. So many people.

'They just want you to know how much he meant to them,' said Katie.

Sara's eyes filled with tears.

The house felt huge. It didn't seem to matter that Ursula and Katie were staying – the rooms echoed with silence. Sara hadn't realised how much space Mike took up. It wasn't just his physical presence – his muscular bulk, his booming voice – but the force of his personality, the way he'd set the atoms of the air spinning. He'd been away so often that she thought she'd be used to his absence. But somehow the knowledge of his imminent return had always kept his outline present. Now that was gone. There was nothing left.

If someone had asked her a few weeks earlier, when Mike's bullying had reduced her to tears on a daily basis, how she would feel if he suddenly disappeared, she would never have said lost or lonely. It would never have crossed her mind. But here she was, wandering about like a child in a maze. Sometimes she'd stare at a blank white wall and think that the past few weeks couldn't have happened, because death and Mike were so obviously incompatible. For a moment she'd be so sure that she'd been hallucinating, and that Mike would any minute come home and shatter the strange, unnatural quiet, that she could almost hear the slam of the front door.

But however long she waited, he didn't reappear.

News of Mike's death spread quickly. Katie said she was

always being stopped by neighbours anxious for updates. Mary Miller used her network of retired NHS employees to spread the word about the importance of medical check-ups for middle-aged men, and much later Sara found out that sudden unexplained death had been the major topic of conversation in Grace's salon for weeks. Gifts appeared daily on the stone steps at the front of the house – flowers, home-made cakes, bottles of sloe gin.

One morning, coming back from the portacabin, Katie said that Sarinda had been talking about the homeopathic remedies that might help with grief. It depended on all sorts of things, like whether you were sighing or sobbing or liked salty food, so Sarinda said it would be best if she could pop in and give her a consultation.

'I can't face seeing anyone,' said Sara.

'I'll tell her,' said Katie. 'She'll understand.'

Sara thought how strange it was that there were people in the village who cared about her at all. Six months ago, she hadn't known any of them.

The bureaucracy following Mike's death almost over-whelmed her. Sara had believed that modern systems worked quite smoothly, and that you no longer made a phone call to a bank only to get a letter the following day addressed to the person who'd died. But she was wrong. Institutions were sympathetic but inefficient. Access to money was a nightmare. A temporary death certificate eventually unlocked some basic accounts, and there was no mortgage to pay, so she was luckier than most. But all the details about savings and investments were hidden away under cryptic file names on Mike's PC, protected by dense security procedures. Even life insurance was complicated, as neither policy paid out

on suicide, so nothing could be settled until the coroner's official ruling on cause of death – which could be weeks away if there had to be an inquest.

At night, Sara lay awake worrying about bills and utilities and how to pay for the funeral.

One Friday evening, Sara opened a bottle of red wine. It disappeared so fast that she opened another. So they sat there at the supper table in a somnolent haze, and Ursula started talking about Mike as a child – silly stories about his paper round, and taking bets on the fastest beetle through a toilet roll, and ruining the paintwork on a neighbour's car by cleaning it with shaving foam. As a teenager, he talked his way out of trouble, charmed his way into clubs, and gate-crashed other people's birthday parties. Her descriptions of him as a young man in his twenties – optimistic, irrepressible, good-humoured – didn't match the Mike any of them remembered, and after a while she must have realised that they all looked sad and uncomfortable, because she stopped talking and stared down at the table.

James fiddled with his wine glass. 'I don't remember him laughing very much.'

'He was in a lot of pain, though, wasn't he?' said Katie.

James kept his eyes on Ursula. 'I don't mean recently. I mean ever.'

Ursula raised her head and looked straight at him. 'I'm talking about the way he was before he met your mother.'

That was a bad moment. Under the table, Sara clenched her hands into fists.

A few days later, Sara was outside in the garden half-heartedly deadheading the roses when James came to find her and said he was cancelling his plans for the summer.

'Are you sure?'

He nodded. 'I can't be on a train across Europe with all this going on.'

'I'm sorry.'

'It's not your fault.'

But she still felt guilty. His life was on hold. He had wanted his independence so badly.

She said, 'After the funeral, there will still be time. I'm sure there will. Before you go off to university.'

James said, 'Maybe I won't go.'

'What do you mean?'

'Maybe I'll take a year out.'

She looked at him with concern. 'Of course you must go.'

For a moment, his usual self-possession deserted him. 'I don't see how.'

She said, with great firmness, 'This isn't the time to make decisions. Let's take it one step at a time.'

Finally, in the last week of July, the wait was over. The coroner's office rang to say that the toxicology results were in, and the post mortem report had given the cause of death as drug overdose. The coroner intended to open the inquest later that day – a formality, and the family wasn't required to attend – and the hearing would be in mid-October. In the intervening weeks, the police would be gathering evidence and talking to witnesses to establish by what means death had occurred.

'Whether he killed himself,' said Ursula, when Sara reported this word for word.

Sara fantasised about giving her a violent shove. Just imagining it gave her a surge of adrenalin. Why did Ursula keep going on about suicide? Apart from anything else, it wasn't

fair to broadcast speculation as fact, especially if James or Edward might overhear.

Sara breathed in and let the air escape slowly from her lungs. 'The good news is that they're releasing the body. They apologised for the delay.'

Ursula was staring into the middle distance. 'Did they give a reason for it?'

'No.'

'And you didn't think to ask.' Her tone was mocking.

Sara felt ashamed. She'd been so relieved that the first stage of the investigation was over that she'd hardly said anything at all. 'It means we can set a date for the funeral.'

'Great,' said Ursula. 'I can't wait.'

Katie had been at the Old Rectory for a month. One morning, as she was helping Sara unload clean clothes from the washing machine, she said, 'Don't you think I ought to go home now?'

Sara looked up. 'Do you want to?'

Katie seemed uncomfortable. 'I just feel I'm getting in the way.'

'You're never in the way. It's lovely having you here. I don't know how I would have managed without you.'

Katie said, 'But maybe it should just be the family now.'

'Why?' Sara paused. 'I know it'll all be different when the summer's over and term starts again. But there's no reason to go back home until then.'

Katie said, in a gabble of embarrassment, 'I might need to get a job. As well as the dog walking.'

Sara's eyes widened. She couldn't believe this hadn't occurred to her. 'Oh, Katie, I'm so sorry. Are you short of money? I should have offered before. What if I paid you to be a kind of live-in housekeeper?'

Kate looked horrified. 'But I didn't—'

'I mean, you're not, obviously. You're a friend. But I'd much rather pay you than some stranger through an agency.'

'But it doesn't—'

'Backdated. Because of everything you've done. It's only fair. And I really do need your help organising the funeral. There's so much to do. You can't be out job-hunting if you're here with me.'

Katie hesitated.

'It's just a temporary arrangement,' said Sara. 'To get us through the next few weeks. You'd be doing me a huge favour.'

It was lucky that Katie decided to stay on. A few days later, Sara came out of the bathroom one morning to find her sitting on the chair on the landing with a face so puffy from crying that she was almost unrecognisable, like a child's toy that's been left outside in the rain.

Sara was shocked. 'What is it? What's happened?'

Katie could hardly speak. She'd been weeping all night. Anna had rung just before she got into bed to warn her that Danny had turned up, out of the blue, at the Goat.

'Danny?'

Katie nodded. Anna and Baz and a few others had been sitting at their usual table, and they turned round, and there he was at the bar. According to Anna, he looked exactly the

same. He was even wearing the long black coat, despite the sultry July weather.

'So what's brought him back?'

Katie said no one had been able to get much information out of him – he'd just been joking around and laughing about how he'd been away all this time, and now he'd come back and they were all stuck in the same place, exactly where he'd left them. He'd had a couple of pints, played a game of pool, and then left.

Katie had badly wanted to know whether he'd asked after her, but hadn't raised it with Anna because she couldn't risk the humiliation if he hadn't.

'Oh, Katie,' said Sara.

'Anna's been saying for months that he wouldn't dare show his face round here again after the way he treated me. But he's back as if nothing ever happened.'

'Maybe he's just visiting. Maybe he won't stay long.'

Katie's eyes filled with tears. 'I never thought I'd have to see him again.'

Shortly afterwards, with extremely unfortunate timing, Maxine cut off all Katie's therapy sessions for the whole of August, as she'd been asked to deliver urgent family counselling – some kind of crisis intervention – to established clients in Edinburgh.

Sara wondered if this was just a euphemism for providing emergency childcare over the long summer break, but she kept her thoughts to herself. It was bad enough that Katie felt abandoned in her hour of need. The last thing she needed was any suggestion that her therapist might be a fraud.

★

The row blew up about ten days before the funeral.

The day was hot and airless. Sara and Katie were sitting in the living room on one of the huge white sofas, doing a final check on all the arrangements – the flowers, the order of service, the reception afterwards. Ursula had taken very little part in the planning and preparation. Sara had asked her, from time to time, what she thought about a particular decision, but she only ever said, 'Whatever you want,' in a cold and listless voice, as if it wasn't worth her attention.

When Ursula came into the room, they both stopped talking and looked up. She settled herself with long-limbed ease on to the sofa opposite and said she'd been wondering what had happened to Mike's watch. She realised she was at the back of the queue, and that someone else in the family might want it, particularly James or Edward as his sons. But she'd love to have something that belonged to him, so she thought she'd ask just in case.

Sara said, 'It got lost, I'm afraid.'

There was no expression on Ursula's face – just her usual blank stare.

'We searched everywhere – cupboards, drawers, underneath cushions. But we couldn't find it.'

'When was this?'

Sara thought back, trying to remember. 'A few months ago.'

Ursula said, 'He must have been upset.'

'He was.'

'He'd worn it every day for years.'

There was a prickling sensation running down Sara's spine.

Ursula said, 'You're such a shit, Sara.'

Next to Sara, Katie gave a little gasp.

'What did you do? Sell it?' Ursula's voice was quite neutral, as if they were discussing the weather.

Sara started talking very fast, telling her about all the things that had gone missing – Mike's watch, his laptop, his car keys. She explained that Mike had reported it all to the police, but that he couldn't be sure they'd been stolen because it was just as likely he'd mislaid them or left them behind at a meeting somewhere. She said it wasn't like him because he was normally so careful about his personal possessions, but she and James thought he might have been distracted because of all the pain he was in. He was so focused on what he had to do to keep the business going that he might have put something down in the wrong place and then forgotten all about it.

The words tumbled out in a great rush, and all the time Ursula just sat there, looking at her.

Then there was silence.

She said, 'Did you ever love him?'

Katie half stood up, but Sara grabbed hold of her arm and pulled her down again.

Ursula said, 'I always supposed it was the money. That's all I could think. But it was such a waste. For both of you. Who knows – you might have been a different person married to someone else. Nicer. Kinder. Maybe Mike let you get away with things too much. Turned a blind eye once too often.'

Sara was finding it hard to breathe.

Ursula said, 'I'm in a difficult position. Mike and I talked a lot, which you probably didn't know – phone, Skype, emails. Usually about Edward. How much it hurt. Wishing it could be different but knowing it never could. You wouldn't discuss it. Everything screwed down tight.'

A shiver ran through Sara's body.

Ursula's tone was cool. 'He told me that he'd made very sure that you and the boys were financially secure. That was important to him, providing for Edward's future. But I'm guessing you don't know how much there is. Maybe you don't have access to all the accounts. And that's why you're so desperate that it was an accidental overdose. I couldn't work it out at first. Then I talked to various people I know in insurance, and they told me that most policies don't pay out on suicide. That helped me to understand. You have to keep saying that it wasn't suicide or you don't get your money.' She paused, her expression quite calm. 'But that puts me in a bit of a quandary. Because accidental overdose doesn't make sense. My brother wasn't stupid. He would never have made a mistake with the pills he was taking. So I'm really confused. And I don't know what to do for the best.'

Sara kept her eyes on Ursula's face.

She said, 'I know you want me to shut up and go away. I do understand that I'm an irritant and I'm making your life difficult. But he was my brother. I loved him. And until I find out what really happened, I'm going to keep on asking questions.'

Sara nodded.

'That's it?' Ursula looked incredulous. 'Nothing to say?'

'I think death is hard to accept.'

Ursula narrowed her eyes. 'What's that supposed to mean?'

'Nothing.'

'Nothing?'

Sara said, 'I think we should get the funeral over with first.'

'What difference will that make?'

Sara spoke slowly and carefully. 'I think we're both still in

shock. Over the next few weeks the police are going to be asking questions. But the priority now is to plan the funeral.'

Ursula said, 'Was he depressed, Sara? Was it the only way out?'

Sara felt Katie shift position. It was a tiny movement, almost imperceptible. 'He wasn't depressed.'

'He sounded depressed. Whenever I spoke to him.'

For a moment, Sara held back.

'He sounded,' said Ursula, 'as if the decision he made years ago to stay with you was slowly killing him.'

She had gone too far. She couldn't sit there saying what she liked, twisting the facts, making mean and cruel accusations. Sara took a deep breath. 'You want someone to blame. I understand that. You don't want to think he made a stupid mistake. You don't want to think that he was tired and drunk and in pain and came home and swallowed too many pills, because that makes it seem meaningless, a waste of a life.' Her voice rose. 'But that's what an accident is. Stupid and wasteful and impossible to understand. Don't you think I go over it in my mind every second of every day? Don't you think I go back over every detail and try to work out what happened? I can't believe I didn't wake up when he came to bed. All night I lay there next to him, and while I was sleeping, he was . . .'

Tears strangled her. Sara couldn't say any more.

Katie, next to her, was trembling.

There was a small silence.

'I have to hand it to you,' said Ursula. 'You've still got it. I've never met anyone able to lie so convincingly.'

Katie let out a little cry of shock.

Sara kept very still. It seemed important not to react.

Languid, unhurried, Ursula got to her feet. 'OK – have it your way. Go ahead and plan the funeral. And in the meantime I'll carry on asking questions. See what I can find out.' She paused. 'You never know, the sight of the coffin might prompt a few memories.'

They watched as she crossed the room, her tall spare figure moving with the grace of a catwalk model.

At the door, she turned round. 'And when you find the watch, let me know, will you? I'd like to have it. Something to remember him by.'

Then she was gone.

For a moment, neither could speak.

Katie said, in a whisper, 'She's mad.'

'I'm sorry you had to hear that.'

'But what are you going to do?'

Sara slumped down further into the soft white cushions. 'There's nothing I can do. We'll just have to hold it together until the funeral. And then she'll go home. For a few weeks at least.'

Katie said, 'I just don't understand why she's saying such horrible things.'

Sara felt exhausted. 'I think it's what they call denial. One of the stages of grief. When you just can't accept what's happened.'

It was Mary Miller who first alerted her. Sara went round to thank her for the flowers she'd left on the doorstep – a bunch

of old-fashioned sweet peas from her garden in velvety shades of pink and mauve – and they settled down at the table, sad and tearful, and had a cup of tea and talked about what a lovely man Mike had been. Despite the open windows, the little kitchen was as usual stiflingly hot, and Sara was drifting off into her own thoughts when Mary said '. . . which is the one good thing about funerals.' Seeing Sara's puzzled expression, she said, looking flustered, 'I mean, there are always wonderful bouquets and hymns and beautiful words about the dear departed, and I'm sure this one will be no exception. But they don't really make you feel any better, do they? It's seeing family that counts. Such a comfort. You must have missed her so much.'

Sara said, 'Ursula?'

'I mean, people always say they'll get together, don't they? And they really mean it at the time. But it takes something big like a wedding or a funeral to make it happen. Life just gets so busy. Especially these days. I asked her how she'd managed to take so much time off work, but she said she's between projects at the moment, which must be such a relief. It means she can stay as long as she likes.'

Sara realised that she should have been paying more attention. 'You've been talking to Ursula?'

'She came round. Just to say hello.'

This was unwelcome news. 'So you had a nice long chat?'

'Oh yes,' said Mary. 'She brought a lovely banana cake with a cream cheese frosting. We enjoyed that, didn't we, Daisy?'

Daisy, in her basket by the stove, was asleep. Her stiff legs stuck out from the great mound of her body like knitting needles from a ball of wool.

Sara said, 'She and Mike were very close.'

'Oh yes. I could tell.' Mary's voice trembled with emotion. 'She said she still couldn't believe he'd gone. I think that's what happens when you've been so far away. It doesn't seem real. Doesn't really sink in. She wanted to know all about his life here – what it was like to live in the village, and what kind of things he got up to. I told her about the time I was coming back from the shop with two big carrier bags, and how he rushed up and took them from me and insisted on walking me all the way to my front door. And she said, that was so like him. Always looking to help others. And we talked about you and the boys, and how hard he worked all his life to make sure you were well provided for.'

Sara could feel a familiar tightening round her temples. Despite the urgency of the conversation, she found herself wondering if homeopathy was any good for tension headaches.

'And she told me about all his charity work. That was amazing. I had no idea. Thousands of pounds he's raised over the years.'

Sara stared.

Mary gave her a warm and reassuring smile. 'Don't worry. I won't tell a soul. Ursula said he never wanted it to be public knowledge.'

Sara's voice sounded faint. 'He kept quite a few things secret.'

'The mark of a modest man, I think.' Mary beamed at her across the table. 'Not everyone wants to shout about their good deeds.'

When Sara called into the salon for a manicure, Grace said that Ursula had popped in several times for sessions of aromatherapy and massage. 'She was all knotted up with

tension. And I said she'd done the very best thing by coming in because you've got to look after yourself at a time like this.'

'Thank God you're here,' Sara said.

'You get a build-up of toxins in the muscle,' said Grace, sniping at her cuticle with what looked like beaked tweezers. 'That's what causes the pain.'

'Did you get much of a chance to chat?'

'Not really.'

Sara said, 'I'm worried about her. I don't think she's really come to terms with what's happened.'

'I know what you mean.' Grace jammed Sara's hand back in the tray of warm water. 'She couldn't believe I hadn't been questioned by the police. She said, that's what you should always do in a case like this. Start with the neighbours. Find out what they know. And I said, well, I live right on the edge of the village, so I wouldn't have seen anything, would I? But she said she didn't mean just on the night itself. She said you have to build up a picture of what was going on before it happened. And I said, like what? And she said, you don't know till you start, because any little detail could be important. That's why the police should be taking their time and weighing up the evidence, not jumping to the first conclusion they think of. And I said to her, but you're not suggesting there was anything funny going on, are you? And she said, I'm not suggesting anything at all. I just think there should have been a proper investigation, that's all, for Sara's sake, to give her peace of mind. Because the last thing she wants is a whole lot of loose ends and everything left up in the air.'

By the time Sara came out of the salon, she was shaking.

She knew, without a shadow of a doubt, that every word of this had already gone round the village.

Worse was to come. Outside Sainsbury's Local, in the modern part of the high street some distance from the salon, she bumped into Rachel. 'Your sister-in-law's very direct.'

Sara forced a smile. 'It's her trademark.'

'I always get told off for asking too many questions, but she could teach me a thing or two. She asked me right out if I thought Mike was depressed.'

For a moment Sara couldn't breathe. 'What did you say?'

'I said I didn't know. I thought it was quite an odd question, if I'm honest.'

'Why?'

Rachel fixed Sara with her usual penetrating stare. 'Because depression is rarely obvious. People are extraordinarily good at hiding it.'

As Sara walked home, she was filled with a strange and disquieting emotion that left her feeling as if her skin was crawling over her bones, squelching and squirming with disgust. It was lucky that there was no one in the house, because she took off all her clothes, piece by piece, as she walked up the stairs, pushed her way into the bathroom, and stood for a very long time under a cold shower.

Sara knew from talking to Mary Miller how common it was. In one of their chats over tea and biscuits, Mary said that her friend Ailsa – who used to be the sexual health nurse at the

GP practice where Mary worked – often said that if she had a pound for every time a patient admitted to playing away she'd be a very rich woman.

Mary said it was so often the little things that caught people out. Obviously, there were the terrible occasions when an unsuspecting partner was diagnosed with chlamydia or gonorrhoea, or discovered genital warts. Sordid secrets often came to light because of sexually transmitted infections. But most of the time the infidelity was betrayed by tiny inconsequential details – a receipt, a misremembered story, texts on a phone.

Mary said you couldn't help wondering if people wanted to be found out. Guilt was hard to bear. It was so tempting to give in to the luxury of confession. Middle-aged men were the worst. They chased after erotic adventures, but then they wanted to be forgiven so that they could slot back into family life as if nothing had happened. Shirts ironed, meals cooked, children upstairs doing their homework – and lovely memories of being a naughty boy to ward off the spectre of old age and decrepitude.

The day before the funeral, Sara gave up on sleep in the early hours. All night she'd been worrying about the way that Ursula was stirring up antagonism against her in the village, and her head was so full of remembered conversations it felt as if she was standing in the portacabin with everyone shouting at top volume.

For a moment, Sara's mind hovered over what had happened in New York, their visit to Ursula in Manhattan just after they married. She felt a plunge of despair. No one knew Ursula the way that Sara did. They saw her as the grieving sister. They didn't know what she was capable of.

Sara turned her head into the pillow.

She had thought of getting rid of the bed. It was too much, lying down on it night after night, thinking of the way he'd drifted from a drugged sleep to death. But at the same time it had seemed somehow cold and callous to let go of her last physical tie with him. She had even thought, in her less rational moments, that a drastic action like that could be wrongly interpreted. Someone might see it as anger, blame, even guilt.

Your mind plays tricks in the weeks after death.

So the bed – the great super kingsize bed – had remained.

Sara lay on her back, trying to calm down and regulate her breathing. But the darkness was suffocating. It felt as if the walls were closing in, making the room small and claustrophobic. After a while, she couldn't stand it any more. It wasn't yet dawn, but she got dressed and went downstairs, careful to make no noise, with the vague intention of taking Bundle out for a walk.

Time should always be put to good use.

Once in the kitchen, she changed her mind. Pulling open the great glass doors on to the garden, she escaped outside into the eerie stillness, breathing in the cool air, feeling the wet grass beneath her feet. The grey light was ghostly, full of shifting shadows. She felt frightened but strangely exhilarated. Bundle, worried by the change in routine, was so subdued that she almost liked him. She sat down on the stone bench underneath the silver birch, and he settled at her feet, quiet and obedient like the dog she'd always wanted.

Katie appeared out of the mist, somebody's old coat over the indeterminate T-shirt she usually slept in. Bundle rose to greet her, tail wagging.

Birdsong echoed in the space around them.

Katie said, 'Couldn't you sleep?'

Dawn is only a beginning. But sometimes it seems to underline your helplessness, the inevitability of a future that frightens you.

Katie said, 'It's all right, Sara. It will all be over soon.'

Sara hadn't been aware that she was shaking until Katie took hold of her hand.

'You've been so brave.' She was leaning forward, trying to give Sara strength from her words. 'It's not for much longer.'

Sara always worked so hard not to give in to weakness. It just made things worse. But Katie's sympathy broke the dam. She buried her face in her hands and started rocking back and forth, making a sort of moaning sound, embarrassing and over the top like something in a bad drama on TV. She almost wished Katie would shake her and make her stop. But Katie just kept saying, 'Oh, Sara, it's OK, it's OK,' which didn't help at all. Bundle, alert to crisis, moved from one to the other, putting his head first on Katie's knee and then on Sara's, and finally, for some reason, this pathetic gesture of solidarity exploded her last heroic attempts to hold it all in. Sara heard herself half shouting, in a voice shaking with emotion, 'No one knows what he did! No one knows!' She could feel the panic rising inside her, that horrible feeling of being out of control. It was getting harder and harder to breathe. For a moment, she felt so sick and faint she thought she was going to black out.

Katie said, 'I don't understand. What don't we know?'

'I can't tell you.'

'Yes, you can. You can tell me anything.'

'It's too late.'

Katie was insistent. 'You have to tell me.'

Sara said, 'You won't believe it. I didn't. I still don't.'

She was bewildered. 'What won't I believe?'

Sara was beyond reason. She couldn't spend another long night staring into the darkness thinking about Mike, the same ugly thoughts going round and round in her head.

So, holding tight to Katie's hand, she told her the whole story.

The week before, on an afternoon when everyone happened to be out – James visiting a friend, Katie with Edward at the shops, and Ursula playing with the heads of gullible villagers – Sara had found herself alone in the empty house with nothing that particularly needed her attention. So she decided to catch up on some basic administration. The road tax on the BMW was due, so she thought she'd look for the MOT. Mike had always been very efficient at keeping track of all the paperwork – normally everything to do with the cars was in his study, in the big grey filing cabinet next to the window. But the MOT was missing. So Sara hunted round the house, in drawers and cupboards, in Mike's briefcase, in the pockets of his suits. She tried to think logically. Maybe Mike had left it in the car – hadn't ever bothered to bring it inside. So she went into the garage and unlocked the BMW, which smelled cold and musty inside because no one, not even Ursula, had used it for a while, and opened the glove compartment.

Right at the back, behind all the petrol receipts, she found a phone. It was just one of those cheap pay-as-you-go ones, so she thought it might belong to James or one of his friends. Maybe Mike had given them a lift somewhere, and found it on the back seat, and put it away for safekeeping. So she picked it up and brought it inside.

She went back up to Mike's study to carry on looking for

the MOT and put the phone in the top drawer of his desk. She thought she'd ask James about it later. But she couldn't get it out of her mind. So after a while, she took it back out of the drawer and looked at it more closely. She tried to turn it on, but it was dead, not surprisingly. So she searched around in the big box of cables and leads and chargers, and found one to fit.

It wasn't hard to get in. Maybe that's what he'd wanted.

'Who?' said Katie.

Sara let go of her hand and rubbed her eyes. They sat in silence for a moment, listening to the clamour of birdsong across the half-light, declaring territory, calling for a mate.

'There were hundreds of texts. Graphic, horrible, explicit texts. I thought, OK, it's phone sex – a middle-aged man having fantasies about women he's never going to meet.' Sara kept her eyes averted. She didn't want to see the shock on Katie's face. 'But then I realised he knew them. He was talking about places they'd been, hotels they'd stayed in. They were making arrangements to meet. Not just bars and cafés. Airports. Train stations.'

Next to her, Katie was very still.

'So I rang them.'

Sara heard Katie's sharp intake of breath.

'I started at the top of the list and worked my way through. I said I'd found this phone in a car park, and I wanted to get it back to the person it belonged to. Just in case it was important. The first one I spoke to was really nice. She said she recognised the number straight away. She hadn't heard from him for a couple of months and wondered if something had happened to him. I wasn't sure what to tell her. I thought the truth might be too much of a shock.'

Katie interrupted, her voice urgent. 'Maybe it wasn't his. Someone could have left it in the car. Someone from work.'

Sara looked up. 'She described him in great detail. So I'd know him if I saw him. So I could give him back his phone.'

Katie was silenced.

'I kept going, working my way through all the numbers. It felt like something I had to do. The same story every time – I'd found a phone and was trying to track down the owner. Most of them didn't want to talk, which didn't surprise me. But I got chatting to a few of them. They talked about him as a friend. Affection in their voices. One of them said she'd known him for years. They met up every few months when he went away on business. Always very generous, she said. Meals out, make-up, jewellery. Even presents for her little boy.'

Katie said, 'Are you sure it was . . .?'

'Prostitutes?' Sara couldn't believe she needed to ask. 'I can show you the texts if you like.'

Katie shook her head, a quick vehement movement.

Sara looked out across the lawn to the sleeping house. 'I'm not stupid. I've always known he had other women. Each time he said he was going away on a conference I guessed what was going on. Working late, running into old friends, the car breaking down – all the old clichés. He was no good at lying. I could always tell.'

'I'm so sorry.' Katie sounded desperate.

Sara felt very tired. It all seemed so pointless suddenly. 'That's not why I'm angry.'

Around them, the garden was waking up, the colour returning.

Sara said, 'I can accept what he did to me. But not what he did to the boys.'

'What do you mean?'

She hated having to spell it out. She took a deep breath. 'I started thinking about the money. How much it must have cost, this secret life. So I went back and looked again. You know how long it's taken me to piece it all together. All the money in different places. But I found it in the end – logins and passwords for two bank accounts I didn't even know existed.' Sara turned and faced her. 'Thousands of pounds, Katie. Over the past five years, he's spent a small fortune. Wiped out two savings accounts altogether. All sorts of regular payments going out every month. Escort agencies, porn sites, hotel rooms, flights. Huge cash withdrawals.' The words were sticking in her throat. 'And you know the worst of it? I can't even ask him how he could do this to us. I can't even sit him down and shout at him. Because he's dead. Because he's gone. Because he's left me behind to sort it all out.'

Katie's eyes were wide with horror.

She said, trembling, 'It's so humiliating. He cared that little. He's spent all the money we'd been saving for the boys' future.'

'Oh, Sara. I'm so sorry.'

'It's as if he took a sledgehammer to our lives and destroyed everything we had. Deliberately smashed it all to pieces.' Sara could hear her voice rising, a wail of emotion. 'So when people stand up at the funeral and say what a great man he was, and how he loved his family and worked hard to make sure that his sons were financially secure, I'll be sitting there knowing that their inheritance has disappeared. That the money I thought was safe has gone. That he threw it all away on sex with random women.'

Faint sunlight shone through the branches of the tree above. She couldn't stop shaking. 'And the irony of it all is that

while I'm trying not to break down, while I'm worrying about how we're going to manage, Ursula will be going round telling everyone his death was my fault, because I drove him to drink and depression and suicide. That he was a saint who could do no wrong. That he always put his family first.' Anger was making it hard to speak. 'Tomorrow will be a day of lies. Lies upon lies upon lies. And I've no idea how I'm going to get through it.'

Outside the Old Rectory, the lawn was dry and brown, like industrial carpet.

In the oppressive heat of her room, Sara put on her black dress. It was linen and close-fitting, and within minutes she wanted to rip it off because her whole body felt constricted. She felt shrink-wrapped, like raw meat. But she made herself wear stockings, too, because bare legs seemed disrespectful.

Downstairs in the hall, the others were waiting for her. Katie had made a huge effort – the hem of her cotton dress was perfectly straight and her shiny brown hair was twisted up and bristled with pins. Ursula, because she was always well dressed, looked exactly the same as usual – elegant and slightly remote, as if she wished she were somewhere else.

The chances of Edward submitting to a jacket and black tie had seemed slim, so Sara had bought new white shirts for the boys and hoped this would be enough. As she said to Katie, it was bad enough burying your father without worrying about what you were wearing.

When the hearse rolled into the drive, and she saw the coffin covered in white flowers, Sara felt frightened. She didn't like thinking of Mike in the suffocating darkness.

The five of them got into the car behind.

Sara said to Edward, 'You know where we're going?'

He said, 'To a funeral.'

'Dad's funeral.'

He repeated, 'Dad's funeral.'

Ursula turned and looked out of the window.

Outside the crematorium, mourners swarmed like flies. There were so many people. New arrivals kept surging forward, milling round her in black suits, khaki jackets, faded dresses, tattoos. She recognised a few faces from the office, and some from the village, but most of the rest were unknown. Who were they all? Where had they come from?

A squat man with a snub nose enveloped her in a hug. The unwanted contact made her recoil. He said, 'Thank you for asking me to speak. It's a great honour.'

She wouldn't have recognised him. It was Charlie the painter. He looked like a bad drawing of himself, a loose pencil scribble of grey lines and cross-hatching.

It's age, she thought. I haven't seen him for twenty years.

It was cooler inside the chapel. Sara sat down on the first row, her sons either side of her. Edward was gently rocking in his seat, keeping himself calm. She wondered how many other women had sat like her, staring straight ahead, trying not to look at the coffin. Her head ached. Her throat was tight. She could feel the pressure of bodies building up behind her, the crowd of murmurs and coughs and whispers. With a sudden lurch of alarm, she couldn't remember where Katie was, and was about to swivel round when she felt a hand on

her shoulder. Katie was sitting just behind her. As always, she was exactly where she was needed.

By the time the service started, all Sara's attention was on trying to keep control. The panic kept rising. Every time she looked away, the coffin pulled her eyes back. She knew he was angry. She could feel it. It didn't matter that he was dead. This wasn't what he'd planned, and he wouldn't let her forget it. She wanted to shout out that it wasn't her fault, that he was to blame, that he had no right to make her feel this way, and her heart began to beat so fast in her chest that she started to shake. There was a moment when she knew that she had to get up and run away, that she couldn't stay in her seat a moment longer, and she almost pushed herself to her feet. But then everyone stood up anyway to sing a hymn, and the strangeness of the movement she'd imagined with such clarity happening as a matter of course, as part of the service, somehow cut the fantasy dead and brought her back to herself – Sara Parsons, a widow, on the front row of her husband's funeral.

Charlie got up to speak. He stood there for a long time, looking down at a piece of paper that trembled in his hand. The silence was thick and sticky. He raised his eyes. He said this was the hardest thing he'd ever had to do. Mike was his best friend. He'd known him for forty years. For half that time, they'd lived at opposite ends of the country. But it didn't matter because Mike was always around when you needed him. In an emergency, he dropped everything. You could rely on him. If you were in trouble, he'd drive all night through a howling blizzard to make sure you weren't alone.

Sara felt hot and light-headed.

Charlie said that Mike was a family man. A wonderful

father. You couldn't spend two minutes in his company without having to look at photos of his sons on his phone. Mike always said that it was a constant surprise to him that James and Edward were so good-looking. He said they'd somehow managed to bypass his genes.

A ripple of amusement ran round the chapel.

Charlie said Mike had always been proud of his baby sister Ursula, and the way she'd forged ahead in a world of fashion and design that he admired but didn't really understand.

Sara stared down at the black weave of linen in her lap.

Charlie paused. 'And by his side for twenty years was Sara. He knew the minute they met that she was the one for him.'

She could feel the skin of her face burning hot.

'He was so excited. Rang me in the middle of the night and asked me how to get her to agree to a date.' Charlie paused. 'As if I'd know.'

Everyone was laughing.

Charlie talked about how Mike's company had grown from one man and a phone to a full-time staff of twenty with contracts all over the world. Mike was a born entrepreneur, because he was creative, and determined, and had the energy to make it happen. But most of all, because he understood people. He supported them, teased them, made them laugh. He believed in fairness and honesty. He believed in working together, looking after each other, helping each other.

Sara felt sick. Who was this man Charlie was talking about? How could anyone think it was true? The air around her seemed shiny, tiny particles of light dancing and glittering so that nothing was straight any more, the edges of everything she could see – windows, walls, wooden chair backs – shifting into jagged, broken lines. At home, Mike had been a liar and

a bully. But no one knew. All they saw was his public face, full of understanding, fairness and honesty. He had fooled them all.

Charlie looked round the chapel. 'This is why so many of us are here today. Some of us have travelled a long way, from New York, from Sydney, from Munich, from Milan. Some of us live nearby, in the village Mike made his home. Some of us knew him all our lives, some for only a few years. But whoever we are, and however we knew him, we had to come today to pay our respects.'

The chapel was silent.

Charlie looked over to the coffin. 'Goodbye, my friend.' His voice broke. 'We're going to miss you.'

Sara pushed her fingernails into the palms of her hands.

Outside, after the service, the crowd of mourners seemed even thicker than before, as if the heat had solidified them into one huge mass.

'Such a gentleman.' Mary Miller was looking up at her, her face wobbling with tears. 'It's so true. We're all going to miss him.'

'I wish I'd known him better.' Sarinda Nunn's little round glasses shone. 'It's been such a privilege to be here today with all his friends, celebrating his life, listening to all the memories.'

The pressure in Sara's head was so strong it felt like a bright light.

Katie said, 'Are you OK?'

She nodded.

By the time they reached the old manor house – much in demand for fashionable weddings – Sara had got herself back under control. The elegance of their surroundings helped. The cream-painted reception room looked out on to a formal

rose garden, and long trestle tables had been set up with chilled white wine, smoked salmon sandwiches, and tiny strawberry shortcakes. Someone guided her to one of the chairs at the side of the room and brought her a cup of tea. Sara was stunned by exhaustion. It takes its toll, night after night of sleeplessness.

Katie joined her. She looked tired, too. Despite all the careful pinning, her dark hair was falling down, and her skin looked almost grey. Sara insisted she drank a glass of wine. 'Funerals are hard.'

Katie said in a low voice, 'Can you imagine what people would say if they knew the truth?'

Sara shook her head and looked away.

'It was so hard just sitting there. I kept thinking about the way he shouted and swore at you, the way he treated you when all you were doing was trying to look after him.'

'Katie—'

'That man Charlie going on and on as if he was some kind of saint! I wanted to stand up and tell everyone what he was really like.'

Sara broke away, unable to listen any more. When she looked back, Katie was staring after her, her eyes desperate with the injustice of it all.

The heat intensified and the afternoon took on the heaviness of a dream. People she didn't know kept coming to talk to her, and she watched their mouths opening and shutting, wondering at the amount they had to say. At one point, she asked them all to excuse her, went out into the corridor and locked herself into the cool tiled toilet. Her face in the mirror looked strange, stretched out and shiny as if covered in plastic.

Katie was waiting for her by the French windows. Seeing them both standing together, Ursula detached herself from a group of Mike's employees and sauntered over. 'Congratulations, Sara.'

'For what?'

Ursula waved a graceful arm round the room. 'All this. The planning. The execution.'

Sara stared back, too tired to speak.

Ursula gave her a mocking smile. 'Anyone would think you cared.'

Sara flinched as if Ursula had hit her.

As Ursula left them, Katie grabbed a glass of wine from the table and took a large mouthful, quivering with indignation. 'She can't talk to you like that.'

Sara was trembling. 'She's just angry, that's all.'

'What are you supposed to have done?'

They watched as Ursula turned to talk to Sally Cook, who shot a quick glance in Sara's direction.

Sara said, 'I trapped her brother in an unhappy marriage and drove him to suicide.'

Katie shook her head, bewildered by such a stupid idea.

Sara said, 'She just wants someone to blame. That's what you do when someone dies – lash out at everyone around you, because nothing makes sense.'

Katie reacted with unusual acerbity. 'She should try blaming herself. If she'd been here, she could have helped you look after him.'

Afterwards, Sara thought about how many factors had been at play – the heat, the wine, the waves of emotion. Katie was young and impressionable. Of course she'd understood that everything Sara had told her had been in confidence. But at

the same time, her loyalty to her friend was strong. She couldn't stand by and do nothing while Ursula wove a web of lies.

Sara didn't see it happen. Charlie had come to say goodbye, because he had a long drive to wherever it was he lived in the north of England, and she'd been so repulsed by the forcefulness of his fleshy embrace just before he left that she'd wandered outside, leaning in to the pink blush of a rose to calm herself with its scent. She didn't find out until much later that it all started with just a few whispered sentences. Katie gave in to the impulse of a moment. Maybe she thought the gossip would stay within the tight village circle – Mary Miller, Grace Knight, Sally Cook, Sarinda Nunn. But it fluttered off almost immediately, settling briefly on shocked lips before flitting across the room to a different social circle altogether. No one wanted to believe it. It was preposterous. It was incredible. But at the same time it fitted so completely with what they had always known – that Mike was extraordinary, unconventional, a man of extremes.

Gemma, Mike's PA, listened open-mouthed. To her, it made perfect sense. Mike's diary had always been a nightmare because he never told her where he was going or what he was doing. A double life of whoring explained it all.

In the space of half an hour, everyone in the elegant cream reception room knew about the prostitutes. They knew about the squandered savings. They knew about Mike's betrayal of his sons. As the implications of the scandal sunk in, titillation was blunted by dismay. Mike hadn't been such a great family man after all.

Afterwards, Sara was thankful that she'd told James and Edward about the games room. When the story broke, they were downstairs in the basement, out of earshot.

How do you talk to the sister of someone who's frittered away his sons' inheritance? It was too shocking to take in. Mary Miller dropped her eyes. Grace Knight looked upset. Sarinda Nunn pretended to be searching for something in her bag. Ursula was suddenly an embarrassment. You could see the confusion on her face. Only days before, all these women were inviting her into their homes, hanging on her every word. Now it was clear from their body language that they wished she'd go away.

Much later, when they were back home at the Old Rectory and Ursula was upstairs in her room with the door shut, Katie confessed. Sara had wandered right to the end of the garden, wanting a moment of calm under the tall trees, and Katie came to find her. She was distraught, sobbing so hard she could barely speak.

There was no way Sara could be angry with her. Katie had merely reacted to events. Of course it was sad that the story about Mike had got out in public. But funerals are emotional affairs, and people understand that things are said in the heat of the moment. Katie mustn't worry about it. The whispers hadn't even reached James and Edward, downstairs in the basement playing table football. The whole thing would probably die down and be forgotten.

Privately, Sara thought the gossip was already halfway round the county. You couldn't keep something like that secret. It was a lasting blow to Mike's reputation. He was no longer the fearless entrepreneur, the doting father, the loving husband, but a figure of fun, a priapic fool. But there was no point in saying this to Katie. She needed comfort, not condemnation.

Sara's one consolation was that Ursula's mischief-making had been curtailed. Her attempts to brand Sara as the witch

who drove Mike to drink and suicide had spectacularly failed.

The morning after the funeral, before anyone else was awake, Ursula and her red suitcase went back to Sydney.

Looking back on the days that followed, all Sara could see was a series of endings. It was as if the funeral had unlocked a door, and everyone made their escape while they could.

First it was Katie. Mortified by having blurted out the secret of Mike's sexual activities, she decided to leave the Old Rectory and move back to her mildewed hovel beyond the back fence. Nothing Sara said could dissuade her.

'I should give you a bit of space.' Katie's kitten-like face was wide-eyed with sincerity.

For a moment, Sara was tempted to sink to her knees and plead with her to change her mind. She couldn't imagine coping – with bureaucracy, with Edward, with life – without her. 'I promise I'm not upset by what happened.'

Katie looked wretched. 'I know.'

'I can't pay you as much if you go.' Sara spoke with unusual sharpness. 'You can't be a live-in housekeeper if you're not here any more.'

But Katie was determined. 'I don't want to get in the way. You need time with James.'

Sadly, this was true – although not, thank goodness, because news of his father's infidelities had reached his ears. Either the villagers were being very careful, or James just wasn't interested, but he didn't seem to have heard anything about

the squandered inheritance. What was uppermost in his mind was the immediate future. In the dark days after Mike's death, James had thought about taking a year out in order to help his mother and brother come to terms with their changed circumstances. Sara had been deeply touched but was adamant that he shouldn't put his academic future on hold. It wasn't fair. He had his own life to lead. She said they all had to get used to living without Mike, so they might as well start now.

'What about the inquest?' James looked uneasy.

'You can come back for it if you really want to. But it's just dry and legal stuff. Statements and reports. They won't need you to stand up and say anything because you weren't even here when it happened.'

'Is Ursula going to be there?'

Sara kept her voice casual. 'I don't know. She didn't tell me what her plans were.'

He was still concerned. 'You shouldn't be on your own.'

'I won't be. All sorts of friends will be there.' Sara tried to reassure him. 'I'm not looking forward to it. But I'll be fine. And it'll be good to have the coroner's decision so that we can all move on.'

To her great surprise, James was eventually won over. Not long after the funeral, he found out that he'd got the results he needed and that his university place was confirmed. There was a lightness about him she hadn't seen for months. He said he'd decided to stick to the original plan and start university at the end of September.

Later, driving the ancient Polo to the shops, Sara was overwhelmed with such panic at the thought of James leaving home that she had to pull over to the side of the road, wind down the window, and take in great gulps of air.

It didn't help that Katie had moved out. Sara mourned the old intimacy. Katie still came round twice a day to take Bundle out, but if she didn't get an answer to her knock, she'd use her key and let herself in. Once or twice, Sara missed her altogether, coming downstairs after doing something noisy and absorbing with Edward, like changing the beds or hoovering the landing, to find the house unusually silent and the hook on the wall empty of Bundle's lead.

Right at the very end of August, there were two odd but unrelated incidents.

One morning, Katie said that she'd seen Anna the night before – not in the Goat, which was still too frightening a place to visit because of the possibility of bumping into Danny, but in the wine bar on the high street – and Anna had told her a very strange story. At the charity shop, Anna had been sorting through a backlog of donations and had found a bag filled with items that should have gone off to be valued. From time to time, people would drop off jewellery or antiques that had the potential to raise quite a lot of money, and it was the manager's policy to send them to a retired auctioneer in one of the villages nearby to ask for his opinion about what kind of price the charity should be looking for. Because of some kind of administrative muddle – or perhaps just basic ineffi-ciency – this particular collection of possibly quite valuable donations hadn't been sent away, but had just been shoved to the back of a cupboard.

Sara had started unloading the dishwasher as Katie was talking – it seemed to be turning into a long story and she thought she might as well be getting on with something useful – so had partially switched off when Katie said, '. . . might be Mike's watch.'

The clean mug she'd picked up fell back into the wire basket. 'What?'

'Anna said they've got an antique Rolex.'

Sara couldn't think straight for a moment. 'Why does she think it's Mike's?'

Katie was flustered. 'It might not be.'

'How could it be? How could it end up in Anna's shop?'

They looked at each other, lost and bewildered.

Sara leaned back against the worktop, trying to think it through. 'How did Anna know Mike's watch had gone missing?'

Katie explained that she'd told Anna weeks before about Mike going through a phase of losing things, and her description of the watch must have stuck in Anna's head. 'I'm really sorry. I know it's upsetting, and there was that horrible row with Ursula. And it may not even be the same watch. But I thought I should tell you.'

'I'm glad you did.' Sara rushed to reassure her – she looked so anxious. 'Where's the watch now?'

'Back in the cupboard. Anna promised to keep it safe until you could get there to look at it.'

A few days later, Sara called into the shop. It was a particularly hot day, and the smell of nylon, raffia and old wool had intensified into something overwhelming, like a scream. Anna's colleague, a rather dowdy-looking woman with a T-shirt tucked into elasticated trousers, conducted an ineffectual search before inviting Sara into the stockroom to look for herself. Sara searched all the shelves, rifled through the cupboards and looked behind the cardboard boxes. But it was no use. The bag of potentially valuable items had gone missing, and the retired auctioneer, when applied to, couldn't remember anything about an antique Rolex, or indeed any kind of watch at all.

'It probably wasn't Mike's watch anyway,' said Katie.

Sara nodded. 'It couldn't have been, when you think about it. There's no way that Mike would have given it away to charity.'

The one silver lining – a thought that Sara didn't share with Katie – was that the watch had definitely disappeared, which meant that Ursula couldn't get her hands on it.

The second strange incident was altogether more puzzling.

One afternoon, Bundle was slumped in the corner of the kitchen, tongue lolling, and Sara and Katie were drinking home-made lemonade in long tall glasses filled with ice and fresh mint from the garden. Katie had just brought Bundle back from a long and enervating walk and her hair was flattened by sweat. She said that now she was sitting down, the heat had stuck her thighs together in one big lump and she felt like a fat mermaid. Sara smiled, seeing a fish tail with shining silver scales. Unfortunately, her mind then drifted to the steely brilliance of the Chrysler building in Manhattan, which reminded her of Ursula and New York, and she hastily brought all day-dreaming to an end.

When the doorbell rang, Sara made a face. She'd had enough of well-meaning visitors. Ever since Mike's death, neighbours in the village had taken to popping round with food and drink in case Sara was too distraught to cook. This was very kind, and Sara was grateful that people were thinking of her and going to so much trouble, but the day before Sally Cook had come round with six stuffed vine leaves. Sara had been mystified as to why anyone would think damp, cold rice wrapped in something that looked like spinach would provide any comfort at all.

Katie smiled at Sara's anguished expression and said she'd

go and answer the door, and there was a small pause while she peeled herself off the chair. Sara leaned back and closed her eyes, and didn't really listen to what was going on in the hall, so it was a surprise when she heard a kerfuffle of footsteps, and looked up to see a short, balding man with wire-rimmed glasses standing in the doorway to the kitchen.

'Sara,' said Katie, 'this is Mr Roslyn. He's a private investigator.'

Sara thought for a moment that this must be some kind of joke. As far as she was aware, private investigators existed only in old crime novels and TV detective shows. But Mr Roslyn held out his hand, and then rummaged in his pocket for his card, and said he was sorry for disturbing them but wondered if he could ask a few questions about someone who used to work as their au pair.

Sara said, 'Hilda?' because they'd only ever had one au pair, and he nodded, his expression friendly but serious.

Sara invited him to sit down. Katie said she ought to be going, but Sara said there was no need to rush off. She felt unnerved by the idea of being alone with this rather seedy-looking stranger. So all three of them settled round the kitchen table, and Mr Roslyn unravelled his extraordinary tale.

It turned out that Hilda, the au pair who had lived with them when Edward was small, had a rich aunt in Tórshavn in the Faroe Islands who had recently died. The aunt had left everything to Hilda, but Hilda couldn't be tracked down, so couldn't claim her inheritance.

Sara was confused. 'What about all her brothers and sisters? Someone must know where she is.'

Mr Roslyn shook his head. 'She was an only child. And her parents died some years ago.'

This was something of a shock. Sara felt a wave of great sadness. Why had Hilda lied about her family? For a while, she stopped listening to the conversation and thought back to all the stories Hilda had told her, the pictures she'd painted of feasts and celebrations, crowded rooms full of friends and relations. Sara shivered, despite the heat of the afternoon. She had a horrible feeling that something had gone badly wrong.

Sara realised Mr Roslyn had stopped speaking and was looking at her with an air of inquiry.

She took a deep breath. 'I'm so sorry. I want to help, but I haven't seen Hilda for years.'

Mr Roslyn said he understood that, but all their enquiries so far had led nowhere so he was starting all over again, building a timeline going right back to when she left school. He said any information Sara could give him would be really useful. So she thought hard, screwing up her eyes, and came up with what she thought were the dates Hilda had lived at the Old Rectory.

Mr Roslyn said, 'And did she leave a forwarding address?'

Sara hesitated.

He waited, pen poised over his notebook.

'The thing is,' she said, 'there was a bit of a row before she left.'

He nodded, eyes full of concern, like a doctor hearing about pain.

Sara glanced at Katie. For a moment, she almost wished Katie wasn't there. It was so humiliating. The last thing she wanted to do was dredge it all up again. But then she realised that Katie already knew what kind of person Mike was, and one more story wasn't going to make any difference. 'I found

out that Hilda and my husband had been having an affair. While she was living here. So I asked her to leave.'

'Oh, Sara,' said Katie.

Mr Roslyn said, 'So it was quite an abrupt departure.'

Katie took a deep breath. 'Mr Roslyn, there's something you—'

But he cut across her. 'Did she say where she was going?'

'No.'

'And were you ever in contact with her again?'

'No.'

'What about your husband?'

Katie gave a little cry.

Sara felt the tears wet on her cheeks. 'He promised it was over. He said he was sorry and that he'd never see her again.'

Mr Roslyn looked sad. 'Mrs Parsons, I'm so sorry to cause you distress. But could I talk to your husband? In case he remembers anything else that could be useful?'

Sara's voice came out much too loud. 'No.'

He opened his mouth to speak just as Katie half rose from her seat, leaning out across the table.

Sara said, 'You can't talk to my husband. Because he's dead.'

In the days before James was due to leave, there was a flurry of activity, getting together all his student paraphernalia – duvet, pillows, cutlery, plates. Sara was grateful that there was so much to do because she couldn't face the thought of living in the house without him.

At the very last minute, she gave him a crash course in basic cooking and food preparation – how to dice an onion and crush garlic, make an omelette, roast a chicken. She didn't want him to spend a whole term eating nothing but chips. He turned out to be a very willing pupil. One night they even managed a sweet potato curry, the spices freshly crushed in the big stone pestle and mortar, the kitchen hazy with cumin, coriander and turmeric.

The morning before he left, Sara said, 'Anything else you want to learn?'

'Risotto?'

So late in the afternoon, when all the rest of the packing was done, she stood with him at the hob, watching him fry chopped onion, garlic and celery, pour in the dry rice, add the white wine, and then the slow addition of hot stock, bit by bit, the grains becoming soft, the rice becoming creamy and thick. A dreamy activity of watching and waiting: the alchemy of chemical transformation.

Outside, the light faded, the sky becoming dark and grey.

The making of risotto can't be rushed. However tired you are, however much your back aches, you have to stand there until it's finished. It's a labour of love.

'And after you've added the Parmesan,' Sara said, 'you can stir in anything else you like – bacon, mushroom, herbs.'

'Anything?'

Grief was never far away. She couldn't speak.

James looked at her more closely. 'Are you all right?'

Risotto had always been Mike's favourite meal – the one he asked for if he'd been away working.

She said, 'It's just hit me that you're leaving home.'

'I'll be back at Christmas.'

She gave him a watery smile. 'So you will.'

When James finally went, getting a lift with a friend who was starting at another London college, Sara felt bereft. If the house had seemed empty without Mike, it now felt limitless, like a fantasy palace with echoing corridors. In the mornings, once Edward had left for school, and she was alone in the vast white rooms, she didn't know what to do with herself. It made sense, obviously, to go back to work. There was nothing to stop her. But she felt she should wait until the New Year so that she could be around when Edward came home on the afternoon bus. It wasn't the time to think of alternative arrangements. Now that his father had disappeared, Katie had moved out, and his brother had gone, Edward was understandably nervous if he didn't know where she was.

When there were only two of them in the house, he became her shadow. Even if she went outside to put plastic packaging in the recycling bin, he came with her, watching her every move. She managed to persuade him that shutting the toilet door didn't herald imminent abandonment, but it was a close call.

The inquest loomed on the horizon. Each time Sara thought about it she felt sick. She had heard nothing from Ursula – she had no idea whether she was intending to come or not.

One morning at the beginning of October, Sara walked into the hall to pick up the post from the mat just as the lock rattled with the turning key and Katie opened the front door. Sara stared in astonishment. Katie was lit up with joy. She radiated bliss. There was a flush to her cheeks and her breathing was rapid with excitement.

'Katie,' said Sara, 'what's happened?'

But Katie's wide smile said it all.

They sat down and had a cup of tea – ignoring Bundle's plaintive whines from the back garden – and Katie told her everything.

Her descriptions were so vivid that Sara almost felt as if she'd been there herself.

The night before, in the mildewed bedroom of her horrible hovel – which seemed even more damp and comfortless after her weeks of luxury at the Old Rectory – Katie had been propped up against the pillows, rather miserably choosing her options for the spring term, when the doorbell rang. Thinking it was probably Anna, because no one else would come round that late without having rung her first, Katie scrambled out of bed, pulled on a pair of socks, and ran downstairs to open the door.

There, in the porch, was Danny.

He said, 'All right?'

She couldn't breathe.

It was such a shock to see him in person. The real thing. The version of him in her head had been, by comparison, just a copy – faded and washed-out, a supermarket own brand, nothing but a ghost of the original. But the Danny in front of her was perfect – immediately recognisable and so exactly what she had longed for, body and soul, that she could only stare.

He said, 'I'll go if you like.'

'No. Don't.' The words were out before she could stop them.

He looked at her threadbare T-shirt. 'You'll catch your death.'

As if in a dream, she stood back and let him in.

Danny, in her living room, was taller than she remembered, but just as thin, like an exclamation mark.

She pulled at her T-shirt, tugging it down so that it covered more of her thighs. 'Would you like a cup of tea?'

'If you're offering.'

Trembling, Katie went out to the kitchen, and all through the familiar process of boiling water and finding tea bags, her head was firing questions at her that she couldn't answer – not even the simple ones, like 'What's he doing here?'

When she opened the cupboard, there in front of her was his favourite mug, one of the joke ones that spelled out a swear word if you had your hand in the right position. She had never had the heart to throw it away.

In the living room, Danny was sitting on the sofa, still wearing his coat, thin legs in black jeans spread out in a V-shape. 'You're not having one?'

'I won't sleep.' She sat down on a pile of cushions on the floor, not too near, not too far.

The room was silent. Danny drank his tea. At one point, he looked up at the ceiling. But he said nothing about the great black cloud of mould.

'You went away.'

He nodded.

'Where did you go?'

'Oh, you know.'

'But you're back now?'

'Got promoted.' He held the mug so that it swore at her. 'I'm a salesman now.'

She thought of all the little old ladies inviting him in for a chat.

'Got my own car. Ford Mondeo. Alloy wheels.'

The room was dank. The darkness was coming in despite the curtains, seeping inside like fog.

She said, 'Anna told me you were back.'

He looked guarded.

She didn't press it. Maybe this was something he didn't want to talk about.

Danny put the mug on the tray.

Katie had forgotten how much they talked in silences. Their conversations were a series of dots. Perhaps that was the reason she stared at him so often – she was trying to understand what he might be thinking by reading the expressions on his face.

Danny leaned his head back against the sofa. 'So what are you up to?'

'Back at uni.'

'Are you now.' His cosy, camp voice made her heart turn over.

'And working.'

'I know.'

Her heart beat faster. 'Do you?'

'Dog walking.'

Her throat was tight, as if someone was strangling her. 'Who told you that?'

'Anna.'

'When?'

'Just now.'

The thought of Danny asking about her in the Goat made it even harder to breathe than before. 'It doesn't pay that well,

dog walking. I should be taking them all out together, really. That's how you make money. But Bundle's a bit manic. And Daisy's so fat she only gets as far as the post box before she has to sit down.'

'You do it every day?'

She nodded.

'How many dogs?'

'Four. Sometimes five.'

'Busy girl.' He smiled, the kind of cracked-face grin that made her think of a clown.

The words fizzled out again.

After a while, Danny shifted in the sofa, spreading his legs more widely. 'My nan asked after you.'

Katie looked up.

'Maybe you could go round some time.'

This was such a strange suggestion that Katie didn't know what to say.

The dots disappeared into a long line of nothing.

Katie stared at the grey wool of her thermal socks, seeing the ribbing of the design and the tiny pinpricks of machining at the toe. She felt a kind of despair. He was sitting there, in her living room, so near she could touch him, so close she could feel his warmth. Everything drew her to him – the way he looked, the way he spoke, the way he kept her at a distance. But the months of weeping were real. She couldn't pretend they hadn't happened. He had hurt her and left her in such a mess that her heart had been mashed into tiny pieces.

'Why are you here?'

He said nothing.

'I mean it, Danny. I haven't seen you for months. What are you doing here?'

Danny's eyes flicked round the room, as if looking for a way out.

'You want something.'

He shook his head.

'So why did you come?'

The air in the room was cold and still.

'I missed you.'

She looked at him, frightened, wary.

He said, in a loud voice, 'I missed you, all right?' He sounded irritated, as if he'd been accused of something he hadn't done. In a sudden movement, he shuffled towards the edge of the sofa, reaching out to touch the very edge of her sleeve. 'I mean it, mate. I don't like it without you.'

Katie started to cry.

Danny dropped down cross-legged in front of her with the careless agility she'd always loved.

She lifted a hand to wipe the tears from her face. 'You missed me?'

He nodded.

'Why didn't you come before?'

They both leaned in closer so that their foreheads were touching, as if they had secrets that no one must hear.

'I did.'

'When?' She couldn't believe her ears.

'Couple of times. I saw you out. Different men.'

'Oh, but that wasn't . . .' Katie, anguished that Danny had seen her with some of her more unfortunate contacts, didn't know how to explain.

'Looked like you were fine. Weren't missing me at all.' His soft voice was back, the wheedling tone that reeled her in.

The misunderstanding was agony. 'But I did miss you. All the time.'

He sounded pleased. 'All the time?'

'All the time.'

He dipped his head and kissed her. His lips were thin, his fingertips cold on her face. She shuffled closer, and he slipped an arm round her and gently tipped her back on to the cushions so that their bodies nuzzled together. It seemed so familiar – the way he smelled, the way he moved, the weight of him.

He said, in a muffled voice, 'You don't know what you do to me.'

It was all so urgent, they didn't even remember to plug in the electric fire.

Afterwards, holding him tightly, she felt safe.

Danny said he could stay, so they went upstairs and got into bed in the muddle of clothes and blankets, pushing the laptop to one side. When she saw him there, lying back against the pillows, she started crying again, because she'd missed him so much. He turned off the light and pulled her head into the hollow of his shoulder, and she started telling him all about the terrible days of misery when she thought she was going under.

He said, 'It's over now.'

She told him about going to see Maxine, and the months of therapy. He wanted to know about the homework tasks. Katie didn't want to tell him at first, especially all the stuff about sexual research through random encounters.

Danny said – she couldn't see his face, because her head was tucked under his chin in the dark – 'You fucked them all?'

She rushed to reassure him. None of them, she said, not

one of them, because they were all disgusting. I didn't fancy any of them. Danny laughed. He said he'd popped back for his nan's birthday a few months ago, and seen her walking along the high street, holding hands with a small dark skinny bloke, a big smile all over her face. Katie changed the subject quickly because she thought he was probably talking about Al who in fact, if she was being honest, was the one person she would have slept with given half the chance.

She told Danny that the therapy had been about much more than meeting random men – it was all about learning to have pride in yourself, and giving yourself permission to enjoy all sorts of selfish pleasures and put yourself first.

'Sounds all right,' said Danny.

Katie explained that Maxine could be a bit fierce sometimes because she said you had to grab what you needed even if it meant taking it away from other people. It was all about pushing yourself to the front of the queue and trampling over everyone else to get there.

'Makes sense to me,' said Danny.

Katie said she wasn't sure. She didn't really want the kind of life that was all about being greedy and making money.

Danny nudged the top of her head. 'You're mad, you are.'

'Do you want to get rich?'

'Fuck off, mate. Of course I do.'

'I'm not sure it makes people happy.'

'Since when?'

Katie didn't want to argue.

All she knew, lying next to him in the dark, was that what made her happy was Danny.

★

Danny's return changed everything. Katie even looked different – there was a dewy intoxication about her, a kind of glowing brilliance that made it almost impossible not to stare. Every morning, Sara sat at the kitchen table and listened, smiling, while Katie – starry-eyed with adoration, brimming over with love – described in detail every conversation she'd had with Danny the night before. He had a way of looking at the world that entranced her. He was funny and clever and thought for himself. She admired his ambition, his drive, his fearlessness.

Sara said, 'So did you find out where he's been living since he went away?'

No, said Katie, that hadn't really come up yet – they'd been too busy talking about his promotion and his mileage allowance and his expenses. She thought he probably felt guilty about leaving so suddenly, because he didn't seem to want to talk about the past nine months, and as far as she was concerned it was all water under the bridge. The important thing was that they were back together again.

Apparently, Katie hadn't told Anna or Baz about the miraculous reunion. She was still a bit worried that they might disapprove, given they were so critical of his previous behaviour. But Katie felt it wasn't fair to be so judgemental.

'It happens all the time, doesn't it?' she said. 'People quite often split up for a while. It's only when you're apart that you realise how much you miss each other.'

Sara nodded in agreement. But privately she was concerned. She had spent too many hours listening to Katie as she spilled out the terrible story of Danny's desertion – the cruel way he'd dumped her in the Goat, irritated by her tears – to feel anything other than a deep sense of foreboding. Romantic

reconciliations happened all the time – of course they did. But it seemed from Katie's descriptions that Danny's original exit had been cold and calculating, which made her wonder if an equal amount of planning had gone into his return. What was he up to?

Her best hope was that he just needed somewhere to live – that his latest girlfriend had thrown him out and he thought Katie might put him up for a while. But even this didn't make much sense. Danny hated emotional displays. He must have known he'd be walking straight back into a volatile situation.

She couldn't bear the idea of Katie throwing her life away on someone who didn't deserve her.

She said, 'So what are Danny's plans for the future?'

Katie looked confused. 'I don't know.'

'You don't know?'

'We haven't talked about it.'

Sara nodded. 'But he's moved back in?'

Katie smiled. 'It's so lucky the house has a drive. Only a little one. But at least he can get his car off the road.'

Sara wondered how Katie could possibly think this was important. 'So he's working locally again?'

'Yes. This is his new patch.'

'Selling windows.'

Katie was rosy with pride. 'He's hoping to make salesman of the month.'

That night, alone in her enormous bed, Sara thought about Katie's loyalty and devotion. Katie had forgiven the past. She bore no grudge. The slate had been wiped clean. Sara found this hard to understand. She wasn't even sure if it was something she should pity or admire.

Her mind drifted to the little house just beyond the back

fence. She imagined Danny leaning in to whisper cosy little secrets, his breath hot on Katie's skin. She thought about the bones of his body, his long fingers, his cool lips on her mouth.

She remembered Katie talking about the excitement of making love in the woods, half hidden by the wet grass – so public, so daring, risking discovery as the dog walkers and joggers and drunks wandered past.

How had he made Katie – conservative, conventional Katie – behave with such recklessness?

The following Saturday, Sara bumped into Rachel in the portacabin.

'I saw that boyfriend of hers the other day.' Rachel fixed Sara with her usual direct stare. 'The one in the black coat. It was quite a surprise. He hasn't been around for months.'

'Yes,' said Sara, keeping her voice light and airy, 'they're back together again.'

She felt envious. Because Katie had described him in loving detail so many times, Danny was very vivid in her imagination. But Sara had never actually seen him in the flesh.

Rachel said, 'I don't hear very good things about him.'

Sara was taken aback. 'He's just got a promotion.'

Rachel looked sceptical.

'And a car. A Ford Mondeo. With alloy wheels.'

Too late, seeing the amused expression in Rachel's eyes, Sara realised that Katie's adoration had rubbed off and that she was gushing about silly inconsequential details.

Danny's return had one good outcome. Katie had been receiving numerous texts from Maxine asking her when she'd like to resume their counselling sessions – Maxine had now come back from Scotland and had once again taken up residence in the small modern house with the cold converted

garage – and had been dithering about what to do. Then, quite suddenly, she made up her mind. One morning, while walking Bundle over Ogden Hill, the whole of the bypass spread out before her, she rang Maxine and said that she didn't think she needed counselling any more.

Maxine was disapproving, explaining that therapy was like antibiotics, and you should always finish the course. 'Or you'll slide back into your old negative ways and end up depressed again. And I can't guarantee I'll be around to pick up the pieces.'

But Katie, in her new-found state of blissful contentment, was adamant. She said to Sara later, 'I know everything's going to be fine from now on.'

Her optimism chilled Sara to the bone.

One Thursday, James rang to say that Ursula was coming to the inquest.

Sara found herself gripping the phone. 'Really? How do you know?'

'She emailed me. Wanted to check she'd got the date right.'

'I'd better make up the bed.'

'You won't need to. She said she didn't want to put you to any trouble. She's going to stay in a hotel.'

After James's voice had disappeared, Sara sat there for a while, still holding on to the phone, staring into space. She had been trying so hard to make herself feel positive about the inquest. Of course, it would be horrible to hear the details of Mike's death all over again – the witness statements, and all the coroner's interrogations, would bring back every moment of the terrible morning when she discovered him lifeless in their bed. But she had comforted herself that at least this formal inquiry would put an end, once and for all,

to rumours and speculation. In addition to this, the coroner's decision on accidental overdose would finally unlock Mike's life insurance policies. There would be no more worrying about money. They'd be financially secure.

But that was the end point. During the journey to get there, she'd have to face Ursula again. This filled her with dread. She'd heard nothing from her for over a month. But she was sure that Ursula's threat to stir things up by asking awkward questions was still very much alive. Ursula hadn't succeeded at the funeral. But maybe Sara wouldn't be so lucky the second time round.

The room was getting dark when Edward came to find her. 'What are you doing?'

'Nothing,' she said.

Luckily, he didn't notice things like tears.

In the weeks before the inquest, increasingly agitated by the prospect of Ursula's return, her memories of Mike grew stronger.

She was frightened by the muddle of her thoughts. There seemed to be no straight paths any more, just roundabouts and T-junctions and the odd bypass hurtling towards a cliff edge. Some days she was quite convinced that Mike was still alive. She knew for certain that she'd be in the kitchen chopping up an onion, and the front door would slam and she'd hear the thud, thud, thud of his footsteps, and there he would be with his habitual scowl, and their evening would proceed

exactly as it always did, the picture of marital discord. She knew this. She knew it for a fact. But then Edward would look up from the sofa and say, 'Why did he die?' with that scared look in his eyes, and she'd be drowning again, drowning, drowning.

In clearer moments, she knew he'd gone. The house howled with his absence. He just wasn't there. But he was still inside her head. To begin with, in the early days, it was just the odd comment that pinged into her mind, sometimes so loudly that she jumped. One afternoon she made a chocolate cake for Edward and must have been distracted at the measuring stage because it came out of the oven looking dense and dark with a distinct dip in the middle. As she stared at it in some dismay, Mike's voice said, 'Not up to your usual standard, Sara.' She whipped round, thinking he was standing right behind her. But there was no one there.

As time passed, comments like these became so much more frequent that she felt like a politician being interviewed by a hostile radio host. When she snapped at the cashier in Sainsbury's Local, Mike was in her ear asking if she was going to apologise. She backed the ancient Polo into a lamppost and he wondered what she was trying to achieve.

Not looking good, Sara.

Not quite what you planned, Sara.

Not going so well, Sara.

She suspected that this was some kind of benign aberration quite normal to the process of grieving and that it was nothing to worry about. Perhaps, like Ursula, she couldn't fully accept that Mike was dead and was holding on to a version of reality that kept him alive in her mind. But this didn't make it any easier to bear. The weight of his disapproval was so heavy.

Once, without warning, he swore at her. He had never before used language that was quite so gross, although the contempt in his face – that blank stare from his pale green eyes – had sometimes led her to wonder if that's what he'd been secretly thinking. But one day, as she picked up a mobile phone in his study – the cheap, disposable, pay-as-you-go phone she'd found in the glove compartment of his BMW – his voice rushed into her head, curt and blunt. It was a terrible shock. She was shaking so badly she had to sit down.

After this, she spent a considerable amount of time and effort blocking out Mike's voice. More often than not, she was successful. But there was the odd occasion, particularly if she was tired or under stress, when she lost control and his booming rudeness filled her head for hours.

Worse than coping with Mike's constant attempts to invade her thoughts was having to worry about Ursula. Vivid images and fragments of speech kept rushing into her head. Sometimes in the evenings when Edward was upstairs watching TV, she could sit at the kitchen table looking at the darkness through the great glass doors and lose a whole hour to unwanted memories from the past.

She remembered the morning in Regent's Park quite soon after she and Mike had got together. Mike wasn't with them. It was probably a calculated ploy on his part to stay out of the way so that they'd get to know each other – it must have been his dearest wish for his sister and new girlfriend to become the best of friends.

They were walking along one of the long straight avenues, surrounded by joggers and mums pushing buggies, the sunlight falling through the leaves and dappling the grass below, when Ursula said, 'Do you ever feel guilty?'

It was a strange question. Her dark hair was falling forwards over her face so Sara couldn't see her expression. 'Sometimes. Why?'

Ursula didn't answer.

Sara was still at that stage of their relationship when she wanted Ursula to like her, so she said, 'I know I should spend more time with my mother. That makes me feel guilty. She wants to see me much more than she does.'

Ursula said, 'I was thinking about Carys.'

There was no obvious way to respond to this, so Sara said nothing. They carried on walking, their steps in time with each other.

Ursula said, 'She's not coping very well.'

They walked on.

'It's not surprising, I suppose.' Ursula's voice sounded high and strained. 'After all those years.'

Sara chose her words with care, 'It was Mike's decision.'

'Oh, I know,' said Ursula, 'I know that. It wasn't your fault. He didn't say when you met that he was living with his girl-friend.'

'No, he didn't.'

'He didn't say that they'd been together since they were at school and they'd just bought their first flat.'

Sara remembered the dresses in the wardrobe, the shoes under the bed, Carys's make-up in the bathroom cabinet.

'He was in the wrong,' said Ursula. 'Not you. I know that. But I just wondered if you were OK with it.'

Sara turned slowly and faced Ursula head on. 'Mike never talks about her. I've never met her. So I'm fine.'

Now, at last, Ursula met Sara's eyes. 'You don't feel guilty?'

'For what?'

'For breaking them up.'

'I didn't break them up.'

For a moment, Sara thought Ursula might argue. She seemed to be struggling to hold back words.

Sara said, 'Mike had moved out by the time we met. I never even saw the flat.'

A white lie, but perfectly understandable in the circumstances.

Ursula looked down at the ground.

Sara said, 'I know you're friends. And I'm sorry she's unhappy. But I can't do anything about it.'

Sometimes, in idle moments, Sara was curious as to why Ursula had thought it was a good idea to raise the spectre of the ex-girlfriend with the woman her brother was currently obsessed with. But she didn't worry about it. She knew Ursula was fiercely protective of her brother, and imagined she was equally loyal to her friends. She never thought that Ursula would take it to extremes. Why would she? In those days she thought Mike's sister was a sane and rational person.

According to Mary Miller, Grace had never really got over Ryan. She wouldn't ever talk about him in anything other than scathing tones – she seemed delighted to be rid of him – but sometimes, in unguarded moments, her beautifully made-up face settled into lines of hopeless misery and, beneath the thick black mascara, a lost and lonely look crept into her eyes.

The rumour was that Ryan was equally unhappy. He hadn't come to terms with the break-up either – Mary said his muscle-pumping in the gym was now so excessive that his biceps had ballooned to Popeye proportions – and would still tell anyone who listened that he had never, on his life, even thought of cheating on Grace.

Once you start telling a lie, thought Sara, you have to stick with it or no one will ever trust you again.

Poor Grace. It was one blow after another.

Outside the village shop, Mary said, 'Did you hear about the bracelet?'

Sara shook her head.

'It was her pride and joy. Rose gold with a heart-shaped padlock. Used to belong to her grandmother. And now it's gone. She can't find it anywhere.'

The gate link bracelet had been in the jewellery box by Grace's bed. She didn't remember when she'd last worn it, but she'd definitely seen it at the weekend when she put her diamond studs away. She hadn't been burgled – there was no sign of forced entry – and no one who'd recently been in the house, from the plumber to her best friend Jade, could remember anything untoward.

She searched pockets and drawers and cupboards, looked in totally stupid places like the fridge and the biscuit tin in case she'd had some kind of eccentric moment, and carefully examined every tiny crevice in the car.

'It's a complete mystery,' said Mary. 'Grace's mum thought it might be something to do with Lulu. But Grace said, I know my dog's clever, but she can't unlock a jewellery box as far as I know.'

Someone unkind started a rumour that Ryan might have

taken it, but Grace said that was ridiculous because she'd changed the locks since she'd thrown him out, so he wouldn't have been able to use his key.

Grace rang the police and was given a crime number so that she could claim on her insurance but, as she said, it wasn't about the money. 'I'd give anything to get it back, Sara. Anything. You know what it's like. If someone dies, the things that used to belong to them are so precious. It's all you have left. Something to remember them by.'

Sara thought about Mike's watch and how much Ursula had wanted it.

Finally, the day arrived.

Sara had expected the coroner's court to be much grander. But it was just a small room with high windows, light wood panelling and a gold coat of arms above the bench where the coroner sat. In the morning when they arrived, neither of the public toilets was working, and everyone had to file through a corridor to get to the staff toilets at the back. This didn't inspire confidence. You could see people thinking that a court of law convened to establish the cause of a sudden death should be able to afford the services of a qualified plumber.

Everyone from the village was there, sitting on the benches at the back, except for Grace, who had asked Mary to say she was really sorry but Kayleigh was off with a stomach bug and she had to mind the salon. Sara was pleased to see all her neighbours, and glad to have their support, but wondered

if they would have bothered to turn up in force if it hadn't been for the revelations about Mike's sordid sexual adventures. No one had tired of the story yet. Sara could tell, when she walked into the portacabin and everyone looked guilty and stopped talking, that the scandal of Mike and the prostitutes still had a long way to run. It was all so exciting, the idea that someone living in their midst – in the biggest house in the village – had been indulging in the kind of shocking lifestyle you only ever read about in the tabloids.

She could imagine all the conversations – how no one could bear to think of the grief, anger and humiliation she must be going through. Poor Sara – she must be devastated. Imagine living with someone for twenty years and finding out he had a whole secret existence you knew nothing about!

Sitting on the hard wooden bench, Sara cringed.

Katie was just behind her, on one of the rows reserved for the witnesses. It was comforting to know she was there. They had driven in together, and Katie had promised she would stay by her side all day. She had got up extra early that morning, rushed Dexter and Lulu out for a quick run, and walked Daisy to the post box. She and Sara had decided that Bundle could manage by himself in the garden until they came home.

High up towards the ceiling, on two sides of the courtroom, the windows let in the autumn light. The sky was bright blue. Sara tried to regulate her breathing. It was nearly over. Just this one day to get through.

It wasn't until they were all settled, waiting for the coroner, that Ursula arrived. Sara didn't need to turn round – she could tell from the murmurings behind her who had walked in. She couldn't quite bring herself to look in Ursula's direction, but

could see, on the edge of her vision, that Ursula had sat down at the other end of the row, as far away from Sara as possible.

Mike's voice in her head said, *She hates you.*

Sara's heart began to beat faster.

You know why, don't you? He sounded sad and resigned. *You know why she hates you?*

It wasn't my fault, she thought. I had no choice.

She blocked Mike's voice from her head.

When the coroner came in, Sara was worried to see how old and thin he was. His spine was bent, as if he'd spent too many years shouldering heavy responsibilities. Was he up to a long day of questioning and analysis? He looked as if he should be tucked up in a wing chair in front of the fire, a tartan blanket folded over his knees.

The coroner began by explaining how the proceedings worked, glancing up at one point to look directly at Sara over the top of his glasses. Sara nodded to show she was listening, but it was hard to concentrate, because of Ursula sitting so nearby, and the constant fear that Mike would interrupt if she dropped her guard for a moment.

He explained that an inquest was not a trial. They were all there to establish the facts surrounding the death of Michael Parsons, and there could be no language of blame or accusation. He said he also had a separate statutory duty to report on any risks to life or health identified during the inquest so that future deaths could be prevented. In a gentle voice, bowing his head as if showing proper deference, he read out a list of the witnesses he was intending to call, explaining that others had not been required to attend as he was going to redact their statements – in other words, just read out those parts that he felt were important. He

would also summarise the post mortem and toxicology reports.

And then, much more quickly than she'd anticipated, Sara, the first witness, was called to give evidence. It was only a few steps to the wooden stand at the side of the court, facing out towards the rest of the room, but it felt like a long slow walk down an endless road. She couldn't stop shaking. So many eyes were staring at her.

The coroner took her through the statement she'd given to the police some weeks before. It was a laborious process. Some sections he read out without comment, but then he'd stop, as if struck by a thought, and ask her to expand. 'Can you explain again, Mrs Parsons . . .?' 'In what way, Mrs Parsons . . .?' There were long pauses while he took notes.

Later, she remembered only fragments of what she'd said. Once, she talked about how much Mike hated being dependent on painkillers, and the coroner looked up and said, 'Can you tell the court a little bit more about this, please?', and she tried to put into words what a physical person he'd always been, and how shocking it had been for him to be reduced to an invalid, and how he kept trying to cut down the dose or manage without his medication altogether in the hope that the pain would somehow disappear if only he tried hard enough to ignore it. On another occasion, she stumbled through the rather sad admission that Mike drank more and more as the weeks passed, but only to dull the pain. He didn't seem to get much pleasure from it. He had a bottle of whisky in his study.

All through her testimony, she was filled with cold dread that she'd say something stupid or illogical. It felt so important to give answers that satisfied the coroner's patient questioning.

During the long pauses while the coroner scribbled away, she glanced up at the high windows and the bright blue October sky.

At one point she worried that the coroner might be slightly deaf, because he asked the same question again and again, rephrasing it slightly each time. Had Mr Parsons ever given any indication that he was thinking of death? Had he ever expressed the intention of wanting to take his own life? She had to fight down the urge to shout out, in a loud clear voice, 'Mike wasn't depressed. He didn't commit suicide. It was an accident.'

But she restrained herself. It seemed better to answer the questions calmly.

Finally, after what felt like hours, he said, 'Thank you, Mrs Parsons. I know this hasn't been easy. You have been very helpful.'

When she sat down, her legs were shaking.

The coroner read out statements from the senior paramedic who had arrived first, examined Mike's body and found no heartbeat, and then from the two police constables and the police sergeant, one after the other – no evidence of foul play, nothing in the room to indicate any kind of disturbance, no blood or obvious wounds on the body, nothing out of the ordinary in the house or grounds.

Sara was flooded with relief when each of the police statements mentioned looking for a note but finding nothing. It made sense that they'd searched so thoroughly. Find a fifty-year-old man dead in his bed, and suicide must be one of your first thoughts.

The police sergeant said that after liaising with the detective inspector, because there had been no indication that any

other persons had been involved, it had been declared a non-suspicious death.

The statement from the GP described Mike's chronic back problem, the various treatments discussed, and the drugs he'd been prescribed. It was good to have a summary of the toxicology report read out in public because it confirmed the high levels of painkillers and alcohol in Mike's blood. The post mortem report said that there had been no pathological features to indicate third party involvement. The cause of death was drug overdose.

The atmosphere in the courtroom was dull and tired as if all the air had been used up. The coroner raised his eyes from the paperwork and suggested they all take a break and reconvene at midday for a short session before lunch.

Outside in the waiting area, one of the toilets was now in operation. But the drinks machine was broken. It took all your coins one by one, but when you pressed 'select' they all rushed out again as if you'd won the jackpot.

'How are you bearing up, dear?' said Mary Miller.

'I've brought Ignatia and Aconite,' said Sarinda Nunn, 'in case you need a remedy.'

Sally Cook said she was a bit confused as to why it wasn't all over now that they'd read out the cause of death, but Mary – who'd been to an inquest before, in the course of her professional duties – said it wasn't just about why someone died, but how it happened.

'But we all know how it happened,' said Sally. 'It was an accident. He took too many pills by mistake.'

Beyond the reception desk, right by the entrance, Ursula was staring out into the car park, her back to them all.

Katie went out to one of the nearby cafés and brought

back a tray of tea in plastic cups. Sara was grateful. She was trembling with cold, as if someone had turned off the heating and the windows were wide open to thick snow and blizzard conditions.

Back in the courtroom, the coroner called Gemma, Mike's PA. She was wearing a bright green bouclé jacket and her silver bracelets jangled as she turned the pages of her statement. It turned out she'd been the very last person to speak to Mike apart from Sara. He'd rung her from Birmingham to relay some action points from the meeting, which had gone well, but he said that if the pain in his back got any worse he was going to have to miss his own party the next day. The coroner questioned Gemma for some time. She was tearful at the beginning but gained in confidence as he congratulated her on the clarity of her responses. She said Mike had sounded angry on the phone, and the coroner asked if that was unusual, and she said, no, pain always made him irritable because it got in the way and took his mind off what he was supposed to be doing next. She said he wasn't a good patient because he was so impatient, and then stopped, tied up in knots by her own bad choice of words.

'He didn't always remember to take his pills. But that was sometimes on purpose. He said they made him feel sleepy and he couldn't concentrate. But then if he didn't take them, he'd be in agony.' Gemma paused. 'It was like he couldn't win. Whatever he did, it didn't work.'

The coroner spent a long time writing this down. Then he asked her to go back to the phone call. 'You say he sounded angry.'

'Yes.'

'But that was normal.'

'Yes.'

'You had no indication that his state of mind was in any way different from usual?'

Gemma thought about this. 'No. He was just like he always was.'

The coroner nodded and thanked her for her evidence and for being so clear. 'Is there anything else you'd like to add?'

For one stomach-churning moment, Sara was frightened that Gemma was going to spill out the story about the prostitutes and the porn sites and the thousands of pounds wasted on sordid sexual adventures. It wasn't relevant – of course it wasn't. It had nothing to do with Mike's death. But she couldn't be sure that the coroner would feel the same way. It might open up all sorts of difficult questions about stress and pressure and mental health.

Sara held her breath.

But Gemma, after a short pause, shook her head.

The coroner said it had been a heavy and emotional morning and thanked them all for their attentiveness and co-operation. He said they would break for lunch and reconvene at two o'clock.

Katie took them all to the café she'd found round the corner. She sat Sara at a table by the window, as if she were an invalid or an elderly lady who needed cosseting, and went up to join Mary and Sarinda in the queue for sandwiches.

Well done, Sara.

She jumped.

Mike's voice said, *You can see the way it's going. The coroner doesn't think it was suicide.*

She shook her head, trying to get him to shut up.

So you'll get your money and keep the house and everything will go on as normal.

She shut her eyes tightly.

Ursula won't be happy, though.

'She's never happy,' said Sara, out loud. In a panic, she looked round in case anyone had heard. But the café was noisy with chatter and scraping chairs and orders shouted to the kitchen.

Without warning, the memories flooded back.

About a year after they married, Mike said that he wanted to meet up with contacts in New York. In some ways it was nothing more than a glorified sales trip, but it was also a chance to see Ursula, who was spending six months there on secondment – her company liked offering their buyers temporary placements in their international offices. As Sara had never been to Manhattan except in her imagination, courtesy of improbable rom coms, she jumped at the chance of going with him. They had planned to rent an apartment or stay in a hotel, but Ursula wouldn't hear of it. She said there was a spare room and plenty of space, and that Lee was really looking forward to meeting them.

'Who's Lee?' Sara was hoping that Ursula might have fallen in love and become less spiky.

Mike looked lost. 'I've no idea.'

What Sara hadn't realised until she was on her own for the third day running – Mike at meetings and Ursula and

Lee at work – was that solitary sightseeing was very boring. She made herself a list, and dutifully looked at landmarks and museums and galleries so that she could say, at the end of each day, 'I saw the Statue of Liberty! I saw MoMA! I saw Central Park!' But as she trudged through the crowded streets, feeling the hardness of the pavements beneath her feet, she realised she'd got out of the habit of spending time alone. She was tired and fed up. She was bored.

Lee turned out to be a tall, athletic Californian who was something to do with brand management in Ursula's office. She said they were just flatmates, but her eyes followed him everywhere.

One afternoon Sara couldn't be bothered to trail round the latest tourist attraction, so came back to the apartment and wandered about looking for distraction. Lee's room seemed to be full of sporting equipment and motivational self-help books. Sara leafed through a pile of letters and invoices on his desk, but they were all to do with gym membership and air travel, so she couldn't be bothered to examine them closely. Ursula's room, on the other hand, was gloriously untidy, with clothes, scarves, make-up and jewellery spilling out of drawers and ending up, like driftwood at low tide, in a long line under the bed. Sara tried on some gold trousers, borrowed some lipstick, and sprayed herself with some of Ursula's scent. Then she pulled out one of the great big artwork folders that were lying under a pile of cushions on the bed.

It was entirely to Ursula's credit that her erotic story about a young woman's secret obsession with a tall, athletic Californian was so compelling – there was a lot of glistening and tumescence – that Sara didn't hear the front door. She

didn't realise Ursula was home until she was standing in the room right in front of her.

Sara grovelled, apologised profusely, and promised never to snoop around Ursula's personal possessions ever again, but it was a long time before Ursula calmed down and stopped shouting.

Afterwards, thinking about the hurt and humiliation in Ursula's eyes, Sara realised there was probably a much deeper story running beneath the whole thing – a deeper story about unrequited love. She was surprised. Even mighty Ursula could be humbled by desire.

On the Friday night, they all went out to a Thai restaurant in the East Village. They had drunk quite a lot of beer by the time Lee arrived, late, with another young man called Simon. They were holding hands.

Sara didn't control her expression quickly enough. Lee caught her looking at Ursula with shocked sympathy, and realisation dawned. He hadn't known about her feelings for him. The air was thick with embarrassment. Ursula stood up, placed her napkin on the tablecloth, and walked out.

The next day, in a voice clipped with anger, she accused Sara of betraying her. She said Sara had deliberately let Lee know. This had ruined not only her personal but her professional relationship with him and would make working together impossible. Mike, who was some way behind, played peacemaker. Ursula turned on him with fury and said he had no idea what was going on. As he stared at her in some astonishment, she said she'd been trying really hard to put the past behind her. She'd decided it was wrong to bear a grudge against Sara for splitting up her friend and her brother – love is messy and unpredictable, and it wasn't fair

to let her loyalty to Carys colour the way she thought about her sister-in-law. But she couldn't keep quiet any longer, because this latest incident with Lee proved what she'd known for some time, which was that Sara was the kind of cruel and vindictive person who deliberately set out to destroy people for her own amusement. She said that Sara had lied when she'd claimed to know nothing about Carys. She'd known about her right from the beginning, right from the first moment she'd laid eyes on Mike. The truth was that Sara had seen a stable, long-term relationship and had set herself the challenge of breaking it up. She hated other people being happy because it was something she didn't understand. She wanted everyone to be as lonely and miserable as she was.

Mike had been staring at his sister open-mouthed. When he shook his head and said she'd got it all wrong, Ursula screamed at him to shut up, to shut up and listen, because he didn't know anything, he was going round with his eyes shut, and it was all because of him that Carys had tried to kill herself.

There was a terrible silence. All the blood left Mike's face. He looked old and almost ugly.

In a much quieter voice, he asked her what she meant. At first, Ursula didn't want to say anything. But he wouldn't let it go. He kept on and on at her. Eventually she said that Carys had jumped in front of a car. She'd broken some ribs. She was out of hospital. She was OK.

Sara felt sick. She made an excuse to leave the room and stood in the bathroom with her head against the tiles, trying to make sense of what she'd heard.

Later that afternoon, Mike rang friends in London. They

told him Carys had got drunk at a party and walked out into the road. Not a suicide attempt. An accident.

Sara said to Mike, 'I want to go home.'

He was distraught. 'I don't know why she's being like this.'

'Why did she lie about Carys? It was horrible. She could see what it did to you.'

Mike said, 'She must have thought it was true.'

But Sara shook her head. 'Even if it was, she shouldn't have told you. She should have protected you. Not passed on some shitty piece of gossip.'

Mike put his face in his hands.

Sara said, 'And what she said about trying to break you up – that wasn't true either. I'd no idea you were with someone when we met.'

Mike looked up. 'I know you didn't.'

'I didn't find out about Carys for months.' Sara's eyes filled with tears. 'I'd never have started seeing you if I'd known.'

He leaned forward and took her hand. 'But that's why I didn't tell you.'

'I never wanted to hurt her.'

'Of course you didn't.'

'I don't know her. I've never met her. But you were together a long time. Of course she was going to be upset.'

He hung his head.

'You should have told me in the art gallery. Right at the very beginning. But you didn't even mention her.'

'I couldn't risk it. I thought if I told you, you wouldn't even let me buy you a cup of coffee.'

They sat in miserable silence.

Sara said, 'Why does Ursula think I broke you up?'

Mike shook his head. 'I've no idea. I've told her so many times.'

'Carys is her friend. I understand that. But she can't go round accusing me of things I haven't done.'

'I'll talk to her. I'll talk to her now.'

Sara sat in the bedroom, listening to their raised voices. The argument went on and on. After a while, Sara heard the front door slam. Mike came to find her. He looked exhausted. The story, when she finally got it out of him, was unbelievable.

Some months earlier, Ursula had shown Carys a picture of Sara on her phone. Carys, shocked, had recognised her straight away. She said they'd all lived in the same block when Mike and Carys were renting a flat in north London.

Sara frowned. 'When was this?'

'It was only a few months. The summer when Carys and I were looking for somewhere to buy.'

'But I've never lived in north London.' Sara was bewildered. 'She must be confusing me with someone else.'

Carys was adamant that she knew Sara well. Sara was house-sitting for a colleague at work who'd gone away for the summer and needed someone to feed his cats – she told Carys she'd never lived anywhere so luxurious and was loving every minute of it. They used to chat in the grand entrance lobby. Sara was really friendly and wanted to hear all about Carys's life, and what she liked doing, and her job at the children's charity, and conversation moved on to Mike, and his IT company, and how long they'd been together. Sara had wanted to know every detail of their relationship because she thought it was so romantic, first love, teenagers at the school gates, still together after all these years. Carys was surprised Mike didn't remember her too.

Mike remembered the block of flats – a 1930s art deco development that looked like an ocean liner from outside, with great sweeping white balconies – but he was sure he'd never met Sara.

'Because I never lived there,' said Sara.

Mike nodded. 'I told Ursula that Carys must have got it wrong.'

'But she won't listen?'

'No.'

Sara felt a little icy clutch of fear. 'So what did you say?'

'I said we were leaving.'

'Oh, Mike.'

'Ursula's stubborn. I've always known that. Decides something and sticks to it – she'll never admit she's wrong. But this is different. This really matters. I said to her, I don't know what Carys's problem is, but Sara doesn't lie. And if you're asking me to choose between them, you know what I'm going to do.' Mike looked desolate. 'Ursula said I just couldn't face the truth, so I said I was sorry, she was my sister and I'd always love her, but I thought we needed some distance between us.'

Sara couldn't bear to see the misery in his eyes. 'I'm sorry.'

'It's not your fault.' Mike tried to smile, but the muscles of his face weren't working properly. 'It's just a misunderstanding, that's all. We'll work it out. We'll look back on this in years to come and wonder what all the fuss was about.'

Ursula was very stupid. She didn't apologise – not then, not ever. Once or twice, when the boys were little, Mike suggested they should go and see her – she was in Australia by then – but Sara always found plenty of practical reasons why it wasn't a good idea. He stopped asking her in the end.

Sara knew that Mike and Ursula patched it up eventually. She knew they spoke on the phone and that Mike had even seen her a couple of times when he was away on business. But she suspected there was always a little crack in their relationship. Ursula could never quite forgive him for what he'd done to Carys.

Sometimes Sara wondered if Mike couldn't forgive himself either. Perhaps that's why he stayed with her, propping himself up with the odd affair, burying himself in his work. He'd already destroyed one woman's life. He couldn't face destroying Sara's too.

It was twenty years before Sara saw Ursula again.

By that time, Mike was dead.

It started innocuously enough. They had all filed back into the courtroom after lunch and were waiting for the coroner to reappear. The usher said, 'All rise,' as the coroner came into view, and everyone settled back down on the pale wooden benches.

Everyone, that is, apart from Ursula. She stayed on her feet, tall and straight, her whole body rigid.

People at the back of the court might not have heard her exact words because she started off in quite a quiet voice. 'I'd like to ask a question.'

The coroner had already shown himself to be a very polite man who recognised how stressful an inquest can be for the recently bereaved. 'Please go ahead.'

'Why is it a non-suspicious death?'

The coroner stared down at the stack of papers in front of him and said the information had been in the police reports, which he was happy to read out again if that would help. Ursula said she remembered the police statements, but that she didn't understand.

'What don't you understand?'

'Why the police made that decision.'

Sara started shivering as if a cold wind was blowing through the room.

The coroner frowned and said that he wasn't clear how he could help her, not because he didn't want to help her, but because the decision about whether or not to treat a death as suspicious is taken by the police officers who first attend the scene, in consultation with superior officers who review their conclusions.

Ursula said – and everyone in the court must have heard this, because her words rang out like a cry of pain – 'And that's it? We just take their word for it?'

Sara's hands were shaking so violently that she had to press down hard into her lap to make them still.

The coroner looked at Ursula over the top of his glasses as if they were the only two people in the room. He said that he'd explained at the beginning of the day's proceedings that the purpose of the inquest was to establish the facts about her brother's death – who he was, when and where he died, and the medical cause of his death. From this, he would decide by what means the death had occurred and record a conclusion. It wasn't a trial, and there could be no language of blame or accusation.

Then he paused for a moment, to be sure he had her full

attention, and said, 'We welcome any information you may have that might increase our knowledge and help us to understand the facts. Is that the case? Do you have further evidence to give us today about Mr Parsons's death that we have not already heard in court?'

Ursula sat down very suddenly as if her legs could no longer support her.

The coroner leaned forwards. 'Is there any further evidence that you would like to tell us about?'

There was a moment of tension, when it felt as if the whole courtroom was holding its breath.

Ursula shook her head.

And at that point, Sara knew it was over.

The ending came quickly after the long and tedious proceedings. It was all dressed up in fastidious legal language, but the decision was quite clear: accidental death.

The relief was so great that Sara couldn't see or hear for a while. It was only after she was outside in the reception area and she had been hugged so many times that she felt like a child's flannel, dirty and slightly damp, that it finally began to sink in. Joy spread through her, running like electricity through her veins.

Mike's death had been an accident. No blame. No horrible repercussions. The period of waiting was over. Life could begin again.

It was, of course, natural that there should be a bit of discussion about Ursula's embarrassing interjection as they all milled about in the lobby afterwards. There were odd mutterings and a few raised eyebrows. But luckily most people hadn't really heard what she'd said, and thought she'd just got in a muddle about one of the police statements. Someone

said they'd always thought she seemed a bit flamboyant, and perhaps she'd just wanted a moment in the spotlight before the final decision.

Ursula herself was nowhere to be seen.

Eventually everyone started to leave. Mary Miller was picked up by her old friend Ailsa – the sexual health nurse – in a small red Audi, and all the others spread themselves out between various cars for the drive back to the village. By the time Sara had found Katie and they were ready to go, the sky was pale grey and there was a sharp wind picking up litter and sending it scurrying along the pavement.

As Sara and Katie left the courtroom, they saw Ursula standing on her own by the iron railings smoking a cigarette. The car park was almost empty – just a few lone cars.

Sara said, 'Do you want a lift?'

It seemed important to be magnanimous in victory.

Ursula turned to face them, her eyes black against the whiteness of her face.

Sara kept her voice neutral and friendly. 'I could drive you to your hotel if you like.'

Ursula stared across the shallow stone steps, her dark hair blown round her head like the brim of a wide hat.

Sara said, 'Or you could come back with us for something to eat.'

Ursula pulled her coat more tightly round her tall, thin body, dropped the cigarette butt, and ground it out with the toe of her shoe.

Sara hesitated, standing there with Katie, both of them buffeted by small gritty gusts of wind.

Ursula said, in a loud carrying voice, 'You killed him.'

She began to walk towards them, each long slow stride

reducing the space between them. Sara couldn't help herself. She looked over to the car, parked by the exit barrier, measuring the distance, wondering whether to run.

Ursula stopped right in front of her. 'I don't know how you did it. But you got him to take an overdose. You crushed up the pills and made him swallow them. And then you lay down next to him all night while the hours passed and his heart beat more and more slowly. And then it stopped. And in the morning he was dead.'

A blast of wind blew round their legs, flapping coats and scarves.

'I thought, if I came back today, someone might listen.' Ursula's eyes were glittering with tears. 'But they didn't. No one listened. They didn't want to know.'

Katie shot Sara a quick glance. But Sara wouldn't look at her. She kept staring at Ursula.

'My brother was a good man. He could have been happy.'

Sara felt very tired. 'You don't know what you're talking about.'

'But I do, Sara. That's the problem. I do know what I'm talking about.'

Katie found her voice. 'I don't think—'

'I know everything you did. All the punishments and humiliations you put him through day after day. For what? I don't know. For not being the man you thought you'd married. For not loving you enough. For not understanding your emptiness and loneliness and self-hatred. But it doesn't make any difference. Because there's nothing I can do. Nothing.' The weariness in her voice was bone cold. 'I can't fight you any more, Sara. I give up. I'm going home.'

Ursula turned and started walking away.

Katie said, 'She can't just—'

'Let her go.'

'But Sara—'

Sara said, her voice sharp, 'Let her go.'

They stood there, shivering, watching as the black line of her body became more and more distant before disappearing altogether round a street corner.

After that final confrontation Sara could hardly stay upright. She wanted to sink down on to the old gravelly tarmac, among all the windblown litter.

Katie insisted on driving. She said Ursula's mad accusation must have been a terrible shock. As she drove, she kept shooting Sara anxious glances, but Sara just sat there on the front seat, staring straight ahead. She knew that Katie wanted to talk – wanted to help neutralise Ursula's latest vile calumnies – but she couldn't face any kind of conversation. Even the thought of it made her feel sick. All she could focus on was getting home. When the silence in the car became oppressive, she turned on the radio. There was a drive-time chat show with a phone-in about the closure of the local psychiatric hospital. No one cares about mental health, said an angry voice, cracked with pain. My wife was so depressed she ended up killing herself.

There were roadworks on the bypass, and they got stuck at the red lights behind a long line of cars and a horse-box.

It was nearly five when they picked up Edward from school. She hadn't wanted him to come home on the bus to an empty house so had arranged for him to stay on. He seemed tired and disoriented, staring at Sara with a blank expression as if he wasn't really sure who she was. The journey home was interminable. By the time they crunched over the gravel past

the stone urns, every part of Sara's body was prickling with misery. The last thing she needed was Bundle's enthusiastic welcome as he hurtled into the hall with a joyous volley of barks.

Katie took charge. 'I'll take him out.'

'You've done enough. You should go home.'

'Just a quick walk.' Katie was determined. 'Or he'll bark all night.'

The silence, once Edward and Sara were alone, was like a cool bandage on a swollen wound.

She took a deep breath. 'It's all over now.'

He said, 'Over now.'

Which, as she thought later, just goes to show how wrong you can be.

Sara and Katie should have talked. That's what should have happened. When Katie got back from walking Bundle, they should have gone to the kitchen and made supper and opened a bottle of red wine. Later it was obvious how much they needed to confide in each other. Sara was at breaking point. If they'd talked, Ursula's accusations outside the court would have been taken apart and seen for what they were – grief that had become ugly and evil and intent on destruction. How could Sara have crushed up painkillers and made Mike swallow them? Was he the kind of man who would meekly do what his wife said? Why would she want to make him take an overdose anyway? The whole thing was ridiculous.

That vicious remark about Sara having no friends was equally stupid. Sara had lots of friends. They'd been there in the courtroom, supporting her.

She and Katie should have pulled apart everything Ursula had said and dismissed it all as a package of lies.

But that night, coming back from the inquest, Sara was terrified. There was too much emotion. Her head was filled with noise, like the sound of crashing waves, and it was only by ignoring it that she had any control at all. If she turned to face it, if she allowed herself to see the force of all that energy, she would have been overwhelmed. She would have drowned.

When Katie returned with Bundle, Sara said she felt unwell and had to go to bed. Katie looked concerned, and sad, but what could she do? She said she'd be back in the morning.

After Katie left, Sara settled Edward in front of the TV and rang James. They'd already had a brief exchange of texts outside the courtroom, but she wanted to tell him exactly what the coroner had said.

He listened in silence. When she told him again about the conclusion of accidental death, he said, 'We always knew it was. But I'm glad everyone else knows too.'

Sara said, 'I can't believe it's all over.'

'But it is. That's it. No more mysteries.'

Sara didn't mention Ursula, or what she'd shouted out at the inquest, or what she'd said afterwards in the empty car park. James didn't need to know about any of that.

When the call was over, Sara went upstairs and ran a bath, and lay there in the deep water for a long time. She knew she should feel relieved. She knew she should feel the tension floating away. But this was the moment, out of all the weeks

and months of pain and anxiety, when she finally hit rock bottom. She felt completely alone. As usual, Mike's voice was around somewhere (*Didn't quite work out the way you planned, did it, Sara?*), but only as background noise, like the radio turned down low. And although Edward was in the house, he'd never been much of a comforting presence. Companionship wasn't something he was able to do. You could be in the same room as Edward, even exchanging the odd word, but he would be in his head, and you would be in yours, and the only communal activity would be breathing the same air.

Sara started weeping into the bathwater. She shouldn't have turned Katie away. She missed her. It's easy to pick up on conversations you've had to abandon halfway through if you live in the same house. But now Katie was in her own house – probably, by now, in her own bed, wrapped round her beloved Danny – and Sara was the other side of the fence, and Katie had no idea how much she needed her.

Sara had always known that it would be hard when Katie left. But she still felt her absence acutely. Her heart hurt. Lying there in the tepid bath, she closed her eyes and imagined what it would be like if Danny went away again, and Katie gave up her damp and mouldy house and came back to live in the Old Rectory. Now that the inquest was over, there would be no anxiety, no financial worries. They would put the past behind them. The house was big enough for each of them to have their own space. They would live together in perfect harmony.

But that's not going to happen, is it, Sara?

An hour or so later, Sara cooked some pasta and she and Edward had a silent supper. Shortly after that, Edward went to bed.

Sara stayed at the table, looking out through the glass of the extension, the black night all around her. Her mind was fizzing with slivers of memory. Ursula was wrong. There was no emptiness, at least not in the early days. It was her confidence that had attracted him. When he finally told her about Carys, she could see why the relationship had been such a mistake. From the sound of it, Carys was clingy and insecure, leaning on him for emotional support. He didn't want someone weak and insipid. He didn't want someone who took up all his time. Sara's cool detachment must have come as a welcome relief.

She had looked at herself in the mirror of his adoration and liked what she saw. And he had gazed back at his calm, composed, self-sufficient wife and had congratulated himself on making such a clever choice.

Soon after they first got together, he said, with the big smile that broke up his rather pushed-together and dough-like face into something startlingly good-looking, 'You really don't need me, do you?'

'What do you mean?'

'I could disappear tomorrow, and you'd be fine.'

She didn't have a clue how to respond. He seemed to want her to agree. But how would that make sense? There has to be a certain amount of wanting the other's presence for a relationship to work at all.

She said, 'Are you planning to disappear?'

He laughed. It was hard to remember where they were when they had this conversation, but she could see the sun shining on the side of his face, lighting up the reddish stubble on his skin. He said, 'I'm going to be around for a long time, Sara.'

Which turned out to be true.

He loved her independence. It meant he never had to worry about her. If you set up your own company, you work long hours. You're hardly ever home.

She said, soon after they married, 'You're just trying to avoid me.'

'You don't believe that.' He looked anxious.

'Don't I?'

He took her face in his hands. 'It's all for you. I'm doing this all for you.'

Was that true? It's a convenient excuse when you're buried in a job you love. Work is selfish. You need enough money to live, to eat, to pay the rent. But after that, it's just extra.

He said, 'I'd give it all up in an instant if I believed that's what you wanted.'

But she'd never asked him to, so she didn't know if that was true either.

Sara stared into the darkness. Towards the end, when she'd got used to living without him, he said his only function was to bring in money and her life would be a lot easier if he wasn't there. It was one of his jokes, of course – his trademark dark humour, flung out on cold winter mornings as he crashed out of the house in a bad mood. She was never quite sure what to say. Disagreeing with him would have been dishonest because, by that stage in their relationship, his analysis was largely correct. She would have preferred a different kind of marriage, but that's what they'd ended up with, seemingly by mutual consent. So she couldn't disagree with him, but she couldn't pretend it was funny either, because it would have been too strange to stand in the hall laughing as her husband told her that he was unnecessary to her happiness. So instead

she just looked at him, and he stared back, and after a while the silence became ominous and unpleasant and he said something angry like, 'For fuck's sake, Sara, I've got to go,' and slammed out of the house.

You would think they would have got the hang of conversational exchanges after twenty years. But it seemed to get harder, not easier.

She didn't want to remember any of it. She wanted to sit at the table and have nothing in her head at all, nothing but cool, empty darkness.

Once, out of the blue, he said, 'You make me feel like nothing.'

She didn't know what to say.

He said, 'Not wanting me. You make me feel like nothing.'

It always came back to sex in the end.

Sara thought, but sex is only a transaction. A contract agreed by both parties. You have to keep it in perspective.

He stayed because he couldn't walk out on his autistic son. That would have felt like failure. He needed his internal image of himself to be squeaky clean. He needed to admire himself.

If he'd been more of a bastard, they would both have been free.

A bastard. A bully and a bastard.

When she finally went to bed, she was sure it would be another night of insomnia. But she must have fallen asleep immediately, because she opened her eyes and there he was, the bulk of him just standing there, silent and accusing. She sat bolt upright in bed and stared straight at him as the outline of his body became less and less distinct, finally swallowed up by the darkness. She lay down again, shivering.

The dreams that followed were vivid and frightening. Part

of her knew they weren't real – just sickening delusions, a kind of waking nightmare. But they seemed so real, more like memory than fantasy. At one point, she was sitting in the grand, polished, black-and-white entrance hall of a block of flats – which she knew, as you do in dreams, was art deco, and that from the outside its sweeping white balconies made it look like an ocean liner – and watched as Mike and Carys came down the stairs. She could see her so clearly – blonde hair, a floppy faded dress in some kind of floral print with tangled tendrils of tiny leaves. Mike always said she was a bit of a hippy. More interested in incense and spiritualism than building up a business from scratch.

Sara marvelled at the detail of Carys's appearance, the way her mind had conjured up something so complete from remembered clothes in a wardrobe.

Mike and Carys reached the bottom step. There must have been something they had to decide about their plans for the day, because they stopped and looked at each other, standing there just in front of her, and their closeness was such that one glance was enough, one brief exchange that summed up all the possibilities, everything they'd discussed, and they laughed and made little clowning gestures as if to say, *Who cares? It doesn't matter*, and the decision was made and they could move on.

But that couldn't be right, could it? When he eventually admitted to Carys's existence, Mike said the relationship was over, that he and Carys had nothing in common, that they were only staying together out of habit and convenience. So how could they be so intimate? How could they talk with their eyes?

As Mike opened the heavy wooden door and stepped out

into the sunlight, his hand was beneath her elbow, guiding her through.

Sara's dream then cut to the same polished entrance hall, but this time she and Carys were sitting together on the curved wooden bench. Was this their first conversation? Their second? Sara was asking her how long she'd known Mike, and Carys smiled with the kind of bashful diffidence that seemed to be her trademark and said, 'Forever. Since we were thirteen. I can't imagine life without him.'

And Sara felt a cut to her heart – loneliness, perhaps, or grief, or a sense that something terrible had happened that could never be repaired and was somehow all her fault.

Just before dawn, she woke, covered in sweat. She could hear someone crying. After some time, she realised that the sound came from her own mouth and that her face was wet with tears. She sat up. The feeling of loss was a physical pain in her stomach, cutting her in two. Rocking backwards and forwards, soothing herself like a small child waking from a nightmare, she found herself shouting to the empty room, 'I never wanted to hurt her!'

Of course you didn't.

She looked round wildly, but he wasn't there – nothing but a grey and uncertain light as the darkness receded.

'She was kind to me.'

She was kind to everyone.

'She was my friend.'

You wanted to step inside her. You wanted to live inside her skin.

Sara shrank back, horrified.

You didn't really want me. I wasn't important – just an accessory, a way of feeling what it was like to be loved.

'That's not true.'

All that planning. All that effort.

She shook her head, trying to get rid of his voice.

Just so that I would look at you the way I'd looked at her.

She said, in a whisper, 'And then you stopped.'

There was no answer.

'Mike?' It was a plaintive cry, an exhalation of grief. 'Why did you stop? Why did you stop?'

But the room was silent.

The next morning, when Katie arrived to walk Bundle, the atmosphere in the house was tense and fractious. Sara's head was thick from dreams that clung to her like wet silk. Edward had only just left for school and Bundle was in particularly high spirits, jumping out at himself from behind hidden corners and knocking over the kitchen chairs.

Katie said, 'Are you feeling better?'

Sara nodded, unwilling to go into detail. 'Just tired.'

'I know what you mean.' Katie looked washed-out, as if she hadn't slept much either.

'Is everything all right?'

Katie hesitated.

'What is it? What's happened?'

Katie said, in a great gabble of words, 'I just wanted to say that I won't tell anyone what Ursula said. None of it, I promise. All that stuff about crushing up painkillers and making Mike take an overdose.'

There was a small awkward pause. Sara said, 'I didn't think you would.'

Katie swallowed. 'I thought you might be worried. Because of what happened at the funeral.' Her voice dropped to a whisper. 'Telling everyone about Mike.'

Sara said, in a cold voice, 'As I've said a number of times, that's all forgotten. We've drawn a line under it.'

Bundle barked, a short imperious yap to remind them that he was waiting.

Katie said, 'You can trust me. I want you to know that. I promise, on my life, I would never do anything to hurt you.'

Sara forced a smile. 'Of course you wouldn't.'

'I hated all the things she said. I kept thinking about them all night. They kept going round and round in my head.' Katie looked desperate. 'It's so frightening. You don't know what she's going to do next.'

'She can't do anything.'

'What if she comes back? What if she comes back and tries to stir things up again?'

Bundle let out a drum roll of barks.

Sara said, 'It wouldn't matter if she did.'

'What do you mean?'

Sara took a deep breath. It was important to reassure Katie that everything was going to be fine. 'We've had the inquest. The coroner heard all the evidence and recorded his conclusion. So we don't need to worry about Ursula's madness and anything she might say in the future. She can rant on all she likes. No one would believe her.'

'You're sure?'

Sara said, her voice calm, 'I think we should forget all about her.'

There was a moment while Katie thought about this. Then the cloud of anxiety lifted from her face and she smiled.

After Katie had left, Sara sat quite still, staring into space.

She hadn't anticipated Katie's reaction. This frightened her. She didn't like feeling out of control.

An hour after this exchange, the doorbell rang. Sara dragged herself to her feet and went to answer it.

There on the stone steps, against the background of red and golden leaves, stood not only a windblown Katie and an over-excited Bundle but a short balding man in a grey coat and wire-rimmed glasses, gazing at Sara with friendly recognition.

'Sara,' said Katie, 'it's Mr Roslyn.'

Sara recoiled. The last time he'd been in her kitchen, he'd gone on and on at her with such ferocity that she'd dissolved into tears.

Mr Roslyn said, 'Would it be convenient to have a word?'

'Not really,' Sara said. 'It was my husband's inquest yesterday and we're all exhausted.'

But somehow after that small explosion of defiance, all the fight went out of her, and she stepped back and let him in.

It was lucky that Katie had come back with Bundle just as Mr Roslyn was leaning on the doorbell. His interrogation would have been much worse if Katie hadn't been there to defend her.

As Sara led Mr Roslyn across the stone floor of the hall, Bundle raced ahead, all the way through to the kitchen extension, and started yapping at the garden. Sara put the kettle on while Katie slid back the great glass doors, and they watched as the dog shot over the lawn and disappeared into the shrubbery out of view. Soon afterwards, they heard his usual manic barking.

'It's the compost heap,' said Katie.

Such was the bewildering surrealism of the morning – a private investigator arriving hours after an inquest – that this remark passed without comment.

It was a relief to sit down with a full pot of coffee. Sara thought she might fade away altogether without an injection of caffeine. After only a small hesitation, because she didn't want to encourage him, she offered Mr Roslyn the biscuit tin. 'So how can we help you?'

Mr Roslyn must have thought they looked tired and distracted, because he went right back to the beginning. He had been hired to find Sara's old au pair Hilda, who had managed to go travelling without telling anyone where she was going. Although she'd tried to impress Sara in her original job interview with stories of a big family and a huge number of brothers and sisters – perhaps to make herself seem like the kind of easy-going person who would be good with small children – she was, in fact, an only child with very few relatives. As a result, the emails, texts and phone calls that normally fly around a close family were non-existent. No one had been in contact with her for some time. Mr Roslyn, because he had very little else to go on, had decided to go all the way back through her life in order to track down where she might have ended up, which was why he'd paid that very fraught visit to the Old Rectory some weeks before.

Although on previous showing a rather pushy interrogator, Mr Roslyn took some time to warm up on this occasion and didn't immediately answer Sara's question as to how they could help him. Instead he began a rather lengthy explanation of standard procedures in the search for a missing person. Because of all the stress and exhaustion of the past few days, Sara found it impossible to concentrate. At some point, she drifted off, only coming to when she realised that both Mr Roslyn and Katie were looking at her expectantly. It was clearly some time since Mr Roslyn had stopped speaking,

and she couldn't recall a single word he'd said. She had no choice but to play the sympathy card. 'I'm sorry. I'm so tired from yesterday that I wasn't really listening. What did you say?'

Mr Roslyn frowned. 'That I haven't been able to find any evidence of her whereabouts since the time she lived here with you.'

Sara was surprised. Most people don't admit so readily to failure. 'So what will you do?'

He fixed her with a serious stare. 'I wondered if we could talk again about what happened on the day she left.'

'Sara is really very tired, Mr Roslyn.' Katie's expression was stern. 'If there's any chance that we could do this another time—'

He cut her off. 'I'm asking a lot. I do understand that. But without more information I'm at a dead end.'

Katie opened her mouth to speak, but this time it was Sara who interrupted. Her voice was high and strained. 'A bargain, Mr Roslyn. I'll tell you what I know. But then you must go. Do you understand? After that, no more questions.'

After a brief hesitation, he nodded.

In fact, there were no great revelations. It all boiled down to such a small story. Sara told Mr Roslyn that she'd known about Hilda's affair with Mike, but had hoped, if she ignored it, that the whole thing would just peter out. She explained that she had been utterly dependent on Hilda, because Hilda had been so good with her autistic son – she was one of the very few people he tolerated when he was small – so Sara had been wary of doing anything to upset her. But then came the day when she came home from shopping, laden down with plastic carrier bags, to find four-year-old Edward lying

on the floor with a livid bruise on his forehead. Sara said that it was hard to explain quite how much that had affected her, except to say that the bond with her son was such that, on seeing the contusion, she felt as if she, too, had been coshed. She felt the pain. She felt dizzy, as if she were losing consciousness. Hilda rushed to reassure her. She and Edward had been in the garden, and she'd been distracted for a moment, just a moment, had turned her back, and he'd fallen down the stone steps near the willow tree. He hadn't cried for very long. It looked worse than it was. He'd let her apply some arnica.

Sara's response had been totally irrational. The whole thing was clearly nothing more than an accident. But she shouted at Hilda. She told her she was stupid and incompetent. She accused her of not caring. She said she couldn't trust her.

Hilda became tearful, and then angry, and at some point in the row that followed, with Edward screaming on the floor with his hands over his ears, she said that Mike was right, and Sara was totally insane. When Sara asked her what she meant, Hilda said, 'You know what I mean.'

They stood there, staring at each other, and Sara said, 'Don't. Please don't.'

And Hilda said, 'What do you care? You don't want him.'

It was hard to explain the significance of that exchange, but both Hilda and Sara knew exactly what it meant. Hilda was challenging Sara to face up to her affair with Mike. Obviously, she had thrown out the words in the heat of the moment. They weren't meant to have any lasting impact. But for Sara it brought everything to a head. As she explained to Mr Roslyn – Katie watching, her eyes huge with sympathy – she realised with sudden clarity that the situation couldn't

continue. She took a deep breath, and asked Hilda to leave. Hilda tried to apologise, but Sara wouldn't listen. She just kept saying that she had to go. Eventually Hilda saw that she wouldn't be able to change Sara's mind, so she went upstairs, packed her stuff together, and left.

'What time was this?' Mr Roslyn was busy scribbling in his notebook.

'I'm not sure. Around lunchtime.'

'Do you remember what she was wearing?'

'No.'

'And where did she go?'

Sara shook her head. 'I don't know. I didn't talk to her again. I was in the kitchen with Edward and heard the front door slam.'

Mr Roslyn looked up. 'She didn't drive, and she didn't have a car, so she must have got a lift? Or a taxi?'

'Or walked,' said Sara.

'With a heavy suitcase?'

Sara felt hopeless. 'I don't know. I don't know what she did.'

'You didn't worry about her? Want to check to see she was safe?'

Quite suddenly Sara couldn't stand it any more. The strain of the day before collided with the stress of remembering an incident she thought she'd buried a long time ago, and she wanted him out of the house. Her voice was shaking. 'We had a bargain, Mr Roslyn. I said I would tell you what I knew. And then, once I'd finished, you'd go. No more questions.'

The light from the window flashed on his glasses. 'Yes, of course. I'm sorry. You've been very kind to give me so much of your time.'

As he fussed about, gathering together his belongings, Sara wondered if she should get up and see him out, but exhaustion seemed to have crept into her bones and immobilised her.

Katie went with him to the door. On the threshold of the kitchen, he turned and faced her. 'Just one more thing, Mrs Parsons. Did anything get left behind?'

'Like what?'

'I don't know. Anything that belonged to her. It can happen when people leave in a hurry.'

'No.'

'Nothing?'

'No.'

As his footsteps echoed in the hall, she felt a clamp around her forehead, and a weight on her chest, making it hard to breathe.

On Saturday morning, coming out of the village shop, Sara found herself face to face with Rachel. Her heart sank.

'I'm sorry I couldn't come to the inquest last week. I couldn't get time off. But I heard it went well.'

Sara nodded.

Rachel said, 'You must be so relieved.'

Sara always found it irritating to be told what she must be feeling. She would much rather come to her own conclusions. What was the point of a conversation if everything was decided before you'd even started? 'I am, yes. I'm really glad it's all over.'

Rachel settled the hessian bag on her arm. 'I saw him in the village.'

Sara was lost. 'Who?'

'That young man of hers. The one in the black coat.'

Sara wondered why this was supposed to be interesting.

'Loitering by the post box talking on his phone.'

'Customers, I expect,' said Sara. 'Talking to customers about windows.'

'You'd think he might want to sit in his car to carry out business negotiations. The Ford Mondeo. With the alloy wheels.'

On the way home, Sara found herself gritting her teeth with irritation. Rachel wanted to make her feel uncomfortable. Why? By the time she'd put away the shopping, Sara had decided that she'd had enough of people altogether. They were too complicated. Much too hard to understand. She was exhausted.

Unfortunately, there was more to come.

When Katie finally turned up, an hour late, to take Bundle for his afternoon walk, Sara was so shocked by her appearance that she insisted she sat down and had a cup of tea. It transpired that Katie had been so busy dog walking that she'd somehow managed to skip both breakfast and lunch.

'Bundle can wait,' said Sara. 'You've got to eat.'

When she next turned round, Katie's face was awash with tears.

It didn't take long to get the story out of her. Katie hadn't wanted to bring it up before the inquest because it seemed so trivial compared with what Sara and the boys were going through, but the worry had been eating away at her. The night before the inquest, she'd met up with Anna in the Goat and

Anna had asked if Danny was looking for a job. Katie had been confused, and said that Danny already had a job, selling windows. Anna had shaken her head, and said, 'Not any more.'

According to Anna – who had heard this from Baz – Danny had come back to the area because he'd been sacked.

Sara was surprised. 'Sacked?'

Katie nodded.

'Why? What happened?'

Katie didn't know. But Baz said that Danny was working out his notice. In a month's time he'd have to give back the Ford Mondeo.

Katie was at a loss to know what was going on. It was true that Danny hadn't exactly lied. Technically speaking, he was still a window salesman with a company car. But shortly he wouldn't be. So he hadn't exactly told the truth, either. On one level, his equivocation was understandable. It's humiliating, losing a job. It's not something that's easy to talk about. But Katie was still upset. She'd thought the reconciliation between them was so complete that they could tell each other everything. Why had Danny wanted to keep this from her? Did he think she'd love him less if she knew?

'I wish he'd told me, Sara. I wish I'd known.'

'He probably didn't want to worry you.'

Katie looked dejected. 'I just don't want us to have any secrets from each other. Not after all we've been through.'

Sara didn't want to trash her romantic illusions, tempting though this was. 'He probably wanted to wait until he had some good news. I bet you he's out looking for a job at this very moment.'

Katie looked up, her face full of hope. 'Do you think so?'

'Definitely.'

After she'd finished her sandwich, Katie took Bundle off to Smith's Field and Sara was left alone to mull over their conversation. She thought about Katie's determined attempts to understand her worthless boyfriend and felt very sad. From what she'd seen so far, the only person who mattered in Danny's life was Danny. He was selfish and calculating, and never stopped to consider Katie's feelings.

With sudden blinding clarity, she knew that he was going to break her heart all over again.

Sara had neglected the garden. She could see that the next day, when she went outside the minute Edward had left for school. The chaos was no longer lovely but threatening and slightly needy, as if the plants were trying to leave the ground and march towards the house. Sara set to, pruning and cutting, taming the penstemons and anemones, the salvia and phlox. The day was brisk and businesslike, with clear skies and a gentle breeze, and she congratulated herself on the wisdom of getting out of the house and doing something she loved. You can analyse too much. You can end up thinking so hard that you miss the big picture altogether. Katie should be her focus. Katie had given her so much love and support, and now it was Sara's turn to repay the favour.

Quite soon, pulling and digging, clearing and weeding, Sara was covered in sweat. She thought about Katie's faith in Danny, her perpetual optimism. Katie was a romantic. She was the kind of person who liked pretty flowers but didn't

want to think of their roots in mould and bacteria. But I know what sins people are capable of, thought Sara, straightening up. I know they're cruel and manipulative and driven by self-interest. Katie is innocent. She sees only the best in people. It's my job to protect her.

She had a sudden sharp memory of an argument with Mike years before. She couldn't remember what it had been about, but he'd been irritated, scornful.

He said, 'Why don't you just try getting on with people for once?'

She had looked at him in astonishment. 'What do you mean?'

'You always act as if someone's out to get you. What's the point? Live and let live.'

But compromise, thought Sara, lifting up an armful of leaves and stems and dank-smelling weeds to put them on the compost heap, has never been in my nature.

On the Monday afternoon after the inquest, Katie crunched back over the gravel, Bundle straining at the lead, to find a police car in front of the house. When she passed the open door of the living room and glanced in to see a uniformed police officer and his crackling radio on one of the big white sofas, her face was the picture of shock.

'Katie!' Sara said. 'Come in! Do you remember PC Bush?'

Katie said something about letting Bundle out into the garden, and while she raced after him towards the kitchen, Sara reminded PC Bush that he'd met Katie before – she was

their dog walker and had been in the house the night Mike died.

Katie came back, looking anxious, and Sara took a deep breath and said, 'We've been burgled.'

'No!' Katie's cry was heartfelt. 'What's been taken?'

'All my jewellery.'

'Oh, Sara.' Katie sat down. 'That's terrible. When did it happen?'

Sara was embarrassed that she didn't really know. 'I found one of my rings on the windowsill in the bathroom, opened the drawer in my dressing table to put it away, and it was empty. Cleaned out. Everything gone.'

'Everything?' Katie's eyes were big with concern.

Sara nodded.

'Someone broke in?'

'Not that we can see,' said PC Bush. He turned back to Sara. 'Is there an alarm?'

She nodded. 'But I don't usually turn it on. Because of the dog.'

What she meant was that she couldn't risk it because Bundle was so unpredictable, leaping up walls and crashing into windows, that he might set it off. But she realised that she'd given the misleading impression that his barking was enough of a deterrent for them not to bother, which sounded so much more mature and grown-up that she let it stand.

PC Bush said, 'Is it possible that you left a window open or a door unlocked?'

Sara felt tears pricking her eyes. 'Very possible. I'm not really thinking straight at the moment.'

'You know about the inquest,' said Katie to PC Bush by way of explanation, and he nodded.

'I feel so stupid not even noticing.' Sara swallowed. 'I can't even remember when I last opened the drawer.'

PC Bush looked grave, as if he completely understood the strain she must be under. 'I'll have another scout round and see what I can find. And we'll send someone over to dust for prints, just in case. Although they usually wear gloves, I'm afraid, so we may not be lucky.'

Boots creaking, he went out to the hall.

Katie said, 'I'm so sorry, Sara.'

Sara could feel her mouth trembling. 'Even my engagement ring's gone.'

Katie reached out her hand.

'I've described everything as well as I can. And given him some pictures I took the last time we had the valuable items insured.' Sara shook her head. 'I just wish I could remember when I last saw it all.'

'With all you've been through,' said Katie with great firmness, 'it's not the least bit surprising.'

After PC Bush had gone, Katie stayed on for a cup of tea. Sara was pleased. Their chats were so infrequent these days. But it turned out that Katie was just killing time. Danny was going to be late home. 'He's gone to London to see a friend.'

'London?'

'I know. I thought it was a long way, too.' She looked anxious. 'But I thought maybe it might be about a job. He's probably pursuing all sorts of leads.'

Over the next few days they kept missing each other, so Sara didn't find out for some time that Danny's London visit had turned into a bit of a holiday. He didn't return for three days. As Katie rather reluctantly admitted to Sara later, this wasn't the first time it had happened – his movements were

fairly unpredictable, and he quite often disappeared for long periods of time. But he got irritated if Katie started making a fuss about where he was going or what he was doing, so she tried not to ask too many questions.

Sara's heart sank. All the old habits were reasserting themselves – and Katie was colluding in it every step of the way. Sara had to keep reminding herself that Katie was very young, and it was natural for her to make mistakes. But it was still hard to see a friend heading off down the wrong path.

Poor Katie. Worse was to come. The next morning, as she followed Bundle through the graveyard on the way to Smith's Field, her mobile rang.

As she told Sara later, it had all begun when she turned on the shower one morning and got nothing but a freezing drizzle. The boiler in her dilapidated house had finally given up the ghost. She left a message with her landlord, asking if he knew anyone who could fix it. She wasn't expecting him to pay to have it mended – that would have been unreasonable, given that she was living there rent-free – but was just hoping for a recommendation or a steer in the right direction. Now, standing in a windswept corner of the field, Katie listened, her mobile clamped to her ear, as he told her that he'd been round to have a look, and the boiler was beyond repair – it just wasn't worth the risk. All the mould was a bit of a shock, too. He'd no idea it had got so bad and was worried it was breaching health and safety – he didn't want her getting sick and ending up in hospital with pneumonia. So basically he thought it was probably time for some major renovation.

'Oh,' said Katie, as she and the phone were buffeted by a sudden gust of air. 'What kind of renovation?'

This was the point in the conversation when the signal dipped, so she kept missing parts of what he was saying, but he seemed to be talking about not getting permission from the council, which didn't make a lot of sense. Then, as the wind howled about her, whipping her hair around her face, Katie suddenly heard his voice clear in her ear. '. . . so I've had a word with a mate, and he's going to go through and do all the basics – damp-proofing, rewiring, re-plastering, the whole works.'

'OK,' said Katie. 'That's fine.'

He sounded relieved. 'I know it's not easy finding somewhere to live. But I'll keep my ears open.'

As Katie rather urgently made it clear that she wasn't sure she'd quite understood, he explained that he needed her out within the month so that the house could be gutted and renovated. For a moment, she felt intense relief. She and Danny would end up with a nice new house. But the reprieve was short-lived. Her landlord was going to do up the house as cheaply as possible because he was putting it on the market. The council wouldn't give him permission to concrete over the garden, and he wasn't allowed to knock it down and build something bigger, so he was just going to sell it. The minute the paint dried, he was getting rid of it.

Katie made a small, brave attempt to suggest that it might be better to have a tenant while he was renovating and selling, but he was quite adamant.

'End of the road, Katie.' He cleared his throat. 'You've got four weeks. End of November.'

When Katie had brought this rather brutal story to a close, she looked utterly defeated. She said, not meeting Sara's eyes, that she had no idea how she and Danny were going to be

able to find a place they could afford and was really scared they were going to be homeless.

There was a small, awkward silence.

Sara said she'd love to help – of course she would – but there was a bit of a problem, which of course Katie knew about already. Edward was fine with Katie, and Katie was welcome any time, but he'd go into meltdown if a strange man came to live in the house. Sara couldn't do it to him – not now, when he was already so fragile because of the recent disappearance of both Mike and James. So she couldn't offer them a room. She was really sorry, but she just couldn't.

After a small pause, Katie nodded.

They sat there as the day gradually died, the silence stretching out in the empty space around them.

The next day, thinking that Mary with all her contacts might have some ideas about how Katie could solve her housing crisis, Sara paid a visit to her cottage on the main road.

As Daisy dozed at her feet, Mary listened to the whole story. She was sorry to hear that Danny had lost his job and wanted to know what he was doing to find another. Sara told her about the trip to London.

'I'm not sure that's going to help.'

She nodded. 'But Katie's hopeful. She has great faith in him.'

Mary sighed. 'I just don't see how they can afford to pay rent if their only income is a bit of part-time dog walking.'

The next morning, Katie arrived at the Old Rectory just before eight o'clock all lit up with happiness. Danny had come back from London with pockets stuffed full of cash.

Sara was astonished. 'How come?'

A little shamefaced, Katie said he'd put money on a horse. 'But it means we can afford a deposit now.'

Just after lunch, Sara fed this back to Mary over a cup of tea. As she chatted on about flat-hunting and how excited they'd be when they finally found a new place and were handed their very own set of keys, Mary seemed distracted.

Setting her cup in the saucer, she looked up. 'Keys?'

'To the front door,' Sara said, wondering what she was missing.

Mary looked worried. 'He's an honest young man, is he?'

'I've never met him.'

Mary was surprised.

Sara smiled. 'I just hear all about him from Katie.'

'When did he come back to the village?'

Sara thought hard. 'About a month ago, I think.'

'Moved straight in with Katie?'

Sara nodded.

'And when did Grace lose her grandmother's bracelet?'

They stared at each other across the table.

As soon as Sara understood the implications of what Mary was saying, she shook her head and said it was impossible. It just couldn't have happened. Mary, pink and flustered, agreed. But they carried on looking at each other with a kind of silent horror. The dates fitted. The facts fitted. It all seemed clear cut.

Sara said, in a hoarse voice, 'My engagement ring.'

'Of course, it might be a complete coincidence.'

Sara nodded.

After a pause, Mary said, 'Where does she keep the keys?'

Sara could hardly bear to answer. 'On little brass hooks in

the kitchen. But he wouldn't do that to her. It's the worst kind of betrayal.'

Mary's face was very sad.

Then Sara remembered what Rachel had said about seeing Danny in the village on the day of the inquest. She told Mary he'd been seen loitering by the post box, just five minutes from the Old Rectory.

'Oh no,' said Mary.

Somehow, at the exact same moment, everyone in the village started to make the same connections between people and events, and the vast beam of their suspicions swung round on to Danny. He had access to all the keys. He could easily have let himself into Grace's house in Meadow Rise – there had been no sign of forced entry – and stolen her grandmother's gold bracelet. On the day of the inquest, when the whole village was sitting in the courtroom listening to the sad story of Mike's accidental death, he could have strolled up the gravelled drive of the Old Rectory, unlocked the front door, and searched the house until he found Sara's jewellery. The trip to London was to get rid of it all. Shortly afterwards, his pockets were full of cash.

It was despicable. It was disgusting. How could he have taken advantage of Katie's neighbours like this?

By the time Katie, blissfully ignorant of all the gossip, had taken Dexter up to the top of Ogden Hill, the rumours had rushed round the village like a small fire.

Poor Katie, looking out over the bypass, knew nothing of this. Her mind was on Danny, and the puzzle of why he was so unenthusiastic about the viewing she'd arranged for a run-down short-let studio flat above the discount carpet warehouse on the industrial estate. She had spent the whole of

the bracing walk wondering how she could persuade him that it was probably the best place they could afford.

When she finally delivered Dexter back home, Rachel sat her down and told her with characteristic bluntness that people were worried that Danny was responsible for all the recent break-ins. The rumour was that he'd gone to London to sell the stuff and was now flush with cash on the proceeds.

Katie came round to the Old Rectory, her eyes red from crying. 'How can people be so horrible?'

She'd had a shock. Sara put sugar in her tea. 'Don't worry. They've just got nothing better to do. It'll all die down very soon.'

But it didn't. Someone tipped off the police. Unbeknownst to Katie, Danny had been in trouble many times before. He had form. Officers went round to his last known address – his nan's house in the terrace by the railway line – and found in her spare room, in old shoe boxes piled high to the ceiling, stolen goods from local burglaries dating back over the past two years.

As Mary said, he'd be lucky to stay out of prison this time. You can try people's patience only so far.

Grace said he must have been kicked out of his job for thieving. It made sense. You only need a few rumours going round about a light-fingered salesman for a company to lose its reputation completely.

Sadly, Danny's arrest didn't help Grace or Sara recover their possessions. Grace's grandmother's rose gold bracelet was never found. None of Sara's jewellery turned up either. Danny must have already sold it. It had all completely disappeared.

★

Katie was heartbroken. She had only just got Danny back. And now, because of his criminal record, he could end up with a custodial sentence.

In the days following his arrest, this was all she could think about. She was desperate to help him. She sat with Sara for hours over cooling cups of tea, talking about books she'd read and films she'd seen, and how a good barrister could argue your case and get you off on a technicality. She was going to stand by him. She would wait for him. He could rely on her.

Sadly, she wasn't able to prove any of this. Danny cut off all contact. It turned out that he'd decided to blame her for the tip-off to the police. Once out on bail, he went back to the hovel when she wasn't there, let himself in, and picked up all his stuff. The only difference was that this time he left the spare key on the draining board by the sink so that she knew his departure was final.

It was torture. There were a couple of days after he dumped her for the second time that Katie didn't even make it in to walk Bundle. Sara went round to the house, but the curtains were drawn and no one answered the door.

In the village, the recent shocking events were endlessly discussed. A sudden death, a scandal about sex workers, a spate of burglaries – daily life seemed to have turned into some kind of soap opera.

Many of the conversations that Sara overheard were deeply unsettling. She once called into the shop to pick up some overpriced white wine and found Mary in full flow, Daisy like a large fur cushion at her feet. When Sarinda looked up and saw Sara standing there, she opened her eyes really wide to warn Mary to stop, but Mary didn't cotton on fast enough

and said, 'You can't live with someone without picking up the odd clue. She must have known what was going on.'

Worse was to come. When Sara heard whispers that Katie had not only known about Danny's burglaries but was also his accomplice, she grabbed her coat, and rushed straight round to the portacabin. She had only been there a few minutes when she heard Sally Cook say that Katie was having a terrible time, what with being evicted from her house, and Mary said that it seemed Katie's parents had just abandoned her and were giving her no support at all.

Sara couldn't hold back any longer. 'That doesn't mean she stole anything.'

A small circle of faces turned towards her.

'There is no way that Katie knew what Danny was doing.' Her voice rang out. 'She wasn't involved at all.'

'Of course she wasn't,' said Mary.

Sarinda looked confused. 'Do the police think she was?'

Later Sara wondered if she'd made the whole thing worse.

It wasn't long before the slanderous rumours reached Katie's ears. Gossip as vicious as that whipped round the village like a virus. Katie wept, sitting at the table in the glass extension, wondering how her friends could think her capable of stealing from them.

'It's all a mistake,' said Sara. 'We'll sort it out.'

Katie looked up, her face stricken with fear. 'What if they decide they don't want me to walk the dogs any more? No one wants to employ someone they can't trust.'

'Don't worry, Katie. It'll all die down.'

'They might ask for their keys back. I would, if I thought someone was stealing from me.'

For her own part, Sara knew that Katie was guilty of only

one thing. She had loved Danny with all her heart. Her infatuation had blinded her to his true nature. It would never have occurred to her, as she hooked the keys on to the little rack in her kitchen, that he would use them to burgle her neighbours' houses.

As the days passed, Sara worried more and more about the febrile atmosphere in the village. Katie tried to ignore it but was constantly aware of people staring at her. She began to look drawn and ill. Sara was concerned that she was turning in on herself, becoming isolated and detached.

One afternoon she asked if Katie had made any progress in finding somewhere new to live.

She hung her head. 'I haven't been looking.'

This was quite a shock. 'But when do you have to be out?'

'About a week.'

'Where will you go?'

Katie swallowed. 'I thought I'd be able to stay with Anna. But it turns out her aunt and the twins are there until Christmas. So they haven't got any space. Not even on the living room floor.'

'So what will you do?'

Katie's eyes filled with tears, as if Sara had pushed her into a bed of nettles.

It was worse than Sara had feared. Depression had settled on Katie like a blanket, depriving her of the ability to act. Sara took a deep breath. 'Come back here. Just till you've sorted yourself out.'

Katie looked despairing. 'You shouldn't have to—'

Sara cut her off. 'Edward and I would love to have you. It's decided. You're coming.'

So Katie moved in, back into her old room, and Sara

heaved a sigh of relief. Now she could make sure that Katie was eating properly and went to bed on time and didn't spend hours staring at her phone, waiting for the text from Danny that never came. Sometimes she drove her all the way into lectures and picked her up again afterwards. She helped her with her coursework and her reading and bought her little treats whenever she went out shopping – dark chocolate truffles, peppermint tea.

Katie said, 'You shouldn't be doing all this.'

Sara smiled. 'Why not? We're friends.'

James sounded cool on the phone when she told him that Katie was living at the Old Rectory again. 'Hasn't she got a life?'

Sara said, 'It's just to tide her over.'

'She's like one of those ear mites that live on dogs. Or a bed bug. Or a tick. Something you can't get rid of.'

'James, stop it.'

'Hasn't she realised there's a world out there?'

'She's like me. She likes a quiet life. She likes living in the country.'

He laughed.

She said, hurt, 'I don't criticise your friends.'

'That's because I don't tell you about them.'

It was meant to be a joke, but it wasn't funny.

Sara ended the call soon after that, feeling unaccountably upset.

With Katie back in the house, the residual tension left over from the inquest – particularly the memory of Ursula's astonishing outburst – began to fade away. But Sara still felt unsettled. She slept badly. Time passed with great speed, even though she didn't seem to be doing anything useful – indeed sometimes, at the end of the day, she was hard-pressed to remember anything she'd done at all. To begin with, frightened by this blurring of hours, she was tensed for some of Mike's more cutting remarks, certain that he wouldn't miss this golden opportunity to point out how much her standards had slipped. But he seemed to have become much less critical in recent weeks. There was a warmth and friendliness about him that made his company enjoyable. Sometimes she could almost feel him smiling.

This was especially true when she was dealing with Edward. Mike was right in her ear then, showering her with praise. She'd always been the one to look after Edward because Mike had been away so much. Most of the time, she rose to the challenge. Edward was her son. It didn't matter whether he was four or fourteen – it was her job to take care of him. But there were days when she was tired and overwhelmed – when he went on and on and on about something new or uncomfortable or surprising or noisy that she just couldn't change, that she just couldn't make go away, so that she could almost see another version of herself, angry and irrational, turning on him, shouting at him, reducing him to tears – and then she could hear Mike saying, *It's all right, Sara. It's OK. You're doing your best* just like he did all the time Edward was small, her lifeline of reassurance when she needed more patience to cope than she could possibly drum up from the bottom of her exhausted soul,

when the only thing that kept her going was his unerring belief that they'd get through it together somehow.

Mike wasn't a saint. He loved business, opportunities, making money. Sometimes he forgot to put his family first. But he had always tried, in his own way, to make things better, to make sure they had enough, that Edward's future was secure. It was true, what Mary had said. He made regular donations to three autistic charities. He said that he and Sara couldn't change the past, but they could try to make sure that other parents had a better experience of diagnosis and support, and weren't left on their own for years struggling to cope. He said, you have to hope for a better future. You have to look after those who need help.

Sometimes, digging outside with a trowel in the garden, Sara would sit back on her heels and think of the early days when the boys were small. They got lost somewhere, she and Mike. It was hard to pinpoint how and where it happened, but there came a time when everyday life was overlaid with a kind of mist. At the beginning, they could talk. He didn't always agree with the way she focused so completely on her younger son, but he understood that she had no choice. Later, as time passed, he was less sympathetic. He couldn't see why everything had to be so rigid, why she couldn't move beyond the designated pathways she insisted upon.

It became hard to remember a time when he looked at her with affection or spoke to her with anything other than irritation in his voice.

Then there was the affair with Hilda. Even now, Sara could close her eyes and see her standing there, blonde hair awry, her sweet expression screwed into pugnacious contempt. She

was in the wrong, and she knew it. The weakness of her position made her spit like a cornered cat.

'Why do you care? You don't want him.'

After that, she had to go.

Sara was the loser in the end. The atmosphere in the house had been quite happy while Hilda and Mike were having it off. Once she'd gone, it became tight and mean. The sunshine had gone out of his life. He became angry and irritable, a default position that became so entrenched that the lines of his face were redrawn.

He had other affairs over the years. She was sure of that. Some months there was a lightness about him again – he would sing in the shower, and take James out to the park to play football, and buy her bunches of flowers. But he was careful never to grind her face in it again. He had learned that much.

His sustenance came from work. He was proud of what he'd achieved. Sara thought that most of his emotional life came from his colleagues and employees – a committed group of people with the same joint goals.

One afternoon, she was dusting the desk in his study – she liked to keep everything clean and tidy in there, just as she had when he was alive – when she came across the phone, the one she'd found in the glove compartment of his BMW. It lay there in her hand, a stubby little silver thing, and she couldn't believe that something so small had started a scandal with such huge repercussions.

He said, *Why did you do it, Sara?*

She didn't jump out of her skin. She had got used to him being inside her head, and nowadays this was a kinder incarnation, a man who sounded as if he genuinely wanted to know what she thought.

She said, 'I had to stop her. For the boys' sake. I had to stop people listening to her.'

But that story – that long story about the texts and the porn and the prostitutes. You made it up. The whole thing.

'It could have happened.'

But Sara, you didn't tell everyone it was a possibility. You said it was true.

She said, a little uncertain of her facts, 'Wasn't it?'

There were no texts. There were no prostitutes. There were no secret bank accounts.

'What about the phone?'

It was Edward's phone. Don't you remember? The first one he ever had. I bought it for him when he started school so he could ring you if he was afraid.

There were faint stirrings of memory. But she couldn't be sure. He might be bluffing, trying to put her off the scent. 'You were away so much. All those conferences. All those hotels. You had to be getting it from somewhere. If you weren't having affairs, you must have been paying for it.'

You blackened my name.

Sara took a deep breath. There was a limit to her patience. 'You deserved it.'

Why?

Her head was hurting, that sensation of something tight round her skull. 'Because you made me feel like nothing.'

She didn't want to hear his reply to this, so she put her hands over her ears, like a child.

That night, when she went to sleep, she curled herself into a ball, as far away from Mike's side of the bed as possible.

*

Because Katie had moved back in, Sara was able to help her through Danny's first appearance at the magistrates' court at the beginning of December. Even on the morning itself, she tried to stop Katie going. She knew that turning up at the hearing would set her back and churn up all the old unhappiness. But Katie was adamant. She said someone had to be there to support him.

As usual, she put other people before herself.

It was a miserable experience. Sara had been keen to see the legendary Danny in the flesh and had to concede, when she finally set eyes on him, that he had a certain louche charm. But she was shocked by the way he stood there smirking, as if the whole thing was a joke. All he had to do was confirm his name and address and put in a plea – he said he was not guilty, which was ridiculous – but he turned the whole thing into an excruciating pantomime, an elaborate charade, raising his eyebrows and pulling stupid faces. Where was his dignity and restraint? Sara was so embarrassed she could hardly bear to watch.

Outside, in the icy cold, Katie's normally dewy complexion had flattened into something papery and grey.

'Why don't we go and find a cup of tea?' said Sara, thinking that Katie looked as if she might collapse at any minute.

Katie shook her head. 'I just want to go home.'

After the hearing, the atmosphere in the house was bleak. It would be at least another month before Danny's trial, so they were stuck yet again in a period of waiting. Sara tried to be sympathetic. She didn't want to appear selfish and uncaring. But there was a tiny part of her that was getting slightly bored with all Katie's moping around. The outcome of the trial was a foregone conclusion. Danny would go to

prison. Because the only possible variable was the length of the sentence, it was time for Katie to accept the inevitable.

More importantly, Sara felt that Katie was missing the crucial point. Danny had never been right for her. He had made it clear he didn't want her and had recently cut off all contact. Surely the time had come to move on. Katie, after all, was living with her best friend in a beautiful house in the middle of glorious English countryside – rent free, all bills paid – and had her whole life ahead of her. Wasn't it time to put the past behind her?

Of course, the intense local interest in Danny's arrest and court appearance didn't help Katie to master her feelings. Her sad coterie of friends in the Goat, excited by the scandal and the drama, gathered round to offer support. But their interest just stoked Katie's despair. She became the centre of attention at a time when she really wanted to hide away and grieve. As she said to Sara with some sadness, it wasn't even any fun going out for a drink any more – every session in the pub turned into an endless discussion of Danny's chances.

Further misery awaited her in the charity shop, where Katie had gone to seek solace from Anna. One Saturday afternoon, Katie looked up from a rail of frayed cardigans to find herself facing Maxine. This was horribly embarrassing. The last time they'd spoken on the phone, Katie had been brimming with confidence. Danny had just returned to her welcoming arms, and she'd told Maxine that everything was going so well she didn't need therapy any more.

When Katie relayed this later, Sara was slightly alarmed. 'But you're not thinking of going back to her, are you?'

Katie looked desolate. 'I don't think she'd want me.'

Maxine had apparently been in a bit of a hurry – some

kind of counselling emergency – so couldn't hang around chatting. But she had given Katie one of her withering glances and said she'd heard all about the arrest. She hoped Katie now realised that she had idealised Danny and projected all her fantasies of true love on to someone totally inappropriate.

As Maxine's gleaming black boots marched out of the shop, Katie had hidden herself in the stockroom and wept.

Somewhat to her surprise, Sara found herself thinking that Maxine was completely right.

Over the next few days, Sara decided that what they all needed to cheer them up was the prospect of a happy Christmas. She felt a little thrill of joy at the thought of James coming home. Katie hadn't mentioned anything about going to Spain to see her parents. Was it possible that she too might be persuaded to spend Christmas at the Old Rectory? Sara could see it now – turkey and Brussels sprouts, silly jokes and paper hats. She imagined them all in the great glass room at the back of the house, sitting round the table laughing.

One afternoon Katie took the Polo to pick up two heavy bags of Bundle's special diet dog food from the vet. Because she disliked him so much, Sara often overcompensated where Bundle was concerned. Even his Welsh wool dog blanket was handmade.

On her return, Katie dragged the bags to the utility room and sat down with Sara at the table, looking thoughtful.

'Tea?'

'Yes please.' Katie hesitated. 'You know that time you saw Grace's Ryan down the alleyway?'

'When he was with that girl?'

'Yes.' Katie screwed up her face, puzzled and confused. 'I was thinking about it when I was driving back from the vet's,

and feeling really sad, because Grace and Ryan are so unhappy without each other. And I was driving past Sainsbury's Local and the Goat, just like you did, and the lights went red, and I stopped. And I looked out of the window and I couldn't see down the alleyway at all. You can't even see the start of it. You have to be a lot further on down the high street.'

'How funny,' said Sara.

'It's strange, isn't it?'

'I definitely saw him. You couldn't mistake Ryan.'

After a pause, Katie said, 'Maybe it was after the lights. Maybe you were stuck in traffic.'

But Sara had got up to open the great glass doors for Bundle who was hurtling towards the house from the end of the garden, hoping it was time for his walk.

Grace found her bracelet. It had fallen down behind the curtains and settled itself into the tiny gap between the carpet and the skirting board. She was lying in bed reading, with just the lamp on by her side, and she'd seen something glinting at the far side of the room. At first she thought it was a trick of the light. But she was curious enough to get up and investigate, and when she realised what it was she was so overcome with joy and relief she burst into tears. She couldn't think how it had got there. She must have taken it off, and put it down on the windowsill, and been distracted perhaps by something going on in the street outside, and drawn the curtains forgetting what she'd done. And then, somehow, it

had slithered off the windowsill, fallen to the floor, and hidden itself from view.

She was mortified. As Katie told Sara later, she took time off from the salon specially so that she was at home in Meadow Rise when Katie came round to walk Lulu. She made Katie a cup of tea, and sat her down at the kitchen table, and said she was really, really sorry. The bracelet had been in the house the whole time. No one had stolen it. Her Danny was completely innocent.

'Oh, Katie,' said Sara, who had been listening attentively.

'He never broke in. It had nothing to do with him.' Katie looked grief-stricken. 'But it's not just that he didn't steal anything from Grace. It's that people jumped to conclusions because of Grace's bracelet and your jewellery, and all sorts of horrible rumours started flying round, and because of that someone told the police, and they went to his nan's house and found all the shoe boxes. If they hadn't gone round there, he'd still be free.'

Clearly the police would have caught up with Danny eventually. But Sara felt this wasn't the moment to point this out. 'It's so sad.'

'Grace was really upset about Danny's arrest. She said she knew what it was like to lose the love of your life.' Katie paused. 'And I said to her that if she still felt that about Ryan, she should go straight round and make it up with him.'

Sara was surprised. There was a different tone to Katie's voice. 'What did she say to that?'

'She cried quite a lot. She said it had hurt so much when she thought he was cheating on her. And I said, well, that was only a rumour, too. A bit of gossip flying round the village. So maybe that wasn't true either.'

Sara bridled. 'I saw him.'

'I know.' Katie kept her eyes on Sara's face. 'I know you saw him. But it doesn't matter, does it? What's important now is that they get back together.'

It was such an unusual experience having Katie stand up to her that Sara was unable to think of a suitable reply.

Sara had the uncomfortable feeling that things were sliding out of control. It didn't help that she was finding it harder and harder to sleep. She tried everything – warm baths, milky drinks, lavender oil on her pillow – but felt so wide awake when she got undressed at night that she found herself gazing at the big, wide bed with despair.

She gave Mike short shrift if he tried to start a conversation in her head. To be fair, he was still being kind rather than critical. But he kept asking questions she couldn't answer, like why she'd tried to make Katie believe that he was up to no good whenever he shut the study door. He said he knew that Sara had a very low opinion of men in general, and that there might be husbands and partners who spent hours every evening watching porn on their laptops, but it wasn't true in his case, and he'd only ever been trying to catch up on work. Sara found this rather whiny self-justification very irritating because it was all water under the bridge and there was really nothing she could do about it after all this time.

Sometimes she was tempted to be quite rude and tell

him he had no right to demand explanations. But then she remembered he was dead, and felt sorry, because he was probably feeling at a bit of a loose end.

There were times when she got tired of lying there hour after hour staring into the dark and decided it would be better to get up and occupy herself with useful tasks. She couldn't keep her mind on reading or listening to podcasts or watching films, but practical jobs like cleaning shoes or clearing out drawers were somehow both soothing and absorbing. The difficulty at night was making sure she was quiet and didn't disturb Katie or Edward. She didn't always manage this. Once, in the early hours, she was rearranging the occasional tables in the living room when Katie appeared in the doorway, anxious and sleepy, wondering what she was doing. Sara had to pretend she'd been tossing and turning worrying about a lost earring and had decided in the end that she might as well just get up and look for it.

Her great joy, of course, was using these periods of wakefulness to prepare for Christmas. Katie said she thought her parents were spending Christmas Day with another ex-pat couple they'd met on the golf course, so she probably wouldn't be going to Spain at all. She was very touched to be invited to the Old Rectory, but a bit worried about barging in on a family celebration. She thought that James might like to have his mother and brother to himself. But Sara was adamant that they'd love to have her and, in the end, Katie tentatively agreed.

In celebration, Sara bought an enormous tree – the ceiling height could take it – and abandoned her usual minimalism in favour of sparkle and bling. Every single branch bristled with decorations, many of them home-made. Sara surprised

herself with creative wellsprings she hadn't even known existed. Many of her more exciting nocturnal adventures involved paper and glue, and she had even experimented with stringing up dried pasta bows that she'd painted red and sprinkled with glitter.

During the day, Sara cleaned the house. She quite enjoyed polishing and dusting. For a while, when she was working in the wills and probate department, they'd employed a cleaner, but Sara had always hated the idea of a stranger snooping through her personal possessions. Quite apart from this, she loved the Old Rectory with such a passion – she had always been terrified that if she and Mike split up she might lose it altogether – that it felt only right she should be the one to buff it to a shine.

Sometimes, standing in the double-height hall as the cold December light gleamed on glass, marble and stone, Sara shivered with delight at the thought that the house, the whole house, now belonged entirely to her. Its lines calmed her. Its spaciousness enchanted her. It was her sanctuary, her refuge, her home.

One evening her phone rang, and James's voice filled her ear.

'Oh,' she said, suffused with delight, 'it's you! When are you coming back?'

'Tomorrow, if that's OK.'

Sara did a quick mental tour of the house. It was ready. Everything was prepared. 'Yes, of course. What time?'

'I was wondering if I could bring a friend.'

'A friend?'

'Yes.'

Sara felt suddenly cold. 'Of course.'

'You don't sound very sure.'

Sara swallowed. 'What kind of friend?'

'What do you mean?'

'Well,' said Sara, in a brisk kind of voice, 'will you be sleeping together?'

There was silence at the other end of the phone.

'I need to know.' Even to her own ears, she sounded much too loud. 'I might need to make up another bed.'

He sounded weary. 'It doesn't matter.'

'Of course it matters. They can't sleep on the floor.'

'Would you rather they didn't come?'

Sara felt a rush of embarrassment, or possibly horror, that made it impossible to speak.

James said, 'Just forget it.'

'No,' Sara was panicking now, 'no, you don't understand.'

'It was a bad idea. I see that now.'

'What do you mean?' Her voice came out as a wail.

'I thought it was Dad. But it wasn't, was it?'

'Please, James, please. Please come.'

He said, 'I don't want an argument. I really don't. I'll ring in a couple of days.'

'James—'

'Say hello to Edward for me.'

After he'd rung off, she stood there, quite still, a statue of ice.

It didn't seem possible that she and James had fallen out.

One afternoon, the doorbell rang. Sara wasn't expecting anyone. Edward was at school and Katie was out somewhere, probably walking one of the dogs.

When she opened the front door and found Rachel standing there, Sara couldn't believe her eyes. They weren't close friends. Sara was pretty sure that Rachel didn't even like her. But, more importantly, it was a weekday morning, and Rachel should have been at school, teaching algebra and percentages and haranguing teenagers about not doing their homework.

She said, 'Can I come in?'

Still dazed, and slightly apprehensive, Sara stood back and let her pass.

Rachel stopped in the hallway, as if struck by something strange. Sara was waiting for the usual comment about the hugeness of the space – the double-height hall, the chandelier, the sweeping stone staircase with the iron balustrade – but all she said was, 'Are you moving?'

'No. Why?'

'All the boxes.'

Sara hadn't really thought until that moment what the results of her recent nocturnal activity would look like to outside eyes. 'Just clearing out a few things.'

Rachel seemed surprised. 'But there's so much of it.'

Sara said, 'I don't like clutter.'

She led the way to the living room and Rachel sank down on to one of the big white sofas. For the first time, Sara was uncomfortably aware that the room looked rather strange. There was almost nothing in it apart from an enormous fir tree covered in rubbish. Had she gone too far? She was just wondering why she'd taken down the mirror above the fire-place, and what she'd done with the little grey button-back

chair, when Mike wandered in and went to sit on the sofa next to Rachel.

Sara stared. Mike looked fit and relaxed, and was smiling the way he used to when they first met. The whole thing was extremely unsettling – it was awkward enough having Rachel in the house – but Sara resolved to carry on as if everything was perfectly normal until the situation became a little clearer.

She said, 'So what brings you here?'

Mike smiled. *Do I need a reason?*

Rachel said, 'I was just passing.'

The last two remarks had come out in stereo so it took Sara a while to work out who'd said what.

'Coffee?'

Rachel said, 'I can't stay long.'

That's a relief.

Rachel said, 'I'll come straight to the point. Katie's a bit worried.'

Sara was taken aback. She didn't think Katie ever confided in Rachel. 'Danny's arrest has been a nightmare for her.'

Rachel leaned forwards. 'She's worried about you.'

Why?

Sara's hands were trembling so much she had to lace her fingers together to keep them still. 'Why?'

Rachel said, 'She thinks you've been under a lot of strain.'

'Well, obviously,' said Sara.

It's only a few months since your husband died.

Sara glared at Mike to shut him up.

Rachel said, 'You're acting out of character.'

Mike laughed.

Sara said, 'It's not funny.'

Rachel looked taken aback. 'I didn't say it was.'

This isn't going very well, is it, Sara?

Sara was finding it hard to keep her temper. 'Keep out of it.'

Rachel looked shocked. 'Of course, if you'd rather I did. I just wanted to know if you needed help.'

Mike was grinning from ear to ear.

'Rachel,' said Sara, with some desperation, 'I don't mean to be rude. I'm sorry. I think it's grief. It makes me very abrupt.'

You were always abrupt.

'I don't want Katie to worry,' she said loudly, trying to drown out anything Mike might begin to say. 'She's probably right, and I'm not myself at the moment. But there's been so much going on.'

She thought, with sudden clarity, that it was very important not to mention James. She didn't want Rachel asking any questions about Christmas.

Rachel took a deep breath. 'She says you don't go to bed at night.'

Sara wanted to disagree but was suddenly unsure. She looked at Mike, who gave her rather a pitying look and shook his head in sorrow, as if this was something she should have worked out for herself. This was quite worrying. Sara knew she had periods of wakefulness but didn't realise she never went to bed at all.

'How does she know?'

Rachel's expression was very gentle. 'She can hear you pacing from room to room. Sometimes you even talk to yourself. When she asked you about it, you said you couldn't go to bed because there was too much to do.'

'I've got a lot on my mind.'

'Of course you have,' said Rachel. 'You've had a very stressful time over the past few months. But if you're having trouble sleeping, why don't you go and see the GP? Just to get yourself checked out?'

'I don't like doctors,' said Sara.

They didn't help me much, did they?

Sara found her eyes filling with tears. 'You know, I still can't believe Mike's dead.'

'That's perfectly natural.' Rachel fixed her with her usual steady gaze. 'But you don't have to cope alone. We're all on your side, Sara.'

Don't believe a word of it.

'I'm not on my own,' she said. 'I've got Edward. And Katie.'

And me.

Rachel hesitated. 'Katie's got her own problems, though, hasn't she?'

That made Sara very cross. Katie hadn't got any problems at all now that Danny had gone. It was just taking her a long time to realise it. She said, in a tart voice, 'It might have helped if people hadn't spread such horrible rumours about her.'

Rachel gave her a very strange look. For a moment, Sara thought she was going to come out with one of her more abrasive remarks. But instead she took a deep breath. 'You're absolutely right. Malicious gossip doesn't help anyone.'

Eventually, after a little more conversation about stress and looking after herself and promising not to empty the house of all its furniture, Rachel said she wouldn't keep her, because she was sure Sara was very busy, but she must promise to call if she needed any help.

After she'd gone, Sara stood in the hall, thinking about what Rachel had said. She couldn't be entirely sure when her

habit of staying up at night had started, but she had an uncomfortable feeling that she hadn't slept properly for several days.

I must ring James, she thought. I'm still not clear when he's coming home for Christmas.

She went into the kitchen to make a cup of tea. Mike had got there first and was sprawled at the table, comfortable and relaxed. When he saw her, he looked up, his expression slightly sheepish.

She said, 'I do wish you wouldn't interfere.'

You've never liked her.

'That's not the point. It was kind of her to visit.'

Was it?

'You shouldn't even be here.'

But I can stay, can't I?

'For the moment,' she said, in what she hoped was a firm voice. 'Just until I've worked out what to do.'

Mike's face stretched into one of his more attractive smiles.

Katie was out when PC Bush turned up.

Sara smiled. He had such lovely blue eyes.

'May I come in for a moment?'

Sara led the way to the huge empty living room.

He said, 'Getting ready to decorate?'

Sara didn't answer.

'My wife's the same. Always wants the house spick and span for Christmas.'

Sara gave a tight little smile. She wasn't sure she liked being compared with his wife, who might be a very nice person, but might equally be someone of limited intellectual abilities.

He hesitated. Sara sat down and he followed suit.

She said, 'So how can I help you?'

PC Bush had taken off his helmet and seemed to be studying it closely. 'We've had a visit. A Mr Roslyn.'

'Oh yes?'

'I believe he's spoken to you a couple of times?'

Sara looked vague but didn't disagree.

'He's making enquiries about a young woman who went missing twelve years ago.' The constable hesitated, choosing his words with care. 'There have been discussions at quite a high level . . .' He stopped, as if he needed to be sure that these were the right words '. . . and our Chief Constable has asked us to make further enquiries.'

Sara put on an expression that she hoped conveyed both surprise and co-operation.

'I do realise this is a busy time of year, and we all know how difficult it's been for you recently. But we wondered whether you might be able to come in to the station and give us some assistance?'

'In what way?'

'If you could answer some questions and make a statement, that would be very helpful.'

'But my son's due home at any moment. His first term at university.'

PC Bush nodded as if he completely understood. 'Maybe one day next week? I said I'd ask, as I was passing. I wanted to explain in person.'

'Next week? The week before Christmas?'

'It wouldn't take long.'

Sara sighed. 'Is it really necessary?'

He looked apologetic. 'I think it might help.'

He really did have such lovely blue eyes. 'I could probably find half an hour. Perhaps when I'm out shopping. Shall I give you a ring when I've had a chance to look in my diary?'

PC Bush smiled. 'That would be very kind, Mrs Parsons.'

In the hall, just as they reached the front door, he turned to face her. 'You can't think of anyone else, can you, who might be able to help with our enquiries?'

Sara shook her head. 'It was all so long ago.'

After he'd gone, Bundle started barking, so Sara opened the glass doors and watched as he raced up the garden. I don't really mind making a statement, she thought. It's only fair. The police were so kind when Mike died. And from a selfish point of view, it might put an end to Mr Roslyn's rather disturbing visits. He did seem very persistent given that there was so little to say.

The frozen garden stretched out in front of her, petrified in the cold sleep of winter. She thought she might just prune the dead wood from the acer, a particularly lovely tree with leaves that turned dark red in the autumn. You had to be very gentle, of course. You couldn't rush in and cut any old how. You had to know when to stop.

When she came in from outside, her face cold, Mike was in the kitchen. It was a slight shock to see him in person again, but at the same time immensely reassuring. He really did look well – so much younger than when he'd died. The lines of pain and anger had disappeared. He had his shirt-sleeves rolled up like he always used to in the old days, and

he seemed relaxed and content, as if he'd just been sitting there at the kitchen table thinking about nothing very much while he waited for Sara to appear again.

She smiled at him, and he looked up and said, *Will you tell them?*

'Tell them what?'

Will you tell them what really happened with Hilda?

She pulled a face to show him what a silly idea that was.

What about me? Can you tell me?

Strangely, she didn't feel surprised or defensive. She didn't rush to change the subject or try to distract him. It seemed for the first time an entirely reasonable request. Why shouldn't Mike know what had happened? So Sara put down her secateurs with the sharp curved blades and bright red handles, and peeled off her thick protective gardening gloves with padding round the base of the thumb so that you don't get blisters when you've been digging in the earth all day, and she sat down opposite him, in the great glass extension at the back of the house, and told him the same story she'd told Mr Roslyn, the private investigator, some weeks before.

But this time she added in a lot more detail. She wanted to give the best account she could. Mike deserved that, after all this time.

She didn't shirk. She told him that she and Hilda had been arguing about their affair, and that her dear little face had been twisted with fury and contempt when she spat out, 'Why do you care? You don't want him.'

Poor Mike. That was hard for him to hear. Years ago, all she'd said was that Hilda had left suddenly, and he hadn't pressed her for details. How could he? He'd been sleeping

with the au pair under their roof. He had to accept whatever she decided to tell him.

But now Sara said that after packing her stuff and coming downstairs, Hilda hadn't walked through the hall and slammed out of the house, as she'd told Mr Roslyn, but had come into the kitchen to say goodbye to Edward. This was a kind and sensible thing to do. It had the potential to upset him, of course, but Edward was going to be upset anyway once he realised she'd gone. Hilda was one of the very few people he could tolerate when he was young.

So Hilda put down her bag and her grey wool coat and squatted down next to his chair. Edward – who still had the livid bruise on his forehead, the original cause of their argument – gave her a quick blank look and turned back to his cars. He had five small metal cars that he carried around with him everywhere – green, red, blue, yellow, black.

She said, 'Goodbye, Edward. I'll miss you.'

He adjusted the fine positioning of the yellow car so that it was exactly in line with all the others.

Sara said, 'It's time to go.'

Hilda stood up, her usual sweet expression back in place – she really was extraordinarily pretty – and said, as if they were talking about something charming and inconsequential like Faroese puffins, 'You know, I wasn't the first, and I won't be the last.'

That hurt, but Sara didn't let it show on her face. She wanted the ending, at least, to be civilised.

Sara followed her back out to the hall. At the foot of the stairs, Hilda stopped to put her coat on, easing her arms into the sleeves. She said, in a speculative kind of way, 'I don't like going without saying goodbye to Mike.'

He was away on business in Berlin.

Sara pushed her. It might have been that she was frightened Hilda was going to change her mind and wanted her out of the house as quickly as possible. But she had forgotten how small and light she was. One shove sent her flying. Her bag at her feet tripped her up and her arms were straitjacketed in her coat, so she fell backwards, unable to save herself. Sara heard the crack as her head hit the black iron banister. She ended up half standing, half sitting, against the curve of the stairs, her blonde hair over her face, like a drunk propped up by a brick wall. Sara tried to pull her to her feet, but she said something angry and incomprehensible, so she backed off. It was humiliating and embarrassing for them both. In the end, because she couldn't get her balance without the use of her arms, Hilda let Sara help her take off her coat, but she was obviously still in shock. Sara said she should sit down for a while.

Edward swivelled round as they came back into the kitchen, Hilda leaning on Sara's arm.

Sara said, 'She fell down, Edward. Just like you did in the garden.'

Hilda looked pale as if she'd hurt herself more than she wanted to say.

Edward said, 'Bang.'

Sara smiled. 'Bang.'

After a while, to her relief, Edward turned back to his cars.

She tried to apologise but Hilda wasn't really listening. After a while she interrupted and asked if Sara could call her a cab to the station, which Sara felt was the least she could do in the circumstances. Because she was flustered, and couldn't find her phone with all the taxi numbers programmed

in, she began one of those hopeless searches that get more and more impossible the longer they carry on. She was in the hall, hunting through a pile of flyers and junk mail, when she heard a noise behind her. Hilda had pitched forwards on to the stone floor and was lying full length on her side, her eyes wide open.

As Sara told Mike all those years later, sitting at the table, it was obvious she was dead. But at the same time it made no sense at all. Can people die like that? One blow to the head? Sara knelt down on the floor next to her, staring at her blank eyes, trying to work out what to do. There didn't seem to be any point in ringing for an ambulance, because no hospital could bring her back to life. She thought of the repercussions of reporting her death. Then she thought about not reporting it at all. James was at school, but due home in a few hours' time. Edward was still in the kitchen, playing with his cars. The boys were her priority.

Eventually, Sara grabbed hold of Hilda under the arms, lifted her shoulders from the floor, and dragged her through to the downstairs toilet. She wasn't heavy, just lumpen and unyielding, as if she was being deliberately unhelpful. Sara covered her face with the hand towel. Then she locked the door from the outside.

Later she said to James, 'Hilda's gone home. Back to the Faroe Islands.'

Edward said, 'Bang.'

She smiled at James. 'Your brother hurt his head. He fell.'

Edward's bruise had turned dark purple.

The next day, she and Edward came home after taking James to school and she spent all day digging a big hole in the garden, about halfway up by the vegetable patch. Edward

was quite happy playing with the woodlice under the terracotta plant pots on the patio, and racing his cars down a wooden plank into a puddle, and they only had to stop a couple of times – once to make a sandwich, and once when the yellow car fell into the drain. James was going out to tea with a friend straight from school, and being brought back home later by the friend's nanny, so at the end of the afternoon, when Edward was inside watching TV and the whole garden was pitch black, Sara dragged Hilda out through the sliding doors.

The Old Rectory was surrounded by very high hedges. And these were pre-Bundle days, of course – there was no dog to get overexcited over a small rigid body.

The following day, Edward and Sara went to the garden centre and bought a very large wooden composter, which they had delivered, for an extra fee, a few hours later. It was quite expensive because it was made of sustainable wood and high-quality durable materials, but Sara thought it was probably a good investment. It looked good on top of the newly dug earth. The delivery men, after she'd tipped them, helped her hammer the posts into the ground so that it was completely secure, a permanent fixture.

Sara said to Mike, 'I had to think of winter weather. Storms and gales and high winds.'

Mike seemed to understand. His expression didn't change.

The next day, she burned most of Hilda's clothes on the bonfire, constantly stoking up the flames to be sure that everything was reduced to ash. Edward watched from a safe distance. He didn't like the sting of smoke in his eyes, or the crack and snap as the wood caught fire.

A few of the better items she took to the charity shop in the nearest town – the one that Anna ended up working in

as a volunteer years later. It seemed wrong just to destroy things that could make money for a good cause.

Sara didn't tell this last part to Mike, because it didn't seem that relevant – all water under the bridge – but she did exactly the same with his antique Rolex after she'd stolen it from under his nose. It had been an impulse to hide his most treasured possessions and watch him lose his temper when he couldn't find them – a silly, childish, pathetic impulse, born out of a desire for revenge. But she had cause. All those weeks of autocratic bullying when he couldn't go in to work and had to run his business from the sofa. All those weeks he shouted at her so that she couldn't think straight and kept locking herself in the bathroom to cry. To make herself feel better during that period of incarceration when she was his secretary, his chauffeur and his personal servant, she carried out all sorts of petty acts of defiance, like pretending she'd misheard and bringing him extra strong mints when he was shouting for his painkillers, and making sure she was out of the house at the exact moment when an important delivery of company documents was scheduled to arrive. It was sad to look back on it. But she'd wanted to hurt him as much as he was hurting her.

Later she couldn't remember whether she'd even got any enjoyment from it in the end, stealing his valuable possessions and watching him stomp round the house in a rage looking for items that had mysteriously slid out of reach. She did wonder whether she should own up, or come up with some story about tidying them away in the wrong place, but she didn't have the courage once he'd reported everything to the police. It seemed easier to let sleeping dogs lie.

The keys and the laptop she took to the council refuse

centre wrapped in a black plastic sack, and hurled them into one of the bins.

But she couldn't bear to trash the watch. It was valuable, and a thing of beauty. She wrapped it in newspaper and posted it through the letter box of the charity shop.

It didn't seem too much of a risk. It really wasn't likely that anyone would suspect a loving wife of playing a horrible trick on her husband.

James wasn't answering his phone. This didn't worry her. He was probably very busy packing up all his stuff and getting ready to come home.

Outside in the cold December air, Sara walked through the garden, leaning down to pick up stray twigs and leaves. It was so peaceful. You couldn't hear any of the neighbours, of course, because the house was so isolated. But you couldn't hear any traffic either. The Old Rectory was much too far from the main road and hardly anyone came this far up the spindly lane. James would be so looking forward to recharging his batteries in the quiet and calm of the countryside. You could really relax when you were this far away from other people.

She wasn't concerned about their slight disagreement. It bore no resemblance to the explosive arguments she had with her own mother all those years ago – standing on the scuffed wooden boards of the hall floor, shouting up the stairs at top volume that she was going to London the minute she finished

school because she was being suffocated, she couldn't breathe, she needed to get out while she could. Sara smiled. She had a very different relationship with James. Her own mother had been frightened and depressed, using every trick in the book to stop Sara leaving home because she didn't have the inner resources to cope alone. Sara, on the other hand, fully accepted James's need for independence. She had completely understood that he had to leave to continue his education – she had even persuaded him to change his mind when he'd been thinking of spending a year at home after Mike had so unexpectedly died.

Of course, when he'd finished his studies, he might come back to the Old Rectory. It was hard to find the money for rent when you were just starting out, and it made sense to take up offers of free accommodation from friends and family. Sara enjoyed picturing the four of them in the house together, pursuing busy independent lives – James and his brother, she and Katie.

Sara could feel Mike on the edge of her consciousness, desperate to know how he fitted in. She blocked the thought.

The secret, she thought, was all in the planning. So many people didn't bother to think ahead. Imagining all those wasted opportunities made Sara feel sad. You can't blunder through life, reeling from crisis to crisis. You need to be sharp. You need to be clever. You need to use your brains.

Sara remembered how Katie had once, with great earnestness, tried to persuade her that they should dig up the compost heap to see what Bundle was barking at. The postman had told her that non-stop noise wasn't normal animal behaviour. He could hear the poor dog all the way round the cul-de-sac.

Sara had said, as gently as possible, 'Do you have any idea what goes on in a compost heap?'

Katie bit her lip.

'All sorts of tiny animals and insects are busy breaking down decaying leaves and rotting vegetable peelings and old tea bags and shredded paper. And all these slugs and snails and beetles and earwigs are attracting birds and frogs and hedgehogs. So what you've got is a warm, smelly, rustling pile of movement and constant surprises. It would be extremely strange if Bundle didn't find this interesting. And unfortunately he's the kind of irritating dog who expresses his interest with continual loud barking.'

Katie looked embarrassed. 'So we don't need to dig it up?'

'No.'

'Because it's completely normal.'

'Sadly, yes.'

'The postman seemed so sure.'

Sara smiled. 'You shouldn't always believe what people say.'

The last thing Sara was expecting was a difficult conversation with Katie. She had genuinely thought that the turbulent events of the past year had been laid to rest, and that they could all look forward to the future with confidence.

A lovely Christmas, after all, was just on the horizon.

But it turned out that she was wrong.

It was a normal, mid-week morning. Edward was at school,

and Sara had just come back from one of the cheaper super-markets on the other side of town where she still went sometimes to stock up on bulk buys of essential food items like tinned plum tomatoes and basmati rice. Since the insurance policies had paid up, money was no longer a problem. She was very well off. But old habits die hard.

It was nearly eleven o'clock by the time she hauled her carrier bags through the front door, so Bundle had already been taken for a walk and was back outside in the garden barking at the compost heap.

As Sara unpacked the last of the shopping, Katie came in to the kitchen. They knew each other very well, so Sara could tell just by looking at Katie's face that something was wrong. But because of Katie's fragile state – she was still so upset about Danny – Sara didn't press her straight away but asked if she'd like a cup of coffee.

Katie nodded in a distracted kind of way.

They sat down at the table underneath the great expanse of wintry grey sky, and Sara asked her what she'd been up to that morning, expecting nothing more than an update on her core module of contemporary business management for hospitality organisations.

Katie said, 'I was looking for some Sellotape in Mike's study and I found all your jewellery.'

Sara stared. It was, of course, a terrible shock. Various possible reactions to Katie's rather bald statement ran through her mind, from outrage that Katie had been snooping through Mike's desk to some kind of simulated astonishment at the miraculous reappearance of stolen goods. But for some reason her usual decisiveness deserted her.

'I don't understand.' Katie's voice was so quiet that Sara

could hardly hear what she was saying. 'It was all there. Everything you reported missing. Even your engagement ring.'

It was a very distinctive ring – Edwardian, Arts and Crafts, with emeralds and diamonds – so Sara wasn't surprised that Katie had recognised it straight away.

Katie's eyes were full of confusion.

Sara said, 'I won't pretend it was for the insurance money.'

It was a rather hopeless attempt to lighten the atmosphere. But Katie didn't smile. In fact, Sara could see from the look of entreaty in her eyes that she was still hoping there was some kind of rational explanation. Katie was, as usual, clinging to the possibility of a favourable outcome long after any sane person would have given up.

'Danny was hurting you.' Sara tried to sound calm. 'I had to do something.'

Katie was trembling. 'So your jewellery was never stolen.'

'No.'

'There was no burglary. It was just like Grace's bracelet. Danny had nothing to do with it.'

Sara leaned forward towards her. 'He didn't steal anything from me or from Grace. But there were lots of other burglaries all over the place. He's guilty, Katie. You told me yourself right at the beginning. And you heard all the charges in court. He's been thieving from old ladies for years.'

'Did you tell the police?'

'You know I did. You were here when PC Bush came round.'

Katie shook her head. 'Did you tell them you thought it was Danny?'

It was tempting to prevaricate. After all, Katie knew the way that gossip worked in the village – a little bit here, a little

bit there. It could have been a collective effort. No one could ever have said, with any degree of certainty, who had finally tipped off the police.

But Sara decided, on the spur of the moment, to tell the truth. She met Katie's eyes with what she hoped was a steady gaze. 'I suggested to PC Bush that they might want to investigate him.'

Katie seemed to slump in the chair.

'For your own good, Katie. I couldn't bear to stand by and do nothing. Not after what he put you through last time.'

Katie just sat there, staring down at the table.

Sara leaned forward. 'I had to make you see what he was really like. You kept blaming yourself. But it wasn't you. It was him. I knew he was going to do it again. He was going to leave you and break your heart. And I couldn't let that happen.'

The silence felt ominous. Sara thought, with some sadness, that honesty came at a price. She'd had a sudden urge to tell the truth, and it had been the wrong call. She was normally so careful. She hardly ever gave in to impulse. It so often played out in her head – crashing the car into the back of someone who'd just taken her parking space, pushing over the cyclist who'd just ridden into her shin. But she had learned over the years that it's far better to think ahead – to work out every possible outcome and adjust your plans accordingly. It takes a little longer, but it leaves you with more control in the end. The last thing you want is a messy, unpredictable result.

Katie lifted her head and looked straight at her, and Sara realised with a pitch of dismay that she was going to pay heavily for her mistake.

Katie said, 'Have you lied about other things?'

It seemed better to be straightforward. 'Yes, sometimes.'

'I mean things that matter.'

'Like what?'

Katie looked serious. 'Everything to do with Mike.'

'Our relationship?'

Katie nodded.

'No, I didn't lie about that. We weren't happy. I wish we had been.' Sara looked down at her hands. Her head hurt, as if she'd drunk too much, or spent hours squinting at strange objects that were just out of focus. She wished she could lie down in a dark room with something cool and comforting pressed against her forehead.

'What about Ursula?'

Sara wasn't really sure how to answer that. 'You saw what she was like.'

'You said she wanted Mike all to herself.'

'Yes.'

'And that she was mad.'

Sara took a deep breath. 'I think she's emotionally unstable. I don't know if that amounts to the same thing.'

Katie was still staring at her across the table. Sara was beginning to worry that she wouldn't have clear enough answers to everything Katie might want to know, when Katie said, 'Was it an accident?'

Sometimes, when you hear something unexpected, you can't immediately work out what's being said. For some reason, Sara had been convinced that Katie was about to ask her about phone sex and fictional prostitutes, so this simple query, which got to the whole nub of the issue rather too quickly, completely threw her. 'What?'

'Mike's death. Was it an accident?'

There was a sudden collapse of time, a flashback so intense that Sara caught her breath. One minute she was sitting with Katie at the long wooden table on a weekday morning in the middle of December, and the next she was standing by the white sink, all alone, on a Friday evening at the end of June. When vivid memories flood back like this, you're almost convinced you can smell and touch, that you can experience all the sensory impressions that imprinted themselves on your mind when they first happened. The window was open, and the night was hot and still, full of the scent of star jasmine and honeysuckle. Sara could remember the heaviness of her eyes, the ache of her muscles, the thick sound of rural silence. Edward and Katie were both upstairs in their rooms – Katie was probably already asleep after her deep and soothing bath.

In his basket by the wall, Bundle was lying stretched out, dead to the world, his throat wheezing with faint, almost inaudible barks.

It had been a backbreaking day of cleaning, polishing, cooking and furniture-shifting in preparation for Mike's fiftieth birthday party. She had pushed herself beyond the point of tiredness. Standing there by the open window, Sara's mind drifted to James, lying somewhere in a grassy field under the serious moonlight, surrounded by friends, drinking beer, listening to music. Of course, she missed him. But just at that moment, she wasn't anxious or afraid. Her lovely house was shining. Everything the guests might need had been prepared. She hadn't wanted to organise a big, expensive celebration. She'd hated the idea of an invasion of strangers. But she'd agreed to do it – out of obligation, out of duty – and now that everything was ready she was proud of what she'd

achieved. It was done. It was finished. She was offering her difficult, irascible, demanding husband the best party he'd ever had.

Sara's phone rang and Mike's name flashed up. 'I'm coming back now.'

She was surprised. He'd said he wouldn't be home till midnight. He was going to take the client out for dinner. 'Is everything OK?'

'I'm not staying. We're going to meet up again next week.'

Her heart sank. His voice was angry. She knew the signs by now. 'Did you forget your painkillers?'

'Don't start.'

Quickly, to distract him, she said, 'Did it go well? The meeting?'

There was the kind of pause that makes you wonder if the signal has gone. Then he said, 'You'll have to cancel it.'

'What?'

'The party.'

'But I—'

'Don't start, for God's sake.'

There was another strange, blank silence.

She said, 'Have you eaten?'

'I'll get something on the way back.'

'But all the—'

'It doesn't matter. It's not important. Sara? Are you listening? Just cancel the party.'

'It's—'

'Get hold of Gemma if you don't want to do it. We spoke earlier. I said it might not happen.'

Her voice came out all floaty and light. 'OK.'

'Sara?'

But now her throat was tight and she couldn't speak.

After she'd ended the call, she stood there at the sink, her hands on the cold white enamel. The night was black all around her, pressing down through the panels of the great glass extension. Various random phrases were floating through her head – *It's just the pain* – *He'll be all right in the morning* – *He didn't mean to sound ungrateful* – *It'll all be fine* – *Don't make any decisions now* – *It's late* – *You need to go to bed.*

He wouldn't find anywhere open at this time of night. Motorway services, maybe, but she couldn't see him dragging himself out of the car for old chips and watery coffee. And he couldn't take the pills on an empty stomach. He'd been told that so many times. She opened the massive great fridge, full from top to bottom with luxury food for the party, and closed it again. With jerky, mechanical movements, she began a fruitless search through both store cupboards for something that might do. She was beginning to move beyond pleasant weariness to a state of fractious exhaustion. She knew him. He was always saying he'd stop off for something on the way, but he never did. He was incapable of doing anything in the kitchen. He couldn't even boil an egg. He'd come back irritable and hungry, expecting a full meal, as usual, to be waiting for him.

For a moment, Sara fantasised about going upstairs and packing a suitcase. She could see herself placing neatly edged piles of ironed clothes against the soft grey quilting, tucking in underwear and socks, adding a silky dressing gown. She thought about leaving this beautiful, empty, shiny house – her creation, her sanctuary, her home – and walking down the lane past the high hedges smelling of laurel and yew. She saw herself disappearing into the darkness.

Bundle, in his basket, sighed.

Upstairs, Edward and Katie were asleep.

She found an onion, some celery, some garlic, half a bottle of white wine, a packet of Arborio rice. She unwrapped a block of Parmesan. She made up a jug of stock. She thought of Mike driving home through the night, his mind screaming with pain.

Around her, the house waited.

Just before she started to cook, she went upstairs and hunted around for his painkillers. He didn't like her doing this. He didn't want her anywhere near his medication – hated any kind of interference. But she couldn't risk the thunderous clash and clatter of furious searching in the early hours as Mike rampaged around, turning the house upside-down. She found a full pack of pills right at the front of his desk drawer. She stood there, staring at it in her hand. Perhaps leaving it behind had been intentional – the continual bravado of self-deception that he was perfectly able to do without painkillers.

Mike hated weakness of any kind.

Downstairs, alone in the kitchen, she chopped and crushed and stirred, and her back – as if in sympathy with his – sang with pain, because the day had been too long, far too long. As she worked, she found herself remembering something from years before, a kind of bright light, a kind of intensity, when he was her future, and she was his, and there was no sniping and misery and disappointment, only his smile and his warmth and the creases round his eyes.

And she knew, at that moment, how tired they were, and how hard they had tried, and how it was time now to let it stop.

Sara stirred in the last ladle of stock.

And when it was done, because he needed to be rid of the agony of the pain as quickly as possible, she pushed the pills out of the little blisters of their flat plastic trays, crushed them in the base of the big stone pestle and mortar, and stirred them into the warm, thick, unctuous risotto. And then she sprinkled it with Parmesan and parsley, and covered the bowl with clingfilm and stood it next to the microwave, just as she always did, so that he'd know it was the same routine, and all he had to do was reheat on full power for two minutes.

She left the empty packet of pills next to the bowl so that he could see what she'd done.

And then she went to bed.

Katie seemed to be waiting for something. Sara said, 'I'm sorry – what did you say?'

'Mike's death. Was it an accident?'

They stared at each other across the table.

Sara felt the past stretching out behind her, blurred and muddled. She felt an overwhelming sense of tiredness.

Katie said, 'I just keep feeling there's something I don't understand.'

'Like what?'

'I don't know. Something that isn't right. It's been going round and round in my head for days.'

Sara said, 'I wish you'd let it go, Katie. It's all over now.'

Katie looked uncertain.

Sara kept her voice calm. 'There was an inquest. Witness

statements, medical reports. The coroner took it all into account and came to a conclusion of accidental death.'

Katie said, 'Why didn't Ursula believe him?'

'Because she wanted it to be my fault.' Sara leaned forwards. 'Don't you remember? She said I drove Mike to suicide. And after that didn't work, she came up with the idea that I'd killed him.'

'She said such horrible things in the car park.'

Sara's voice was cold. 'Which you promised you'd never repeat.'

'I won't.'

'On your life, you said. You promised on your life.'

Katie nodded, eyes wide with sincerity.

Sara looked out through the big glass doors. She wondered if she should go out into the garden after lunch and cut back the ivy on the fence. But she wasn't sure she had the energy.

Katie said, 'It's just that everything feels different now.'

With difficulty, Sara dragged her mind back to the present. 'What do you mean?'

Katie said, her voice indistinct, 'Because of what happened with Danny. It's all changed.'

They could hear Bundle barking.

With great weariness, Sara said, 'You're angry with me.'

Katie looked up.

'But you must understand I was trying to protect you. He was going to hurt you and I couldn't let that happen again. All those weeks, Katie, all those weeks we sat here talking about him because you couldn't accept what he'd done. I couldn't bear to see you go through that a second time.'

It was, of course, tedious to have to run over all the arguments when the whole thing was so glaringly obvious, but

Sara tried once more to explain, as gently as possible, why Danny was so wrong for her. Poor Katie. Even after all this time, the hold that Danny had on her was so strong that she couldn't be rational and objective. Sara touched on his grandiose delusions, his unpredictability, his criminal tendencies. She said that it was all to Katie's credit that she had been so loyal and stood by him, but there was a danger that her open and trusting nature was blinding her to all his faults. Danny had preyed on Katie's gullibility and abused her trust. It was time to face up to the truth.

Katie was silent.

Sara said that Katie was kind and good-hearted and determined to see the best in everyone. But she had to understand that there were people in the world who would happily take advantage of that and manipulate her to their own ends. She had to see through lies and exploitation and learn to stand up for herself.

This finally prodded her into speech. Katie said, her mouth trembling, 'You sound like Maxine.'

'I'm saying it for your own good.'

'But don't you see?' Katie's eyes were huge. 'None of this is important.'

Sara was lost.

'You took Danny away. I thought you understood. I thought you understood how much I loved him. But you took him away from me.'

Sara felt a small flash of irritation. 'I didn't take him away. I suggested that the police might want to investigate him.'

'And they arrested him.'

'Katie, I don't know how to get through to you. Danny wasn't right for you. He didn't deserve you.'

'But wasn't that up to me? Wasn't that my choice?'

Sara looked at her with exasperation.

Katie said, 'You've been so kind, and I don't want to sound ungrateful. I know you were trying to do the right thing when you told the police about Danny. But I wish you hadn't. I wish you'd kept quiet.'

Sara glared at her. 'It didn't make any difference. The police would have caught up with him sooner or later.'

Katie wouldn't back down. 'You don't know that.'

Sara was having to work very hard to keep her temper. Bubbles of rage kept blistering through her mind, shouting words that she could only just keep silent. Katie was being obtuse. There was no logic to anything she was saying. Clearly Sara had saved her from an abusive relationship that would have destroyed her. It was stupid to pretend anything different. For a moment, she stopped listening, lost in a grey mist of irritation, and only came to when Katie said, '. . . and they think I shouldn't be spending so much time with you.'

'Who?'

'Anna and Baz.'

Sara looked at her with astonishment. 'Why?'

Katie was clearly finding this difficult. 'They say it's been a bit intense.'

'Intense?'

'With the funeral and the inquest, and now all this with Danny.'

Sara said, 'It's been a very difficult time for both of us.'

But she could see from Katie's expression that this wasn't enough. With a great effort of will, Sara pulled herself back under control. It seemed these vacuous friends from the

foul-smelling Goat had said something that Katie had decided was important. 'Why shouldn't we spend so much time together?'

Katie was hunched over. 'Because you're so much older than I am.'

Sara stared.

'They say you're old enough to be my mother.'

Sara felt a cold shiver run down her spine.

'And in the pub,' said Katie, wretched with embarrassment, 'people are saying it's more than that. More than just being friends.'

There was an awkward silence.

Sara said, 'It's just gossip. You should never listen to gossip.'

They could still hear the distant sound of Bundle barking. No one, it seemed, was taking any notice of what he was trying to tell them.

With a stab of sadness, Sara realised that everything was about to change. She could feel it in the air. It had crept up when she'd been looking the other way, when her attention had been distracted by trying to explain. For the first time, Katie was making her feelings plain. She was daring to criticise, to risk offence, to say the unsayable. It seemed – incredibly – that her love for the ridiculous, pathetic, insignificant Danny had suddenly made her brave. She was finally speaking up for herself.

Perhaps if you have your back to the wall, the only choice is to turn and fight.

Katie looked up. 'I was talking to Rachel the other day. She said that people are always changing their minds about where they're living, even halfway through the year, and it's worth asking around to see if there are any spare rooms in

any of the student flats. Or even a shared house somewhere in town.'

Sara could hardly bear to listen.

'She said you get more of the student experience that way.'

Sara felt a band of tightness in her throat. Why was Rachel interfering?

'I may not be able to find anywhere.' Katie was having trouble meeting Sara's eyes. 'But I thought I could have a look and see what's out there.'

Sara said, keeping her voice neutral, 'Can you afford it?'

'I can get a loan. Lots of students get loans to cover their rent.'

'It seems a shame,' said Sara carefully, 'when there's so much space here.'

There was a kind of pleading in Katie's face, a longing to be understood. 'It just seems a good idea.'

Sara couldn't speak.

'I'll carry on with the dog walking. Maybe not twice a day. But as often as I can. I love Bundle. I don't want to let him down.'

Bundle? Bundle? With difficulty, Sara said, 'So you're looking now?'

Katie was clearly finding this hard. 'I've talked it over with Anna, and she says I can stay with her. So I can grab things when they come up. View straight away and put down a deposit.'

'I thought there was no room at Anna's.'

Katie swallowed. 'Her mum said there's always room.'

'So when will you go?'

'I'm not sure.'

Sara said, forcing herself to sound calm and sensible,

'It's entirely up to you, of course. You must go whenever you like.'

Katie bit her lip. 'Maybe I should go now.'

'Now?' There was a kind of pressure in Sara's ears as if she was being held underwater. It made it hard to speak. 'What about Christmas?'

Katie still couldn't look at Sara directly. 'I think I should probably go and see my parents. Mum was really upset when I said I wasn't coming. She said they'd been really looking forward to it.'

Sara said, 'So you're going to Spain.'

Katie nodded. 'Anna's for a few days. Then Spain.'

'This is all happening so fast.' Sara smiled. 'I didn't know you were making so many plans.'

'I wasn't, really. They've sort of made themselves.'

Sara tried to look as if she knew exactly what Katie meant. 'So you're going to leave now?'

'I think so.'

'Won't it take you a long time to pack?'

'Not really. It's just clothes and a laptop.'

'And they're all expecting you?'

Katie shifted in her chair. 'Not exactly. But Anna said I could stay whenever I wanted. And Mum said, just turn up when you can. It'll be a Christmas surprise.'

Sara thought it all sounded rather vague and slapdash. The last thing anyone wants is uncertainty about dates in the middle of the festive season – Katie was being extremely inconsiderate. But it seemed the decision had been made. She cast around for something to say, feeling that the only important thing was to save face and maintain a façade of normality. 'We'll miss you. Especially on Christmas Day.'

'Is Polly coming?'

This was almost her undoing. 'Polly?'

'I thought James might bring her home for Christmas.'

'Oh,' said Sara, her heart plunging in shock, 'I don't think they've decided yet.'

'Maybe they'll do Christmas Day here and Boxing Day in Wales.'

Sara nodded as if she had even the slightest clue what Katie was talking about. The thought that James might be seeing someone – someone with whom he was so intimately involved that her family played a significant part in Christmas festivities – made her feel sick.

The conversation had brought itself to a close. Katie remembered, with sudden panic, that she'd half arranged to meet Anna in the charity shop, which would work out really well because then they could go back to Anna's house together when she finished work. Katie stood up so quickly that her chair fell backwards and clattered to the floor. Everyday life flooded back into the room and the tension – the awkward, tortuous silences, the pauses filled with hidden meaning – vanished without trace.

It was astonishing, really, quite how much had been communicated in such a short time.

'Sara?' Katie – rushed, dishevelled – stopped on the threshold.

'What?'

She hesitated. 'You're not upset?'

'Of course not. I completely understand.' Sara glanced up at the kitchen clock. 'If you're sure about going straight away, I can give you a lift into town if you like. As long as we leave in the next half hour, I can still be back in time for Edward.'

'Really?' Katie's face lit up. 'Yes, please.'

Sara tried to find just the right level of warmth and indifference. 'Of course, I'm still hoping I can change your mind.'

Katie shook her head. She seemed so grown-up suddenly, so certain of her decisions. 'I think it's time to go.'

'You're sure?'

'Yes.'

'Quite sure?'

Katie nodded.

Sara smiled. 'Promise me one thing.'

Katie waited, her face full of the old eagerness to please.

'I know you want to look around and see what's out there. But remember that the Old Rectory is your home. Forever. There's always room for you here.'

Katie's eyes were solemn. 'Thank you.'

After Katie had gone upstairs, Sara stayed at the table, looking out into the garden. She sensed Mike was around somewhere, wanting to speak, but she wouldn't let him get a word in. He had no place in this moment. It would just make everything more complicated, because it really had nothing to do with him. It never had.

Sara felt very calm. It was a relief to have some clarity of thinking at last. Of course it had all come as a bit of a shock, because she hadn't expected Katie to surprise her with a radical change of plans, but there was no point in getting emotional. The important thing now was to act in Katie's best interests, whatever the personal cost. She felt a rush of anticipation, a fluttering of her heart. It was time to face up to what had to be done.

Sometimes it takes a good friend to push you in the right direction.

Overhead, she heard drawers opening, cupboard doors shutting, the thud and crash of haphazard packing. She imagined Katie throwing her clothes into a bag – in an untidy, messy way, because she was hopeless at anything practical – and gathering up the chaos of bottles and make-up from the bedside table. Sara wondered how long it would take for her to clean Katie's room once she'd gone – to wipe away the finger marks and coffee mug rings, the blobs of foundation, the ash from her incense sticks. She thought about the splodges of nail varnish on the duvet cover and the smears of mascara on her pillow. It all seemed so sad. For a moment Sara was filled with a sense of weariness, as if she were doomed like some kind of fairy tale character to repeat the same tasks again and again, the work never-ending, the job never done.

She heard footsteps walking over the floor above, the creak of a floorboard, and then silence as Katie made her way across the landing and down the stairs. The house was so big, you couldn't ever really hear progress from one room to another. Sometimes you just had to imagine it.

She thought about Katie walking down, step by step, her hand on the black iron balustrade. She thought of her putting her heavy bag on the floor and lifting her coat to push her arms into the sleeves.

Sara took a deep breath. This was so hard. But it was time to go out into the hall to say goodbye.

Acknowledgements

Thanks to Nicholas Rheinberg, PC Stephen Bush from the Metropolitan Police, Professor Annie Bartlett and Dr Gwen Adshead for their professional advice – all errors that have crept in despite their best efforts are entirely my own. Thanks to friends and family for their love, support and editorial suggestions – Alexandra Fabian, Yvonne Wilcox, Sally Eden, Gabriel Firth, Luke John Oxlade, Tamsin Kelly (who read every draft), Joe Kavanagh, Ben Kavanagh, Alice Kavanagh, and my husband Matt Kavanagh. Finally, thanks to my agent Veronique Baxter and all at David Higham Associates, and to everyone at Hodder & Stoughton – particularly my kind and brilliant editor Ruth Tross.

THRILLINGLY GOOD BOOKS FROM CRIMINALLY GOOD WRITERS

CRIME FILES BRINGS YOU THE LATEST RELEASES FROM TOP CRIME AND THRILLER AUTHORS.

SIGN UP ONLINE FOR OUR MONTHLY NEWSLETTER AND BE THE FIRST TO KNOW ABOUT OUR COMPETITIONS, NEW BOOKS AND MORE.